DOING
BUSINESS
in ASIA

SAGE was founded in 1965 by Sara Miller McCune to support the dissemination of usable knowledge by publishing innovative and high-quality research and teaching content. Today, we publish over 900 journals, including those of more than 400 learned societies, more than 800 new books per year, and a growing range of library products including archives, data, case studies, reports, and video. SAGE remains majority-owned by our founder, and after Sara's lifetime will become owned by a charitable trust that secures our continued independence.

Los Angeles | London | New Delhi | Singapore | Washington DC | Melbourne

Gabriele Suder,
Terence Tsai &
Sumati Varma

DOING BUSINESS in ASIA

Los Angeles | London | New Delhi
Singapore | Washington DC | Melbourne

Los Angeles | London | New Delhi
Singapore | Washington DC | Melbourne

SAGE Publications Ltd
1 Oliver's Yard
55 City Road
London EC1Y 1SP

SAGE Publications Inc.
2455 Teller Road
Thousand Oaks, California 91320

SAGE Publications India Pvt Ltd
B 1/I 1 Mohan Cooperative Industrial Area
Mathura Road
New Delhi 110 044

SAGE Publications Asia-Pacific Pte Ltd
3 Church Street
#10-04 Samsung Hub
Singapore 049483

Editor: Matthew Waters
Assistant editor: Jasleen Kaur
Production editor: Martin Fox
Marketing manager: Abigail Sparks
Cover design: Francis Kenney
Typeset by: Cenveo Publisher Services
Printed in the UK

Library of Congress Control Number: 2020933414

British Library Cataloguing in Publication data

A catalogue record for this book is available from the British Library

ISBN 978-1-5264-9450-4
ISBN 978-1-5264-9449-8 (pbk)

At SAGE we take sustainability seriously. Most of our products are printed in the UK using responsibly sourced papers and boards. When we print overseas we ensure sustainable papers are used as measured by the PREPS grading system. We undertake an annual audit to monitor our sustainability.

To David, Caroline and Chantal and all of my incredible family. With a special dedication to my parents and to Rudolf. (Gabriele)

To my family and loved ones who supported me through a particularly difficult time in life. (Terence)

To Arvind and Anirudh for all the love, support and encouragement. (Sumati)

CONTENTS

LIST OF FIGURES

LIST OF TABLES

PREFACE

AN AGILE AND FRAGILE REGION: WHAT THE CORONAVIRUS PANDEMIC AND 'BLACK SWAN' EVENTS REVEAL

This business textbook addresses the Asian business environment and provides a cross-border, regionalization-focused strategy perspective. It sheds light on Multinational Enterprise (MNE) strategy and action across Asia or part of Asia and in key locations. Its broad regional perspective is not random.

Just as in other parts of the world, certain risks and uncertainties inherently spread across borders and have an impact locally, regionally and internationally. These include key considerations of our times, covering a range of ethical, humanitarian, climate change-enhancing fires and flooding, and major health issues – and the role of private enterprise in this. This role encompasses a moral responsibility, as agents of cross-border collaboration, to be part of the solution rather than the problem. To mitigate threats is to keep workplaces and consumption safe and ethical, and to keep supply chains resilient for their own sake and, even more, for that of the stakeholder community they operate in.

The most recent illustration of the need for this value-driven approach is the outbreak in China of the coronavirus, and its spread as a pandemic worldwide. The World Health Organization declared this a global emergency. The virus has caused a range of respiratory illnesses from the common cold to more dangerous conditions like Severe Acute Respiratory Syndrome, or SARS, making more victims than the 2002 SARS crisis did. In addition to the tragic human toll, from a company view, the most visible part of its business impact is linked to Asia-focused dependencies as the region serves as a major supplier of components and parts to supply chains around the world, and as a continuously growing consumer of goods and services at home and abroad. Let's focus on the supply chain impact for a moment: to get a sense of what this encompasses, note that in 2018, China was reported to have shipped nearly $35 billion worth of auto parts, mainly for assembly lines and some directly into retail, according to UN data. Robert Bosch GmbH, the world's largest maker of car parts, is just one of the major players directly affected due to its main Asian facilities located in Wuhan, the geographical epicentre of the virus, not forgetting their own and affiliated very numerous small and medium-sized suppliers.

Disruption to virtually every industry through the virus directly or indirectly is due to labour availability, factory closures and city blockages, travel and flight restrictions, lockdowns, and shrinking consumption despite panic buying, i.e. detrimental for employees, consumers and communities that the companies do business in. The disruptions have been shown to have a rapidly cascading effect on contracting and order delivery, which will be mitigated by strategic investments in the region that are focused yet provide for agility and resilience. The impact is wide-ranging:

- from delaying film, games and consoles releases to the relocation of conferences and summits, or installing safety measures, for example for the Mobile World Congress in Barcelona, Spain (typically attended by 100,000 plus business participants)
- from total business travel bans for staff imposed by some major companies, to university semester/term delays and back-up or quickly designed online solutions
- from flight cancellations into and from China – then elsewhere across the world – to temporarily stopping production lines at factories located elsewhere in Asia, such as Hyundai, the world's fifth-largest auto-maker, in South Korea because of shortages of Chinese parts
- from retail businesses that had to keep stores closed or adapt opening hours to the health threat and the lack of local and international consumer confidence, to firms like Nike, Burberry, Tapestry (owners of Kate Spade, Coach and Stuart Weitzman) and Estee Lauder informing investors of the material impact to operations and turning to digitalization and online tolls to maintain and leverage customer experience.

Financial forecasts, and therewith investment or investment modification plans, have been dramatically amended to take this impact into account. The business impact is now reported to be significantly worse that the impact in the aftermath of the 9/11 terrorist attacks in 2001, and the 2016 Fukushima earthquake and tsunami, and the October 2011 Thailand floods, which affected regional and global supplies, or the Global Financial Crisis. The UN Office for Disaster Risk Reduction estimated that Thailand's 2011 flooding reduced the world's industrial production by 2.5 per cent. Other human-made and natural disasters are not risk-managed by most organizations because they are typically classified as 'uncertainty' and less quantifiable and predictable. This points to so-called 'black swan' events becoming increasingly challenging to mitigate. They also damage market performance – due to real issues but also some market irrationality, aggravation through the speed and (at times, non-expert) quality of information and a general mistrust of accurate data coming from some countries' governmental sources.

Cross-Asian supply chains import about 40 per cent of their intermediate goods from China. The diversification of business investment across Asia, including agile partnership arrangements, allows for firms to find alternative supplies during the peak of a crisis and, at a minimum, as a containment strategy. Further out, Australia (and even further, Brazil) as a commodity exporter to China, expects to see a growth 0.3 percentage below forecasts at the time of writing – and will likely be well below this level for some time – which did not factor in the virus yet are highly foreign-trade dependent. Multinationals are adjusting rules, behaviours and processes. Putting customers and employees first is becoming more and more key to corporate survival; doing so digitally has become crucial. Managing uncertainty, in contrast to risk, requires a broader and more comprehensive customer and employee-focused strategy for firms. And though globalization has retracted to a focus on local and national levels, trade and investment continue to be exposed to risks and uncertainty that remain global: they require (at a very minimum) a region-wide cross-border mitigation in Asia.

ACKNOWLEDGEMENTS

The authors would, in particular, like to thank the following great supporters for their invaluable patience, help, suggestions, submission of opinions of materials, and/or all of this combined: our families and spouses; our colleagues at our respective universities and across our International Business scholarly communities; the team at SAGE Publications – with a special mention to Matthew and Jasleen who have yet again been an amazing, highly supportive publication team; the anonymous reviewers; and the research grant support and assistants at CEIBS, in particular, Gemma and Jasmine; and to organizations granting permissions.

While every effort has been made to trace the owners of copyrighted material and to cite scholarly and professional contributions to the highest degree of academic and publication ethics, we do apologize if this may have proven impossible in some circumstances and we may unwittingly have infringed rights. We would in those circumstances appreciate any information that would enable us to rectify and trace owners of such copyright so that we can acknowledge their contribution.

The book idea and concept were initially created and designed by the first author, who would like to very warmly thank Terence and Sumati for their enthusiastic uptake of the idea and the highly effective cross-border work collaboration – at a distance for all of us – that has made this book what it is. The journey has been particularly smooth and enjoyable, as we all share a passion and a work ethic that beautifully combine to create a unique and hopefully highly valuable contribution to readers' understanding of how to do business in the Asia of today and tomorrow.

ONLINE RESOURCES

Doing Business in Asia is supported by a wealth of online resources for both students and lecturers to help support learning and teaching. These resources are available at: https://study.sagepub.com/suder.

FOR STUDENTS

- Read Journal Articles to extend your knowledge and support your assignments.
- Use Weblinks to gain insight from real world examples.
- Revise what you have learnt with Discussion Questions and suggested answers that accompany each chapter.
- Test your understanding and prepare for exams with interactive Multiple Choice Questions.

FOR LECTURERS

- Support your teaching each week by using PowerPoint slides prepared by the authors for each chapter.
- Encourage discussion in class by making use of the comprehensive Case Study Teaching Notes provided.

INTRODUCTION

OBJECTIVES OF THE BOOK

This chapter will cover:

- The objectives of this book
- An introduction to the Asian business environment
- Insights into a diverse Asia, and its geo-economic and geo-political clusters
- The context of the international business environment within a transforming Asia
- The international firm, examining the size patterns of firms doing business in and across Asia, including multinationals, transnationals, large and small and medium-sized enterprises (SMEs).

This business textbook addresses the Asian business environment with a cross-border, regionalization-focused strategy perspective. It sheds light on multinational enterprise (MNE) strategy and action *across* Asia or part of Asia, rather than focusing on a single location.

It is meant to be used by a readership of Master's and MBA students, as well as in Executive Education. Also, it will appeal more broadly to the well-informed general public interested in Asia-specific strategy, International Business and International Marketing, Asian Studies and International Relations, and in case studies that illustrate the business practice of well-known companies and leaders in their field. For the academic readership, the book is structured to follow the typical course outlines that focus on the issues we analyse and illustrate, from chapter to chapter, for ease of adaptation to existing courses.

We are using a holistic and a 'key locations' approach to texts, and present examples and cases from a wide range of Asian locations, ensuring that future and current business leaders in our readership gain the most useful insights into Asian cross-border location advantages that span highly developed, emerging and less developed economies. Yet we also bring more focus onto the Far East than is used in most other textbooks.

The overall structure of the book is similar in logic to the lead author's *Doing Business in Europe* series, with a focus on key themes that are highly relevant in the region today and tomorrow, in contemporary Asia, including investment strategy, location choice and modes of entry, as well as regional integration, supply chain leadership and

global value chain (GVC) participation, cross-cultural diversity and inclusion best practice across Asia and in Asian teams, and more.

Just as with *Doing Business in Europe* and its three editions, this textbook is therefore meant to provide a comprehensive solution for Asian business training.

When you 'enter' a given chapter of the book, you will gain insights into a world that is made from underlying concepts and theory, and will then be led through case study examples, to finally ponder strategic implications for Asian business management. In this way, the textbook covers the most relevant topics that shape the Asian business environment and business practice today. The case studies offered help transpose the theory and conceptual learning into a practice-focused understanding. Each section concludes with review questions, so you can check your understanding.

On its online support, lecturers will be able to access the book's teaching notes for the case studies as well as suggested responses to the questions and multiple choice questions (MCQ) suggestions.

A particularly useful feature of this textbook is that it offers a truly Asian perspective, in that the three co-authors are not only located in three different countries across Asia-Pacific, but have also worked and trained as international and local business executives across Asia in a variety of other locations over more than two decades, and hence are particularly complementary in the perspective that they bring together. There is no other book that is written with the complementarity that these three international business professors provide: this book is the fusion of their unique integrated teaching and research strengths, their locations and perspectives, and their combined all-Asian/Asian-Pacific international business experience.

This volume offers the most suitable, applicable, real-world insights yet found in international business textbooks that focus on Asia, to best serve future managers and leaders in international business in – and with – Asia and presents them with best practice while not holding back on the challenges (and solutions) that are often required to yield competitive advantage in a highly diversified and competitive region. It hence serves the needs of a readership already located in Asia as well as students in non-Asian locations preparing to do business in Asia.

Doing business with and across Asia is always simultaneously stimulating and challenging, and particularly multifaceted. Within most of the region, growth rates are expected to continue rising in the next decade, in contrast to most other regions in the world. Regional business leaders forecast significant international (Asian cross-border) market expansion activity in the short and medium term. Yet some parts of Asia continue to suffer from economic crises, natural and human-made disaster, poverty and major institutional challenges.

It has been acknowledged that business in Asia is marked by an ongoing, accelerating integration of its economies on an internal and external level. This is additionally altering the Asian business environment, its societies, industry dynamics and with that, corporate strategies when going across borders. This includes paying increasing attention to global value chain participation, free trade, international trade agreements, preferential market access conditions, market entry and expansion, and how to use regional capabilities effectively.

Some of the issues addressed by the book are: How does the Asian business environment function? What are the market mechanisms that have to be considered when doing business with, within and across Asia? What are the trends, opportunities and challenges that shape the most vibrant business opportunities – now and in the future – and hence, that shape strategy, marketing and ultimately the success of internationalization in and into this region? What planned set of actions do managers take to obtain or maintain a competitive advantage in and across Asia, and often beyond, when making efficient and effective use of the MNEs' assets and resources and while combining them with core competences – that is, what are the proven concepts and strategies that work for Asia?

What you are holding is an up-to-date holistic international business-focused textbook: a unique contribution that fills a gap where advanced business readers explore the need to recognize the importance of recent developments in Asia overall and expand their crucial understanding of key locational advantages of cross-border business strategy in Asia. It is crucial to recognize, acknowledge and manage the dynamic nature of a key regional business strategy in a context that includes economies of multiple status and growth, within a distinct diversity of cultures and resources. The readings will help you keep track of the many evolutions that have shaped the contemporary Asian marketplace.

ABOUT THE AUTHORS

Professor Gabriele Suder is a business advisor, professor and distinguished, award-winning, highly prolific author with more than 50 peer-reviewed scholarly journal articles and 12 international business and strategy books. In addition to this book, they include *International Business, Doing Business in Europe* (Sage Publications, three editions), *The Routledge Companion to European Business* and a book series on the impact of terrorism on internationalization (Edward Elgar Publications). In addition to her own publications, she has co-authored and co-edited several books, always across countries and time-zones: effective international collaborations, in all sorts of ways, are Gabriele's passion.

She is a reviewer for leading international business and strategy journals, and has published in many of them including, among others, *Journal of World Business, International Business Review, European Journal of International Management, Australian Journal of International Affairs, International Journal of Human Resource Management, Journal of Knowledge Management Practice, PS: Political Science & Politics*. She also has more than 70 corporate and sector case studies in training and practitioner journals and serves as an editorial board member at the *Journal of International Business Policy* and *International Business Review.*

Gabriele is currently holding professorial and adjunct roles at the University of Melbourne, the Faculty of Business and Economics and Melbourne Business School, and at RMIT University, Melbourne, Australia. She is an active member of the Centre for Asian Business and Economics (CABE), and on the Board of the EU Centre on Shared Complex Challenges. Gabriele has also served as an external research fellow and expert in different capacities at the most prestigious governmental and multilateral institutions including JETRO (Japan), the EU, UNCTAD and OECD, and as a World Investment Report Expert. She regularly advises on free trade agreements (market access and expansion for multinational companies) at governments across Asia. She is Past President of the Women of AIB (Academy of International Business) Association and is currently Vice President of the Australia New Zealand International Business Academy (ANZIBA). In Asia, she has worked in academic and advisory capacities across more than 12 countries, with major projects based in China, Japan and India. In her practitioner capacity, at Gartner, Inc., Gabriele helps foreign-owned multinational companies strengthen and leverage their capabilities to overcome mission-critical challenges and hence to drive influential subsidiaries for the good of the corporation and of society. She also publishes for Gartner.

Dr Terence Tsai is an Associate Professor at the China Europe International Business School (CEIBS) with extensive teaching, research and working experience including at the University of Cambridge in the UK, the University of Western Ontario in Canada, and the Chinese University of Hong Kong in Hong Kong SAR, People's Republic of China (PRC), and Shanghai Jiaotong University in PRC. His areas of teaching and research include Chinese management, international business, strategic management, strategic business simulation, cross-cultural management, organization theory, foundations of management and environmental management and sustainability. He is also a front-line scholar who has professionally interacted with various key stakeholders and immersed himself specifically in the Asian environment.

Currently, Terence holds the position of Associate Professor of Management at the Department of Strategy and Entrepreneurship at CEIBS (Beijing, Shanghai, Shenzhen, Zurich and Accra) and the former Director of the School's Case Development Center. He also edited the School's first Corporate Social Responsibility Annual Report.

Dr Tsai's research has been published in top business and management journals and his papers have secured honours in several international management and international business conferences. Terence has also been a member of several academic and industrial committees and editorial boards across Asia, including Mainland China, Taiwan (Republic of China/Chinese Taipei), Hong Kong, Japan and in the US.

His most recent research projects include 'SINET' (the Small and Medium-sized Enterprises International Network), which investigates the challenges and opportunities that SMEs face when they expand their business abroad. The research has been built on data collected from interviews with 30 SMEs in nine countries: China, Denmark, Egypt, India, Jordan, Poland, Taiwan, UAE and the UK. Some research outcomes of this project have been published in the *International Business Review* and *Journal of World Business*. Terence also initiated a research project on how digital platforms revolutionarily changed the ways of doing business and the traditional value creation model. This in-process research project 'Digital Platform Economy' will examine successful digital platforms in China, which include some of the world's leading platforms in terms of business models innovation and profit generation, and to provide practical insights for both traditional and digitized businesses.

Dr Tsai has also developed a great number of award-winning case studies based on his real-world business experience and close observation and business advisory services. These case studies have been used for EMBA or an equivalent level of executive education purposes and been published in leading practitioner-oriented journals or incorporated into book series.

Besides his current academic activities in China, Terence also served as a member of the Board of Directors at the International Schools of Business Management (London, UK), the Senior Consultant at the International Business Ethics Institute (Washington DC, USA), and the Senior Partner at MZ & Partners (Shanghai, PRC) where he offers expert advices in areas such as strategic consulting and policy analysis.

Dr Sumati Varma is an Associate Professor at the Department of Commerce, University of Delhi. She has 30 years' experience of undergraduate and postgraduate teaching, including positions as visiting faculty at leading business schools in India such as the Faculty of Management Studies (FMS), the Delhi School of Economics and the Department of Financial Studies, Delhi University, for their MBA programmes.

Sumati was awarded the prestigious International Visitor Leadership Program (IVLP) fellowship in 2011 by the US Department of State for her contribution to curriculum development for the first ever programme on 'American Studies for Indian Universities' introduced in different Indian universities.

She has worked as a consultant with the World Bank, and has contributed to its flagship publication *Investing Across Borders* (2012).

Sumati is a prolific author with seven books to her credit in different areas of international business published by Pearson International. She has also contributed as co-author in the international edition of *Money, Banking, and the Financial Systems* (with R. Glenn Hubbard, 2nd edn, Pearson), to the Horizon edition of *International Business* (with J.J. Wild and K.L. Wild, 6th edn, Pearson) and as adaptation author for the global edition of *Preparing Effective Business Plans: An Entrepreneurial Approach* (Bruce R. Barringer, Pearson-International, 2nd edn).

She has over 30 papers published in reputed national and international journals such as *Journal of East West Business, Asia Pacific Business Review, International Journal of Emerging Markets, Transnational Corporation Review, Decision,* and *International Journal of Technology Learning and Change.*

She has been a member of the executive team for Project X-Culture (2015–2019), an international experiential learning project at the University of North Carolina, involving over 10,000 students from 400 universities across 40 countries. She is also a member of the Research Team of Lab ReTMES (Research Team for Mediterranean Entrepreneurship and Startups), Department of Law and Economics, Mediterranean University of Reggio Calabria, Italy.

Dr Varma has contributed to the content development of the e-PGPathshala project under NMEICT, Ministry of Human Resource and Development (MHRD), India. She is also a consultant in curriculum development at the American Centre and at the National Council for Educational Research and Training (NCERT), a nodal agency for the curriculum development of Indian schools.

Her research interests include born global firms, where she has done pioneering work in the Indian context. She is also interested in various facets of firm internationalization, international entrepreneurship and cross-border M&As.

She has also presented papers at national and international conferences of repute, including the Academy of International Business (AIB), AIB India chapter, UNU MERIT Netherlands, Copenhagen Business School, European Group for Organizational Studies (EGOS) and Asia Pacific Researchers in Organization Studies (APROS).

THE UNIQUE COMBINATION OF THREE PERSPECTIVES

The three authors have combined their unique perspectives in *Doing Business in Asia* to provide you with a comprehensive, theoretically insightful and practically impactful guide for your international business in this fascinating market.

We have covered the key issues in this sense. To add to this, you may (or not) wish to consider some additional reading, as non-core reading options. We could, for example, suggest:

- The textbook *Doing Business in Emerging Markets* (Sage, 2013) by S. Tamer Cavusgil, Pervez N. Ghauri and Ayse A. Akcal, mainly focuses on India over the other BRIC countries.
- For an additional, pure marketing perspective yet less focused on specific Asian cross-border strategy, you may wish to have a look also at *Principles of Marketing* (Pearson, 2015) by P. Kotler, G. Armstrong and P. Agnihotri.
- There is also a 2010 textbook by Andrew Delios, Paul W. Beamish and Jane W. Lu, *International Business: An Asia Pacific Perspective* (Pearson, 2010), which at the time took a country by country view.
- *The Oxford Handbook of Asian Business Systems* (Oxford University Press, 2014), edited by Michael A. Witt and Gordon Redding, provides interesting additional material on a comparative approach to the region to identify similarities and differences in the region, with a focus on business systems.
- In *Dynamics of International Business: Asia-Pacific Business Cases* (Cambridge University Press, 2013), the editors Prem Ramburuth, Christina Stringer and Manuel Serapio offer several interesting additional case studies from that time period,
- Finally, Peter Verhezen, Ian Williamson, Mark Crosby and Natalia Soebagjo have published *Doing Business in ASEAN Markets: Leadership Challenges and Governance Solutions across Asian Borders* (Springer Nature, 2016). It provides several useful additional insights for our readership predominantly on issues of governance and leadership standards.

We hope this book will prove extensively useful and wish you all the best in your cross-Asian business endeavours.

1
AN INTRODUCTION TO DOING BUSINESS IN ASIA

1.1 THE ASIAN BUSINESS ENVIRONMENT

Introduction

Asia as a marketplace and business environment is multifaceted and heterogenous in many of its aspects. It is the home to some of the most vibrant economies of the world, and some of the most exciting multinationals (MNEs), such as Samsung, emerging market multinationals (EMNEs) such as Tata, and innovators, such as Alibaba and many others.

China, Japan and India are among the world's top ten economies, placed second, third and sixth respectively (WEF, 2017). The majority of gross domestic product (GDP) is generated outside of the USA and Europe, who used to be seen as the traditional growth engines and economic leaders. Notwithstanding growing domestic strengths in trade and investment capabilities over time, 'none of these economies has developed in isolation,

---

Asia: Home and host of international (=cross-border) business

- Home to the emergence of regionalized business leader firms (in addition to/versus local or globally active firm strategy).
- Host to a vast range of non-Asian multinationals, eager to keep exploring and utilizing the advantages that the diversity of Asian locations hold as markets, suppliers, or increasingly, partners and owners.

with production networks across national borders engaging extensively in intermediates trade, often at the regional level' (Suder et al., 2015: 404)

In this dynamic environment, cross-border market expansion activity of corporations accelerates and extends the momentum to a regional level, and often, globally. Asia as a region is both home and host to intense international business activity.

The Asian business environment has proven to be challenging for some MNEs: some of these firms have lost reputation, resources, **intellectual property** (IP) and more while learning how to best do business in or across Asia. They also struggle with the nuanced economic inequality affecting individuals, societies and organizations.

When firms internationalize, they possess and utilize specific resources, assets and characteristics that provide them with their own rare firm-specific advantage (FSA). This shapes their capability to succeed with their cross-border trade or investment, and their knowledge of how to internationalize effectively.

The internationalization decision is based on various motives, including market, rent and resource-seeking behaviours. The location decision, that is, which country, region and market the firm decides, is determined by the advantages that the location can provide, i.e. through country-specific advantages (CSAs) such as resources, and region-specific advantages (RSAs) such as market grouping benefits that may be a source of FSA variations:

> Country and region-specific advantages (CSAs and RSAs) that firms encounter across borders (are interconnected through) FSAs for successful international business if firms are to leverage on operations and experience in one country for application in another. (Suder et al., 2015: 414)

This combination of advantages leads to immense opportunities when strategically managed. Taken as a whole, Asia provides for a unique diversification bundle. Just one part of it, the **Association of Southeast Asian Nations (ASEAN)**, is set to become the equivalent of the world's fourth largest economy by 2030 (State Government of Victoria, 2018). As a crucial part of the 'global factory' (Buckley, 2011), Asia is predicted to become the world's largest economy before 2030 (World Bank, 2019).

This reveals the potential for international business operations in Asia, whether by Asian firms across their region, or non-Asian business doing business in Asia. Asia continues, on a multi-country basis, to consolidate its pre-eminence in attracting production and services activities from internationalizing firms inside and outside the region. Multinationals today opt for the widespread use of diversification strategies across this unique regional business environment.

Locational diversification across Asia

Advantages of locational diversification strategies in Asia: the multi-country strategy:

- reduction of risk and uncertainty impacts
- access to a variety of CSAs (market, talent, innovation, funding, etc.) and to RSAs
- provision and consolidation of international business relevant intelligence and opportunity
- agility across regional trade and **foreign direct investment (FDI)** options.

Asia offers a fast-paced, rapidly evolving business environment. Much happens in this region that impacts cross-border (international) business strategy. In particular, the progress in the transition of China from a centrally planned command economy to an efficient market economy is a complex process, when at the same time values of liberal bilateral and multilateral trade arrangements are challenged, and when leadership brings political ideology into economic decision-making at all levels. Other countries take very different paths.

We count more than 40 years of China's 'reform and opening', providing evidence of a unique path towards adapted gross domestic product, standards of living, income distribution, accompanied by institutional change and technological advancement. Other countries are also undergoing their own reforms to promote trade and investment, for 'sustainable and inclusive growth'. Trade between the **Asia-Pacific Economic Cooperation (APEC)** members has been found to be their most important vector of growth in addition to household consumption (APEC, 2018a: 15). India will be one of the most populated countries in the world though struggles with fragmentation of its regulatory environment.

Yet it is China's rise that business sees as pivotal and catalytic to the positioning of Asia as one of the world's leading regions in business, economic and potentially geopolitical terms. This goes well beyond the considerations of the flying geese model or the Asian 'miracle'/Asian 'tiger' phenomenon led earlier by Japan.

Challenges in this progress are numerous and similarly influence the way in which corporations determine their Asian internationalization path. These include demographic, social and environmental issues, as well as the impact of the coronavirus pandemic to name only a few. Such challenges also reveal resilience and sometimes opportunities.

Comprehensively, trade and investment linkages flourish for most parts of Asia. The golden triangle of China, Japan and South Korea has improved its connections to account

Opportunities arising from Asia's challenges

- Sustainability contributions.
- Disaster resilience capacity building.
- Climate change-focused solutions.
- Stimulation of start-up ecosystems and SME growth.
- Investments, for example in health, energy efficiency, innovative waste reduction and water management.
- Reverse innovation (innovation is seen or used first in the less developed markets than applied in developed markets).

for a quarter of the world's output of goods and services. The APEC region has paid particular attention to inciting a trend in key private sector engagement. The ASEAN's 2017 trade figures between China and the ASEAN's Big Five – Indonesia, Malaysia, the Philippines, Singapore and Thailand – have multiplied by factors of 500 per cent. Market integration without precedent shapes an increasingly stable and prosperous regional marketplace. Yet several locations miss out. In Pakistan, the 'average tariff on imports is 300% higher than the average tariff prevalent in some countries in Southeast Asia' (OECD and World Bank Group, 2015: 71). Isolationist policies hinder APEC's connectivity, maintain high prices and limit consumer choice, despite APEC's important capabilities in manufacturing and exporting. This is not an exclusive case across Asia. Section 2.1 will shed light on the geo-economic and geo-political clusters that help distinguish (and better strategize) some of the region's most distinctive parts.

1.2 CENTREPIECE: DIVERSE ASIA – GEO-ECONOMIC AND GEO-POLITICAL CLUSTERS

Geo-economics analyses interplays between geo-political factors and business strategies. Companies are continuously driven to collect and analyse geo-economic data in order to obtain an overview of market conditions. This is particularly vital for business strategists doing business in Asia, as countries in Asia embrace diverse cultural origins and economic and political heritages.

Home to 50 countries and an estimated population of 4,462.7 million, or nearly 60 per cent of the total population of the world (UN DESA, 2018), the continent of Asia stretches to some 44,614,000 square kilometres, roughly one-third of the land surface of Earth (Chandrasekhar et al., 2018). A brief division of Asia is introduced in the box below.

Geographic divisions of Asia

Eurasia: The continent that stretches from the Atlantic Ocean to its west and the Pacific Ocean to its east.
Central Asia: Located along Europe's eastern borders and in the middle of the Eurasia continent.
Eastern Asia: Refers to Asia's north-east region, which is bordered by Central Asia to the west.
Southern and Southeast Asia: Regions that include the south of Eastern and Central Asia.
Northern Asia: Mainly consists of Russia, located north of Mongolia and east of the Ural Mountains.
Western Asia: Located in the western-most region of Asia and across the Red Sea, overlooking Northern Africa.

Geo-economic clusters of Asia

Grounded on geographic conditions, countries in the same region are tied together to embrace **globalization** drift and to seek mutual economic growth. A typical arrangement is to foster **free trade zones** (FTZ) and promote **free trade agreements** (FTAs). One example in Asia is the Asia-Pacific Economic Cooperation, an organization of 21 member countries (APEC, 2018b), sanctioning its member countries fewer entry barriers. APEC is used by some scholars as a basis to define Asia-Pacific as a geo-economic region that includes both developed and developing countries alongside Pacific coastlines, such as the US and countries in Eastern, Southern, Southeast Asia and Oceania.

Although Asia grew by 5.5 per cent in 2018, accounting for nearly two-thirds of the global figure (IMF, 2018: 11), it is experiencing increasing gaps in terms of levels of development. As shown in Table 1.1, some representatives of Asia-Pacific countries can be categorized by their economic status (IMF, 2018).

The complexity and population base of Asia make it the most exciting yet challenging place to do business. Knowing the geo-economic data helps businesses to better grasp opportunities and challenges and enables them to thrive in some of the world's most rapidly growing economies. The top ten economies in Asia with the highest growth rates as of April 2018 are shown in Figure 1.1.

Table 1.1   Divisions of Asia by economic status

Areas	Countries	Economic Status
Developed Asia	Australia, Hong Kong SAR, Japan, Macao SAR, New Zealand, Singapore, South Korea, Taiwan	Growth remains strong and is expected to continue, along with world trade
Emerging Asia	People's Republic of China (China), India, Indonesia, Malaysia, the Philippines, Qatar, Saudi Arab Emirates, Vietnam	Projected to gain further momentum but facing risks such as border disputes, unstable or unpredictable government policies
Developing Asia	Armenia, Bangladesh, Bhutan, Cambodia, Cyprus, Iran, Lao PDR, Myanmar, Nepal, Sri Lanka, Turkey	Optimal growth is projected but with uncertain factors, including unstable or unpredictable government policies
Under-developed Asia	Afghanistan, Azerbaijan, Iraq, the Maldives, Pakistan	No data on growth is specifically given, under-developed Asia experienced real GDP growth rates varying from 2% to 5.6% as of early 2018

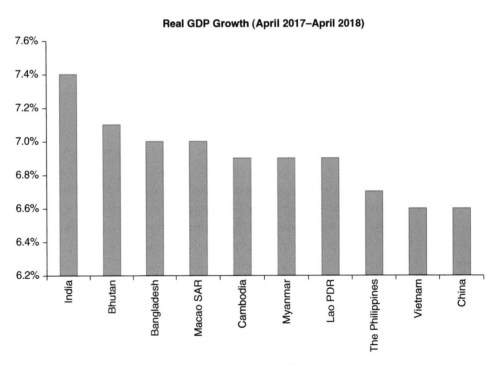

Figure 1.1   Top ten real GDP growth economies in Asia

Source: IMF DataMapper, 2018

To enhance deeper cooperation between countries of different economic status, various trade agreements were formulated and signed. There were 262 trade and investment agreements in Asia (UN ESCAP, 2017). Some of the examples are shown in the box below.

Examples of Asian RTAs

Asia-Pacific Trade Agreement (APTA)
ASEAN Free Trade Area (AFTA)
Pacific Islands Countries Trade Agreement (PICTA)
South Asian Free Trade Area (SAFTA)
The Comprehensive and Progressive Agreement for Trans-Pacific Partnership (CPTPP)

Geo-political clusters and border disputes of Asia

Notwithstanding increasing regional cooperation, parts of the region were also prone to disagreements that were illustrated, among others, by intermittent border disputes.

Asia witnessed numerous disruptive border disputes, of which some have caused geo-political risks and uncertainty, which affected the business environment. Eighteen major border disputes are shown in Table 1.2.

Table 1.3 further explains selected border disputes in Asia.

Table 1.2   Asia's tangled borders

1. Fergana Valley	The Fergana Valley is a snarled border with ethnic enclaves claimed by the neighbouring states of Kyrgyzstan, Tajikistan and Uzbekistan. Since the collapse of the Soviet Union, the border has been contested because of the valley's valuable transportation routes and natural resources, as well as the stranding of ethnic populations outside of their respective states. This led to large-scale ethnic violence between Kyrgyz and Uzbeks in 1990 and again in 2010.
2. Durand Line	The Durand Line, which demarcates the border between Afghanistan and Pakistan, is a colonial legacy from when the British controlled Pakistan. Although the international community views the Durand Line as an official border, Afghanistan has complained since the 1940s that the border cuts the ethnic Pashtun population in half. Tensions over the border have led to artillery exchanges between the Afghan and Pakistani militaries as recently as May 2013.

(Continued)

Table 1.2   Asia's tangled borders (*Continued*)

3. Kashmir	Kashmir has been a point of contention between India and Pakistan since the Muslim-majority region's ruler opted to stay within India when bother countries became independent in 1947. Since then, the nations have fought three wars over the region and have engaged in multiple skirmishes, including one in 2014. The rival claims have also contributed to ongoing insurgencies in the region that have resulted in terrorist attacks.
4. Aksai Chin	Aksai Chin is a contested border between China and India. China claims the region as part of its Xinjiang province, while India insists that the area is part of greater Kashmir. The two countries fought a war over the area in 1962 but agreed to demarcate the border in the 1990s. However, China has continued to challenge India and vice-versa, with a border standoff occurring between the two sides in 2014.
5. Sikkim	In 1967, China and India agreed to designate the former autonomous monarchy of Sikkim as an official part of India. However, China has continued to position soldiers more than a kilometre into Sikkim in a sliver of land called the Finger Point. China's reopening of the border there is thought to be aimed at putting pressure on India to recognize China's territorial demands elsewhere.
6. Bhutanese Enclaves	Following the conquest of Tibet in the early 1950s, China took control of numerous enclaves along the border with Bhutan. This led to close military collaboration between Bhutan and India before China defeated India in a 1962 border war. Bhutan continues to protest the inclusion of its areas, though China has signalled it is willing to reach an end to the ongoing deliberations over the border.
7. Indian and Bangladeshi Enclaves	The India–Bangladesh border is rife with isolated enclaves in each other's territories. There are more than 150 such enclaves between the two countries, with rampant crime and poor access to medical care because citizens must cross international boundaries to reach their respective country for assistance. An agreement for the countries to exchange the enclaves took place in 2011, but it has yet to be ratified by the Indian parliament.
8. Arunachal Pradesh	Arunachal Pradesh is one of the 29 states that make up India, while China views a significant portion of the state as part of the larger South Tibet. The Tibetans and the British demarcated the current border in 1914, although China does not recognize the agreement.
9. Preah Vihear	Preah Vihear, a 900-year-old Buddhist temple perched on the Thai–Cambodian border, has led to decades of violence between the two counties. The Thai and Cambodian militaries have routinely exchanged fire, and ultranationalists from both sides have used the temple as a rallying cry. In 2013, the International Court of Justice ruled that the site belonged to Cambodia.

(Continued)

Table 1.2 Asia's tangled borders (*Continued*)

10. Paracel Islands	The Paracel Islands have been a point of contention between Vietnam and China since at least the 1970s. China deployed an oil rig within Vietnam's exclusive economic zone in May 2014 and added a second rig in June. China removed the rigs, but these actions led to an increase in tensions, with Vietnamese and Chinese ships ramming one another around the island chain.
11. Spratly Islands	The oil- and gas-rich Spratly Islands have a checkerboard of competing claimants. China and the Philippines each lay claim to the entire chain, but Malaysia, Indonesia and Brunei all claim some part of the islands as well.
12. Scarborough Shoal	The Scarborough Shoal is a particularly rich area for fishing, which is significantly closer to the Philippines than to China. However, China has claimed the area, partly because of claims that Chinese sailors discovered the island. China restricted access to the island following a standoff in 2012.
13. Pratas Islands	The Pratas Islands are claimed by both China and Taiwan. However, this dispute is especially complex, as China claims sovereignty over all of Taiwan. Taiwan houses a military outpost and a civilian airport on the Pratas Islands.
14. Senkaku Islands	Both China and Japan claim the Senkaku Islands, though the islands are under the administrative control of Japan. The islands are uninhabited, although they are rich in fishing areas and sit in an area of potential natural gas deposits. China and Japan have frequently dispatched vessels to the islands, but China recently began sending fewer military vessels and more fishing vessels in an attempt to bring the islands under de facto control.
15. The DMZ	Despite an armistice that ended the Korean War, North and South Korea technically remain at war. This is nowhere more apparent than along the demilitarized zone, the tentative frontier separating the counties that is the most armed region in the world. Despite numerous clashes and exchanges of fire between the north and the south, the DMZ has remained as the de facto border since 1953.
16. Mount Baekdu	Mount Baekdu is a mountain of near-sacred significance for Koreans. Korea's first kingdom was established at the mountain, while the North Korean regime reveres it as the birthplace of Kim Jong-il. Control of the mountain is now split between North Korea and China. However, South Korean nationalists frequently insist that the whole mountain belongs to Korea.
17. Liancourt Rocks	The Liancourt Rocks are a small group of islets in the Sea of Japan between the Korean peninsula and Japan. South Korea, North Korea and Japan all lay claim to the area, which is currently administered by South Korea. In April 2014, Tokyo reaffirmed Japanese sovereignty over the rocks.

(Continued)

Table 1.2   Asia's tangled borders (*Continued*)

18. The Kuril Islands	The Kuril Islands are an island chain linking Japan's northern Hokkaido island to the Russian Kamchatka Peninsula. Japan and Russia have disputing claims over the four islands closest to Japan. Russia insists that the islands are theirs following annexation by the Soviets during World War II. The islands continue to be a major point of contention. In August 2014, Russia held military exercises in the islands, and Japan has said that in 2014 it had to scramble its jets in response to possible Russian aerial incursions more than at any other time in the past quarter-century.

Table 1.3   Selected border disputes in Asia

Disputes (selected)	Involved Parties	Main Challenges
Korean Peninsula	North Korea and South Korea	• Division of the Korean Peninsula between the Democratic People's Republic of Korea (North, advocating socialism) and the Republic of Korea (South, advocating capitalism and democracy) in 1950, the conflict between two different political regimes is still ongoing
South China Sea	China, Taiwan, Malaysia, Indonesia, the Philippines, Vietnam and Brunei	• Island and maritime
Senkaku Islands	Japan, China and Taiwan	• Island and maritime (East China Sea area)
Himalayas	China and India	• Territorial issue
Jammu & Kashmir	India and Pakistan	• Territorial issue

Cultural clusters of Asia

An important indicator of a shared culture is the shared language and dialect. Table 1.4 displays the main geographical distribution of Asian languages, listed in descending order of speaker number.

A widely advocated cultural and social value throughout Asia is **collectivism**. Business units from Western countries, where people generally cherish individualism, almost always find this to be one of the biggest barriers when they come to do business in Asia. Asian companies often make business decisions based on group opinions and consensus, whereas in most Western countries individual input is more valued. Collectivism in some countries (Chapter 7) explains why most Asian countries are more comfortable with power inequalities than Western countries (Schweitzer and Alexander, 2014: 14–16).

Table 1.4   Divisions of Asia by language

Category	Language Represented	Areas of Usage
Sino-Tibetan	Chinese Mandarin and Chinese Cantonese	Eastern, Southern and Southeastern Asia
Indo-European	Indo-Iranian, Slavic languages	Mainly in Central and South Asia, and part of Northern Asia
Altaic	Korean, Japanese and Turkish	Northern Asia and Central Western Asia
Afro-Asiatic	Modern Arabic	Southwest Asia

According to Edward T. Hall, two forms of 'time' are important to international business: **polychronic** and **monochronic**. In a polychronic time system, engagement and completion of human actions are far more important than schedules. On the contrary, a monochronic time system is in favour of segmented time and thus highly respects schedules and appointments (Hall and Hall, 1977: 13–14).

People from polychronic and monochronic time systems correspondingly fall into two types of communication systems: high and low 'context'. Since polychronic people spend great amounts of time in building relationships, information and communication become implicit and intangible when it comes to completing work tasks (high context). Meanwhile, monochronic people need extra information and communication to conduct their tasks (low context) (Hall and Hall, 1977: 6–7).

Table 1.5 explains and compares some differences between Asian and Western culture in these two respects (Schweitzer and Alexander, 2014: 19–20).

Table 1.5   Asian culture versus Western culture

Culture Respect	What Is Typical in Asia	What Is Typical in Western Countries
Time	Polychronic: • Attention is given mostly to: • relationships • clients, patrons, customers • friends, colleagues and family members	Monochronic: • Attention is given mostly to: • the project • priorities • procedures
Context	High context: • indirect, non-verbal messages • finessed, vague, indefinite • situation and people are more important than words spoken • disagreement is personalized	Low context: • direct, verbal message • specific, to the point, definite • great importance is placed on words spoken • disagreement is depersonalized

It is important to understand that the value of collectivism which is socially recognized in most Asian countries that we just discussed does not necessarily refer to the political element that influences or leads to nations' economic system such as a **planned economy**. For example, in China, once known as the biggest socialist country in the world, government no longer plans goods for the welfare of the country. The planned economy has gradually been diluted since the reform and opening-up policy in China started in1978. In fact, different political systems are not mutually exclusive, and nowadays 'mixed economic systems are observed more often than pure economies' (Cavusgil et al., 2013: 30–31).

In summary, no other continent has its coastlines and inner lands shared by the same multitude of countries as Asia. The clusters presented in this chapter help businesses to better comprehend and formulate their marketing and internationalization strategies, which will be discussed in the following chapters. The book will focus mainly (though not exclusively) on Eastern, Southern and Southeast Asia, and on selected market groupings.

1.3 THE CONTEXT: THE INTERNATIONAL BUSINESS ENVIRONMENT IN A TRANSFORMING ASIA

Introduction

This sub-chapter provides you with a comprehensive perspective on key trends that are transformative to most of Asia. We will focus on the themes that are most relevant to the Asian cross-border business environment. Within this region, transformation is ongoing and demonstrates certain important commonalities.

Key transformational trends

- Growth and the continuing emergence of the Asian middle class.
- Demographic issues and skills development.
- High tech and servicification patterns.
- Acceleration and facilitation: Asia-focused international market expansion activity.
- Indispensable: intermediate products and services.
- Capacity building payoffs.
- Moving together: market integration trends.
- Challenging trends.

Growth and the continuing emergence of the Asian middle class

Across Asia, growth rates continue to rise. It has proven to be relatively resilient to global crises effects and impacts in the long term compared with other parts of the world. Market growth is mainly driven by expanding populations and by income. An increasingly large, wealthy middle class continues to emerge across the region. The 'golden triangle' of Japan and South Korea, followed by China, came first. India and large parts of Southeast Asia are following. In Southeast Asia, growth results from consumption growth due to the increasing purchasing power of consumers, rather than from population growth (Potia and Remes, 2016). This is accompanied by consumption shifts from limiting purchases to staple commodities to also including high value and quality produce, products and services. Simultaneously, urbanization is growing, and offers business opportunities in infrastructure, smart cities development and much more.

Demographic issues and skills development

Demographic trends separate Asia into particularly young and particularly aging economies. Japan, for example, not only needs to open more **export** markets to stimulate its economy, but also, given an aging population, there is a dire need to attract highly skilled foreign labour along the Singapore example or that of Hong Kong. This provides for labour mobility and expatriation opportunities. While major parts of Asia (e.g. ASEAN) engage into educational reforms focusing on quality and technical skills, skill gaps remain, especially in healthcare, manufacturing, engineering, construction, hospitality and tourism, retail, ICT, banking and financial services.

High tech and servicification patterns

Economically well-developed parts of Asia are highly connected, high-tech savvy and transition from manufacturing to advanced manufacturing and services and the digital economy. In particular, Southeast Asia invests to leverage the benefits of digital transformation. Varying trends in skills reveal a skills gap in this field though. Although less developed countries show high connectivity through information and communication technology (ICT), having leapfrogged into the mobile phone and digital world in many cases, user skills exceed producer and programmer skills with only some exceptions. This gap is blatant in advanced information technology (IT) (especially artificial intelligence – AI) in most countries other than the highly developed Asian economies. An emerging trend is that of Southeast Asia's upskilling through capability building, which provides strategic opportunity for business. In Indonesia, for example, this has led to the digitalization of some business-focused administration (e.g. company name registration). In India, the success in demonetization revealed ongoing exciting digital potential. Its Fintech sector is booming, and innovative start-up **mergers** and **acquisitions** are taking place that sustain these trends.

Acceleration and facilitation: Asia-focused international market expansion activity

Among facilitating factors, various countries have moved towards more international, more diverse, and more welcoming trade and FDI policies. One example is Japan. Debt-ridden for many years, it remains limited in its capacity to fully tap into the benefits of international trade and investment, despite very significant value-adding capabilities. Yet its international free trade pacts with ten Pacific Rim countries and with the European Union (EU) are helping its reposition, and in particular, are increasing its participation in global value chains across the region. Australia, as a different example, has benefitted for many decades from the commodities boom across Asia. As its economy is transitioning, it focuses on other Asia-Pacific regions and 'Indo-Pacific Asia', also through trade agreements to access Industry 0.4 via international business and research partnerships.

Indispensable: Intermediate products and services

Asia's role in GVCs shows continuous growth trends, meaning that more firms are engaged in intra-and inter-firm production and trade of unfinished goods and services across borders. Among developing regions worldwide, Southeast Asia participates most in GVCs, as well as (with Europe) Central Asia (OECD, 2015: 17); yet South Asia shows the lowest participation rates, though also growing. The Organisation for Economic Co-operation and Development (OECD, 2015: 18) notes that this may be linked to lesser regional trade integration.

Asia has a vast array of production advantages. Its locational interdependence of developed and less-developed countries across the region 'leverages on the heterogeneity of location specific advantages within the region' (Suder et al., 2015: 404). This leads to greater inclusion of peripheral economies, given their factor advantages, e.g. labour costs. In turn this is expected to lead to greater development through automation, AI and upskilling.

Capacity building payoffs

Capacity building continues to be an important feature of cross-border engagement across those Asian economies that are highly diverse in economic status. Indonesia, the largest of the ASEAN economies, and Malaysia are examples where capacity building provided by other countries, e.g. Australia, pays off. Among improvements, a reduction of red tape for cross-border trade and investment yields greater micro-and macro-economic benefits also for trade partners. Both countries are among the top APEC countries for FDI increase, together with Vietnam. In Vietnam, for example, minority investor protections and electronic customs clearance systems increase international trade opportunities. On-going industrial capacity building, infrastructure investment and resources investment support these trends.

Moving together: Market integration trends

A great part of Asia is increasingly connected through market integration. Among new FTAs in the region, seven are intra-APEC. Another 14 FTAs in the region involve at least one APEC economy.

The Trans-Pacific Partnership takes integrational benefits to unique cross-fertilization levels, through a unique set of comprehensive **tariff** and **non-tariff barrier** reductions across parts of Asia and part of the Americas. This is expected to help counterbalance issues that hold back South Asia's participation in the trade of intermediate goods and services, which constitute more than 75 per cent of international trade. Southeast Asia, with the most comprehensive and deepest regional integration agreements, continues its dynamic approach to multilateralism.

Table 1.6   The rise of the Asian FTA

FTAs	2000	2017
Bilateral (across Asia and with non-Asian countries)	9	97
Plurilateral	5	38

Source: PWC, 2018

Challenging trends

Regulatory challenges are among the regional trends that are specifically, though not exclusively, visible in the example of India. Particularly complex environments for FDI are due to an unpredictable regulatory landscape and often vastly differing rules between locations. In addition, Asia's third-largest economy suffers from uneven governmental policy results, for example in goods and services taxation, where the services sector suffers from up to 3 per cent increases (from 15 to 18 per cent in 2017).

Corruption is a recurring challenge across Asia and adds to the challenge of red tape. While the latter trend is weakening, corruption trends appear harder to solve. Concentrated ownership is one aspect that challenges corporate governance, from a cultural and institutional perspective. Parts of Asia, especially some parts of Central Asia, suffer from particularly weak institutional contexts and consequently lagging economic and social development. Ongoing, long-lasting geo-political, geo-economic and social turmoil means that tapping into locations such as Afghanistan, for example, requires unique capabilities and knowledge (Suder et al., 2016).

The diversity of political systems is equally challenging. While there has been a sustained trend towards democratic systems, monarchies persist and dictatorships remain. Geo-political issues stemming from North Korea's regime withhold some of Asia's capacity to fully benefit from regional connectivity. Such issues expose a context in which world powers convey their diplomatic strength throughout the continent.

Ready to dive into in-depth analyses and case study illustrations? The following chapters of this book will explain and analyse business impacts stemming from this context, in detail, and illustrate them through case studies.

1.4 THE INTERNATIONAL FIRM: MAIN SIZE PATTERNS IN ASIA

The **multinational corporation (MNC)** is typically the face of international business. It is also known as the **multinational enterprise (MNE)** and the transnational corporation (TNC). This is an organization that has business operations or investments in two or more countries. The earliest MNEs emerged from the developed world and were business corporations with huge resources and operations across multiple business sites. These continue to dominate the world of international business but are now supported by the emergence of firms of varying sizes from across the world.

The evolution of the modern MNE is linked to industrialization and expansion of trade and the earliest MNEs thus emerged from the industrialized countries. The Dutch

East India Company is often considered to be the world's first MNE, formed for the purpose of trade and other colonial activities that marked the beginning of the era of modern international business. The growth of international trade relations, facilitated by industrialization and improvements in transport in the late nineteenth century, led to the growth of international business. Asia played a significant role in the earliest international business activities as the source of raw materials such as cotton and tea for the factories of Europe.

Technological advances and inventions such as the steam engine, electric turbine and the railway locomotive enabled the earliest European companies to establish overseas production. MNEs from USA industrialized much later, driven by technological innovation, the use of electrical power and the internal combustion engine, which helped to transform factory production processes. This allowed them to produce goods of a consistent quality for vastly expanded markets and to reap the benefits of economies of scale. The large American conglomerates, such as United States Steel, American Telephone and Telegraph (presently known as AT&T), General Electric (GE), Standard Oil, Ford and General Motors, are symbols of American dominance in the world economy in the first half of the twentieth century.

The earliest Asian MNEs emerged from Japan in the period following World War II. The Japanese economy went through an 'economic miracle' of rebuilding its industrial base and infrastructure from scratch, facilitated by the government's supportive role and the ability to exploit technological advances in production and information. This led to the emergence of the Japanese MNE as a strong player in key sectors like automobiles and electronics.

The 1980s and 1990s saw the rise of East Asia as an industrial power, based on technological learning, adoption and adaptation, combined with a determined focus on penetrating Western markets. Despite the setback of the financial crisis of the late 1990s the Asian MNE continued to make rapid inroads into the manufacturing sector, in basic sectors like steel, in services like hotels and trading operations, and in high-technology sectors like semiconductors and flat panel displays. The rise of Asian MNEs from India and China changed the nature of international business and the face of the traditional MNE. Some of the MNEs from Asia include Lenovo (China), Acer (Taiwan), Petronas (Malaysia), Samsung Electronics (Korea), LG (Korea), Jardine Matheson (Hong Kong), Neptune Orient Lines (Singapore), and Li & Fung (Hong Kong), often known as emerging market MNEs (EMNEs).

Types of MNEs

The traditional MNE

The early MNEs from the developed countries existed in a relatively closed and domestically oriented world economic system. They made their foreign expansion through mini versions of themselves as more or less self-contained national subsidiaries. These MNEs exploited their ownership advantages, in foreign locations through internalization, to establish their global presence. These were large business firms with operations in multiple locations which replicated their domestic business operations. Typical examples include US MNEs such as General Electric (GE) and General Motors.

Dragon TNCs

The **dragon TNCs**, also called latecomers, are a cluster of firms, which originated from the peripheral regions of the global economy (such as the Asia-Pacific region) in a phase of catch-up industrialization. They emerged as challengers to the existing large TNCs, and successfully established themselves in the global marketplace. They are also known as latecomer TNCs because they arrived late on the international stage and used strategies that were different from those of their traditional developed country counterparts.

Born global firms

Born global firms, also called global start-ups or international new ventures, are SMEs that almost bypass internationalization as a process as they start and operate from day one in global markets as global players, servicing their customers wherever they are to be found. They are characterized by a strategy of accelerated internationalization, which has changed the dynamics of international competition. Firms from the Indian information technology sector, such as Mphasis, have made their global entry through a series of mergers and acquisitions, enabled by prior learning (Varma, 2011). Geo Search from Japan was established in 1989 as a manufacturer of high tech equipment for road construction. It designed the world's first land mine detector in 1997, which made it a global player in the markets of Kuwait, Cambodia, Afghanistan and Lebanon.

Global niche players

Global niche players have a 'global' orientation, and concentrate their efforts, on maintaining a leading position in a very narrowly defined niche market. Firms like Hauni, which is the chief manufacturer of the world's cigarette-making machines, show that suitably focused geocentric firms can sustain their world position against the efforts of huge multinational competitors (Mathews and Zander, 2007).

Micro MNEs

Micro MNEs (Ibeh et al., 2004) or infant MNEs (Lindqvist, 1991) are a body of smaller MNEs in terms of resources, staff and capital, which originate from the industrial countries and use vigorous, innovative strategies to enter the global market. Examples include the Dutch animal nutrition and fish feed manufacturing firm Nutreco, or Fresenius, the German manufacturer of renal dialysis machines (Mathews and Zander, 2007), and Alibaba (China).

State-owned MNEs

State-owned MNEs, or state-owned enterprises (SOEs), are an important feature of the current international business landscape. They are defined as separate legal entities established or acquired by governments to engage in commercial activities, including FDI operations, by way of having affiliates abroad or engaging in non-equity modes. An additional criterion is that a government entity should either own at least 10 per cent of the capital, be the largest shareholder or benefit from a 'golden share' (UNCTAD, 2017).

At present there are about 1,500 state-owned MNEs (1.5 per cent of all MNEs) with more than 86,000 foreign affiliates and these are engaged in 11 per cent of the total global **greenfield investments**. In Asia, China has the largest number of SOEs (18 per cent), followed by Malaysia and India (UNCTAD, 2017). The largest non-financial SOEs in 2016 are COSCO (China), Petronas (Malaysia) and ONGC (India).

Internationalization strategies

Asset exploitation

The asset exploitation perspective explains the strategies of incumbents from the developed world. These firms leveraged their existing FSAs in new locations for international venturing, to get a **competitive advantage** over indigenous firms in the host country (Caves, 1971; Hymer, 1976).

Asset seeking/augmenting

The asset augmenting or asset seeking perspective is an alternate viewpoint that explained the rise of MNEs from the **emerging markets**, especially from Asia. It explains the strategies of latecomer EMNEs to seek resources and overcome their competitive disadvantages (Makino et al., 2002; Mathews, 2002, 2006). These alternate perspectives explain

FDI as a tool for enhancing **competitiveness** through the acquisition of resources and capabilities that are lacking in EMNEs, rather than exploiting an existing set of advantages.

Linkage, Leverage, Learning (LLL) strategy

The emergence of the latecomer firms, discussed above, is best understood in terms of the LLL theory (Mathews, 2002, 2006). These firms have leveraged the linkages on existing global value chains and used the learning from these networks to establish themselves as successful players in the global economy. Ispat (now Mittal Steel) is the world's largest steel producer. It began its life as a tiny steel producer in Indonesia but grew through the exploitation of its latecomer advantage in utilizing mini-mills and electric arc technology, combined with a new feedstock technology termed direct reduced iron (DRI). Its growth strategy was built around leveraged acquisitions of former state-owned steel plants around the world. These strategies have been further elaborated on in detail in Chapter 2.

The springboard strategy

The springboard strategy (Luo and Tung, 2007: 18) uses international expansion as a springboard to acquire critical resources for improving a firm's global competitiveness. Springboard is a long-term strategy that involves a series of systematic outward foreign direct investment (OFDI) activities, aimed at acquiring strategic assets such as technology, brands and access to global consumers. The strategy is revolving, since it is integrated with domestic business activities, aimed at strengthening domestic capabilities for further international expansion. Firms engaging in the springboard strategy are EMNEs from newly industrializing economies such as Taiwan, Singapore and South Korea as well as MNEs from the advanced economies.

The leapfrogging perspective

The leapfrogging strategy helps latecomer MNEs to catch up with the competitive position of early movers through the use of radical technological innovations and by taking on more risk. This helps firms to avoid the risk of technological obsolescence and proprietary technology diffusion to rivals.

Parental networks/business groups

The use of strategic networks (Chen, 1998) helps small and weak firms to make their foreign market entry. These networks include parental networks and business groups which provide member firms with the necessary information, knowledge, resources, markets and technologies to enable their internationalization.

REFERENCES

APEC (Asia-Pacific Economic Cooperation) (2018a) *APEC Regional Trends Analysis: Trade, Policy, and the Pursuit of Inclusion.* APEC Policy Support Unit, May.

APEC (Asia-Pacific Economic Cooperation) (2018b) Member Economies. Available at: https://www.apec.org/About-Us/About-APEC/Member-Economies (accessed 18 June 2018).

Bender, J. and Nudelman, M. (2016) Asia's tangled border. Available at: https://www.businessinsider.com/asias-disputed-borders-2016-03 (accessed 17 August 2018).

Caves, R.E. (1971) International corporations: The international economics of foreign investment. *Economica*, 38: 1–17.

Cavusgil, S.T., Ghauri, P.N. and Akcal, A.A. (2013) *Doing Business in Emerging Markets*, 2nd edn. London: Sage Publications.

Chandrasekhar, S. et al. (2018) Asia Continent. *Encyclopaedia Britannica*. Available at: www.britannica.com/place/Asia (accessed 18 June 2018).

Hall, E.T. and Hall, M.R. (1977) *Understanding Cultural Differences*. Yarmouth, ME: Intercultural Press. Available at: http://teaching.up.edu/bus511/xculture/Hall%20and%20Hall%201990,%20ch1.pdf (accessed 17 August 2018).

Hymer, S. (1976) *The International Operations of National Firms: A Study of Direct Foreign Investment*. Boston, MA: MIT Press.

Ibeh, K., Johnson, J.E., Dimitratos, P. and Slow, J. (2004) Micro multinationals: Some preliminary evidence on an emergent 'Star' of the international entrepreneurship field. *Journal of International Entrepreneurship*, 2(4): 289–303.

IMF (International Monetary Fund) (2018) Asia Pacific Regional Economic Outlook. Available at: www.imf.org/en/publications/REO (accessed 18 June 2018).

IMF DataMapper (2018) Real GDP Growth Annual Percentage Change. Available at: www.imf.org/external/datamapper/NGDP_RPCH@WEO/OEMDC/ADVEC/WEOWORLD/APQ (accessed 20 August 2018).

Lindqvist, M. (1991) 'Infant multinationals: the internationalization of young, technology based Swedish firms', dissertation, Stockholm School of Economics, Institute of International Business, Stockholm.

Luo, Y. and Tung, R.L. (2007) International expansion of emerging market enterprises: A springboard perspective. *Journal of International Business Studies*, 38(4): 481–498.

Luo, Y. and Tung, R.L. (2018) A general theory of springboard MNEs. *Journal of International Business Studies*, 49(2): 129–152.

Makino, S., Lau, C.M, and Yeh, R.S (2002) Asset exploitation vs asset seeking: Implications for location choice of foreign direct investment from newly industrialized economies. *Journal of International Business Studies*, 33(3): 403–442.

Mathews, J.A. (2002) Competitive advantages of the latecomer firm: A resource based account of industrial catch-up strategies. *Asia Pacific Journal of Management*, 19: 467–488.

Mathews, J.A. (2006) Dragon multinationals: New players in 21st century globalization. *Asia Pacific Journal of Management*, 23: 5–27.

Mathews, J.A and Zander, I. (2007) The International Entrepreneurial Dynamics of Accelerated Internationalization. *Journal of International Business Studies*, 38(3): 387–403.

OECD (Organisation for Economic Co-operation and Development) and World Bank Group (2015) *Inclusive Global Value Chains: Policy options in trade and complementary areas for GVC Integration by small and medium enterprises and low-income developing countries*. Report prepared for submission to G20 Trade Ministers Meeting, Istanbul, Turkey, 6 October.

Potia, A. and Remes, J. (2016) Who are the future consumers of South-East Asia? World Economic Forum, 26 May. Available at: www.weforum.org/agenda/2016/05/who-are-the-future-consumers-of-south-east-asia/ (accessed 20 June 2018).

PWC (PricewaterhouseCoopers) (2018) *Free Trade Agreement Utilisation Study*. Report prepared for the Department of Foreign Affairs and Trade's (DFAT), Canberra.

Schweitzer, S. and Alexander, L. (2014) *Access to Asia*. Hoboken, NJ: John Wiley & Sons, Inc.

State Government of Victoria (2018) ASEAN Trade and Investment Statement Consultation Paper. Doing Business in East Asia Workshop, March, Melbourne.

Suder, G., Birnik, A., Nielsen, N. and M. Riviere (2016) Extreme case learning: The Manager perspective on rare knowledge and capabilities development. *Journal of Knowledge Management Practice*, 15(1): 130–145.

Suder, G., Liesch, P., Inomato, S., Jormanainen, I. and Meng, B. (2015) The evolving geography of production hubs and regional value chains across East Asia: Trade in value-added. *Journal of World Business*, 50(3): 404–416.

UN DESA (United Nations, Department of Economic and Social Affairs, Population Division) (2017) World Population Prospects: The 2017 Revision. Available at: http://esa.un.org/unpd/wpp/ (accessed 24 August 2018).

UN DESA (United Nations, Department of Economic and Social Affairs, Statistics Division) (2018) Methodology: Geographic regions. Available at: https://unstats.un.org/unsd/methodology/m49/#fn1 (accessed 24 August 2018).

UN ESCAP (United Nations, Economic and Social Commission for Asia and the Pacific) (2017) Trade and Investment Agreement Database. Available at: www.unescap.org/content/aptiad/ (accessed 18 June 2018).

Varma, S. (2011) Born global acquirers from Indian IT: An exploratory case study. *International Journal of Emerging Markets*, 6(4): 351–368.

World Bank (2019) *Global Economic Outlook: Slow Growth, Policy Changes*. Washington DC: World Bank. Available at: www.worldbank.org/en/publication/global-economicprospects (accessed 6 April 2020).

2
INTERNATIONAL BUSINESS STRATEGY: ASIA

2.1 INTERNATIONAL BUSINESS STRATEGY INTO AND ACROSS ASIA

This chapter focuses on international business strategy typically utilized to do business in and across Asia. It covers:

- international business strategy into and across Asia
- a case study on going to India – opportunities and challenges for APUS's globalization
- a case study about the Charoen Pokphand Group – the strategy of a cross-border 'latecomer'
- it concludes by highlighting strategic implications.

A key issue in international business is the strategy for entering a foreign market. It is held that the world of international business has gone through a transformation in the last few decades – with shrinking economic distance, lower transaction costs and de facto economic integration. As we saw in the last chapter, there is a variety of new actors from SMEs to born global firms, and from private equity to state-controlled enterprises and sovereign wealth funds using varied strategies to gain access to new markets and territories.

A major hurdle to be overcome by the MNE in making a foreign market entry is the **liability of foreignness**, which is the disadvantage suffered by the MNE in the host country due to its non-native status. A major cause of the liability of foreignness is the differences in the business environments between home and host countries. The business environment has three major dimensions – economic, political-legal and social-cultural – which create a unique background in which business firms operate. Differences in the economic, political and legal systems in the host country as compared to the home country environment give rise to regulatory and operational risks arising out of trade and investment barriers between countries. The host country also has a different cultural environment and MNEs must adapt to these differences as well, in order to survive and grow in the host country. Chapter 4 will shed further light on these essential components of the business environment.

In a changing global order, the MNE has to constantly adapt itself to changing environments. The years from 2017 to 2020 have seen a new wave of de-globalization (or 'slowbalization' as *The Economist* termed it in 2019) in the world economy, manifested as initiatives of increasing nationalistic expansionistic tendencies mainly led by Asian powers, protectionism for trade and investment mainly led by the USA, and a transformation of global and regional integration and des-integration, the latter mainly led by the United Kingdom's exit from the European Union and observed with much attention worldwide as to impact. This has created new rules of the game for MNEs.

A firm's business strategy has four major aspects as it examines the feasibility of entering a new market. These are concerned with decisions relating to the following issues:

- drivers of foreign market entry (WHY)
- location (WHERE)
- timing (WHEN)
- mode of entry (HOW).

All these decisions taken together determine the MNE's competitive position in a new business environment. These entry strategy decisions are important since they determine the MNE's investment environment, resource commitment and evolutionary path.

Drivers of foreign market entry (why enter a foreign market)

There are two kinds of factors driving a firm towards foreign market entry:

Pull factors are proactive motivations, which provide the stimuli for a domestic firm to explore a foreign market. Proactive factors pull a domestic business firm into foreign markets, by giving them the stimulus to move into new unexplored markets. For instance, changes in the World Trade Organization (WTO) rules governing quotas on the **import** of textiles into developed countries, which were lifted in 2005, created such an opportunity, and led to an increase in the ability of Indian firms to produce apparel for foreign markets.

Push factors arise out of reactive motivations, which provide a domestic firm with the stimuli to move abroad arising out of environmental factors.

Profit maximization

Profit maximization is the most cited goal of a business enterprise through increased revenues and/or reduced costs. Entry to the international market through international trade and investment is the means through which a business firm is able to benefit from differences in labour costs, availability of resources and capital as well as differences in regulatory frameworks such as tariff barriers and taxation. The rapid growth of the out-sourcing industry is an example of firms in developed parts of the world being able to take advantage of the low-cost, skilled labour force in countries such as India, Ireland and the Philippines to maximize their profits.

Specific knowledge about a foreign market and its culture helps to provide a huge proactive stimulus. Firms such as Amway and Avon were pulled into the fast-growing Chinese market in the early 1990s in the direct marketing business and made huge profits, helped by the Chinese culture of personal connections and large close-knit families.

Growth

A firm's ability to grow is subject to its profit-making ability, which depends to a large extent on the opportunity to avail itself of large-scale economies. Since the domestic market is often saturated, limited or overcrowded, a firm can increase its scale of operations only by tapping into the demand in foreign markets. This not only leads it to newer consumers but also helps in cost reduction and increased profits. Firms are thus able to reap the benefits of location economies through the dispersal of activities to different global locations so that they can be performed efficiently and effectively. Thus, we can see that the global footwear industry, which found China to be a low-cost manufacturing destination, is now relocating to other Asian countries. Leading brands like Adidas and Nike have therefore moved their production base away from China, into Vietnam and Indonesia, as the cost of production is lower in these countries as compared to China (Bain, 2018).

Firms are pushed into foreign markets if they have *excess production capacity* that remains under-utilized for domestic markets but can be used to enter a foreign market. Changing domestic market conditions and declining sales may also propel a domestic player into foreign markets. The proximity to customers is also a push to explore a foreign market, as lower geographical distance leads to lower transaction costs for the MNE. Another important determinant is the cultural distance between the home and host country, which arises out of common cultural factors between the home and host countries. The existence of a home country diaspora in a region creates an assured market, which pushes a domestic firm into a foreign market. Marico, an Indian firm, began foreign operations by exporting coconut hair oil to Dubai, which had a huge Indian diaspora, which was a potential consumer base of its popular brand *Parachute* (Knowledge @Wharton, 2010).

Strategic factors

A firm's ability to participate in international business is often based on its core competencies. Core competence refers to skills possessed by the firm which cannot be imitated and are the source of its competitive advantage. A firm can capitalize on its distinctive resources or capabilities, which have been developed at home to enter a foreign market. Leveraging these capabilities can help a firm to establish itself through a 'first mover' advantage, leading to advantages of technological leadership, brand image, customer loyalty and a competitive position. Take, for instance, firms such as the Microsoft Corporation (USA) and Infosys (India) from the software industry and Volkswagen (Germany) and Toyota (Japan) from the automobile industry, who have penetrated the global market through products developed at home and marketed worldwide. Firms such as Toyota have been able to enter the large markets of the United States by offering products that are superior and more reliable than those of their local US rivals such as the Ford Motor Company and General Motors.

To enter a foreign market, the MNE needs a set of resources and capabilities that will help it overcome its liability of foreignness and give it the competitive advantage needed to succeed in an unfamiliar business environment.

International location choice (where to enter)

A firm's choice of foreign location is based on the existence of location and region specific advantages present in the host country, which attract foreign firms to these foreign markets. These factors are also the basis of the country competitiveness of the host country. A crucial factor that determines the firm's location choice is the motive driving its decision to enter a foreign market. There are four basic firm motives that act as determinants of its location choice – resource seeking, market seeking, efficiency seeking and **strategic asset seeking**. Firms choose their foreign market destinations driven by any one or a combination of these motives and tend to choose locations that integrate these motives effectively with greater favourable resources and institutional endowments.

Natural resource seeking motives

Natural resource seeking is usually associated with firms in the primary sector. The resource seekers are motivated by their need for cheaper resources including the associated transport and communication infrastructure. Rising prices for international raw materials and rapid economic growth have intensified the competition for these natural resources, such as the search for oil in the Middle East region. Australian MNEs are an important source of resource seeking FDI in the ASEAN region, and almost 90 per cent of the investment is directed at three countries – Singapore, Thailand and Indonesia. Leading Australian MNEs in the region include BHP Billiton Ltd and Rio Tinto for metals and minerals and Woodside Petroleum Ltd and Origin Energy Ltd for oil and gas resources (ASEAN Investment Report, 2018).

Market seeking motives

Market seeking is driven by the need to protect an existing market or to exploit new markets, motivated by prospects for growth and large market share. A firm may be driven to establish a presence in a new market prior to competitors or to counteract similar action by competitors. A firm's desire for market power may also be realized through access to a local network of suppliers and customers through investment in a local market. For instance, sea food exporters from around the world – from countries such as China, Korea, and faraway Peru and Norway – have been targeting the Japanese market, since there is a huge demand for the best varieties of seafood there.

Efficiency seeking motives

The intention of efficiency seekers is to take advantage of different factor endowments, economic systems, policies and market structures to concentrate production in a limited number of locations. Efficiency gains are the result of synergies – both static and dynamic. Static synergies include the pooling of management resources, revenue enhancement by using each other's marketing and distribution networks, purchasing synergies, economies of scale in production leading to cost reductions and the avoidance of duplication of production, research and development (R&D) or other activities. Dynamic synergies involve the matching of complementary skills and resources to enhance a firm's innovatory capabilities with a long-term positive effect on sales, market share and profits.

China has been the chosen destination for products ranging from shoes and toys, to high-end electronic products such as DVD players, cameras and mobile phones on account of its ability to offer the advantages of being a low-cost producer.

Strategic asset seeking motives

Firms engage in this form of FDI as a means for sustaining or enhancing their international competitiveness. Assets such as R&D or technical know-how, patents, brand names, local permits and licences and supplier and distribution networks, may usually take time to develop and are crucial to increase a firm's income-generating resources and capabilities (Dunning, 1977). The ASEAN region has seen significant FDI inflows in countries with competitive ecosystems and rapidly growing industry clusters, such as in the automotive and the electronics industries. Investing firms include Apple (United States), which established an R&D facility in Indonesia, Dyson (United Kingdom), which opened a technology centre in Singapore, and Nissan (Japan), which set up an R&D facility in Thailand. Table 2.1 provides a snapshot view of investing firms and their destinations.

Asset exploiting or asset seeking/augmenting motives

An alternate classification of the motives specified above is based on the asset exploitation versus the asset seeking/asset augmenting perspectives.

The *asset exploitation view* is the traditional perspective, which viewed foreign market entry as the transfer of a firm's proprietary assets across borders in the search for markets and resources based on its existing firm specific competitive advantages. This viewpoint explained the behaviour of the earliest MNEs that came from the developed

Table 2.1 FDI in the ASEAN region

Investing Firm	Home Country	Type of FDI	Home Country
Apple	USA	R&D facility	Indonesia
Dyson	UK	Technology centre	Singapore
Nissan	Japan	R&D facility	Thailand
Osram Opto Semiconductor	Germany	R&D facility	Malaysia
Samsung	Republic of Korea	R&D facility	Vietnam

world (Caves, 1971; Hymer, 1976). The most popular explanation in this category is the Eclectic Paradigm (Dunning,1977, 1993) also known as the **Ownership, Location, Internalization (OLI)** framework. According to this theory, firms choose FDI as their mode of foreign market entry based on existing ownership specific advantages which are exploited in foreign locations through the process of internalization.

The asset augmenting or asset seeking perspective seeks to explain foreign market entry for MNEs from the emerging markets. These MNEs were known as 'latecomers' and 'challengers' since they made a late appearance in foreign markets, using strategies that were quite different from those which had been used by developed country MNEs. This category of MNEs used foreign market entry as a strategy to build capabilities that they did not possess and to enhance their competitiveness (Makino et al., 2002; Mathews, 2002, 2006). These include Acer (Taiwan), Ispat International (Indonesia), Li & Fung (Hong Kong) and the Hong Leong Group (Malaysia).

Firm internationalization may therefore be driven by capabilities that the firm possesses (asset exploiting) or it may be driven to acquire the capabilities that it is desirous of possessing (asset augmenting/asset exploiting). The resource seeking, market seeking and **efficiency seeking motive**s are considered to be asset exploiting and the strategic asset seeking motives have been considered asset seeking/asset augmenting (Makino et al., 2002). Table 2.2 below explains these concepts.

The strategic motives that determine location choice for the MNE are not of the 'either/or type' – they are not mutually exclusive, and a firm may choose a foreign location based on its desire to achieve more than one strategic goal.

The attractiveness of a location may also change over a period of time, due to withdrawal of benefits such as tax incentives by the government, or increased costs of operation in areas that were previously considered cost effective. As we saw earlier sports manufacturers such as Nike and Adidas have shifted production from China to more cost-effective destinations such as Vietnam and Indonesia over time.

The choice of an international location involves making the choice of a region (such as the ASEAN or Southeast Asia) or country and also choosing a region within the country.

Table 2.2   Motives of foreign market entry

Asset Seeking	Asset Augmenting
Developed country MNEs	Developing country MNEs
Use existing capabilities	For acquiring capabilities
Resource seeking, market seeking, efficiency seeking motives	Strategic asset seeking

The country selection determines the macro environment for operations for the MNE, but the choice of region determines operational conditions for the MNE in a foreign land. The choice of both country and region should be made on the basis of locational determinants that are likely to influence future operations and expected returns.

For instance, firms investing in the information technology sector in India tend to choose two of the following locations: the northern cities of Delhi, Gurugram and Noida and the southern location of Hyderabad, Chennai and Bengaluru. This is due to the benefits of agglomeration – defined as the clustering of economic activities in a particular region. These benefits are as follows:

- Knowledge spillovers between closely located firms as individuals move across jobs
- Industry demand, which creates a skilled labour force that is mobile across the region
- The nature of the industry, which creates a pool of specialized buyers and suppliers who also locate within the same region.

Some of the MNEs located in these regions include Microsoft (USA) and Apple (USA) in Hyderabad, IBM (USA) and HP (USA) in Bengaluru and Google (USA) in Gurugram.

Timing of entry (when to enter)

This question relates to whether the MNE should be a first entrant into a new market and gets the benefits of the **first mover advantages** or a late entrant to avail **late mover benefits**. Both strategies have their advantages and have been used by firms to enter a new foreign market.

First mover advantages

The early entrant into the market gets the benefits of using proprietary technology, which has not been used elsewhere. This also allows them to reap the benefits of scale and scope economies in a new market.

First movers can create entry barriers for the late entrants through loyalty, which their brand gets as a first entrant into a new market. McDonald's (USA) was the first mover into the Indian market in the early 1990s and established itself as a favourite, since it learnt early lessons on how to adapt its menu according to local taste and other factors such as the consumer's ability to pay.

Domestic competition in the home market pushes some firms into foreign markets as early movers. Japanese MNEs Sony, Honda and Epson all made an early entry into the US market, to escape stiff domestic competition, beating their industry leaders Matsushita, Toyota and NEC respectively.

Early market entry also allows the MNE to establish relationships and network with both the consumer and the government. Motorola (USA), for instance, made an early entry into China and reaped the benefits as its technology was adapted by the Chinese government as the national standard for paging devices. In India, Motorola (which was acquired by Chinese MNE Lenovo in 2014) has set up a manufacturing plant for both Lenovo and Motorola smartphones, by integrating their supply chains but keeping the brand identity distinct and separate (Dhapola, 2015).

Late mover advantages

The late mover firm gains the advantages of learning from the experience of the first mover. Thus we find that although McDonald's (USA) became a favourite in the Indian market, it also gave other US MNEs such as Pizza Hut, Domino's and Burger King, who were late entrants into the Indian fast food market, important lessons that helped them to customize their menu to suit the taste of the Indian consumer.

The late entrant accesses the benefits of learning from the early movers' technological infrastructure and mistakes. Latecomers like IBM (USA) and Matsushita have a deliberate strategy of being late comers to take advantage of established market conditions when they enter a foreign market.

However, the first mover may also face some disadvantages and lose out to late-comers – such as the early mover Netscape, which lost out to Internet Explorer which was a late entrant into the market.

Experience shows that it is difficult to predict which market entry timing strategy will be successful. Take the case of first movers in the automobile industry in China in the early 1980s – Volkswagen (Germany) met with huge success, Chrysler (USA) got a moderate share of the market and Peugeot (France) was a failure and had to leave the market. Late entrants in the 1990s also saw mixed success, as General Motors (USA), Honda (Japan) and Hyundai (South Korea) achieved significant market shares, but many other firms continued to struggle to gain a foothold in the market.

Entry mode selection (how to enter)

Entry mode is the specific path taken by the MNE to enter a foreign market. Modes of entry fall into three categories: trade-related, contractual or transfer-related, and

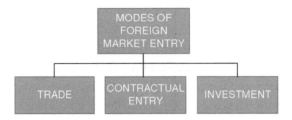

Figure 2.1 Modes of foreign market entry

investment-related entry mode. There are different degrees of resource commitment, organizational control, risks and expected returns associated with each of these modes of entry. Figure 2.1 gives a snapshot view of the above.

Trade as the mode of entry

Trade-related entry modes refer to foreign market entry through the purchase and sale of goods and services across national borders. Trade-related entry modes include exporting, **entrepôt trade** and **countertrade**.

Exporting may be direct or indirect:

- *Direct export* is the sale of goods or services produced within the organization in a foreign market, without assistance from any other party. This may be through the sales department in the initial stages of export and may later be via an export division or department that is specifically set up for this purpose.
- *Indirect export* is the sale of goods in foreign lands through different kinds of export, commission agents or intermediaries. Export intermediaries are third parties that specialize in facilitating import and export services, through support in transportation, documentation and customs claims, or they may perform more extensive services, including taking ownership of foreign-bound goods and marketing and financing functions.

Entrepôt trade refers to the import of goods for the purpose of re-exporting them.

Countertrade enables a seller and a buyer from different countries to exchange merchandise with little to no cash or cash equivalents changing hands. It can take the form of barter, **counter purchase**, offset, switch trading or buyback.

Contractual entry modes

Contractual entry modes or transfer-related entry modes are those associated with transfer of ownership or utilization of specified property such as technology or assets from one party to the other in exchange for royalty fees. They differ from trade-related entry modes in that the user in a transfer-related mode 'buys' certain rights for the use of property such as technology from the other party. These modes are extensively used in technology-related or intellectual/industrial property rights-related transactions. This category includes entry modes like **international leasing, international licensing, international franchising** and **turnkey projects.**

International leasing is an agreement in which a foreign firm (*lessor*) leases out its new or used machines or equipment to a local company (the *lessee*) often in a developing country). International leasing is used as a mode of doing international business largely due to the financial capability of manufacturers to pay for heavy production equipment. It is an opportunity for the owner of such equipment, which may be sitting idle, to put it to productive use by leasing it out. In this mode, the foreign lessor retains ownership of the property throughout the lease period during which the local user pays a leasing fee.

International licensing is an entry mode in which a firm (the *licensor*) grants to another firm (the *licensee*) the right to use any kind of expertise, know-how, blueprints, technology and manufacturing designs for a specified period of time in exchange for a royalty fee to market and manufacture the licensed products in the licensed territory. It is a commonly used mode of foreign market entry which enables foreign products and brands to reach a wide consumer base without setting up production facilities in the host country.

International franchising is an entry mode in which the foreign franchisor grants use of the intangible property rights, such as a trademark or brand name, to the local franchisee. It usually includes strict and detailed instructions on how to carry out the business operation and often production equipment, managerial systems, operating procedures, advertising and promotional materials, and even loans and financing. The world's most popular franchised products come from US MNEs McDonald's, Kentucky Fried Chicken (KFC) and Pizza Hut. However, the product being sold has to be customized to cater to local taste and culture – thus McDonald's does not sell beef burgers in India and has customized the menu to include potato patties for India's large number of vegetarian consumers. It is interesting to note that the company's vegetarian menu in India has now found its way to other countries as a result of the increasing trend of people opting for a vegan lifestyle (*Indian Express*, 2018). Franchising as the entry mode may also suffer the pitfalls of learning and imitation by the franchisee, as Pizza Hut discovered to its dismay in Thailand, when its agreement was not renewed. There is also the danger of the local 'copycat' – so in India for every Burger King restaurant in a neighbourhood, there is also a local Burger Singh (Das, 2015).

The franchisor receives a royalty payment, which is a percentage of the franchisee's revenues, in return for the use of its name. Sometimes the franchisor has specific requirements about the method of production, such as Burger King and McDonald's, which require the franchisee to buy the company's cooking equipment, burger patties and other products that bear the company name.

A *turnkey project*, also called build–operate–transfer (BOT), is an investment in which the entire design and construction of an operation is done by a foreign investor who hands it over after completion, for management by a local team. This involves the export of technology, management expertise and capital equipment. In return for completing the project, the investor receives guaranteed periodic payments. BOT is useful for very large-scale, long-term infrastructure projects, such as power generation, airports, dams, expressways, chemical plants and steel mills, which require special expertise. These projects are often undertaken by a consortium of firms such as the Metro Rail Transit Corporation (MRTC) in the Philippines, which signed a turnkey agreement for railway projects, with a consortium comprised of Mitsubishi Heavy Industries, the Sumitomo Corporation and the EEI Corporation.

Investment-related entry modes

In contrast to trade-related and transfer-related entry modes, investment-related entry modes involve ownership of property, assets, projects and businesses invested in a host country. Foreign investment takes two forms: foreign direct investment and **foreign portfolio investment**.

Foreign direct investment as a mode of entry refers to long-term investment in the productive assets of a company for the purpose of control. FDI-related entry modes are more sophisticated than trade-related modes and involve a higher risk and longer-term contribution than both trade- and transfer-related choices. The country making the FDI is called the home country and the country receiving the FDI is called the host country.

Greenfield investment is an investment process that results in the creation of new assets and production facilities in the host country. It is a long-term proposition in which an overseas production facility is set up from scratch.

A *merger* is the amalgamation of two existing enterprises. It is a voluntary and permanent combination of two businesses, which integrate their operations and identities with those of the other. The merged enterprise then functions as a new entity. For example, both Daimler-Benz and Chrysler ceased to exist when the two firms merged, and a new company, Daimler Chrysler, was created. Asia witnessed several big mergers in 2018, with India and Japan taking the lead in this business activity. Some recent mergers include Walmart Inc.'s $16 billion investment in India's Flipkart Group, for a 77 per cent stake in the Indian e-commerce market leader. Hong Kong-based conglomerate CK

Hutchison Holdings Ltd gained its biggest acquisition when it made a $9.6 billion bid for the Australian gas pipeline operator APA Group (Baigorri, 2018).

An *acquisition* is the purchase of an existing business venture in a foreign country. It allows a firm to establish itself in a short period of time since it takes over a running enterprise. An acquisition can be hostile if the acquired company is unwilling to be bought, or it can be friendly and with the consent of the acquired enterprise. As we read earlier in the chapter, Motorola was initially acquired by US MNE Google and later by Chinese MNE Lenovo and has thus lost its own original identity. Indian technology MNE Wipro Ltd has used an acquisition strategy that it calls 'string of pearls'– an approach focused on buying several small companies that are a strategic fit. It has acquired several firms in both the USA and Europe using this acquisition technique to get quick access to customers and technology, and acquisitions in Vietnam, Hong Kong, China, Indonesia and Malaysia have enabled Wipro to access these markets and also given it a low-cost manufacturing base (Mishra and Raghu, 2007).

Brownfield investment is a combination of greenfield investment and mergers and acquisitions. It denotes an investment where an existing firm acquires another firm and infuses it with fresh capital and assets after the acquisition.

Foreign portfolio investment (FPI) is investment in financial instruments such as stocks and bonds through the stock exchange and other financial markets only to earn a return on the investment.

Although we have discussed one entry mode at a time, in actual practice firms choose to enter different markets using different modes of entry. For instance, IKEA has used **joint ventures (JVs)** as its mode of entry into China but has used the franchisee mode of entry for Hong Kong and Taiwan. We discuss this is greater detail in Chapter 5.

The path of foreign market entry: Evolutionary or accelerated process?

Incremental process model

Traditional theory views international entry not as a one-step action but rather as an evolutionary process involving a series of incremental decisions during which firms increase their commitment to a foreign market by shifting from low- to high-commitment entry modes. This **incremental process model** is also known as the **stage model**, which states that a firm chooses to enter a culturally close country as its first step in internationalization and follows this with entry into culturally distant countries. This explanation fits the path taken by the earliest MNEs who followed the learning curve of accumulating competence, knowledge and confidence in the international entry process. They moved sequentially from no international involvement to export to overseas assembly or sales subsidiaries (sub-contracting, branches or franchising) to overseas production via contractual or equity JVs (they also move from minority to majority equity positions), and, ultimately, to overseas penetration and integration through wholly owned subsidiaries or umbrella companies. Increasing levels of involvement in foreign markets help a firm to accumulate experiential and local knowledge for further and distant foreign market entry.

However, as you saw in Chapter 1 there is now a new variety of MNEs, called the latecomers, which have emerged from the peripheral regions and view the global market as their natural home from the day they are born. These small to middle-sized firms from various industries skip the evolutionary path and use alternate strategies of internationalization, which are discussed in detail here.

Ownership, Location, Internalization (OLI) strategy

The OLI hypothesis (Dunning, 1977, 1993) (cf p. 29) is the most popular explanation of foreign market entry. It elaborates that firms' FDI behaviour is determined by ownership, location and internalization advantages. Location advantages can be investigated through host country specific variables, while both ownership and internalization advantages are examined by firm specific factors. Arising from the business environment associated with a particular geographical location, these location specific advantages define the degree of attractiveness of a host economy to the investing MNEs. Focusing on the rationale of economic efficiency, the eclectic paradigm suggests that foreign firms are motivated to exploit location specific advantages provided by the host country through internalizing their firm specific advantages. Firms with different motivations choose locations with different sets of location advantages.

Linkage, Leverage, Learning (LLL) strategy

The Linkage, Leverage, Learning (LLL) theory (Mathews, 2002; 2006), which was introduced to you in the previous chapter, explains the emergence of latecomer firms. These firms emerged in the international market by leveraging the linkages on existing value chains and used the learning from these networks to establish themselves in the global economy. Hong Kong-based Li & Fung has developed a business model around the creation of global value chains as it receives orders from buyer firms in the advanced countries, and has thus become a global player.

The springboard strategy

EMNEs use international expansion as a springboard to acquire strategic resources and reduce their institutional and market constraints at home. This helps them to overcome their latecomer disadvantages and also helps to compensate for their existing competitive weaknesses. Springboard is a long-term strategy that involves a series of systematic OFDI activities, aimed at acquiring strategic assets such as technology, brands and access to global consumers from mature MNEs to compensate for their competitive weaknesses. The strategy is revolving, since it is integrated with domestic business activities, aimed at strengthening domestic capabilities for further international expansion (Luo and Tung, 2007: 18). Asian firms from Taiwan, Singapore and South Korea have used the springboard strategy to make a foreign market entry. China's Haier has successfully used springboarding to expand into developed markets by gaining access to valuable strategic assets. It has also upgraded its home-centred capability to combine the foreign technologies it acquired with its own innovation in product features and customization.

The leapfrogging strategy

The leapfrogging strategy is used by latecomer MNEs to catch up with the competitive position of early movers. This helps them to avoid the risk of technological obsolescence and proprietary technology diffusion to rivals, as well as having to educate a changing market. The leapfrogging strategy is different from springboard as it does not involve the recursive or revolving dimension of international operations and is only a complex and revolving latecomer catch-up strategy (Dore, 1990; Anderson and Engers, 1994). Arçelik (Turkey) is an example of MNE growth through leapfrogging. The firm made its foreign market entry through OEM in 1988, but saw accelerated growth from 2002 through a series of targeted acquisitions and new openings in Europe and Russia to expand its geographical, product and brand range. In 2006 it had two overseas production plants (Romania and Russia), a design centre in Italy and sold in 101 countries, increasing its share of foreign sales from 16 to 39 per cent (between 1999 and 2005), and becoming the third largest appliance company in Europe.

The institutional perspective

This is one of the most popular explanations for foreign market entry of EMNEs. It explains that EMNEs enter foreign markets to escape from or avoid weak institutional environments at home (Witt and Lewin, 2007; Boisot and Meyer, 2008). Since EMNEs are accustomed to a home environment with weak institutions and knowledgeable in handling such hardship and uncertainty, they are able to survive in similar environments in other developing countries (Cuervo-Cazurra and Genc, 2008). EMNEs thus leverage institutional arbitrage as they utilize their skills developed in weak institutional environments by adapting to institutional pressures that Western firms find difficult to manage, or just benefit from better institutional environments when they invest in advanced markets where property rights are better protected.

Strategic networks

Small and weak firms lacking in the resources necessary to compete, often use strategic networks (Chen, 1998) for entering foreign markets. These include parental networks or business groups which provide member firms with access to the information, knowledge, resources, markets and technologies, which will enable their internationalization.

2.2 Case study: Going to India – opportunities and challenges for APUS's globalization

Overview

Gaining a million users within its first week of launch, APUS, a Chinese mobile internet technology company, had accumulated over 600,000 followers on Facebook and 1.2 billion global users across 200 countries and regions in 2017. Tao Li, the founder and chief executive officer (CEO) of APUS, established the company one month after his resignation from China's leading internet security company, Qihoo 360. APUS expanded so fast that in just one year after launching, it had appeared on the *Wall Street Journal*'s '$1 Billion Dollar Club of Venture Companies' list, being the world's youngest **unicorn company**. In 2016, APUS vowed to make a $44 million fresh investment in India, and as of 2018, the company had four revenue generating overseas subsidiaries, including one wholly acquired software developer.

Learning outcomes

By the end of this case study, students should be able to:

1   Identify four essential aspects of globalization: why, where, when and how.
2   Understand how external factors might affect the implementation of cross-border expansion in Asia, e.g. how the evolving of industry or geo-economic conditions influence a company's adoption of globalization strategies.

Introduction

APUS is a Chinese mobile internet technology company that offers free user systems for smartphones. As of the end of 2017 and early 2018, 99 per cent of APUS's total users were from overseas markets. Table 2.3 shows the proportions of the company's revenues by region from 2015 to 2017. APUS has been generating revenues by charging third party advertisement fees. Globally, APUS had 0.2 billion, 0.4 billion and 0.5 billion new users in 2015, 2016 and 2017 respectively. The steady growth of users made it possible for the company to start monetizing its user traffic in 2016. As shown by Table 2.3, due to the large base of users in Asia, APUS generated most of its revenues in this region when it first started monetizing, accounting for 47 per cent, compared to 25.2 per cent in North America. The number was still the highest in Asia but decreased a little in 2017 because of the growth of users globally, while an increase for North America was largely due to the rise in advertisement charges for companies from that region. From simply offering free apps to directly investing in India, APUS is gradually building up an ecosystem of its own across Asia.

Table 2.3   Proportions of revenues by regions

Year	2015	2016	2017
Region	Revenue proportion	Revenue proportion	Revenue proportion
Asia	41.5%	47%	37.8%
North America	32.6%	25.2%	34.7%
Europe	13.5%	13.1%	14.1%
South America	8.6%	11.5%	10.5%
Africa	2.8%	2.3%	1.7%
Others	1.2%	1.0%	1.2%

Source: APUS Group IPO Prospectus, 2018: 277

APUS's globalization

APUS was born out of a profound knowledge of the software and internet industry, and the rich experience of product development and distribution channels by Mr Tao Li, former Overseas Markets VP of Qihoo 360. Throughout his years with Qihoo 360, China's biggest internet security solution company, Li had experienced the rise of

(Continued)

(Continued)

China's internet market. As an overseas business VP, Li had gained profound knowledge of the industry and markets both inside and outside of China. Back in 2012, Li had already foreseen the growth limit of China's mobile internet industry: 'The size of internet users in China will not exceed 8 billion', said Li in a magazine interview (*CEIBS Review*, 2015: para. 5), relying on his experience in the industry and the demographic structure in China. He predicted that despite the financial prosperity, China's internet companies would eventually encounter a bottleneck.

Just as Li had predicted, in 2014, the net profit of China's mobile internet industry hit its bottom, with 95 per cent of the revenues generated from the domestic market. Meanwhile in other parts of the world, for example Brazil, a gradual transition from feature phones to entry-level Android smartphones was in progress. The *World Internet Development Report 2017*, stated in 2017 that there were 3.9 billion internet users globally, among which smartphone users were 2.6 billion. The report estimated that smartphone users would be 3.6 billion in 2020, nearly 50 per cent of the global population (MIITC, 2017). According to what Statista revealed in the global mobile operating system (OS) market share report, 1.16 billion Android smartphones were sold by 2015 and Android accounted for around 85 per cent of all smartphone sales to end users worldwide at the beginning of 2016 (Statista, 2018). On 25 June 2014, Google announced at its annual I/O developer conference that Android had 1 billion 30-day active users, sending 20 billion texts a day and 93 million selfies a day (Huet, 2014).

'Just like peach-picking', said Li: 'You should focus on picking those fully grown and fine ones first and worry about how peach trees are planted later – when there are no more peaches to be picked' (*China News*, 2015: para. 20). The 'fully grown and fine peaches' referred to the new users in the global markets for APUS, the 'trees' were the mobile internet industry in the emerging markets. Li was aware that even if the industry was not at an equal state globally, the users were ready. He aimed to be one of the first movers to win those users immediately.

Seeing the tough and saturated domestic market and the optimized growth of figures and possibilities on a global scale, Li was confident that the aforementioned 'untapped' overseas markets would host the greatest business opportunities for new smartphone business, particularly when the big Chinese players were not yet to be found there. 'I knew for sure that my new direction would represent two core traits: the first would be mobile Internet; the second would be international markets', said Li before he officially founded APUS (Tencent Technologies, 2014). In contrast to Qihoo 360, where the core business was about internet security and he used to hold significant shares, Li embarked a different route for his new company to avoid direct competition. A month after he left Qihoo 360, forgoing his high-ranked position and shares, in June 2014, APUS, abbreviated from 'A Perfect User System', was launched as a smartphone user system developer, providing faster and more convenient internet access solutions for smartphone users, initially for those using Android.

Li's former experience of managing vast amounts of customer data at Qihoo 360 rendered him the requisite knowledge to deal with the sore spots for smartphone users. In the case of Android smartphones, these meant slow and unstable operating systems, and unfriendly interfaces. APUS deliberately developed their products to tackle these problems. Three main features of APUS products were small (in file size), fast (in responding), and simple (to use). The memory space required for installing APUS products was as small as 1 MB as compared with over 10 MB for other similar products. Along with many other features that APUS gradually developed to offer, such as desktop archive management, themes, proximity scanning, smart centre, smartphone lock, etc., its series of products drastically increased internet accessing as well as phone operating speed, hence improved users' experience. Not only for Android, APUS products could also adapt to more than 20,000 mobile phone brands and models. By solving major problems for smartphone users, APUS attracted large numbers of new users in the emerging markets outside of China.

Strategic considerations

When Li considered the choice of which foreign market to enter, he emphasized two points: the culture of the target markets and the maturity of the industry there. Li had travelled across the world for months, hoping to find the best and most appropriate foreign markets in which to initiate his new business. Those trips helped him realize that, unlike cultural and linguistic factors, market maturity was not easily influenced or determined purely by human will: 'All of the core points are rooted in the ability to successfully adapt psychologically', said Li: 'In venturing overseas, the most important factor to consider is the degree of market maturity: one should seek first to enter mature markets' (Tencent Technologies, 2014). He divided the global internet industry into three major markets: the US, indisputably the most mature market in the world, China, and the rest of the world. He believed that firms in the first two markets were already experiencing fierce and brutal competition, leaving scarcely any room for new players. The remaining parts of the world, accounting for billions of potential customers, would become an attractive playground for budding entrepreneurs and ultimately grow into healthy and prosperous markets for more lucrative businesses. As early as 2012, Li saw business opportunities evolving in Southeast Asia, South America, Russia, the Middle East and Africa, among which India became his first location choice for his new business due to the following reasons.

The process of psychological adaptation was easy: both India and China represent the world's oldest cultures, and the economies of both countries had grown at a drastic speed through the opening up of their markets. Moreover, Buddhism, which originated

(Continued)

(Continued)

in India, had played a decisive role throughout the development of China's civilization and culture, and had gradually and subtly influenced the social and business behaviours in those two countries. For example, building long-term relationships and trust is vital in business, and it is not uncommon to see personal issues involved in business activities as well.

The company was able to exploit relative government policies and taxation benefits. Ever since 2013 China had begun to promote its economic development strategy, namely the **Belt and Road Initiative**. The goal was to systematically engage mutual development with nations in the Belt and Road regions, such as Central and South Asia, Southeast Asia and East Africa. Li mentioned that one of the important and reliable 'pulling factors' for Chinese companies to expand overseas was the policies of the Chinese government. Since its launch in 2014, 69 per cent of APUS users are located in 65 countries within the Belt and Road regions, compared with 20 per cent of its users located in North America and Europe (APUS Group IPO Prospectus, 2018: 40). In 2016, the State Administration of Taxation of China amended tax regulations which granted the eligibility to APUS for remission of value-added tax (VAT) in regard to its overseas sales of consulting services, along with other related taxation reduction benefits for APUS technology transformation services. The company, claiming itself as the pioneer in this national economic development strategy, had since further expanded its business and planned to enter more countries in the Belt and Road regions, abiding by the nation's digital development of Belt and Road guidance, and aimed at becoming the major supplier of internet portals in these countries.

User behaviours and interests in India were more suitable for a technology advanced internet company. Li's experience with overseas markets provided him with the knowledge that India's end users were generally more interested in internet tools. APUS's 2015 Global Mobile Internet Report revealed users' interests and preferences based on app downloading ranking. For example, users in China were believed to be more interested in **e-commerce platforms** for online purchasing, while in Singapore users were more interested in social media. Users in the US tended to like online games whereas users in India paid more attention to internet tools (YiCai, 2016). 'India is going through one of the most exciting shifts with mobile at the moment, with its rapidly embracing 4G and smartphones', Li also once stated: 'India has the best computer scientists amongst all in the world' (Tech in Asia, 2016).

As of 2016, APUS had 50 million users in Southeast Asia as a whole, many of whom were daily active users (DAUs). By mid-2017, the same number represented users in India alone. Witnessing its great success, APUS, together with five other venture capital firms, announced a fresh investment of US $44 million in India in 2016. The investment was for setting up APUS's new R&D centre and a sales and business development office specifically for its Indian market. Further, the company elaborated on this investment and business outlook with respect to its cooperation with India in a statement in the 2016 annual statement: 'Much was written in 2016 about the investments made in Indian start-ups [...] the real reason is that Chinese companies see India as a major opportunity. It is at the same point that China was at perhaps five or six years ago, with the same tantalizing, untapped potential for mobile internet to revolutionize the lives of billions' (APUS Official Website, 2017). In this statement, APUS introduced the wave of investment in India by many big and powerful Chinese technology companies such as Tencent and Alibaba with billions of dollars. Though APUS did not possess the same resources as these big players, it also benefited from doing business in the Indian market and planned to further invest US$152 million in India besides its dissolved partnership with InMobi, a mobile advertising technology company, and Hotstar, a video platform.

Challenges

Even for Li, an 'internet old timer', cross-border expansion is still challenging. Product-wise, as an internet company, APUS constantly faces the unprecedented pace of technological change. Also, in this ever-evolving industry, time means not just money but sometimes a key element to survival. Li's philosophy about app products is that a company should never delay their launch because of slight imperfections. 'You finish the product at 60 percent, and it is ready to go', he said. And the market will refine and complete the rest of it' (*CEIBS Review*, 2015: para. 9). The ability to attract on-going funding and persistently investing in R&D have been two important means to maintain APUS's competitiveness.

But beyond dealing with industry specific challenges, how to launch a Chinese brand successfully in a foreign market is also crucial. Li once explained that, depending on local conditions, the company could choose from one or any combination of the following four modes simultaneously for foreign market entry: exports of products to local users, strategic collaborations with local suppliers, the launch of subsidiaries or offices in the target market, and direct investment or merger and acquisition (M&A).

In general, internet technology is apt to export once it is well developed and refined in its home market. Li was confident that the internet technology-derived products in China were suitable to export to emerging markets. From the foundation of APUS in 2014 to 2016, the company exposed itself by entering user-generated content (UGC) platforms such as app stores and social media platforms, offering free apps for users and charging advertisement fees to the third (content-carrying) parties (platforms). Once users downloaded and used the products on their phones, these products would be rated and reviewed on these platforms. These ratings and reviews, and its UGC, were critical measurements for new products and key reference indicators for new users. UGC helped to maintain APUS at the top of app charts on these platforms. As more UGC

(Continued)

(Continued)

was created, more new customers were acquired by APUS. As mentioned earlier, Indian users' UGC was extremely important and helpful for a technology company such as APUS – a focus was put on the technological attributes of APUS products and reviews were professional.

Besides 'asking' users to promote their products, APUS also engaged its users in the target markets to grow with the company's products, so that the users subtly helped to localize the brand, or in other words APUS products followed the pattern that most software would follow, namely engaging the users in testing the products and helping to improve them. APUS also did a little more than that by allowing users to customize their own software on their phones, for example, uploading their favourite photos to create their own themes. This helped the company lower costs (specifically in this case, to lower the costs of graphic designing), while avoiding cultural barriers by inviting local users to attach their chosen features to a foreign brand.

The results from APUS' marketing approaches were encouraging: the first series of products, APUS Launcher, was available for download at app stores on 2 July 2014, and within the first week, the company had gained 1 million users, and within one month the number reached 10 million. Within the first six months, following its official debut on Google Play, the company had 1 billion users. In its first year, APUS's user number hit 2 billion, covering 50 countries and regions globally.

Besides gaining new users through UGC at Google Play, APUS also established symbiotic relationships with global platform suppliers such as Google, Facebook and Twitter for advertising to attract new users. Although these platforms are officially banned in China, APUS has not been affected because its business focuses only on overseas markets. According to Li's calculation, the switching cost (from non-Android) per user would be 20 times that of developing a new user. Hence, the strategic objective was to keep acquiring new users in the new markets. APUS attracts new users with its basic 'all-in-one' products. These products have features to meet every function that customers want from a mobile app and the radar system was based on APUS big data computing technology. For example, an auto scanning and searching function helped users to discover software or games used or played on other phones nearby. An automatic news generating function helps to save users' time spent headline searching. APUS also offers 'user hot points' for loyal customers to watch online videos freely on their phones. By offering these customer needs oriented functions, APUS creates value for users but also generates great profits by collecting its customers' mobile user data. These data are fundamental to the company later establishing its massive user database, which provides the content for APUS's computing and analysing. The result of analysing this database is the key for APUS to push precisely relative advertisements to its users.

Doing business across Asia also triggered fiercer competition for APUS. Rivals did not only appear from overseas but also from home. Since late 2015 and early 2016, the domestic market in China has sensed the changes in the industry. More Chinese companies started to go abroad and enter the same Asian markets as APUS did with similar app products. At the same time, the soaring number of 'copycats' from China started to threaten market positions for industry leaders like APUS. One example is Hola Launcher, a theme and wallpaper app launched at Google Play in November 2015. Hola Launcher has some features similar to APUS Launcher – its 'all-in-one' speed booster, battery saver and charger protector, and it claimed to be the fastest and smallest Android app in the world. To many users, Hola Launcher was a younger and condensed version of APUS Launcher, not to mention the fact that Hola Launcher was developed by Hola Team, which was a **wholly owned subsidiary** of Qihoo 360 where Tao Li used to work.

Years earlier, though, Li had made the following statement: 'We have become a bridge and a platform: other companies can simply build on what we have created in order to enter these new markets. The first to flourish in international markets will certainly face greater challenges than those who come after, these markets need a company like us' (Tencent Technologies, 2014). Having foreseen these challenges, Li knew exactly what was necessary for him to do after simply exporting abroad for two years: developing an APUS ecosystem.

The prerequisite for building an ecosystem was APUS's highly integrated products, all focused on user-internet linkages, which were used only as a data inflow platform before. Since June 2015, APUS had begun to establish its big data platform and embed a 'radar system' in its products, allowing it to trace and compute app utilization and make a precise push notification service based on its 10 billion user database. Another utility of this big data platform was to develop it into an open-source platform to integrate more third-party apps and services with its international partners. Such collaboration also assisted APUS's partners to expand their global business. For example, APUS planned to partner with at least 20 smartphone manufacturers in India, aiming at bringing in another 75 million users by the end of 2018. As of December 2017, some of APUS's global partners, including Google, Facebook (USA), Amazon (USA), Twitter (USA), Huawei (China), ZTE (China), Yandex (Russia) and InMobi (India), had grown their overseas market shares through not just cooperating with but also investing in APUS's open-source platform.

This was probably the **business model** Li was seeking from the beginning; after all, APUS was once the world's youngest unicorn company with rich connections and experience with venture capitalists and investors. Based on the integrated products, a fully developed ecosystem with an in-depth financial nexus became the next phase of APUS's globalization. For example, APUS has been refining its data analytics and push service, aiming at recommending highly precise financial service apps to its users since 2015. Through working with suppliers in this field, APUS had the opportunity to

(Continued)

(Continued)

choose and collaborate with top finance agents and suppliers across Asia and beyond. Li believed that when a Chinese company went abroad, its growth trajectory would be affected by policies and laws (especially in Asia, where unstable and unpredictable regulations are endured by most emerging markets), religions and cultures. Hence, to be successful, localization – blending yourself into your target markets – became the key strategy. In Li's opinion, investment, including direct investments, and mergers and acquisitions, is a valuable component for building the APUS ecosystem and a long-term goal. He believes that setting up its own branches – making direct investments in overseas markets – is one of the more in-depth collaboration and localization tactics: 'The best way to open a foreign market, is to localize yourself' (Sohu Technology, 2017).

As a long-term strategy of the company, APUS set up the APUS Fund in 2014. In 2016, when India became APUS's biggest and most successful overseas market, APUS Fund led Northern Light Venture Capital (a China-focused venture capital firm interested in companies with ground-breaking ideas), Redpoint Ventures (an American venture capital firm), Chengwei Ventures LLC (one of China's oldest independent venture capital firms that prefers to invest in scalable businesses in the global Chinese economy, specifically interested in communication software enterprises), SIG Global (a US based venture capital firm that is well known for financial derivatives pricing and trading), and Qiming Venture Partners (a China-based venture capital firm that specializes in building new companies in China) in announcing the aforementioned US$44 million investment in India. During this investment, APUS set up APUS APPS to function as its R&D centre and marketing office in India. In the same year, GLORY SUN was set up in Singapore as a server base. Several other capitals were shareholders of GLORY SUN before it was fully acquired by APUS and later merged with APUS APPS in 2017. APUS APPS is now wholly owned by APUS as an overseas subsidiary. As of 2018, APUS had established four overseas subsidiaries, of which three generated revenues through advertisement fees and one software developer.

The development of the industry further pushed APUS to launch overseas investment. Following the phase of direct exporting (2014–17), the mobile internet industry has stepped into the phase of content managing in forms of online news, video clips, online reading, music and games (2018–20). E-platform (a collection of software and hardware services used to implement its digital strategy to end users), e-payment (methods of electronic payment or customer–vendor money transactions), O2O (offline-to-online, a digital transformation of traditional business), and FinTech (financial technology, technology used to offer financial services to users), to name a few, were at this time influencing the trends of mobile internet, creating new challenges and opportunities for companies like APUS (2020–future). With the help of its investment in India, APUS has been able to develop longer-term and deeper relationships with its users and potential users from more social and cultural angles. For example, APUS participated in the fourth Career Fair & Confluence for Women in Bangalore, advocating for Indian women's equal employment rights. According to Li, an effective and sustainable business model should contain three value goals: gaining financial benefits, satisfying customers, and creating values for the communities. Through refining its ecosystem, APUS was able to offer its users better experience with its products. By working with more top technology companies in Asia and worldwide and further reliance on supportive regulations from home, APUS was more capable of reaching its goals of generating more profits and creating value for its communities. Last but not least, through activities like 'Women Game Changer', APUS not only approached more customers, but also attained sustainability.

Case questions

1   What traits of the Indian market discussed in this case have made it APUS' most successful market?
2   What external elements were especially important for doing business in Asia?

2.3 Case study: The Charoen Pokphand Group – the strategy of a cross-border 'latecomer'

Overview

The Charoen Pokphand (CP) Group is Thailand's earliest multinational enterprise. The group was born with an international orientation and has grown and expanded into a global agribusiness based on its firm specific advantages and by developing capabilities leveraged from connections with diverse networks. The business originated as a small shop selling vegetable seeds and grew into an integrated global agribusiness. It is presently a diversified conglomerate with business interests in animal seed production, livestock farming, meat processing, retail, telecommunications, e-commerce, automotives, pharmaceuticals, real estate and finance and banking.

This case study is a classic example of an emerging market latecomer MNE from a small Asian country. It clearly outlines how a latecomer can grow into a global giant through aggressive diversification based on the exploitation of existing resources and accumulating new ones. It also brings out the significance of using networks and alliances as an internationalization growth strategy.

(Continued)

(Continued)

Learning outcomes

By the end of this case study, students should be able to:

1   Identify the internationalization strategies of latecomer MNEs from Asian economies like Thailand.
2   Understand the factors that helped the CP Group in its cross-border expansion in Asia and across the world.

Introduction

The Charoen Pokphand Group is Thailand's largest diversified conglomerate. The group operates in 15 countries through group companies and affiliated business units and exports to over 100 countries across the world. Its core interest is in agribusiness, represented through CP Foods, which accounts for about 30 per cent of the group's revenue. The agribusiness has two main segments: livestock and aquaculture. The livestock segment comprises of chickens, ducks and pigs, and the aquaculture business segment consists of shrimp and fish. Its products include animal feed, animal farm products, processed food and ready meals.

CP's claim to be the 'Kitchen of the world' began with domestic operations, which continue to remain a dominant aspect of its total business. At a typical poultry-processing site located at Korat, a few hours' drive north of Bangkok, vast quantities of birds are processed for the domestic and foreign market. Korat produces about 36,000 tonnes of fresh meat each year and more than 65,000 tonnes of cooked products. While the bread-crumbed chunks of chicken from the facility appear in outlets of Kentucky Fried Chicken, the birds' wings often go to Japan.

Its diversified business range currently operates through 13 business groups, in a wide array of businesses such as agro-industry and food, marketing and distribution, telecommunication, pharmaceuticals, finance, automotives and industrial products and property development.

The CP Group presently has holdings in more than 200 subsidiaries around the world, employing 300,000 people, and had total revenues of 1.8 trillion baht ($54 billion) in 2018 (CP Group, 2018, www.cpfworldwide.com/en/investors-map).

The CP Group's organizational structure (Figure 2.2) is clearly divided into domestic and foreign operations. The domestic operations are organized into three units: Feed, Farm and Food. Exports are also included as a part of domestic operations. The international operations are managed by listed and unlisted firms across the world.

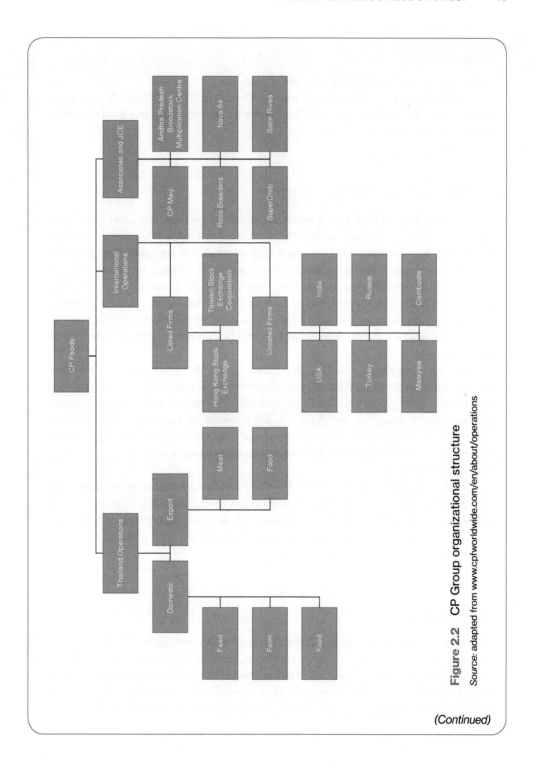

Figure 2.2 CP Group organizational structure

Source: adapted from www.cpfworldwide.com/en/about/operations

(Continued)

(Continued)

The group is listed on the Hong Kong and Taiwan stock exchanges.

The CP Group is a family business, with the founding patriarch Dhanin Chearavanont, who started the conglomerate over five decades ago, occupying the top position as chairman since inception.

Origin and domestic growth

The CP Group began life as a small seed shop in 1921 on the Song Wat Road in Bangkok. It was started by two brothers who moved to Thailand to escape the downturn in China. In the next two decades the business began international expansion into Southern Thailand, Penang and Singapore since these were geographically proximate markets, initially, and later into all parts of Asia. This conforms to typical explanations for internationalization such as the Uppsala model, where a firm initially expands into neighbouring markets through exports, and later uses the experiential knowledge gained here for higher entry modes such as alliances and acquisitions for geographically and culturally distant markets.

During the 1950s and 1960s, the group began its diversification from seed trading into animal feed milling. This development was in response to the increased demand for gunny bags from Thai commodities exporters, with the largest demand coming from the Bangkok Feedmill Co. in 1968. Animal feed milling remains the core activity of the group today. Growth in business was the result of adopting modern technology, connections with the overseas Chinese trading networks and local political connections.

Government policy and changes in the military regime were the two major factors that contributed to the growth of group business in the 1960s and 1970s. The government policy to promote poultry farming was a boon and pushed the group towards developing alliances to augment its capabilities. Alliances have continued to be a vital aspect of the CP Group's business strategy through the years.

International growth and expansion

CP was born with an international orientation – it started its business life by importing seeds from China, and seed trading has continued to be part of its core operations. However, its actual internationalization journey began in 1972 with the establishment of its first overseas feed mill in Indonesia. Indonesia was suited to CP operations, since it had an abundant supply of raw material for animal feed and the growing economy would provide a large market for CP products. This investment enabled its subsequent entry into poultry farming and fisheries in the country.

It subsequently expanded its feed mills to Hong Kong in 1974, Singapore in 1976 and Taiwan in 1977. It also invested in insurance, investment and finance companies in Hong Kong in the 1970s, all of which became sources of funding for its ventures in China. This was a vital source of finance, given the strict currency control followed by Thailand at that time.

China has been an important investment destination for the CP Group. CP's initial links with China have held it in good stead and gave it the first mover advantage when China opened its markets in 1979. The CP Group became the first investor in China's Shenzhen SEZ. The investment was a joint venture between CP, Continental Grain (USA) and a local Chinese company. This investment was the outcome of the sustained efforts made by the CP Group to maintain business connections in China and capitalize on its diaspora status. The *guanxi (networks)* that the CP Group had developed led to subsequent investment in China in the form of joint ventures, wholly owned subsidiaries and cooperative agreements with firms in the host country. CP's investments in China were a diversified portfolio across different sectors – unlike most other foreign destinations, where it confined itself to its core business of animal feed and integrated livestock industry.

CP's investments in China included aquaculture, petrochemicals and real estate development. Manufacturing investments included two beer breweries in collaboration with Heineken (Germany) and Boonrawd Brewery (Thailand). It also established several retail outlet projects, such as Lotus Supercenter, which it operated on its own, and Makro, the Mall, in partnership with local players. By the early 1990s, CP had launched 200 subsidiaries in China.

CP followed its tried and tested domestic business strategy in developing its internationalization path. It used its firm specific capabilities in establishing feed mills as the point of first entry, which then attracted poultry farming and meat processing. It later diversified into other areas such as setting up a motorcycle manufacturing unit. CP also continued to use technology partners such as Honda to strengthen its position in foreign markets.

The use of networks and alliances has been a key feature of the CP Group's internationalization strategy; its first alliance was with the US-based agricultural multinational Arbor Acres to invest in a joint venture in 1970. The 60:40 joint venture, Arbor Acres (Thailand), was established to import chicken breeding stock from the US. The alliance served the interests of both parties – CP was looking for technology and Abor Acres was looking for investment opportunities abroad. The subsequent collapse of the military government allowed CP to expand further into chicken slaughtering and processing activities, which had earlier been under state control. This also led to vertical

(Continued)

(Continued)

integration with the help of the knowledge gained from the Arbor Acres alliance. The integration not only increased domestic demand for animal feed, but also paved the way for entry into the Japanese market through exports in the early 1980s.

The group also expanded into farming through the contract system, where farmers were provided with credits by CP for the purchase of inputs and were bound to sell their produce to the firm. This made the CP Group into what some reported as an 'exploitative monopoly', since it could control farmers through its superior technology and production chains. By the end of the 1970s, the CP Group had established itself as a complete supply chain for controlling activities ranging from animal feed production, livestock farming and meat processing.

The decade of the 1980s saw the rise of Asia as an economic power. Thailand emerged as a major food exporter, driven by the growing demand for raw and processed food in the neighbouring Asian economies. The CP Group further internationalized into Asia as it found markets in Japan and East Asia for its products.

The poultry model of contract farming was replicated in shrimp farming in the 1980s. CP gave shrimp farmers larvae and feed of a superior protein variety at four times the price of chicken feed, and bought the entire production for export to Japan, Europe and the USA. CP was a successful shrimp exporter and helped to bring Thailand onto the map of the world's largest shrimp producers. CP's success in shrimp farming was also attributed to its alliance with Mitsubishi (Japan). Japan is a major market for shrimps and the Japanese were interested in getting involved in its production. CP's shrimp farming later spread to other parts of the world such as Indonesia, Mexico, India, Vietnam and Cambodia (Winichagoon, 1992).

Diversification

The late 1980s saw the CP Group diversify out of the agribusiness space into marketing and distribution. It entered into a joint venture with Oscar Mayer (USA), a giant in the production of meat and allied products, in 1986, for help with food processing technology. The alliance enhanced its capability to increase its variety of processed food exports. The group's main product in the export market was frozen chickens. As a consequence of the joint venture it launched its own brand, CP, for different processed meat products such as meatballs and sausages. It also ventured into the retail space and set up stands for the sale of grilled chicken in high pedestrian traffic areas near fresh markets and supermarkets, and later started a fast food chain called Chester's Grill.

The CP Group's favourite growth strategy was based on developing capabilities through the use of alliances and joint ventures for both domestic and foreign operations.

Some of these alliances included a joint venture with the SHV group of the Netherlands, the owner of the cash-and-carry Makro stores in 1988 and the setting up of Siam Makro in Thailand. It also got into a licensing contract with Southland Corporation for the 7-Eleven convenience stores in 1989. The group also established a chain store, Lotus Supercenter, and recruited former employees of Wal-Mart to help overcome initial management issues in the domestic market. CP Group currently runs cash-and-carry businesses in Thailand, China, Cambodia and Myanmar. It has 123 Makro cash-and-carry outlets in Thailand, and 60 outlets in China under the brand Lotus.

CP had been Walmart's source of Chinese goods and Walmart was hopeful that the CP Group's Chinese connections would help it gain a foothold in China. However, Walmart's unwillingness to share management control and technology with their partners, and the difference in corporate cultures, led to a breakup of an intended CP–Walmart alliance to enter China (Handley, 1997).

The next steps in CP's diversification were in the infrastructure sector, which was in the process of privatization. The first in the series was in petrochemicals, which has been the key to Thailand's energy needs since the discovery of natural gas in the Gulf of Thailand in the late 1980s. CP Telecommunication (later Telecom Asia) was formed as a joint venture with British Telecom in 1990. The project won all government concessions for the installation of 3 million lines without a single cabinet approval.

The group later established Telecom Holding, a 99.99 per cent subsidiary, as the telecom group's holding company and investment arm. It also invested in other telecom projects within the country and also abroad, in China, Indochina and India. The group also entered into a technological alliance with Nynex (USA), which resulted in the use of fibre optics in its telephone lines. This gave them a technological edge and a first mover advantage as compared to other competitors in the field. CP later set up cable TV networks and offered Thailand's first pay-per-view programming and other interactive programs (Far Eastern Economic Review, March 2, 1995).

The CP Group continued its global expansion in the 1990s, with significant investments in India, Vietnam and Canada. CP entered India in 1992 with the aim of making the country its innovation hub for technology and digitization. It established a new chicken processing plant in Chittoor, Andhra Pradesh, in 2016. The plant was strategically located to serve two of the largest cities of South India: Chennai and Bangalore. Established under the 'farm to fork concept', the plant manufactures both vegetarian and non-vegetarian ready to eat snacks. CP invested $18 million in the Chittoor facility, which has a capacity of 20,000 tonnes per year for primary processing and about 4,000 tonnes for secondary processing.

The CP Group further expanded into the retail space in India through its company Siam Makro PCL, in 2018. It established itself in the wholesale cash-and-carry business

(Continued)

(Continued)

under the brand, Lots Wholesale Solutions. The company has an investment target of INR1,000 crore in setting up its wholesale distribution centres and back-end supply chain over the next five years in North India.

CP Foods entered Vietnam in 1993, and since then it has invested over $1 billion in the country. Vietnam continues to remain an important investment destination for CP foods, and accounts for 15 per cent of the company's total sales. CP Foods announced an additional investment of US$200 million in Vietnam to make it an export hub for its poultry and pork business in 2017. The investment is aimed to take advantage of Vietnamese access to the Trans-Pacific Partnership (TPP), which offers Vietnam advantageous trading terms with Asian countries such as Japan and Australia, as well as Mexico and Canada. Thailand has yet to join the TPP, but it has an existing export quota with the EU. It is hoped that CP's investment in Vietnam will double that quota.

Vietnam became the seventh country to ratify the TPP in November 2018, and the agreement is expected to boost Vietnamese exports by 4 per cent. CP Foods investment in Vietnam intends to use the country as an export hub for chickens and shrimp, to both Asian destinations such as Japan and the Middle East, and also to Europe and North America. CP Foods intended to boost shrimp exports through Vietnam, by increasing its shrimp farming capacity in the country to 50 billion units a year from the current 12 billion. This is aimed at increasing its annual production capacity of shrimp feed from 300,000 tons to 500,000 tons over two years.

CP's investment in Vietnam is also aimed at taking advantage of it being a low-cost production base. Manufacturing wages in Vietnam are lower than those in Thailand and China, giving it a competitive edge in production as compared to these countries. CP's current investment in meat processing plants is aimed at further strengthening its business bonds in Vietnam. The completed chicken factory will have a processing capacity of 1 million chickens per week, and the enhanced capacity is intended to be on a par with domestic production in Thailand.

CP Foods' recent acquisitions also include Canadian pork producer HyLife for $372.79 million in April 2017, aimed at establishing a firmer foothold in the North American market. CP Foods has acquired a 50.1 per cent stake in the Canadian company, with a Japanese partner Itochu acquiring the remainder.

The CP Group's growth and expansion is attributed to competitive advantages derived from its own industry specific technological skills combined with strong networking capabilities. The industry specific skills were derived from economies of scale and scope developed through its domestic business experience. CP achieved complete vertical integration in agribusiness and other food industries based on the benefits of scale and scope economies of production in Thailand and also in the other neighbouring developing countries it expanded into.

Networks

The use of alliances and networks has been a key feature of CP's strategy for both domestic and international expansion. This is similar to other East Asian MNEs, which supplemented their competitive advantages with technological and other capabilities through networking (Mathews, 2006). Over a period of time, MNEs needed to enhance their home country industry specific technological skills with value adding activities. This pushed them into developing and using personal networks to begin with, and subsequently building and nurturing more formal and transparent alliances (Pananond, 2009). The group's survival and growth are attributed to brand building, integration of its operations and service provision based on its owned competitive advantages, supplemented with capabilities developed through networking.

Internationalization of the CP Group has been based on different types of network relationships: social and ethnic ties, alliances with foreign technology partners and relationships with both home and host country governments. This is a key feature of other East Asian MNEs also (Mathews, 2006) and a primary factor for their rapid growth into diverse geographical markets.

Ethnic ties and ancestral loyalty

The CP Group started its business life with close links to China. It has successfully leveraged its social and ethnic ties and diaspora status with China, for successful growth and expansion. China has been an important investment destination of the CP Group. It started business by trading seeds from China, and later expanded into various other businesses based on their common ethnic background. In later years, the connection with the Chinese trading network was a strong factor in its growth. This helped the business group to get a first mover advantage and establish a presence in China in 1979 before firms from other parts of the world could enter.

CP's China connections also made it a partner of choice for other MNEs desirous of entering the country. This included Walmart, which wanted to piggyback on CP to enter the Chinese market.

Technology alliances

Technology partnerships have been a key feature of the growth of the CP Group. It has chosen technology partners for both domestic and international growth and exhibited

(Continued)

(Continued)

the necessary absorptive capacity ability to adapt that technology for its growth. CP's earliest alliance in 1970 was with US firm Arbor Acres, which had been one of the pioneers in selectively breeding for the purpose of producing a meatier, faster-growing bird. CP imported its first chickens in 1973, launching the company's nursery operation. At the same time, the company hired foreign nutritionists to help it develop new, higher-yield feed formulas.

CP's alliance with Arbor Acres helped its vertical integration efforts in chicken farming and processing and became the basis for its subsequent entry into Japan. By the mid-1970s, CP had succeeded in developing a bird that reached maturity after only seven weeks, compared to up to four months for other breeds. At the same time, the company's improved feed formula meant that chickens could be brought to maturity with only half the amount of feed. The CP Group's other technology imports of animal farming, which were developed in different climatic conditions, were successfully adapted by it for warmer weather and subsequently exported to countries like Indonesia and Vietnam.

In 1980, the company partnered with another US company, Avian Farms, to begin breeding ducks. The company also added pig breeding operations that year, importing livestock from Belgium, Holland and the United States to develop its own pig hybrids. In 1986, the company spotted another food opportunity and launched a research centre for the development of new breeds of shrimp that would be adaptable for fish-farming methods. The company's success in that area enabled it to become the world's leading supplier of black tiger shrimps.

It also used alliances for diversification into diverse business portals such as retail and telecommunications. The company's entry into the restaurant sector came in 1988 with the launch of Chester's Grill. That same year, CP launched its own supermarket group, Makro, which quickly became a leader in Thailand's retail sector. The following year, CP entered the dairy market, partnering with Japan's Meiji group to launch the CP Meiji line of dairy foods for the Thai market. The company also added convenience stores that year, getting a Thai franchisee for the 7-Eleven retail format. The company quickly began building that format into a national chain, adding as many as 20 stores each month and reaching a total of 1,000 by the end of the 1990s.

Yet the company's diversification went even further. In 1989, CP joined with Solvay, a Belgian manufacturer of polyvinylchloride, to launch Vinythai Co. Polyvinylchloride is a synthetic plastic polymer, used in a variety of applications in buildings and construction. This joint venture enabled the entry of CP into the construction sector, to meet the increasing demand in a growing Thai economy (Bossier et al., 1999). The following year, the company made an even bolder move, forming a partnership with the US telecommunications firm of NYNEX (later Verizon) to launch Telecom Asia (TA), in a move to compete against the government's former telephone monopoly in the Bangkok market. A list of its major alliances is given in Table 2.4.

Table 2.4 Alliances of the CP Group

Year	Firm	Country	Purpose
1970	Arbor Acres	USA	Import of seeds
1981	Dekalb Company	USA	Development of maize
1981	Continental Grain, local company	USA, China	Chicken farm and feed mill in China
1986	Oscar Mayer	USA	Food processing technology
1986	SHV Group	Netherlands	Siam Makro – cash-and-carry retail
1988	Meiji Group	Japan	Dairy business
1989	Southland Corporation		7-Eleven stores
1989	Solvay	Belgium	Polyvinylchloride
1990	British Telecom	UK	Telecom Asia – telecommunication
1993	Mitsubishi	Japan	Shrimp farming
1993	Heineken Group	Germany	Beer brewery – China
1994	Boonrawd Brewery	Thailand	Beer brewery – China
2005	Yonekyu Corporation	Japan	Pork processing technology

Source: Pananond and Zeithaml, 1998; www.cpfworldwide.com

Government connections and policy

The CP Group has also capitalized on cultivating political and government connections. It has been known for its connections with different political parties and with the military government, which has been a significant player in Thailand's political economy. These connections have been in varied forms, ranging from direct donations, participation on company boards and employment of high-level retired government officials (Pananod et al., 1998).

The group has also capitalized on changes in government policy and political changes, which have worked in its favour. In the 1960s, for instance, the government was strongly promoting poultry farming to help with rural development. This was a strong development that favoured the CP Group's business.

The collapse of the military government in 1973 further helped, as it removed the government monopoly on poultry slaughtering, and the business further expanded into the processing of chicken meat. CP's close connections with the government also helped it

(Continued)

(Continued)

to enter into the telecommunication sector when it was privatized in the 1990s and its subsequent growth and expansion in later years.

Acquisitions

The decade beginning 2000 onwards saw a change in the internationalization strategy of the CP Group, which has continued its global expansion through a series of acquisitions in both the regional neighbourhood and the distant countries of North America, South America and Europe. Its major acquisitions are listed in Table 2.5.

Table 2.5   CP Group acquisitions

Year	Firm	Country	Business	Stake holding
2005	Animal Feed	India	Animal feed	100%
2005	Shrimp Farm	Malaysia	Shrimp Farm	100%
2009	Animal Feed Co.	Taiwan	Animal feed and farming	32%
2011	Animal Feed Co.	Cambodia	Animal feed and farming	25%
2012	Chester's Food Co. Ltd	Thailand	Fast food	100%
2013	CP-Meiji Co. Ltd	Japan	Milk products	100%
2013	Russia Baltic Pork Invest ASV	Russia	Swine business	100%
2014	BHJ Kalino Food AB	Sweden	Frozen meat and food products	29%
2014	Tops Foods NV	Belgium	Ready to eat food	80%
2014	Kaifeng Chia Tai Co. Ltd	China	Production, distribution animal feed	100%
2014	Hefei Chia Tai Co. Ltd	China	Production, distribution animal feed	100%
2015	CP Cambodia Ltd	Cambodia	Integrated chicken business	75%
2015	Severnaya Woyskovitsy	Russia	Integrated chicken business	80%
2015	CP Chozen Limited (CP Chozen)	England	Restaurants, street kiosks	80%

(Continued)

Table 2.5   CP Group acquisitions *(Continued)*

Year	Firm	Country	Business	Stake holding
2016	COFCO Meat (Suqian) Co. Ltd	China	Chicken products	100%
2016	Bellisio Parent, LLC	USA, Canada	Market entry into North America for frozen foods	100%
2016	Fujian Sumpo Foods Holding Co. Ltd	China	Animal feed, farming and trading of poultry	70%
2016	Norfolk Foods (Private) Limited	Sri Lanka	Entry into ready to eat food business; exports	80%
2016	Hubei Chia Tai Co. Ltd (Hubei)	China	Animal feed, breeder animals and processed food products	100%
2017	Paulsen Food GmbH ('PF')	Germany	Expansion into Germany and Europe for chicken and duck products	
2017	Westbridge Food Group Limited (WFGL)	England	Expansion into England and Europe for retail, food services and food manufacturing	
2018	CP Hilai Harbour Co. Ltd	Thailand	Restaurant	
2018	Camanor Produtos Marinhos Ltda	Brazil	Shrimp farming	

Source: www.cpfworldwide.com/en/about/milestones

Summary

The CP Group is Thailand's earliest multinational enterprise. The group was born with an international orientation and has grown and expanded into a global agribusiness based on its competitive advantages derived from its own industry specific technological skills combined with strong networking capabilities. The industry specific skills were derived from economies of scale and scope developed through its domestic business experience.

The growth of CP Group, in both the domestic and foreign market, has been strongly based around diversification of the agro industry **value chain**. It achieved complete vertical integration from feed material production to retail distribution in agribusiness, developing a strong competitive advantage which was difficult for domestic and foreign players to replicate.

(Continued)

(Continued)

The international expansion of the CP Group has initially been market seeking, driven by rising opportunities in the booming and growing regional market. The CP Group began international expansion in its neighbouring countries of Indonesia and China before stepping onto distant foreign shores. This is consistent with the regional focus of Thai MNEs in general (Hiratsuka, 2006; UNCTAD, 2006), which have expanded into neighbouring countries driven by economic growth and development. The CP Group started with agribusiness in China, but later expanded into aquaculture, downstream petroleum projects, real estate development, banking, brewing and retailing (Pananond and Zeithaml, 1998), and then telecommunications.

CP's later investments were efficiency seeking in nature. It initially moved into shrimp farming in Vietnam, Malaysia and India pulled by the benefits of lower costs of operations in these regions as compared to Thailand. It also consolidated its business to create efficiencies and synergies within the overseas subsidiaries. For instance, Thailand was the base for cooked and processed meats, China became the base for poultry exports to Japan, and Turkey was established as the base for the EU (Pananond, 2009).

The CP Group thus stands out as a classic MNE from the developing world, which has grown into a global MNE based on characteristics and strategies quite different from those of its Western counterparts.

Case questions

1   What are the key features of the internationalization strategy of the CP Group, and how has it evolved over time leveraging its Asian basis?
2   Discuss the role of alliances and networks in the growth of the CP Group. Why have acquisitions become dominant in CP Group's growth strategy?

2.4 STRATEGIC IMPLICATIONS

Market entry can be the riskiest but most rewarding decisions a business can make.

Internationalization is an integral part of multinational companies. This chapter introduced you to the rationale, motivations and strategic considerations that shape why, how and when businesses expand across borders. We have seen in this chapter that in selecting the most suitable entry and investment strategy, businesses can reap the benefits of new and/or expanding markets. In this manner, companies change their own capabilities while also changing the dynamics in the local and international business environment.

The impact of this process is dependent on the selection of the market, the entry and/ or investment mode (the latter potentially meaning upscaling or downscaling of extant business operations in the region), and aligning corporate capabilities with local market capabilities, assets and needs. Asia has been shown to constitute a range of markets at different stages of maturity. Heterogeneity exists in terms of languages, physical and online market maturity, commerce and e-commerce buying culture, purchasing power parity (GDP per capita), and much more. This region therefore requires solid market research and assessment, and ongoing adaptation of the MNE's operations, assets and resources.

From a strategic perspective, Asia as a region is growing too rapidly to ignore. This means that Asian companies, in particular EMNEs, leverage the region through a cross-border regionalization strategy, often thus strengthening their capabilities before internationalizing into other regions of the world. Similarly, non-Asian firms are found to leverage their regional and international footprint through a strategy that is multi-locational, tapping into a range of advantages while mitigating risks that may stem from regulatory or market conditions that may widely differ from those of their home country.

Strategy is a planned set of actions that managers take to obtain or maintain a competitive advantage by making efficient and effective use of the company's assets and resources combined with core competences. International strategy can thus be defined as the company's strategy that is employed across borders, i.e. across at least two countries: its home country and at minimum one host country. The first step in going to market across Asia is to understand the market opportunity in each country of that region, to strategically assess their combined strength and fit with the corporate objectives, and then consider the best approach to entering the markets in a sequential or simultaneous effort depending on the resources, capabilities and entry modes selected.

Among the multiple ways to successfully invest in each of these different countries, the diversity of the individual market's state of maturity helps firms acquire an increasingly extensive set of 'internationalization knowledge' (IK) that emanates from market diversification, locations, timing and venture modes (Riviere and Suder, 2016).

When venturing across Asia in manufacturing sectors, you will most likely consider trade (import or export) type engagement with new markets at the start of your venture or when commitment is kept low as risks remain high; and you will increase your investment mode and upscale your engagement as your capabilities increase and/or advantages can best be accessed through partnerships or direct investments.

When planning to establish a viable online venture, you will most likely consider starting by selling directly via e-commerce or a managed service provider (MSP), or via a publisher or a value-added reseller (VAR), i.e. a company that adds features or services to an existing product, and then resells it (usually to the end users) as an integrated product or a 'turnkey' solution. Finally, when upscaling investment or in a market considered highly attractive with fairly low risk, selling directly through a wholly owned local entity is the option of choice. Do consider also that many firms use a hybrid strategy, which depends on how strong a firm's presence is or aims to be in a given market at a given moment in time, and hence applies one or more of these marketing modes. For example, you will find that some companies manage local subsidiaries for direct sales, customer support and promotion in one country yet partner with distributors only in others.

Interestingly it was found by a range of research studies that only one in four market entries succeed. This is a fairly low number, which illustrates that a cross-border strategy has to be well prepared, planned, executed and updated. This failure rate is mainly due to a lack of internationalization knowledge and the inexperience of companies venturing abroad in this highly complex market, as well as failing to correctly assess and manage key factors including timing, scale (especially scale relative to the competition), scope (especially regarding product adaptation, diversification and localization needs) and the ability to leverage assets. Those companies that have best practice records will typically boast important learning and adaptation capabilities and leverage insights from similar decisions that other companies have made in the past. That is, these companies use internationalization as a key component of their strategy rather than as a simple marketing exercise. This relies on the analyses of the firm's value proposition and capabilities, the potential of the market (including size, linkages to other attractive markets, pricing and elasticity assumptions, etc.), competition (including the anticipation of competitive response), sales/market share revenue, and cost.

Businesses often vary the use of different market entry methods for different countries so as to mitigate risk in cross-border markets in Asia. Also, this shows the adaptation of strategy in terms of the macro perspective, in that some countries will only allow a restricted level or type of imports but may welcome some form of investment, for example building manufacturing facilities that consequently provide jobs, allow for knowledge – and technology – transfer and limit the outflow of foreign exchange. Additionally, some market entry methods may not suit on a practical basis, for example when there is a lack of suitable distributors or agents to sell and service the product.

As determined in the chapter, firms seek some very specific advantages through foreign market entry. When these advantages are limited to a specific country, market entry into one host market may suffice at least in the short term, either through trade – on a more superficial engagement level of import and/or export – or though some type of investment that is typically held on a low-risk level.

Why do companies then tend to look at Asia with a multi-country lens? Companies will aim to yield the multiple advantages of a regionally (multi-country) focused strategy, because it allows them to combine a number of country and region specific advantages with the capabilities of the firm as it seeks more than one type of competitive advantage, leverages its resilience and secures the investment made in Asia, no matter whether this is its home or host region.

Emerging market MNEs, in their internationalization strategy, tend to seek to exploit existing resources, and even more so, to augment their resource base or pursue a combination of both. You will have noted in this chapter in what manner the timing of market entry or expansion, upscaling or downscaling of a MNE's investments in Asia, is correlated with an organization's learning capability and its internationalization knowledge, and with the business environment. In a region of great diversity, the question of ownership advantages that often distinguish EMNEs from developed country MNEs, has been greatly debated by international business scholars in the past decade or so, showcasing that strategic assets can be obtained by companies from resource-challenged home markets through focusing on partnerships and M&A strategy while building their own through increasing strategic knowledge and innovative capabilities.

Resource-dependency is an important focus for Asian firms that do business across the region and shapes their process. This underpins the exponential role of China, India and the ASEAN in the capacity to explore and exploit cross-border business advantage across the region.

This resource-dependency focus and development of relevant strategic knowledge is key to the survival and inherent strategic renewal of organizations that do business in Asia. That is, it leverages the ability of the multinational to maintain its fit with its business environment. For example, the need for local responsiveness varies across the diversity of Asian markets and allows firms to secure revenue from a given similar market while yielding innovative capabilities and new lessons of customer needs and customer-centricity in another that may require more adaptation. From a strategy perspective, this means a comprehensive set of advantages can be obtained and can leverage further organizational capabilities. This is key to a successful international marketing strategy.

Learning from the diversity of markets is seen as a 'must' in the search for new ideas (Chesbrough, 2003) and to avoid complacency, by driving innovation. This stimulus for innovation can also be observed in the role of the international context in regard to reverse innovation, for the sake of early positioning in new technological trend exploitation. Using this one region in the world that consistently shows growth, can hence significantly add to competitive advantage while managing risk.

Overall, it has been found, when knowledge is important, then collaborative modes of internationalization are preferred: this centres on firms being driven less by cost minimization than by 'the aim to maximize the value created by transaction' (Meyer et al., 2009: 558), i.e. the most value-creating choice in the long run. Along this path, patterns of internationalization expansion may foster or hinder a 'searching and learning': alternatives compete for an organization's resources, time and capabilities. In Asia, the importance of a firm's ability to acquire and sustain resources through cross-border strategy is increasingly crucial to its survival and ability to compete. This is even more so as in Asia, developed country MNEs continue to leverage their strengths through tapping into resource advantage across multiple locations, and at the same time, developing countries have emerged as significant sources of outward FDI and globally influential MNEs.

How has this been demonstrated in this chapter? The case of APUS, a Chinese mobile internet technology company, illustrates the opportunities and challenges stemming from continuous changes in globalization, and how external factors can affect implementation of cross-border expansion in Asia, e.g. the development of industry or geo-economic conditions and how they influence the company's adoption of globalization strategies.

The APUS case shows an example of an Asian MNE that formulated export strategies utilizing its core competence. The key focus of the case reflects the characteristics of industry development stages in emerging markets, each with their peculiar oversaturated and overheated competitive environment. APUS successfully captured first mover advantages and set up its roots in several foreign markets, often Asian, ahead of its competitors including several Chinese tech tycoons that dominated the domestic market in China. The company also extended its investments through various means in those markets after competitors arrived in succession.

APUS was based on the founder's rich knowledge of software technology. Its Android smartphone optimizing software was initially designed and developed in its home country, China, and adjusted and refined for direct exporting to overseas markets.

When APUS was founded, both pull and push factors induced the company in starting and growing its business abroad. The pull factors included the national economic development plans that greatly encouraged and benefited APUS to expand its business into several Asian regions, while the push factors arose from the overcrowded smartphone industry in China, marked by a relatively robust and mature industry structure with several Chinese technology tycoons splitting the market and leaving little room for smaller and newer players. These factors resulted in APUS's proactive and reactive strategic decisions to export its advanced technology abroad – receiving benefits from policies and regulations from the home country and avoiding direct competition and imitation in its home market.

As for a target market choice, several location advantages made India APUS's biggest overseas market and most important business centre. Among those advantages, the maturity of the industry was a key element for APUS and its founder. Because APUS's products were perceived to be constantly advancing its technology in optimizing Android smartphone performance and its user-friendly operations, the praise and reputation from users would play an important role in promoting the company on UGC platforms. Considering the following aspects of Indian – relatively high penetration rate of computer and software technology in the market, more tech-leaning user behaviours when using mobile phones and apps, and the rise of a substantial amount of smartphone users – APUS believed that India was the most appropriate target market for its products.

The case also demonstrates that FDI can strengthen the tie between the company and target markets in which it expands its businesses. For example, as direct exporting progressed, APUS started to extend its investment in India through setting up R&D centres and a series of mergers and acquisitions, with the purpose of establishing a longer-term relationship in the market and expanding its businesses into wider-scaled fields in order to garner maximum benefits.

What is specifically told by the case of APUS is not only the importance of understanding the contextual factors in various Asia regions but also the importance of recognizing the advantages that could be undertaken through specific 'localized' strategies in order to succeed in market entry.

The case study that followed looked at the Charoen Pokphand Group (CP Group), Thailand's largest diversified conglomerate. It is a classic example of an emerging market latecomer MNE from a small Asian country, which grew into a global giant. The group was born with an international orientation and has grown and expanded into a global agribusiness based on developing its firm specific advantages and further developing capabilities leveraged from connections with diverse networks. Its global strategy had elements of both traditional internationalization and of the latecomer MNE.

The business originated as a small shop selling vegetable seeds and grew into an integrated global agribusiness. It is presently a diversified conglomerate with business interests in animal seed production, livestock farming, meat processing, retail, telecommunications, e-commerce, automotives, pharmaceuticals, real estate and finance and banking.

The international expansion of the CP Group was driven by rising opportunities in the booming and growing neighbouring regional markets of Indonesia and China. This is in line with traditional explanations of firm internationalization, such as the Uppsala model, where a firm initially expands into neighbouring markets through exports, and later uses the experiential knowledge gained here for higher entry modes such as alliances and acquisitions for geographically and culturally distant markets.

Networks and alliances have been a key feature of the CP Group's global growth strategy, for both domestic and foreign operations. This is characteristic of strategies followed by East Asian latecomer MNEs, which have used connections to various networks to expand into global markets.

The CP Group began by leveraging its social and ethnic ties and diasporas status for doing business in China. This was followed by technology alliances with various MNEs across the world. CP also successfully leveraged its political and government connections. It had strong connections with different political parties and with the military government, which has been a significant player in Thailand's political economy.

The last phase of the internationalization strategy was through a string of global acquisitions, aimed at further strengthening the CP Group's presence in the global market and further developing its capabilities.

It is also evident that the strategic implications of doing business in Asia rely on extraordinary scale, the speed of technological upgrade and digitalization, the increasing overall political stability, and the rising rates of savings. Asia, and in particular its three economic powerhouses of China, India and the ASEAN, provide a unique opportunity as platforms for regional and global growth. The next chapter will shed light on how the strategic selection of business locations into and across the Asian markets drives competitive advantage, especially when aligned with the relevant organizational structure.

REFERENCES

Anderson, S.P. and Engers, M. (1994) Strategic investment and timing of entry. *International Economic Review*, 35(4): 833–853.

APUS Group IPO Prospectus (2018) www.csrc.gov.cn/pub/zjhpublic/G00306202/201806/t20180608_339587.htm (accessed 15 January 2019).

APUS News (2018) Available at: www.apusapps.com/cn/news/qi-lin-he-sheng-apus-fu-chi-yin-du-nu-xing-jiu-ye-yu-chuang-ye (accessed 31 March 2020).

APUS Official Website (2018) APUS supported women in India in employment and entrepreneurship. Available at: www.apusapps.com/cn/news/qi-lin-he-sheng-apus-fu-chi-yin-du-nu-xing-jiu-ye-yu-chuang-ye (accessed 7 March 2019).

Baigorri, M. (2018) Record $734 billion in Asia M&A spree led by Takeda, Walmart. Blomberg, 6 July. Available at: www.bloomberg.com/news/articles/2018-07-06/record-734-billion-in-asia-m-a-spree-led-by-takeda-walmart (accessed 30 March 2020).

Bain, M. (2018) To see how Asia's manufacturing map is being redrawn, look at Nike and Adidas. Quartz, 10 May. Available at: https://qz.com/1274044/nike-and-adidas-are-steadily-ditching-china-for-vietnam-to-make-their-sneakers (accessed 30 March 2020).

Boisot, M. and Meyer, M.W. (2008) Which way through the open door? Reflections on the internationalization of Chinese firms. *Management and Organization Review*, 4(3): 349–365.

Bossier, A., Cuyvers, L., Leelakulthanit, O. and Van Den Bulcke, D. (1999) Vinythai: A case study on the establishment of a petrochemical joint venture between a Belgian and a Thai company. *ASEAN Business Case Studies*, No. 15. Available at: https://repository.uantwerpen.be/docman/irua/73d0a0/4022.pdf (accessed 31 March 2020).

Caves, R.E. (1971) International corporations: The international economics of foreign investment. *Economica*, 38: 1–27.

Caves, R.E. (1996) *Multinational Enterprise and Economic Analysis*, 2nd edn. Cambridge: Cambridge University Press.

CEIBS Review (2015) Avoided battles in China, APUS found blue sky in overseas market. Available at: www.ceibsreview.com/show/index/classid/122/id/3261 (accessed 10 January 2019).

Charoen Pokphand Group (2004) *International Directory of Company Histories*, Vol. 62. St. James Press. Available at: www.company-histories.com/Charoen-Pokphand-Group-Company-History.html

Charoen Pokphand Foods Public Co. Ltd. Available at: https://asia.nikkei.com/Companies/Charoen-Pokphand-Foods-Public-Co.-Ltd

Chesbrough, H.W. (2003) The era of open innovation. *MIT Sloan Management Review*, 44: 35–41.

China News (2015) Chinese mobile internet goes abroad, APUS' target in Android new users. Available at: www.chinanews.com/cj/2015/08-13/7465999.shtml (accessed 16 March 2019).

CP Group (2018) Geographical footprint. Available at: www.cpfworldwide.com/en/investors-map (accessed 31 march 2020).

Cuervo-Cazurra, A. and Genc, M. (2008) Transforming disadvantages into advantages: Developing-country MNEs in the least developed countries. *Journal of International Business Studies*, 39(6): 957–979.

Das, G. (2015) Burger wars. *Business Today*, 20 December. Available at: www.businesstoday.in/magazine/features/fast-food-brands-mcdonalds-kfc-dunkin-donuts-burger-king-vie-for-indian-burger-market/story/226498.html (accessed 6 April 2020).

Dhapola, S. (2015) Lenovo, Motorola start smartphone manufacturing in India with Moto E. *Indian Express*, 19 August. Available at: https://indianexpress.com/article/technology/mobile-tabs/lenovo-motorola-start-smartphone-manufacturing-in-india-with-moto-e (accessed 30 March 2020).

Dore, R.P. (1990) *British Factory – Japanese Factory*. Berkeley, CA: University of California Press (originally published in 1973).

Dunning, J.H. (1977) Trade, location of economic activity and the MNE: A search for an eclectic approach. In B. Ohlin, P. Hesselborn and M. Wijkman (eds), *The International Allocation of Economic Activity*. New York: Holmes and Meier, pp. 395–418.

Dunning, J.H. (1993) *Multinational Enterprises and the Global Economy*. Wokingham: Addison-Wesley.

Economic Times (2016) Charoen Pokphand Foods forays into packaged foods business in India. Available at: https://economictimes.indiatimes.com/industry/cons-products/food/charoen-pokphand-foods-forays-into-packaged-foods-business-in-india/articleshow/52639453.cms?from=mdr.

Finance (2016) Platform firms are more advantaged in overseas VCs, 21 Finance. Available at: http://m.21jingji.com/article/20160402/c820d33752019540103cd58b92e612ee.html (accessed 15 January 2019).

Huet, E. (2014) Google I/O: Keynote Live Blog, *Forbes*, 25 June. Available at: www.forbes.com/sites/ellenhuet/2014/06/25/google-io-2014-keynote-live-blog/#4957b5f7e287 (accessed 24 April 2019).

Hymer, S. (1976) *The International Operations of National Firms: A Study of Direct Foreign Investment*. Boston, MA: MIT Press.

Indian Express (2018) McDonald's aloo tikki secures place in American menu with vegan tag. Available at: https://indianexpress.com/article/lifestyle/food-wine/mcdonald-aloo-tikki-american-menu-vegan-tag-5502151 (accessed 30 March 2020).

Kafouros, M.I., Buckley, P.J., Sharp, J.and Wang, C.Q. (2008) The role of internationalization in explaining innovation performance. *Technovation*, 28(1–2): 63–74.

Kim, C. and Park, D. (2015) Emerging Asian MNCs. *Asia Pacific Business Review*, 21(4): 457–463.

Kindelberger, C. P. (1969) *American Business Abroad: Six Lectures on Direct Investment* New Haven, CT: Yale University Press.

Kishimoto, M. (2019) CP Foods taps into Vietnam's TPP access to drive poultry exports. *Nikkei Asian Review*, 23 April. Available at: https://asia.nikkei.com/Business/ Companies/CP-Foods-taps-into-Vietnam-s-TPP-access-to-drive-poultry-exports (accessed 30 March 2020).

Leiponen, A. and Helfat, C.E. (2010) Innovation objectives, knowledge sources, and the benefits of breadth. *Strategic Management Journal*, 31(2): 224–236.

Luo, Y. and Tung, R.L. (2007) International expansion of emerging market enterprises: A springboard perspective. *Journal of International Business Studies*, 38(4): 481–498.

Makino, S., Lau, C.M. and Yeh, R.S. (2002) Asset exploitation vs. asset seeking: Implications for location choice of foreign direct investment from newly industrialized economies. *Journal of International Business Studies*, 33(3): 403–421.

Mathews, J.A. (2002) *Dragon Multinationals: A New Model for Global Growth*. New York: Oxford University Press.

Mathews, J.A. (2006) Dragon multinationals: New players in 21st century globalization. *Asia Pacific Journal of Management*, 23(1): 5–27.

Meyer, K.E., Wright, M. and Pruthi, S. (2009) Managing knowledge in foreign entries strategies: A resource-based view analysis. *Strategic Management Journal*, 30(5): 557–574.

MIITC (Ministry of Industry and Information Technology of China) (2017) *World Internet Development Report 2017*. Available at: www.cac.gov. cn/1122128829_15135789293581n.pdf (accessed 3 March 2019).

Mishra, P. and Raghu, K. (2007) Wipro puts cash to good effect as its acquisitions get bigger. LiveMint, 9 August. Available at: www.livemint.com/Industry/ kvSnIbWixdDVgzxS9zXq8M/Wipro-puts-cash-to-good-effect-as-its-acquisitions-get-bigger.html (accessed 30 March 2020).

Narula, R. and Kodiyat, T. (2016) How weaknesses in home country location advantages can constrain EMNE growth: The example of India. *Multinational Business Review*, 24: 249–278.

Pananond, P. (2009) Thai multinationals: Entering the big league. In R. Ramamurthy and J. Singh (eds), *Emerging Multinationals in Emerging Markets*. Cambridge: Cambridge University Press, pp. 312–351.

Pananond, P. and Zeithaml, C.P. (1998) The international expansion process of MNEs from developing countries: A case study of Thailand's CP Group. *Asia Pacific Journal of Management*, 15: 163–184.

Riviere, M. and Suder, G. (2016) Perspectives on strategic internationalization: Developing capabilities for renewal. *International Business Review*, 25(4): 847–858.

Sohu Technology (2017) Six take-aways and inspirations from APUS' successful overseas experience. Available at: www.sohu.com/a/205978763_343044 (accessed 15 January 2019).

Statista (2018) Global mobile OS market share in sales to end users from 1st quarter 2009 to 2nd quarter 2018. Available at: www.statista.com/statistics/266136/global-market-share-held-by-smartphone-operating-systems/ (accessed 7 March 2019).

Sydow, L. and Cheney, S. (2018) 2017 Retrospective: A monumental year for the app economy. Available at: www.appannie.com/en/insights/market-data/app-annie-2017-retrospective/ (accessed 15 January 2019).

Tech In Asia (2016) APUS finds India 3 times bigger than China, vows $44m fresh investment. Available at: www.techinasia.com/apus-finds-india-3-times-bigger-china-vows-44m-fresh-investment (accessed 15 January 2019).

Tencent Technologies (2014) Tao Li, Former Vice President of Qihoo360, discusses his 'overseas experiences'. Available at: www.apusapps.com/en/news/tao-li-discusses-his-overseas-experiences/ (accessed 15 January 2019).

Winichagoon, W. (1992) Formation and behaviour of Thai industrial capitalists: A case study of Charoen Pokphand Group in agro-industry. IMA Thesis, Faculty of Economics, Thammasat University, Bangkok.

Witt, M.A. and Lewin, A.Y. (2007) Outward foreign direct investment as escape response to home country institutional constraints. *Journal of International Business Studies*, 38(4): 579–594.

YiCai (2016) Understanding APUS' Global Mobile Internet Report: Why Singaporeans like social media while Indians like the tools. Available at: www.yicai.com/news/5008490.html (accessed 7 March 2019).

Zeschky, M., Widenmayer, B. and Gassmann, O. (2014) Organising for reverse innovation in Western MNCs: The role of frugal product innovation capabilities. *International Journal of Technology Management*, 64(2–4): 255–268.

3
LOCATION DECISIONS AND MARKET EXPANSION IN ASIA

3.1 INTERNATIONAL LOCATION CHOICES

This chapter provides essential learning focused on international location choices, market expansion and organizational structures that enable business ventures into and across Asia. It covers:

- an introduction to international location choices
- a case study about Unilever – changes in organizational structure
- a case study illustrating how organizational structure can be aligned, focusing on 'fast retailing' in East Asia
- it concludes by highlighting the resulting strategic implications.

International location choice is a crucial aspect of a firm's international business strategy. As we saw in Chapter 2, the choice of location is based on the existence of country and region specific advantages present in a geographical location, which attract foreign firms. Country specific factors determine the macro environment for the MNE, and region specific factors determine its operating environment. Sometimes these factors may be overlapping and common, but it is possible that regions within a country offer different specific location benefits.

India, for instance, emerged as a favoured emerging market business location after the macro-economic reforms of 1991. However, within the country, certain regions such as the state of Gujarat have emerged as an investment hub on account of favourable investment policy changes that are specific to the region. The automobile industry was among the earliest to take advantage of these state specific industrial promotion policy initiatives and several MNEs such as Hero Motocorp (Japan), Peugeot (Italy) and Maruti Suzuki – a joint venture between Maruti (India) and Japan's Suzuki – have set up manufacturing units in the state. Ford India is said to have selected Gujarat because of its location – its ports allow for possible exports to Western markets – its cost and logistics considerations, business environment and the state government's 'transparent and competitive' offers to start and implement a business proposal. Gujarat has better labour–industry relations than other Indian states, infrastructure that includes good roads and ample electricity and water and a central location between Delhi and Mumbai.

Locational determinants may therefore be classified at the macro and micro level.

Macro level determinants

Regulatory environment

A firm's decision to choose an international location is driven by a favourable regulatory environment. This includes policies that determine the outward orientation of the country such as FDI and trade policies and also those that determine its internal business environment such as industrial policies, tax policies and labour laws. A leading example of this is Singapore, which has transformed itself from a racially divided third-world seaport into one of the world's most sought-after investment destinations (DeBold et al., 2015) due to its outward oriented approach towards trade and FDI. The focus on attracting FDI through a well-regulated internal business environment has led to its emergence as an exporter of aerospace, semiconductor and biotech products and has made it the regional headquarters for some of the world's largest and most innovative companies, such as BMW (Germany), Roche (Switzerland), Novartis (Switzerland), Microsoft and Apple (USA)(Christensen et al., 2019).

Socio-political factors

The socio-political environment is responsible for creating a smooth working environment for the MNE. Political stability is a strong pull factor for the foreign MNE. Similarly, factors such as the general attitude towards foreign business and permission to repatriate profits create a positive image of a country as a business location. However, regional variances may exist, such as in the context of India, where the southern state of Kerala, which has traditionally had a socialist government, has been a less favoured destination for foreign MNEs as compared to other states. McDonald's (USA) opened its first restaurant in Kerala in 2013, almost 17 years after it established its first restaurant in India.

Infrastructure

Infrastructure plays a major role in attracting foreign business. The existence of a network of roads, railways and communication facilities helps to create a favourable business destination. The state of infrastructure in the ASEAN region varies across countries, given that the region is a diverse mix of high-income and low-income economies with several large middle-income economies as well (World Bank, 2018). In the past decade, Asia-Pacific countries have constructed more infrastructure than any other developing region. However, there are huge differences in the condition of infrastructure across different Asian countries. Infrastructure is woefully inadequate in countries like Malaysia, Laos and Indonesia, whereas Singapore is a favoured business location on account of its state-of-the-art infrastructure facilities.

China's Belt and Road Initiative released in 2015 aims to encompass land routes (the 'Belt') and maritime routes (the 'Road') with the goal of improving trade relationships in the region primarily through infrastructure investments. It aims to involve infrastructure development and investments in 152 countries and international organizations in Asia, Europe, Africa, the Middle East and the Americas.

Special economic zones (SEZ)

Developing countries attempt to attract FDI by setting up **special economic zones**, which provide preferential treatment for taxation, land use, infrastructure access and government assistance to MNEs. These special enclaves offer location advantages that are not available in other regions. China created its first SEZs in the towns of Shenzhen, Zhuhai and Shantou in Guangdong province and Xiamen (Amoy) in Fujian province. These new SEZs soon attracted foreign investment and became the hub of rapidly expanding light and consumer goods industries and growing populations. Shenzhen transformed into a megacity and became a world-class tech hub, home to the Shenzhen Stock Exchange and one of the busiest financial centres in the world. The earliest investors in Shenzhen were US MNEs Intel and IBM, and also Toshiba (Japan) and Samsung (South Korea). Similarly, the Pudong area within the Shanghai municipality became a special economic zone with policies that were even more flexible than those already in force in the original four SEZs.

India has introduced free trade zones (FTZs), export processing zones (EPZs), free zones (FZs), industrial estates (IEs), free ports and urban enterprise zones in the last two decades to promote exports and FDI. Recently, several Chinese investors have shown interest in setting up business in different SEZs across the country. These include Beiqi Foton Motors for setting up an auto industrial park in Pune, Maharashtra; China Development Bank Corporation (CDB) and China Small and Medium Enterprises (Chengdu) Investment Limited (CSME) for setting up a multi-purpose Chinese industrial park in Gujarat; Dalian Wanda Group and China Fortune Land Development (CFLD) Co. Ltd for development of an integrated entertainment park-cum-industrial township and industrial park in Haryana (Singhania and Rao, 2018)

Government efficiency and corruption

MNEs are also attracted by the soft infrastructure such as government efficiency and a lack of corruption. Efficiency in government functioning translates into a responsive work environment, assistance and support in various issues and quick ratification of projects without taking bribes or using delaying tactics. The Corruption Perception Index is an annual tabulation of countries across the world based on public sector corruption. The Index is an annual ranking based on the relative degree of corruption for countries from all over the world. Singapore (3), Hong Kong (14) and Japan (18) were in the list of top 20 least corrupt countries in 2018.

Sustainability and ethical attitudes

The attitude of the host country towards sustainability and ethical practices may attract MNEs. There is a general notion that countries in the developing world have weaker laws and enforcement as compared to their developed country counterparts. This has resulted in the setting up of manufacturing sweatshops for MNEs like Nike (USA) in Vietnam and Cambodia (Bain, 2017) where these Western MNEs can get away with a lax attitude towards working conditions for workers.

Microlevel determinants

Markets

The existence of a large and growing market is the greatest attraction for an MNE. This finds evidence in the increasing investment flows to countries such as Indonesia, Malaysia, Singapore, Thailand, Cambodia, Laos, Myanmar and Vietnam, which have been identified as outperforming emerging economies of the Asian region in the last decade. Growth in the region has been driven by a conscious pro-growth policy creating a 'virtuous cycle of productivity, income and demand' (Vanham, 2018). Vietnam, for instance, has an economic growth of 6–7 per cent, which rivals that of China, and its exports are worth as much as the total value of its GDP. The small ASEAN nation is emerging as a manufacturing hub, with products ranging from Nike sportswear to Samsung smartphones. It has emerged as the largest exporter of clothing and the second largest exporter of electronics in the region in 2017 (Vanham, 2018).

Earlier in the 1990s, pharmaceutical MNE Pfizer chose to establish its multi-vitamin production plant in India since it was a growing middle-class market. Similarly, Toys-R-Us chose to enter Japan in the 1990s since the strong Japanese economy and increased consumer spending were a huge attraction for investment.

Consumer base

MNEs choose to locate in regions that have a large potential consumer base. Manufacturing MNEs would like to base their operations as close as possible to the consumer, to take advantage of cost efficiency and marketing effectiveness. Royal Enfield, India's largest motorcycle manufacturer, chose to locate its first foreign production base as a wholly owned subsidiary in Thailand. The choice of destination was driven by the fact that a large section of Thai commuters is moving up the income ladder, leading to increasing demand for the two wheeler, alongside an emerging trend of long distance leisure riding among youth in the country (Ghosh, 2019). US soft drinks MNEs Coke and Pepsi chose to base their China operations in the eastern part of the country because of the large consumer base present there. United Parcel Service (USA) similarly chose Taipei in Taiwan as its Asia-Pacific air hub, since it had easy accessibility to customers.

When entering a new region, MNCs choose to begin in a mature market and then expand outward. Bosch (Germany) is an engineering and technology company that started its Southeast Asia operations in 1923, in the British colony of Malaysia. It formed a joint venture in Indonesia much later, in 1994, and also opened a representative office in Vietnam in that year. It expanded into Laos in 2012 and Myanmar in 2013, and at present Bosch has a presence in all ten ASEAN member nations, in businesses spanning automotive, consumer goods and energy (Lang et al., 2018).

Cost of production

Costs are the most important variable of the MNEs location decision choice. These include wage costs, which are often a substantial proportion of the total cost of production.

The phenomenon of outsourcing has emerged as a result of the search for low-cost destinations, as MNEs located production in global locations where labour was available at cheaper rates than in their home country. The emergence of India as the outsourcing hub for IT, and countries like Bangladesh, Indonesia and Thailand for apparel manufacturing, is due to the low-cost labour force in these parts of the world. Within a country also, there may be regional differences in costs. Nike (USA) chose to locate its manufacturing units along the Pearl River Delta in China to take advantage of the low wage rate in that part of the country.

China has similarly been investing in Malaysia over the last two decades. This includes Huawei and ZTE's entry into Malaysia's telecommunications sector in 2001 and 2004 respectively and automobile producer Chery's investment in 2008. Chinese FDI in Malaysia increased after 2014, after the launch of the One Belt and One Road initiative and is spread over diverse sectors (Yean, 2018).

Agglomeration benefits

MNEs often choose regions that have a concentration of industrial units to take advantage of a common labour pool and spill over benefits of learning from regional networks. In India, for instance, the IT industry is concentrated in two locations in north and south India. Similarly, the automobile industry, which is a key driver of India's manufacturing, is located in the southern city of Chennai, which is also known as the 'Detroit of Asia'. US automobile giant Ford Motors set up its plant in Chennai in 1995, marking the arrival of the city as an auto hub. Since then, the region has manufacturing plants established by BMW (Germany), Renault (France), Hyundai (South Korea), Mitsubishi (Japan) and Daimler (Germany). The Indian state of Tamil Nadu is one of the top ten automobile hubs in the world, with Chennai having an installed capacity to produce 1.4 million cars per year.

It was seen that firms from Taiwan's electronics industry established a foothold in Thailand in the early 1990s as a consequence of the agglomeration benefits arising out of previous associations with other Taiwanese investors who were already operational in that country (Sim and Pandian, 2003).

Labour productivity

International production is hugely dependant on high labour productivity and a skilled labour force. As production has become technology intensive, it needs just the right combination of labour skills and technological competence as an important determinant of its location. The availability of a skilled managerial, marketing and technical workforce is crucial for the firm to gain or continue to reap the benefits of competitive advantage. As an example, take the case of Apple, which decided to shift the production of the Mac closer to home in Austin, Texas, as a fallout from the tariff war with China in early 2019. However, the decision had to be reversed because the US could not produce the adequate number of screws required for seamless production, which were being easily produced in China. The screw shortage highlighted the importance of China as a manufacturing base with the advantages of skill, scale, infrastructure and cost.

Aligning organizational structure

Organizational structure is a formal arrangement of individuals, activities and relationships to achieve a common goal. It helps to clearly determine formal power and authority relationships and is represented in the company's organization chart. Organizational structure is developed to enable the effective implementation of strategy. Organizational strategy is the firm's desired plan of action, and the structure is critical in ensuring that the desired goals are met efficiently. Multinational enterprises thus need an effective structure for successful strategy implementation.

Once an organization decides to go international, it has to align its organizational structure and its implementation and control systems to reflect new strategies. Internationalization means diversity in products and services, geographical markets and human resources. The firm needs a reconfiguration of its competencies and resources to cope with the dispersal of its global activities. This may often lead the organization through an evolutionary process commensurate with the stage approach of internationalization.

Internationalization thus translates into different challenges for the MNE. It has to identify the best organizational structure for operational effectiveness. This should lead to an optimal approach for the implementation of corporate strategy globally, regionally and locally. It explores how MNEs choose appropriate structures so that they can be successful both locally and internationally. MNEs have to learn country tastes, global trends and market transitions that call for structural changes.

Global organizations have tried to realize scale benefits by centralizing activities that are similar across locations and tailoring then according to the needs of local markets. Today, as more and more companies shift their weight to emerging markets, the boundaries between those activities are changing for many organizations.

At some point, they will need to adapt their structures and processes to acknowledge this boundary shift, whose nature will vary across and within companies, depending on their industry, focus and history. In one recent case, an international publishing company created global 'verticals' comprising people who work on content and delivery technology for similar publications around the world. But it was careful to leave all sales and marketing operations in the hands of local country managers, because in publishing these activities can succeed only if they are tailored to local markets.

Take the case of IBM in Asia, which has globalized its business services but left the businesses local. IBM realized that there was too much duplication of effort if it had a complete suite of business services to support different product brands in various Asian countries. It therefore identified 11 services with common features in functional areas: supply chain, legal, communications, marketing, sales management, HR and finance. Each function was assigned a global 'owner' with the task of consolidating and refining operations to support businesses in the region's different countries. The MNE then kept essential elements of each function and discarded the redundant ones. So now, for instance, IBM's growth market operations are served by HR specialists in Manila, accounts receivable are processed in Shanghai, accounting is done in Kuala Lumpur, procurement in Shenzhen, and the customer service help desk is based in Brisbane. This created the new 'globally integrated enterprise model' for Asia and later evolved into an entirely new structure for IBM's global operations.

Organizational designs

The basic function of the organization is to provide a framework for decision-making, co-ordination, reporting and communication to ensure learning from the global marketplace through the company's different units. As the firm moves into the international market, it adapts its structure according to its degree of internationalization in different geographical locations. These structures can be broadly divided into three categories: early organizational, international division and global organizational.

Early organizational structures

When a company first begins international operations, it is typical for these activities to be extensions of domestic operations. A domestic firm begins its life as a small organization with a structure based on the functional division of activities such as production, marketing and sales, which is coordinated by top management. Decision-making in such an organization is usually centralized. The firm's international activities are so insignificant that they do not require any organizational adjustment.

Its decision to tap the international market has an ethnocentric orientation, as its primary focus continues to be the local market, with international involvement having secondary importance. International transactions are conducted on a case-by-case basis, and there is no attempt to consolidate these operations into a separate department. Under this arrangement, international sales are viewed as supplements to the income earned from home-country operations.

As the firm's international operations expand, it brings about changes in its organizational structure to reflect those changes. As a first step, the MNE establishes a separate marketing department to handle international sales, and all overseas operations are coordinated through this. This helps the company to develop marketing specialists who learn the specific needs and marketing techniques to employ in overseas selling.

Alternatively, the firm may set up a separate export department that reports directly to the CEO or it may be a sub-department within the marketing area. Consider for instance, TAL Apparel, which is a private, family owned garment manufacturer based in Hong Kong. It was set up in 1947 as the first spinning mill in the country and later diversified into apparel manufacturing for leading brands such as Calvin Klein (USA) and Banana Republic (USA) (Barrie, 2018). The firm uses a combination of overseas marketing representatives and direct export sales as part of its domestic marketing department.

Another possible arrangement is the establishment of overseas subsidiaries to manage individual ventures in different geographies of the world. In this arrangement, the head of the venture has a great deal of autonomy and reports directly to the CEO.

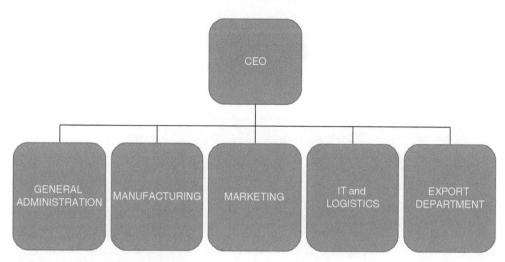

Figure 3.1 Export department

International division structures

The international division structure is established to handle all the international operations of a business firm. This aims to do away with the possibility of treating international operations as secondary in importance as compared to domestic operations. The international division focuses on international expertise and information flows in the context of the international market and its activities. However, the firm continues to keep manufacturing and its related functions under domestic control to avail itself of the benefits of large-scale production. This structure also helps the MNE to develop a cadre of internationally experienced managers. As an example, take the case of Marico (India), which established an international division to manage its basic business of exporting hair oil to the countries of the Middle East. The knowledge of the local market gained by Marico then helped to expand its business into other areas such as beauty clinics in the region. It also moved into North Africa by establishing wholly owned subsidiaries for production (Marico, 2019).

However, the international division structure often faces problems of coordination and control between domestic and foreign personnel. The head of the international division is usually considered to be at the second tier of the organizational hierarchy, with less authority and decision-making power than his or her domestic counterparts. It is therefore important that there is frequent, close interaction between domestic and international personnel to remove possible conflict. This is also important because the domestic units are usually organized along product or functional lines, but the international division has a geographical orientation.

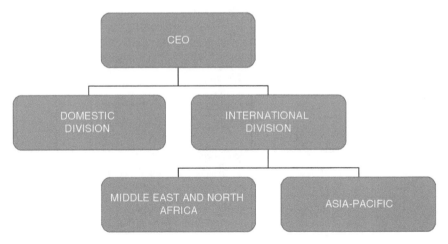

Figure 3.2 International division

Global organizational structures

As firms continue their international expansion, they move towards adopting a more global structure, driven by competitive compulsions and changes in strategy. It is well known in the literature that 'structure follows strategy'.

There are five basic types of global structures discussed here.

Global product structure

A global product structure is a structural arrangement in which domestic divisions are given worldwide responsibility for product groups. It is adopted by firms that have a reasonably diversified product portfolio and are organized along product division lines even as domestic companies. Figure 3.3 provides an example of the global product structure of such a firm. Just as with domestic divisions, international divisions are also autonomous, self-contained units responsible for their profits. The structure is commonly used by consumer product firms and has historically been used as a strategy to deal with consolidation.

The product structure allows the firm to focus individual major product lines and specific customer needs and requirements. It also helps the firm to develop a niche cadre of specialized managers with an in-depth understanding of a particular product line, and to match customer needs with different stages of the product life cycle across the home and host country market.

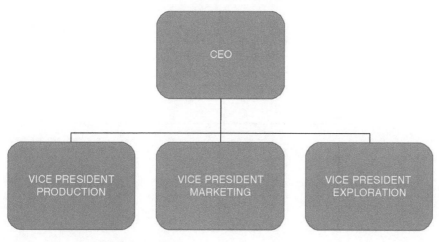

Figure 3.3 Global product structure

However, it causes duplication of effort and personnel, and wastage of resources for the organization. It also needs a management team with a specific geocentric orientation to handle products in different markets. Coordination is a basic hurdle in this structure as different units operate independently without cooperation of effort and resources.

Firms are meeting international challenges through reorganization as in the case of Li & Fung, Hong Kong's largest export trading company and an innovator in the development of **supply chain management**. The company has global suppliers worldwide that are responsible for providing the firm with a wide range of consumer goods ranging from toys to fashion accessories to luggage. In recent years Li & Fung reorganized and now manages its day-to-day operations through a group of product managers who are responsible for their individual areas.

Global area structure

The **global area structure** is an organizational arrangement with a highly decentralized structure. The primary operational responsibility in this organizational form is delegated to area managers, each of whom is responsible for a specific geographic region. It is usually adopted by firms with a low degree of diversification and a domestic structure organized along functional lines. In this polycentric (host country oriented) structure, the area manager reports directly to the CEO. Figure 3.4 provides an example of this structure. Under this arrangement, each regional division is responsible for all functions

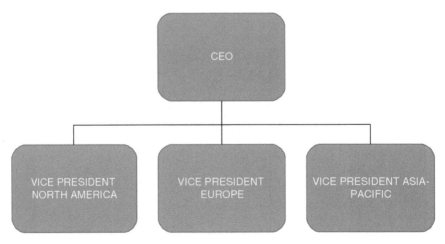

Figure 3.4 Global area structure

within its area, that is, production, marketing, personnel and finance. Operational authority and strategic decision-making are decentralized to individual area managers, but overall strategic direction and financial control remain with the headquarters.

A global area structure is commonly used by MNEs with mature businesses and stable product lines.

Advantages:

- These organizations have a geocentric approach while achieving local adaptation on a regional basis. The regional managers have the authority to modify products and strategy according to local needs.
- The structure is useful for firms that are marketing oriented and need to adapt their product to local tastes and preferences.

Disadvantages:

- There is limited communication and knowledge sharing among different regional managers.
- Regional managers often lack a global orientation.

An important issue in geographical structures is the location of its regional headquarters. For instance, firms in the Asia-Pacific region have a preference for Singapore on account of its infrastructure and human resources. It was estimated that almost 4,200 firms had their regional headquarters in Singapore in 2016. This includes engine-maker Rolls-Royce, technology company Microsoft and pharmaceutical firm Bayer Pharmaceuticals. Bayer set up its regional headquarters in Singapore in 2000, and it has used this location to forge research partnerships with local and regional academics and government agencies, to successfully develop treatments for diseases commonly found in the region. Other MNEs such as furniture retailer Ikea (Sweden) and consumer goods company Unilever have chosen Shanghai and retailer Walmart (USA) prefers Hong Kong as its regional headquarters (EDB Singapore, 2017).

However, since the focus is on regional management, global issues of product development and product management may be neglected. This is seen in the case of McDonalds (USA), which changed its traditional geographical structure in 2015 to an alternate form where business units were classified into four groups based on the maturity of its presence in the market: the flagship US market, established international markets such as Australia and the United Kingdom, high-growth markets such as China and Russia, and the rest of the world. The change was driven by falling profits in markets in Asia and Europe and was accompanied by a revamp in the menu to include healthier food options (CBS News, 2015).

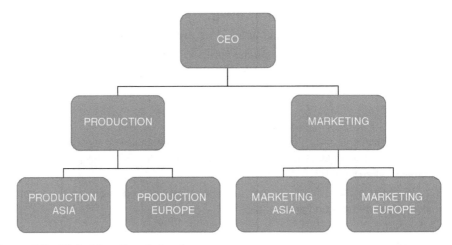

Figure 3.5   Global functional structure

As firms change their organizational structure in response to their changing strategic imperatives, the changeover may not be the same across the globe. Ford Motor company, for instance, changed its organizational structure from a geographic oriented to a product oriented one in 1995. However, it continued with a geographical structure for its Asian and Latin American markets, since regional adaptation as needed in these areas was easier to achieve than in other parts of the world.

Global functional structure

This structure is built around the basic functional tasks of the organization. Figure 3.5 shows such an arrangement. In a **global functional structure**, the head of the production department is responsible for all domestic and international manufacturing. Similarly, the head of marketing is responsible for the sales of all products both in the domestic and foreign market. This structure is most commonly used by MNEs that have a narrow product line and have reached a stable level of demand that is not likely to face major competitive changes.

Advantages:

- The global functional structure allows tight centralized control as a small group of managers are responsible for all managerial functions.
- The structure has a focused global strategy with a high degree of functional expertise.
- This also helps to save resources as there is very little duplication of facilities.

Disadvantages:

* However, it may be difficult to coordinate different areas such as production and marketing since each one operates independently of the other. This can be particularly troublesome if the TNC has multiple product lines.
* It may be difficult to respond to specific customer needs in individual markets.

Matrix structure

A **matrix structure** is a *geocentric* organizational arrangement that blends two organizational responsibilities such as functional and product structures or regional and product structures.

It attempts to combine product, regional and functional expertise while maintaining clear lines of authority. The functional emphasis pays attention to the activities to be performed, whereas the product emphasis focuses on the goods that are being produced.

This structure is characterized by a dual command system. For instance, a functional area manager, say, from marketing, has a multiple reporting relationship. He will report to his area manager in his geography and to an international or worldwide marketing manager at headquarters. This helps the organization to develop a geocentric attitude.

There are three types of managers in this geocentric matrix structure: regional managers, product managers and matrix managers.

> *Regional managers* are charged with business in their markets. Budgets for these operations include selling any of the products made by the TNC, subject to the decision of each regional manager. These regional managers have a *polycentric focus*.
>
> *Product managers* are accountable for coordinating the efforts of their people in such a way as to ensure the profitability of a particular business or product line. These managers have an *ethnocentric attitude*.
>
> The *matrix managers* are responsible to both regional and product managers; they have two bosses.

Singapore-based Olam International is an exporter of agricultural products such as cashews, grains, sugar and palm oil as well as rubber, fertilizer and wood products. It is one of the world's leading suppliers of cocoa and coffee. Olam is a highly diversified organization spread across 60 countries, 20 products and 10 functions. This highly coordinated, cross-functional and high-performance organization is organized as a matrix structure, and is integrated across multiple businesses, geographies and functions. Its corporate centre has been the catalyst for the integration of its multi-business company by developing a shared vision and agenda, installing common operating systems, and embedding a common culture across the organization.

Sony's electronic businesses, including personal computers and cable television set-top boxes, have been unified in one group. The MNE has created a new division that will focus exclusively on the mobile phone business. It also has a management group called the 'Global Hub' that coordinates strategy across a host of Sony units including financial services, games, internet services and entertainment.

Advantages:

- It seamlessly blends the benefits of global strategy while responding to local needs.
- It combines the best elements of the global area, product and functional structures.
- There is a focus on sharing of organizational knowledge and learning across all sub-units on a global level.

Disadvantages:

- There are multiple levels of command creating a dual authority structure for the employee.
- This complex structure creates problems of coordination and control.

Transnational network structure

The **transnational network structure** is among the newest forms of international organizational arrangements. It combines elements of the functional, product and geographical organizational structures and uses a network arrangement to link together its various subsidiaries all over the world. This huge interlinked structure is held together at the centre by *nodes*, which are units that act as the chief coordinators for the product, functional and geographical structures within the superstructure. Within the larger organizational structure, the product group units and geographical area units can choose their own organizational design according to their own requirements. This structure helps TNCs take advantage of global economies of scale while also being responsive to local customer demands. An example of how the transnational network structure works was provided by Royal Philips Electronics in the 1990s. This firm, with its headquarters in the Netherlands, is a diversified TNC with operations in more than 100 countries and produces a diverse product line ranging from light bulbs to defence systems. The company's functions, businesses and markets represented at the highest levels are innovation, strategy, human resources, legal and global markets, with a dedicated representation for China as a major growth market. Some of its units specialize in manufacturing, others in sales; some are closely controlled by headquarters, others are highly autonomous.

The basic structural framework of the transnational network consists of three components: dispersed sub-units, specialized operations and interdependent relationships.

> *Dispersed sub-units* are subsidiaries that have geographical locations based on the advantages of those locations for the organization. These advantages could range from low costs and new technology to emerging consumer trends, and they determine the geographical position of the subsidiary.
>
> *Specialized operations* are focused activities carried out by sub-units that make the best use of specialized expertise or other resources. These activities focus on specific product lines, research or marketing areas.
>
> *Interdependent relationships* are used to share information and resources throughout the dispersed and specialized sub-units.

The transnational network structure is difficult to draw in the form of an organizational chart because it is complex and continually changing. It is also cumbersome to coordinate and control and is continuously changing to suit changes in the global market.

3.2 Case study: Unilever – changes in organizational structure

Overview

This case examines the evolution and growth of Unilever as a transnational MNE and the changes in its organizational structure and strategy in response to growth imperatives in the global marketplace. The core argument here is that enterprise profitability is based on the ability of the MNE to find a fit between organizational architecture and strategy. This fit should match the needs of the firm's competitive environment and push it to adapt itself accordingly. Unilever has evolved through actual practice as a business responding to the dictates of the marketplace. Its global journey began with entry into Asia and was accompanied by necessary changes in its organizational structure. The success and growth of Unilever into various global markets including Asia is based on conscious changes made in strategy and organization in response to the changing business environment.

(Continued)

(Continued)

Learning outcomes

By the end of this case study, students should be able to:

1   Examine the growth and evolution of Unilever as a transnational MNE, and the organizational changes associated with its growth into Asia and other parts of the world.
2   Understand the key elements of Unilever's *glocal* strategy for growth into Asia and other markets.

Introduction

Unilever is British-Dutch transnational consumer goods MNE. It was formed through the merger of the Dutch margarine producer Margarine Unie and the British soap-maker Lever Brothers on 2 September 1929. Its product range includes food and beverages, cleaning agents, beauty products and personal care products. It is a dual-listed company consisting of Unilever plc, based in London, and Unilever N.V., based in Rotterdam. The two companies operate as a single business, with a common board of directors.

Unilever currently owns 400 brands, including Lipton, Knorr, Dove, Axe, Hellmann's and Omo, which are available in 190 countries, including 19 countries in Asia. It is said that a Unilever brand can be found in seven out of every ten households in the world. Several of these brands have been customized for local markets of Asia – for instance Brooke Bond caters to the specific needs of the Indian consumer.

Unilever established a presence in Asia as early as 1885, when the first bars of Sunlight soap were shipped to Kolkata (then Calcutta) as Lever Brothers' products. Unilever set up its first Indian subsidiary in 1931, known as Hindustan Vanaspati Manufacturing Company, followed by Lever Brothers India Limited (1933) and United Traders Limited (1935). These three companies merged to form Hindustan Unilever Limited (HUL) in November 1956. HUL offered 10 per cent of its equity to the Indian public, this being the first time a foreign subsidiary was being opened to the local public.

Unilever obtains 59 per cent of its current business from emerging markets and had a turnover of €51 billion in 2018. It is currently organized into three divisions: Beauty and Personal Care, Foods and Refreshment and Home Care. Beauty and Personal Care had a turnover of €20.6 billion, accounting for 40 per cent of total sales and 33 per cent of operating profit. Foods and Refreshment had a turnover of €20.2 billion, accounting for 40 per cent of total turnover and 58 per cent of operating profit. Refreshment and Home Care generated turnover of €10.1 billion, accounting for 20 per cent of total turnover and

9 per cent of operating profit. It aims to be a sustainable business at all stages of the product life cycle, making efforts to reduce its environmental footprint, use sustainable sourcing of raw material and help its consumers improve their health and wellbeing (Unilever, 2019a).

Unilever currently has a matrix organizational structure, based on products and regions. This case study shows how MNEs like Unilever adapt their organizational structure to manage and direct their global operations profitably in their global expansion beginning with Asia. The core argument here is that enterprise profitability is based on the ability of the MNE to find a fit between organizational architecture and strategy. This fit should match the needs of the firm's competitive environment and the firm should adapt itself accordingly. We explore the growth of Unilever into various global markets with a focus on Asia to investigate whether this growth is based on strategic changes based on internationalization across this region that is today crucial to Unilever's business, and how the organization responded to its changing competitive environment.

A decentralized organization

Unilever was launched as a manufacturer of home products – soap and margarine (a substitute for expensive butter) – using its inherited capability in the use of fats and oils from its original Dutch and British parent firms. The MNE started life with an international orientation, since its two parent companies, Margarine Unie of the Netherlands and Lever Brothers of the United Kingdom, had a long tradition of expanding their businesses through both export and local production (Maljers, 1992). It had established strong and significant international links in Africa for the procurement of palm oil. It made use of these links to launch new businesses in Asia, Africa and Latin America in the 1930s.

During the war years (1940–49), Unilever found its businesses in Germany cut off from London and Rotterdam. This led to the development of a corporate structure that would allow local Unilever subsidiaries in host markets to gain a high level of independence and to gain and maintain sufficient autonomy to focus on the needs of local markets.

It thus started out in 1929 with a decentralized organizational structure, which was necessary since it competed in markets where local responsiveness was crucial, since the production and marketing of home products have traditionally been tailored to the tastes and preferences of consumers in different national markets. Unilever catered to the needs of local responsiveness by pursuing a localization strategy that was reflected in its organizational structure. Unilever's decentralized structure was designed to ensure

(Continued)

(Continued)

that responsibility for various functional areas such as production, marketing and sales was delegated to autonomous national units. The British and Dutch components of the organization coexisted loosely with one another. This structure was based on the multi-domestic approach and ensured that the huge number of brands and factories owned by Unilever were organized nationally, and functioned on limited central direction.

Unilever began international expansion into Asia, Africa and Latin America in the 1930s, and later into the USA, as a manufacturer of home products such as margarines, cooking fats and laundry soaps.

Unilever's expansion into Asia began with setting up a subsidiary in India in 1931. This was followed by business operations in Sri Lanka in 1938 and in Pakistan in 1948. It also established operations in Bangladesh in 1971, China in 1986 and Nepal in 1992.

Unilever products have always been characterized by a combination of global with local features, and its marketing efforts have focused on important social issues of the region. This has been followed since its inception in the late nineteenth century, when Sunlight bar soap was introduced to address the hygiene problem in Victorian-era Britain. Sunlight made its way to the Indian market in 1888, much before the Indian subsidiary was established. Since then, various products introduced by Unilever have focused on social issues of the region. These include Lifebuoy, which addresses the problems of life-threatening diseases associated with poor hygiene, and Domestos, which seeks to improve sanitation for millions of people who do not have access to a toilet.

The decade of the 1960s was the beginning of an era of globalization marked by the onset of economic integration in Europe. Laundry soaps and edible fats were the main products in Unilever's portfolio at this time, contributing to almost half of its profits and making these products a part of household consumption across the globe. The production and marketing of the home care portfolio led to the adoption of a localization strategy that was tailored to meet the demands of consumers in different national markets.

The Unilever organizational structure in the 1960s was so decentralized that it was almost fragmented. The historical legacy of decentralized authority led to the creation of a huge business lacking in cohesion, but which had a huge operating cost. However, Unilever's decentralized structure was successful in its expansion into the overseas markets of Asia, Latin America and Africa, where it successfully established a strong presence in the detergents and personal care markets (Jones, 2005a).

Unilever's story from the 1960s was based on juggling the benefits of local market knowledge and decision-making, against the disadvantages of excessive decentralization and fragmentation. Until the mid-1960s, it was organized on the basis of national markets. Every country was an individual profit centre, and the national management team was fully responsible for the profits of all units in its territory. Product groups worked only in an advisory capacity, and all management decisions on the marketing and distribution of different products were based on local priorities.

Unilever went through its first organizational restructuring in 1966, as it created product groups into profit centres for all countries in Europe. The national management team now assumed an advisory role. The products were organized into three different food units: an edible fats group, a frozen food and ice cream group, and a food and drinks group that took care of everything else – mainly soup, tea and salad dressings. This reorganization ensured the existence of a decentralized structure that had the advantage of providing a deep understanding of local markets with a degree of centralized control (Maljers, 1992).

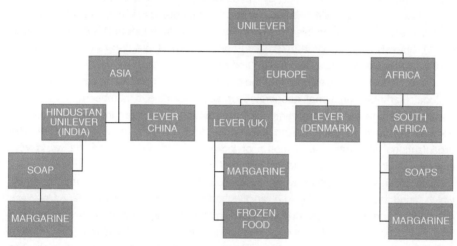

Figure 3.6   Unilever – a decentralized organization

Diversification

During the second half of the twentieth century Unilever began following a policy of diversification, which was the managerial strategy in fashion during that time. It diversified in response to specific threats to its core business, since there was stagnation in the consumption of yellow fats and increased competition in laundry soap and detergents from its rival, US-based Procter & Gamble, which had gained a technological advantage in the manufacture of synthetic detergents (Jones and Miskell, 2007).

The diversification of the Unilever business model was driven by a string of acquisitions, which enabled the MNE to build successful businesses in new product categories. It diversified into ice cream, tea, and also personal care and specialty chemicals businesses. Unilever also acquired paper manufacturers, ferry companies

(Continued)

(Continued)

and home decorating companies. It used its West African affiliate, the United Africa Company, to acquire several small and medium-sized firms in Europe across a range of sectors such as automobile distribution, medical devices and even garden centres (Jones and Miskell, 2007). While most of these acquisitions were subsequently divested during the 1980s, ice cream and tea remained lasting components of the Unilever business empire. Given that a simple product like tea is consumed in multiple different ways across the world, the popularity of Lipton as a brand is indeed commendable. The British consumer likes it hot and highly diluted with milk, the Americans usually like it iced and in India it is cooked with milk, spices and condiments to resemble a thick beverage.

Unilever's prominent acquisitions over the years include Lipton (1971), Brooke Bond (1984), Chesebrough-Ponds (1987), Best Foods (2000), Ben & Jerry's (2000), Alberto-Culver (2010), Dollar Shave Club (2016) and Pukka Herbs (2017).

Over the years, it was evident that the nature of Unilever products required proximity to local markets. Functional economies of scale justified a number of head-office departments and the free movement of information across organization boundaries allowed everyone to benefit from experience and creativity at a global level. The organizational structure was a matrix of individual managers around the world who shared a common vision and understanding of corporate strategy.

This resulted in an unwieldy organization, based on the multi-domestic approach, which found itself falling behind in a rapidly changing competitive environment. Unilever's decentralized organization meant duplication in manufacturing, a lack of scale economies, a high cost structure and delays in decision-making. It faced competition from giant retailers like Walmart with its low prices, and from Proctor and Gamble, which had similar sales but with half the work force. Adopting a new product in a regional market meant that it had to convince all the regional subsidiaries – which could be a matter of four to five years. Similar decisions by its competitors Nestlé, Proctor and Gamble and L'Oréal took much less time. Advertising and branding were handled amateurishly by local managers. Unilever needed to purchase 30 different types of vanilla for its ice cream in Europe and its Rexona deodorant had 30 different packages and 48 different formulations. The decentralized structure of Unilever's international organization had a domestic orientation, which led to unnecessary duplication and multiple obstacles in the manufacturing of its global products.

Geographical reorganization – 1990s

Unilever went through a major organizational restructuring in the 1990s, designed to centralize authority in response to changing realities of competition. It adopted a more transnational strategic orientation, which could balance the need for local responsive-ness in marketing and sales with the centralization of manufacturing and product development. The change hoped to bring in the benefits of scale economies and make product decisions at a regional level.

Unilever introduced a new structure based on regional business groups. Each business group contained a number of divisions, which focused on a specific category of products. These divisions made decision-making centralized for manufacturing and product development activities. The main aim of this reorganization was to reduce operating costs and speed up the development and introduction of new products.

The restructuring created four core business areas: Home Care, Personal Care, Foods and Specialty Chemicals. The new structure was led by a new team, and included 12 business groups, each responsible for a mix of geographical and product areas. It discontinued 1,200 brands and focused attention on 400 remaining brands with the greatest potential. Development of new global products was done by global teams on the basis of common features in major country markets. The positioning of global brands such as Dove soap was done on a global basis. Local management teams did not have the authority to take decisions on its packaging, formulation or advertising strategy.

Unilever made several acquisitions during the 1990s, which were aligned with its core products. These included Breyers ice cream and the Helene Curtis hair care business in the US and Kibon ice cream in Brazil. It sold the United Africa Company, Unilever's huge West African trading, brewing and textiles company, and all its chemicals businesses including National Starch and Quest International.

A major development in the Asian region was the merger of Hindustan Lever and Brooke Bond Lipton India, to create the country's largest private sector company. The MNE also launched Organics shampoo in Thailand, which was being sold in over 40 countries within a year.

In response to changing consumer sentiment and the increasing preference for healthy food, Unilever decided to eliminate trans-fats from food production. This decision was taken in response to new research that suggested the adverse impact of this category of fats on blood cholesterol.

Figure 3.7   Unilever – a regional reorganization

(Continued)

(Continued)

Creating a balanced matrix organization

Unilever embarked upon another organizational transformation in 2000, attempting to create a more balanced matrix organization for its international operations, in response to the challenges in its business environment. The 'One Unilever' programme aligned the organizational structure with a single strategy, aimed at simplifying the business and leveraging scale economies more effectively. It created two global divisions: Food products and Home and Personal Care products. This was aimed at reducing Unilever's brands from 1,600 to 400, and for consolidation of production in fewer, but more efficient production units.

Its brand portfolio was reshaped and enhanced through both acquisitions and the sale of several brands. Its prominent sales included Diversey Lever, Elizabeth Arden and Unipath. Unilever Cosmetics International (UCI) was sold to Coty Inc. of the US, in line with Unilever's strategy to focus on core categories. Other important sales included the North American laundry business, the edible oil business in Côte d'Ivoire, business interests in local oil palm plantations, Palmci and PHCI, and the Bertolli olive oil and vinegar business to Grupo SOS.

Unilever acquired Best Foods (USA) – which was the second-largest cash acquisition in its history – and added Skippy peanut butter, Hellmann's mayonnaise and Knorr soups to its product portfolio. This acquisition established Unilever as a significant player in the US market, filling a much-needed gap. Other US acquisitions included Slim-Fast Foods and Ben & Jerry's, allowing Unilever to become the world's largest food conglomerate. It also acquired the Amora-Maille culinary business in France.

There was a renewed focus on health issues with the launch of the Unilever Health Institute in 2000, which aimed to be a centre of excellence in nutrition, health and vitality. The Institute opened regional centres in Bangkok, Thailand and Accra, Ghana in 2003.

Unilever also maintained its commitment to sustainability and protection of the environment. It was committed to sourcing all its tea and palm oil from sustainable, ethical sources.

It continued to maintain a regional structure under its two divisions, since it recognized the importance of localization in all its markets. These reorganizations aimed to establish a fit between organizational strategy, architecture and the business environment, to help it face new competitive realities.

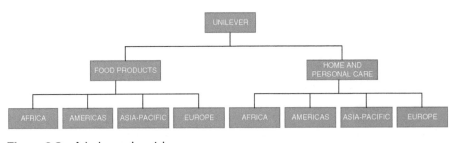

Figure 3.8 A balanced matrix

Transnational focus

The emphasis on having a *glocal* (global with a local emphasis) strategy continues to be the hallmark of Unilever operations. It introduced Annapurna iodized salt in India in 1995, which had a huge impact on redressing iodine deficiency in the country. In 2008, the Indian subsidiary, Hindustan Unilever, developed Pureit, a line of water filters in response to the needs of clean water and sanitation for India's large population. The MNE later introduced Pureit to China and other parts of Southeast Asia.

Unilever brands also aim to act as a catalyst to promote positive cultural norms in both a global and local context. The Brooke Bond tagline – 'Common ground is only a cup away'– is highly relevant in an increasingly divided world and is equally applicable in a local context. In India, it addresses religious tensions, in the Gulf region the focus is on divorce issues, and in Canada it is aimed at same-sex relationships.

Unilever brands also take on an activist stance, aimed at mobilizing citizens to change policy or create social movements. Ben & Jerry's for instance, builds movements around issues such as climate change and the refugee crisis. Seventh Generation – with its plant-based products – campaigns for renewable energy. The deodorant brand Rexona is aimed at helping to reverse physical inactivity, a big issue for societies facing increasingly sedentary lifestyles.

In 2015, Unilever introduced the Indian cosmetic brand Lakme to Indonesia and customized it by getting *halal* certification for the products in accordance with Islamic law (Koyanagi, 2017). In 2017 it launched body moisturizers named Hijab targeting the Indonesian Muslim female consumer who wears a full body covering garment called a hijab (Maulia, 2017).

Unilever also re-entered the Myanmar market with the launch of a new manufacturing facility and new headquarters in Yangon. It is among several MNEs which have found potential in the mountain country's youth, high growth and limited exposure to big international brands, following political transition.

In March 2018, the company sought to end its dual Anglo-Dutch structure, with a proposal to move its headquarters completely to Rotterdam. A shareholder vote was planned to decide for the listing of a new Unilever Dutch entity, which would have seen Unilever dropping out of the FTSE 100 Index. However, when it appeared that the vote would fail the scheme was cancelled.

Unilever announced changes to its leadership and organization as it continued its transformation into a faster, leaner and more agile company. The changes resulted in the creation of three global divisions last year – Beauty and Personal Care, Foods and Refreshment, and Home Care – organized around geographical regions into a more balance matrix structure (Unilever, 2019b).

(Continued)

(Continued)

Final remarks

Unilever is a transnational corporation, with a matrix form of organization, organized on product and regional lines, which combines local initiative with some centralized control. The rapid pace of environmental change, increased complexity and demands and the need for cultural adaptability have presented overwhelming challenges for the MNE. Unilever has emerged as a successful transnational organization, which has constantly adapted its structure and strategy in order to keep pace with the challenges of the marketplace.

Unilever began life as a decentralized organization, based on the multi-domestic approach, and had a local strategic emphasis for its basic products. It grew through diversification of products across regions, into a huge, unmanageable and cost heavy organization with slow decision-making skills.

This led to major organizational restructuring efforts as its strategic thinking became more focused, with an emphasis on reconfiguring the geographical basis of its business. Unilever brands became household names across global markets. Dove, Sunsilk, Omo, Surf and Lipton were great consumer products, but they became worldwide brands because of the capabilities of Unilever. Their success rested on the choices made in strategy and organization.

A crucial aspect of its ability to adapt is its managerial workforce, which was encouraged to think in a transnational manner since the inception of the organization. It started a policy of local managerial recruitment to replace the Dutch and British executives from head office who were managing most of its local units. Starting with the Indian subsidiary in 1931, Unilever put into place a management process known as 'ization'. In other words, filling local executive and technical positions with Indian managers led to the 'Indianization' of that subsidiary – along with 'Australianization', 'Brazilianization' and other examples of localization of management in various countries with Unilever operations (Maljers, 1992).

The Unilever story has several lessons – the most important being that in order to be a successful transnational organization, the MNE's structure and strategy must constantly adapt, regardless of internal and external difficulties, in order to keep pace with the changing marketplace. Unilever has successfully weathered numerous changes over the course of its lifetime. Its organizational restructuring in response to new market trends illustrates a successful combination of structural formality and managerial flexibility in response to the dynamics of a changing competitive landscape.

Case questions

- What form of organizational structure does Unilever have? Explain its growth and evolution from inception until the present as it expanded into Asia and other parts of the world.
- What is the role of localization and local responsiveness in the transnational matrix structure followed by Unilever, in its operations in Asia?

3.3 Case study: Organizational structure aligned – 'Fast retailing' in East Asia

Overview

Fast Retailing is a Japanese global company that operated several fashion brands including UNIQLO, GU and Theory. As of November 2019, the company was the world's third largest fashion manufacturer and retailer, ranked after INDITEX (Zara) and H&M. Unlike those of Zara and H&M, apparels sold in Fast Retailing, chiefly through UNIQLO, were seen as less trendy and more as simple-styled well-designed functional pieces at a lower price for daily use. In a high consumer opinion-influenced industry like fashion, Fast Retailing competed head-on with other trend-leading fashionable brands with its standard and no-nonsense products through its management system. This case seeks to understand the rationale for differentiation and the success of Fast Retailing, which was often attributed to its unique corporate culture and organizational structure. While adhering to the basic principles imposed by the headquarters in Japan, Fast Retailing derived good business results partially from adapting its organization via a carefully designed global area structure. This was achieved with the deployment of flexible layers of sub-committees and modules and giving autonomy and authority to each store to fit the local conditions wherever it expanded. The global area structure was important given the widely varied institutional and environmental circumstances in Asia.

Learning outcomes

By the end of this case study, students should be able to:

1   Identify Fast Retailing's culture and understand how this culture has exerted an impact on the company's global expansion choices of location, organizational structure and management system in response to different local conditions in Asia.
2   Identify the characteristics of a typical global area structure and understand its roles in shaping the management system that has been adopted by the company in an Asian setting.

Introduction

On 18 October 2019, UNIQLO, a subsidiary of Fast Retailing, became the world's second biggest apparel manufacturer and retailer, just behind Zara, the leading global fashion

(Continued)

(Continued)

brand. In fiscal 2019, UNIQLO had a revenue of US$21.51 billion, moving up from third to second place (Fast Retailing, 2019h). UNIQLO is an Asian brand, from Japan, while Zara and H&M are both from Europe where the modern sense of fashion thrives. The biggest difference between Fast Retailing and its two main rivals is that its products come embedded with Fast Retailing's unwavering philosophy, which is to avoid blindly following the runway fashion trends and try to innovate to produce high-quality and reasonably priced day-to-day clothes. Fast Retailing aims to establish a connection between its apparel and nature, which is termed 'LifeWear' (Fast Retailing, 2019b). To achieve this, UNIQLO, the core brand of Fast Retailing (see Table 3.1), tried to differentiate and construct its image through unified store designs and universal products. While its competitors Zara and H&M's apparel pinpoints modernity and fashion, UNIQLO's window displays stress simplicity (SOHO, 2019). The models found in a UNIQLO store window are dressed in 'simplified but not simple' clothes. The layout of UNIQLO's shop windows is designed with eye-catching lighting exhibiting the effect of installation art. Artistically ornate and graceful lamps

Table 3.1   Performance by group operation (billions of yen or stores)

Year		2017	2018	2019
UNIQLO Japan	Revenue	810.7	864.7	872.9
	Operating profit	95.9	119	102.4
	Direct-run stores	831	827	817
UNIQLO International	Revenue	708.1	896.3	1026
	Operating profit	73.1	118.8	138.9
	Direct-run stores	1089	1241	1379
GU	Revenue	1991	211.8	238.7
	Operating profit	135	11.7	28.1
	Direct-run stores	372	393	421
Global Brands	Revenue	141	154.4	149.9
	Operating profit	0.5	−4.1	3.6
	Direct-run stores	1002	984	972

Source: www.fastretailing.com/eng/ir/financial/excel/20191010_group_gyoseki.xls

are applied to the whole background to achieve the unexpected visual aesthetic effect, filled with a sense of simplicity (SOHO, 2019). The theme is bright and bold. Rather than adding too much room for imagination, UNIQLO's window displays use the most intuitive way to showcase the current hot products and fashion trends in the store. Its service is also unique in that it advocates service with a Japanese gesture, like greeting with a raised voice and in a cheerful manner, 'Welcome to UNIQLO! Help yourself!' when you enter the store. In contrast, you often do not find anyone to serve you at Zara stores except when approaching fitting rooms or check-out counters.

History

UNIQLO is a relatively young company. When Tadashi Yanai, the CEO of UNIQLO, was born in 1949, his father owned a suit shop in Yamaguchi Prefecture, a former trading port with a long history of openness and cultural exchange (Fast Retailing, 2019i). As Japan's economy recovered and its domestic spending power improved, his father successfully opened 22 stores. By 1984, Tadashi Yanai had succeeded as the president of the company, and opened a shop in Hiroshima called Unique Clothing Warehouse the same year (Fast Retailing, 2019i).

UNIQLO was not originally called UNIQLO. It began as 'UNICLO' for 'Unique Clothing Warehouse' but was accidentally written as 'UNIQLO' by a Chinese partner in Hong Kong (Vision Critical, 2019). Instead of blaming him, Tadashi Yanai thanked him because he thought 'Q' looked cooler than 'C' and decided to change all the registrations and advertising campaigns from 'UNICLO' to 'UNIQLO.' The name 'UNIQLO' thus came about as a result of a coincidence (*NSS Magazine,* 2019).

Tadashi Yanai had long admired retailers such as Marks and Spencer (Britain), Benetton (Italy) and GAP (America), wondering why there were no similar retailers in Japan. Back in the 1990s, he told friends UNIQLO would overtake GAP (Vision Critical, 2019). A close friend said: 'He never hides his dreams, even if it feels a bit arrogant. It's very un-Japanese.' In the 1970s and 1980s, Tadashi Yanai seized the opportunity associated with Japan's economic take-off and the appreciation of the yen, but he also suffered from the dire situation after the Japanese economic bubble burst in the late 1980s and early 1990s. Under the effect of the great depression in the 1990s, he decided to bypass intermediaries and deal with the suppliers directly. He challenged the point of view that 'Japanese customers do not favor the products made in China'(SOHO, 2012). Indeed, 90 per cent of UNIQLO's clothing was made in China; at the same time, relying on a 'high quality but low price' strategy. This quickly captured

(Continued)

(Continued)

customer loyalty, and accurately grasped the pulse of globalization, and UNIQLO grew at a fast pace, 'crazily' (SOHO, 2019).

On a breezy April afternoon in 2012, a corporate trainee stood at the back door of UNIQLO's flagship store in Tokyo's plush Ginza district, where it opened just a month before, interviewing customers. The first question he asked was always the same:

What word comes to mind when you think of the UNIQLO brand?

'Yasui.'

'Yasui.'

'Yasui.'

Person after person – 28 in a row – uses the same Japanese word, which does not mean 'cool.' It means 'cheap.' (Fast Company, 2012)

Perhaps the advertisement, which embodied the elements of *yasui*, worked particularly well: UNIQLO was never reported as 'cool' in Japan. UNIQLO had enriched its brand story, ensuring that 'cheap' at UNIQLO meant affordable, not poor quality or low grade. 'Cool is good, but too much of a good thing', said Naji Takizawa, UNIQLO's famous contract designer, in his workshop. It was an L-shaped three-story space with many windows, stacked with hundreds of samples and two headless models in tennis suits, just below Tadashi Yanai's office. 'In addition to being trendy, consumers have a desire for functionality. The product should be strong enough, easy to wear on a daily basis. Everything needs a fashion element, but fashion is just an ornament' (Sina, 2015).

From a nearby shelf, Naji Takizawa took a parka with a colour between dark green and light brown, embellished with vertical zipper bags that echo the catwalk styles of Burberry Prorsum and Marc Jacobs in autumn/winter 2015. But even more interesting was the evolution of the product. Pointing to a single seam on the left, he said: 'Double seam is much more complicated. A single line is easier and takes 20 seconds less' (Sina, 2015).

Before joining UNIQLO, Naji Takizawa was chief designer at Issey Miyake. He said, 'In Issey Miyake, its philosophy is plus. In this case, the philosophy is subtracting. Less, less and less!' UNIQLO took 90 seconds less to make the parka. The time and cost saved by making 600,000 parka coats were significant, which explained why UNIQLO's products were cheap. 'It's similar to what I used to do at Issey Miyake, which was all about good design but different kind of design', said Naji Takizawa (Sina, 2015).

In 2009, on his sixtieth birthday, Tadashi Yanai received the best birthday gift. With a net worth of $6.1 billion, he became Japan's richest man according to the Forbes list. As Tadashi Yanai said: 'Poor people buy UNIQLO, and rich people buy UNIQLO, too. We advocate "all-matching". "All-matching" needs taste. People with good taste will buy UNIQLO, and people with average taste will buy UNIQLO. Our products have good quality and at low prices, which is the key to our success in this economic crisis' (SOHO, 2012).

It can be said that the financial crisis of 2008 made UNIQLO. Bill Gates, the world's richest man, lost $18 billion in 2009, Warren Buffett, $25 billion and Nintendo's former President, Hiroshi Yamauchi, $4.5 billion (SOHO, 2019). Tadashi Yanai was the exception, bucking the trend with Fast Retailing's stock up 63 per cent in 2008, UNIQLO's sales soaring and new stores popping up around the world (Fast Retailing, 2019f).

The world's second largest manufacturer and retailer of private-label apparel, Fast Retailing offers high-quality, reasonably priced clothing by managing everything from procurement, design and production to retail sales (SOHO, 2019). UNIQLO, its pillar brand, generates approximately $17.3 billion in sales from 2,196 stores in 24 countries and regions (Fast Retailing, 2019a). Without a soul, a company is nothing (Business of Fashion, 2019). The soul of UNIQLO is 'cheaper clothes but in good quality, let it be UNIQLO!' (Southeast of Wealth, 2019).

Global expansion

UNIQLO's global strategy did not happen naturally (Martin Roll, 2019). The economic downturn of the 1990s made it difficult not only for companies but also for the Japanese domestic market. The Japanese domestic clothing market became saturated (Vision Critical, 2019). To overcome this, UNIQLO embarked on a journey of global expansion, but this journey has not been smooth (Fortune, 2019).

In September 2001, UNIQLO entered the British market and opened a branch in London, which was the first time it had explored overseas markets (Fast Retailing, 2019g). In May 2002, its number of stores in the UK increased rapidly to 15, and then expanded to 21. Although the number of stores was increasing, the operation suffered losses. Hence, UNIQLO began to reduce the number and scale of its stores and closed those outside London's city centre that did not perform well. This setback did not affect its confidence in exploring international markets, especially the British market. In 2013, it launched its children's clothing line in ten UK stores, which turned out to be very popular. After more than ten years of development, there were 15 UNIQLO stores in the UK as of November 30, 2019 (Fast Retailing, 2019b).

(Continued)

(Continued)

On its entry into the US market in 2005, UNIQLO believed that the US would account for a fifth of its parent company's sales and reach its target of $20 billion by 2020 (Fast Retailing, 2019f). UNIQLO opened stores in three suburban New Jersey malls in 2005, only to close them within a year. The first New York store opened in 2006 in Manhattan's SOHO business district, and in autumn 2011 it opened two mega-flagship stores on Fifth Avenue and 34th Street, with aggressive advertising across multiple platforms. In September 2012, it opened a 43,000-square-foot store in Paramus, New Jersey, which was then the largest overseas branch. In October 2012, it opened a 29,000-square-foot store in San Francisco's Union Square, officially entering the West Coast. Between October and November 2013, UNIQLO opened ten new stores in US shopping malls. The new stores were strategically located near UNIQLO's flagship stores on the US East and West Coasts, with four in California, three in New York, two in New Jersey and one in Connecticut. In addition, the flagship UNIQLO store in New York, which opened in April 2014, became the first clothing retailer in the United States to introduce a Starbucks Coffee shop in the store. To attract customers, UNIQLO set up relaxation areas with sofas, tables and chairs, and iPads in the store. In July 2014, UNIQLO launched a 'push into the American heartland' with a range of cheap, brightly coloured sweaters. As of 30 December 2019, UNIQLO had 52 stores in the United States (Fast Retailing, 2019d).

The company's entry into other Asian markets took place almost simultaneously. In its early days in mainland China, UNIQLO developed and designed all products in Japan and then commissioned local Chinese companies to manufacture its products. Through the signing of long-term and strategic cooperation agreements with Chinese manufacturers, stable relationships were formed (Fast Retailing, 2019f). UNIQLO had a rocky start in China, too. It first opened stores in Shanghai in 2002, sacrificing quality there to maintain its low-price position in the domestic Japanese market. By the end of 2005, it only had seven stores in China and no profit. Unlike Japan's M-shaped social structure, China had more 'middle classes' with good spending power (Martin Roll, 2019). As a result, UNIQLO repositioned itself above the middle-income level, with prices about 10–15 per cent higher than in Japan, safeguarding instead of sacrificing quality in pursuit of lower prices. After defining the 'middle class' in China, it began turning around its status in China and gradually expanded (Fast Retailing, 2019d).

In recent years, UNIQLO has made China the focus of its international expansion, adopting a different strategy in China with further subdivision of the consumer market and opening up the markets that other competitors had not yet entered (Martin Roll, 2019). UNIQLO turned its development orientation towards the average family, valuing the consumption demands of its community customers. Its medium and small shops gradually entered community shopping centres, and then community markets, breaking into the second- and third-tier cities, making good use of the differences in information flow between second- and third-tier cities and first-tier cities, and grabbing the local mass market, which paid more attention to practicality. As more and more Chinese got to know, understand and like UNIQLO, it was gradually more and more appreciated among its Chinese customers (Fast Retailing, 2019b).

UNIQLO sold men's, women's and sportswear in China and announced it would open 100 new stores there annually, mainly in commercial complexes, shopping centres and commercial streets. The site selection criteria were areas with a large flow of people, namely downtown areas with frequent commercial activities, near public gathering areas, and close to its arch-rivals. The space requirement was generally 500–1,500 square metres with a rental contract duration lasting 5–10 years. As of 30 December 2019, UNIQLO had 738 stores in the Chinese mainland (Fast Retailing, 2019f).

UNIQLO entered the Hong Kong market later than mainland China, in 2005, successfully shifting its customer base to the middle class there too. On 26 April 2013, it opened its seventeenth store in Hong Kong, which covered a total area of 3,500 square metres. As of 30 December 2019, it had 30 stores in Hong Kong (Fast Retailing, 2019f).

According to UNIQLO's annual report for the fiscal year 2018 (see Table 3.1), the performance of UNIQLO International was spectacular, with a 26.6 per cent rise to $8.1 billion, placing UNIQLO International revenue ahead of UNIQLO Japan for the first time (Martin Roll, 2019). Operating profit soared by 62.6 per cent year on year to $1.08 billion, reaching UNIQLO Japan level (Fast Retailing, 2019b). As Tadashi Yanai said in the annual report for the 2018 fiscal year:

> I put UNIQLO's comprehensive success down to a growing embrace of our LifeWear concept worldwide. LifeWear is clothing that offers true comfort, high quality, and fashionable touches at a price everyone can afford. Unlike trend-chasing apparel firms, the UNIQLO brand seeks to become an essential part of life. LifeWear is forged out of long-held Japanese respect for superior crafts-manship. LifeWear means bold new materials born from revolutionary technolo-gies. LifeWear means simple, highly finished clothing that accentuates the wearer's style. (Fast Retailing, 2019b)

UNIQLO's globalization was a success story (see Table 3.1). But what was the secret to its success, and how did it succeed in spreading its philosophy and brand concepts globally?

(Continued)

(Continued)

UNIQLO's global area organizational structure

UNIQLO's global strategy has kept consistent with its stores in Japan where its customers can find products at lower prices and with good quality. In order to maintain this consistency, it has established at least one subsidiary in each and every region in which it operates and established its global management under a typical geographic-oriented corporate structure (Fortune, 2019). Those subsidiaries constitute its international business segment, besides UNIQLO Japan and other business segments of the corporate structure (Jiang, 2019). All of these subsidiaries have their own regional head offices, which are authorized to make regional decisions. It is through this organizational structure that UNIQLO successfully brings its clothing philosophy to the world, and its products to the home and host market. To date, it has been embraced by consumers globally (Fortune, 2019) especially in Asian markets (Fast Retailing, 2019d).

An organizational structure can be seen as a formal arrangement of individuals, activities and relationships to achieve a common goal, which helps to clearly determine formal power and authority relationships in a company. This is represented in a company's organization chart (Fortune, 2019). An organizational structure is developed to enable the effective implementation of strategy. Organizational strategy is the firm's desired plan of action, and the structure is critical in ensuring that the desired goals are met efficiently. Multinational enterprises thus need an effective structure for successful strategy implementation. Once an organization decides to go international, it has to align its organizational structure and its implementation and control systems to reflect new strategies. UNIQLO needed to design and implement an effective global organizational structure rapidly to support its global strategy. Among the six generic global organizational structures, UNIQLO has chosen a global area organizational structure. As you learnt in section 3.1, the global area structure is an organizational arrangement with a highly decentralized structure. The primary operational responsibility in this organizational form for UNIQLO was delegated to area managers, with each one responsible for a specific geographic region. This is usually adopted by firms with a low degree of diversification and a domestic structure organized along functional lines. In this polycentric (host country oriented) structure, area managers report directly to the CEO. Under this arrangement, each regional division is responsible for all key functions within its area, that is, production, marketing and sales, personnel, and finance. Operational authority and strategic decision-making are typically decentralized to individual area managers, but overall strategic direction and financial control remain with headquarters (Jiang, 2019).

Figure 3.9 is a schematic diagram of UNIQLO's globalization organization. We take UNIQLO Greater China as an example to illustrate how UNIQLO's global organizational structure works.

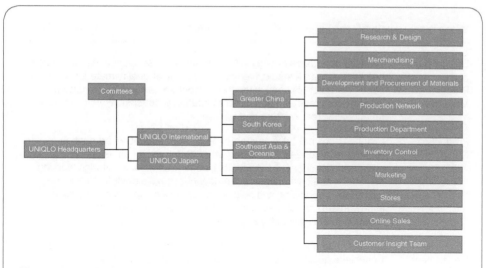

Figure 3.9   UNIQLO's global organizational structure

Source: Fast Retailing, 2019c

UNIQLO headquarters has jurisdiction over UNIQLO Japan and UNIQLO International, which is divided into greater China, South Korea, Southeast Asia and Oceania, South Asia, North America and Europe based on its geographical location. The greater China region is sub-divided into three modules based on functions: design, production and sales, each of which is further divided into the business modules outlined in Table 3.2 (Fast Retailing, 2019c).

Table 3.2   UNIQLO's business modules

Research and Design	UNIQLO's research and development centre is constantly researching the latest new materials and global fashion. A year in advance, the R&D department holds a concept meeting with representatives from the marketing and materials development teams to determine the correct design concept for each season, prepare design proposals and refine samples.
Merchandising	The sales force plays a vital role in the production of the product, communicating closely with the various departments before determining the plan, design, materials and marketing required for each season. Another important responsibility of a salesperson is to determine the product line and volume for the year.

(Continued)

Table 3.2   UNIQLO's business modules *(Continued)*

Development and Procurement of Materials	UNIQLO negotiates directly with material manufacturers and places large orders to secure a stable, high-volume supply of quality materials at low cost. The materials used in its core project are particularly important, with in-depth research and experimentation producing layers of improved functionality, feel, contour and texture.
Production Network	UNIQLO does not have any factories and outsources all production to partner factories in China and other countries. It has established a strong relationship of trust with its partner factories, monitoring working conditions and environmental protection for textile manufacturers and major fabric suppliers, and helping the factories implement necessary improvements to maintain a win–win relationship and ensure the production of high-quality products.
Production Department	UNIQLO has about 450 production teams and textile craftsmen. In order to achieve quality improvement, customer concerns are communicated to the production department. The production team visits the partner factory on a weekly basis to resolve production quality or management issues.
Inventory Control	The biggest task of the inventory control department is to maintain optimal inventory levels. UNIQLO achieves this by monitoring sales and inventory on a weekly basis, distributing necessary inventory and new products to fulfil orders. At the end of the quarter, salespeople work with marketing to coordinate and monitor the timing of any price changes.
Marketing	UNIQLO regularly promotes its core products, advertising their unique qualities and noteworthy features on television and other media.
Online Sales	Online sales are increasingly important. In mainland China, online sales account for more than 15 per cent and 20 per cent of total sales, respectively.
Customer Insight Team	UNIQLO's customer insight team analyses the volume of requests and comments from online customers that are critical to improving its core product line.

Source: Collected and compiled from the Fast Retailing Group official website data

All of these business units were merged into three major modules that ultimately formed the core organizational structure of greater China. UNIQLO's headquarters controls the global uniform standards of the brand, including clothing and brand philosophy, and regional subsidiaries conduct brand localization on the premise of abiding by the global brand standards. For example, UNIQLO introduces 'tailored' product mixes in different regions of mainland China, facilitating timely delivery of the items that customers need most. This has led to a significant increase in both revenue and operating profit (47.1 per cent and 2.3 per cent respectively in FY 2018) (Fast Retailing, 2019b). UNIQLO has also introduced 'Global One' to inspire all group businesses to share their success stories of global best practices (Fast Retailing, 2019f). Managers worldwide gather at the Tokyo head office for a global conference to discuss the new challenges and problems in their countries or regions every six months (Fast Retailing, 2019f). It is through centralization and decentralization of power that UNIQLO renders the subsidiary the due constraints and the rights of autonomy, which subsequently enable the subsidiary to successfully realize the globalization strategy of the head-quarters. In this way, its corporate philosophy and business vision are fully translated to each employee of Fast Retailing from head to regional offices and to each and every store. Both regional managers and their store managers are greatly empowered to decide and modify strategies according to local needs. Listening to the voice of con-sumers at the front line, each store forecasts consumer demand and then combines with its own professional managerial experience to launch products that are popular with consumers.

For UNIQLO, each store is decentralized. As the company expands, management issues will become more prominent, while the store manager is regarded as the company's 'top manager' in UNIQLO. CEO of UNIQLO Greater China, Pan Ning (who progressed from store clerk to store manager and then CEO) has passed on such a culture to UNIQLO in China: 'Each store is a relatively independent operating body, and the store manager is the one who has the final say' (SOHO, 2012). Headquarters should provide the marketable goods, information and guidance to the store accurately and quickly. In 1999, UNIQLO began to implement the 'Superstar Store Manager'. The Superstar store managers can adjust and determine the order quantity according to the location of the store and the level of customer needs. They can independently determine the product display, the store operation, advertising leaflets, etc. Having worked as a store clerk initially, Kosaka Takeshi, CEO of UNIQLO Taiwan, explained the role of 'Superstar Store Manager': 'When I was promoted to the store manager, I felt "this store is mine". No matter what happens, I will make the decisions' (SOHO, 2017). The bonus of the 'store manager' is completely linked to performance. It is very important to become a 'Superstar Store Manager' to drive other stores to gain good performance (SOHO, 2017).

At the same time, UNIQLO showcases how a 'flat' organization works, in which there are few or no levels and functions in between management and staff level employees. Compared to UNIQLO, Amazon's structure is hierarchical, Google's is clear but interwoven between products and departments, and Microsoft's is reported by some scholars as 'separate kingdoms'. In the fast fashion industry, it is important to respond quickly to trends to build core competitiveness. UNIQLO can always gather

(Continued)

(Continued)

the latest information about different trends from different subsidiaries worldwide (UNIQLO, 2019). Its flat organizational structure can effectively help to quickly respond to market changes, and optimize organizational capabilities while emphasizing business capabilities and developing both individuals and teams.

UNIQLO advocates the ultimate service spirit 'Zenin Keiei', which seeks to inspire the entrepreneurial spirit of every employee, and provide customers with the best service wholeheartedly. The pursuit of details to achieve perfection is repeatedly emphasized. UNIQLO stores are extremely detail-oriented, with all clothes folded in a specific way to ensure that the customer can easily see the information they need, such as the sizes. Another detail of UNIQLO is its mirrors and lights, which are carefully designed in its Chinese stores. The facial contour of the Chinese is flatter than that of Caucasians. If the light is directly drawn from above, facial contour defects are thought to become rather obvious. In UNIQLO China, in fitting a mirror, the light is slanted down from the front or the back, which is reportedly seen as more suitable. The colour of light choice is also considered essential in that it should not be dazzling, but rather the light should be soft and should function to beautify the image of customers' skin (SOHO, 2019).

Physical organizational structure in itself is not enough to help with strategic deployment and ensure the smooth implementation of the strategy.

The committees

According to the UNIQLO 2018 Annual Report:

> In line with Fast Retailing's corporate auditor governance model, the majority of our Board of Directors is made up of external directors in order to enhance the Board's independence and strengthen its oversight ability. Our executive officer system aims to separate management supervision and execution functions to ensure swift and effective business operations. Individual committees support the Board by facilitating frank, open, and timely discussions and decision making. (Fast Retailing, 2019b).

To ensure the company's strategy is correct and its subsidiaries can successfully implement the headquarters' strategy, Fast Retailing has set up various committees (Martin Roll, 2019).

UNIQLO overseas offices' operation decisions are made by these committees, assisting regional subsidiaries to carry out business based on headquarters' strategy, responding to important trends affecting the business environment.

Table 3.3   Fast Retailing's committees

Human Resources Committee	The human resources committee decides on important organizational changes and adjustments to the human resources system of Fast Retailing and makes its recommendations directly to the Board of Directors.
Sustainability Committee	The sustainability council, composed of external directors, auditors and other experts, determines Fast Retailing's overall sustainability strategy, annual sustainability report, environmental activities, social responsibility activities and diversity initiatives.
Disclosure Committee	The disclosure committee is responsible for improving transparency in the disclosure of information relating to business, finance, etc., promptly disclosing information to the Tokyo stock exchange and the stock exchange of Hong Kong, and proactively disclosing information that may have a material impact on the investment decisions of investors and shareholders.
IT Investment Committee	The IT investment committee investigates the effectiveness of individual investments and discusses and advises on investments to drive the group's system reform.
Code of Conduct Committee	The code of conduct committee is responsible for educating executives and employees on how best to address any violations of the Fast Retailing Code of Conduct (CoC).
Business Ethics Committee	The business ethics committee ensures that the group advises departments on the basis of field inspections and partner company surveys. It does not use its position to exert undue pressure on business partners such as partner factories or suppliers.
Human Rights Committee	Chaired by an outside professional, the human rights committee conducts human rights due diligence, provides advice and education, investigates human rights violations and considers relief measures.
Risk Management Committee	In order to strengthen the detection and management of major risks, this committee analyses and evaluates the impact and frequency of risks on enterprises, discusses countermeasures, and takes measures to prevent or contain risks.

Source: Collected and compiled from the Fast Retailing Group official website data

In July 2019, for example, Fast Retailing announced it would cut unnecessary plastic use throughout its supply chain, reducing the use of single-use plastic bags by 85 per cent by

(Continued)

(Continued)

2020. About 7,800 tons of plastic can be saved each year. Customers and business alike have come to understand the importance of sustainability, and the impact on climate change.

Fast Retailing started by introducing eco-friendly paper shopping bags and rethinking product packaging. By September 2019, UNIQLO stores in Greater China had already replaced their paper bags with FCS-certified eco-friendly versions. The reform of shopping bags was decided by UNIQLO's sustainability committee (Martin Roll, 2019). In addition, the committee promotes UNIQLO's initiative of leading a sustainable lifestyle with technology. UNIQLO's 'fast' is mainly about capturing customer demand, quickly commoditizing, and swiftly delivering products to customers, not about making disposable clothes.

On the product side, UNIQLO sees sustainability as two-fold. The first layer is sustainability of product technologies, such as recyclable materials. UNIQLO has started making clothes with recyclable materials on a large scale. Cooperating with Toray, it has realized the traceability of PET plastic bottle recycled polyester fibre through a unique recycling identification system. Starting in the spring of 2020, it uses this new recycled material to produce a line of high-performance quick-dry garments. In addition, UNIQLO stores in Japan are now recycling customers' Ultra-Light Down jackets, using Toray's newly developed automated equipment to sort, extract, clean and reuse the jackets (HBRCHINA, 2019).

The second layer is the sustainability, or durability, of the products themselves. Despite the fact that UNIQLO clothes can last for more than a decade, it is constantly improving its products, offering new and ageless designs with better quality every year. It is the mission of UNIQLO to make clothing that customers wear the most and the longest (HBRCHINA, 2019).

Final remarks

The decentralized organizational structure works well for a customer centric MNE in industries such as fashion and retail, where customer intelligence and the agile adaptation to local, regional and global market needs are determinants for business success. It is particularly valuable for Fast Retailing because of its 'tone-settled' products which do not always reflect the most popular fashion trends but rather need the valuable input of customers' experience and feedback from every specific region. However, risks also exist within a corporation's reliance on regional management: those risks lie in the potential business performance challenges if and when regional staff fail to perform, to implement the appropriate adaptations, to provide global headquarters with the most needed intelligence to receive adequate resources and shape global and regional strategy, or to deal with margin issues, for example the growing cost of labour in China where the company's production takes place.

Case questions

1   What strategies had been adopted by Fast Retailing in its product design and what is UNIQLO's clothing philosophy?
2   What strategy has UNIQLO adopted to cope with the saturation of its domestic market? How did UNIQLO's globalization come about?
3   In the case of fast retailing, how did Fast Retailing reconcile globalization and localization? What can globalized Asian companies learn from Fast Retailing?

3.4 STRATEGIC IMPLICATIONS

This chapter first reviewed how multinationals select business locations in and across the Asian markets, and then focused on how they align organizational structure. Strategic decision-making in both directly related areas is typically made by the leadership of the multinational, and is based on the study of the existence and availability of country and region specific advantages present in geographical locations and the necessary alignment of capabilities to do business across borders and yield competitive advantages broader than those gained on a country to country basis.

It is considered that the sum of regionally obtained advantages is greater than those obtained by a multitude of country to country engagement, that is, coordinating market expansion across Asia as a region is advantageous from a strategy perspective – and choices of locations in investment decisions and the organizational structures to support those, need to be strategic and well-focused.

We recognize even more in this chapter in what way Asia represents an extraordinarily dynamic and changing market in which macro-economic environments evolve continuously and require companies to adapt. Those changes on a macro level include increasingly business-appropriate developments across the regulatory and infrastructural environments that constitute Asia, and a mostly increasingly broad and stable socio-political environment, with less notable exceptions than just a decade ago. Infrastructural connectivity between locations has significantly improved and continues to provide for FDI in connectivity initiatives across, into and beyond the region. This includes physical, digital and people-to-people linkages that at the same time facilitate in-bound FDI in other sectors as well as supply chain integration and underlying social understanding: this has great potential to further promote peace, human rights and the eradication of poverty.

Additional macro factors such as corruption were explored in section 3.1, which are key components to decisions by multinationals to invest or upscale or downscale their activities in or across a given location.

At the micro level, growth trends have been shown to have a major role to play in exploring and exploiting capabilities. In particular, the rise of the middle class and the associated increase in consumer spending have been reported for most of South, East and Southeast Asia, while the whole region continues to expose a diversity in income, and in local versus foreign consumption preferences. A large and/or wealthy consumer base is hence key to location decisions, especially when it comes to large-scale investments; so are production costs, labour productivity, capabilities and their connectivity or conglomeration/clustering.

Also, factors such as foreignness come into play. Strategic implications stem from a given location's likelihood to accept and adopt foreign goods or services compared to the locally owned offer at hand. This 'Liability of Foreignness' (LoF), the disadvantage of being foreign in and to the market, results typically from a social and economic cost disadvantage versus local firms. Firm specific advantages are key to overcoming such barriers, in mitigating the impact of differences between home and host country, and in overcoming host country disadvantage whether cultural, institutional (e.g. labour regulations, HR practices, corporate governance practices, management styles), logistical, political or other. In business across Asia, while this LoF is combined with the cost of multinationality, which refers to the costs of an MNE to transfer firm specific advantages from home to host country dependent on organizational structure, the networked nature of cross-border expansion can help counterbalance those effects.

The multinational's organizational structure is instrumental in capturing those advantages that the firm hopes to create, maintain and leverage through its combination of foreign branches and subsidiaries. The given structure needs to be best aligned to tap into the locational mix so as to implement and control systems to reflect global strategies and objectives, that is, to perform and influence on a corporate level while respecting and leveraging local and regional specificities.

This requires, in its best case, the organizational capability to reconfigure competencies and resources to cope with the dispersal of cross-border activities and stimulate growth. This chapter has provided you with insights into the organizational designs that supply frameworks for decision-making, coordination, reporting and communication. They aim to ensure that value and, often, learning from the foreign marketplaces are provided through the company's different units.

Depending on the vision, mission, corporate strategy and internationalization experience and knowledge of the firm, structures have been shown to vary from product-focused to functional structures, decentralized global areas to hybrid structures. The most common organizational structure of firms that use Asia with a cross-regional strategy is the matrix structure, in which leadership has simultaneous regional and product responsibilities. This structure indicates a high commitment of the company to cross-border business, in that significant resources are dedicated. We can assume that management has gained significant experience and competence in running subsidiaries across a variety of countries or regions, and that the firm is present in increasingly complex markets, using entry and investment strategies that include FDI and collaborative ventures within a refined international network strategy.

The diversity of Asia's business environments requires due attention to the planning and management of any cross-border venture with a focus on questions of management, decision-making and control, to preserve managerial, financial and technological resources effectively.

This means a decision on autonomy of locations needs to be taken, and this is typically prone to adaptation over time. A centralized organizational design means that headquarters in the home country retains considerable authority and control over the firm's cross-border activities. This illustrates a strategy focused on integration and standardization. However, a decentralized design translates into broader autonomy and decision-making authority delegated to the subsidiaries in a host country or region. This allows for local and regional responsiveness, and a greater degree of host market adaptation as well as locally sourced learning and innovation.

For manufacturing firms and firms with relatively lesser experience with internationalization, exporting is typically the first choice when making locational choices, or partnerships with foreign distributors or agents with international divisions such as those noted above. Some firms use an export department, meaning their involvement with the foreign location is – from a structural perspective – very low.

On the basis of this chapter, it has become clear that the organizational structure serves as a tool that enables (or hinders) the implementation of strategy across its international activity. As it is fairly usual to see Asian EMNEs using joint venture investment modes in most of Asia, and wholly owned subsidiaries in the most developed Asian markets only, their strategy is driven by tapping into competitive advantage through network models. The autonomy that JVs and subsidiaries have is hence reliant on their capability to develop positions and connections that allow them to utilize not only their own but also their network's capabilities.

This differs from multinationals from developed countries, whether from Asian or non-Asian home markets, that are embedding their strategy primarily into the existence of their own capabilities, though this may differ when operating their investments mainly in developing or emerging Asia.

This means that EMNEs are typically seen as more attuned to using their learning capability as a resource, to share and tap into other firms' learning, and to seek learning opportunities as well as market diversification. They may also be more sensitive to barriers to entry due to a lack of, or a different experience of, cross-border expansion than their developed country competitors or they may use cross-border expansions to target different types of markets. They also often suffer from lesser brand awareness, and misperceptions regarding quality, as found for example in the so-called 'Liability of Indianness' phenomenon.

Network relations in Asia bring significant advantage through complementary resources, better leverage with and access to financial and technology providers, funding sources and even political connections, as well as knowledge and management skills, and reduced transaction costs. On the downside, when ties are too close and become elite networks, they have been found to lead to inefficiencies, undesired if not unethical behaviour and possibly corruption. This is specifically the case when the legal frameworks in the locations are particularly weak and local autonomy on organizational structure is extensively high. However, when legal frameworks become stronger, network ties become looser, which provides advantages of heterogeneity leading to better efficiencies, competition and innovation.

From a resource-based view, strategic implications of locational and structural decisions directly impact the way in which the company can utilize internal inimitable resources as the main stimulus of performance and gain additional and more effective access to resources than their competitors can. This results in competitive advantage when the resource is valuable, rare, immobile outside the company and cannot be substituted. Together with coordination capabilities through structure and network access, this gives cross-Asian business a solid basis to perform on.

Especially for small and medium-sized EMNEs, embeddedness in networks forms their process of international learning and growth. Also, EMNEs tend to acquire SMEs and firms that hold specific assets (in the so-called asset-seeking behaviour), for example valuable intermediary resources for their supply chain, to accelerate their learning, local embeddedness and overall innovation capabilities.

The Unilever case study illustrates the topic of this chapter as it examines the evolution and growth of a Dutch-British transnational MNE and the changes in its organizational structure and strategy in response to growth imperatives in the global marketplace, with a focus on Asia. The case highlights that enterprise profitability is based on the ability of the MNE to find a fit between organizational architecture and strategy. This fit should match the needs of the firm's competitive environment and push that firm to adapt itself accordingly. Unilever has evolved as a business responding to the dictates of the marketplace. The success and growth of Unilever into various global markets including and leveraging Asia are based on conscious changes made in strategy and organization in response to the changing business environment.

Unilever was formed through the merger of two European firms, and has grown into a global TNC with a presence in 190 countries through ownership of 400 brands. It gets 59 per cent of its current business from emerging markets, with a prominent presence in Asia. It has a matrix organizational structure, based on products and regions, developed over the years to manage and direct their global operations profitably.

Unilever began its operations through a decentralized organization, with a strong strategic focus on the local business environment for its basic products. It grew through diversification of products across regions, into a huge, unmanageable and cost heavy organization with slow decision-making skills. You will have learned that this led to two major organizational restructuring efforts as its strategic thinking became more focused, with an emphasis on reconfiguring the geographical basis of its business. Unilever brands have become household names across global markets. Dove, Sunsilk, Omo, Surf and Lipton are great consumer products, but they became worldwide brands because of the capabilities of Unilever. Their success rests on the choices made in strategy and organization.

A crucial aspect of its ability to adapt is through its managerial workforce, which was encouraged to think and act in a transnational manner and mindset since the inception of the organization. It started a policy of local managerial recruitment to replace the Dutch and British executives from head office who were managing most of its local units. In other words, filling local executive and technical positions with Indian managers led to the 'Indianization' of that subsidiary – along with 'Australianization', 'Brazilianization', and other examples of localization of management in various countries with Unilever operations.

Unilever has evolved as a successful transnational organization. It is insightful to study how its structure and strategy have constantly adapted, to keep pace with the changing marketplace. It has successfully weathered numerous changes over the course of its existence, and this is ongoing. Its organizational restructuring in response to new market trends illustrates a successful combination of structural formality and managerial flexibility in response to the dynamics of a changing competitive landscape.

The Fast Retailing case then discussed how an Asian MNE has expanded into multiple global markets by taking a regional organizational structure-based strategy, which focuses on specific geographic traits and local needs for its global locations with its head office taking control of major business decisions. The case also demonstrates how organizational structures of MNE serve to assist in conveying the corporate culture and achieve business goals, yet in a rather different space and context from those of Unilever.

Founded in 1984, well-known UNIQLO, now a subsidiary of Fast Retailing, expanded into the global markets as its home market, Japan, became saturated. In 1999, the corporate established its Shanghai (China) office to explore more production capability and enhance production management. In 2001, the first overseas UNIQLO store was opened in London, marking its first step towards global expansion. Fast Retailing's global strategy was consistent with the one in its Japan office, offering stores where its customers could find products at lower prices with good quality. In order to maintain this consistency, Fast Retailing established at least one subsidiary for each and every region in which it operated and established its global management as geographic-oriented. These subsidiaries constituted the UNIQLO International business segment, alongside UNIQLO Japan and other business segments. All these subsidiaries had their own regional head offices, which were authorized to make regional decisions.

As the world's third biggest apparel manufacturer and retailer, Fast Retailing ranks just behind Zara and H&M, two leading fashion brands both from non-Asian regions. The biggest difference between Fast Retailing and its two main rivals is the products imbedded with its unwavering philosophy, which is to not blindly follow fashion trends from the runways but to persist in innovating to produce high-quality and reasonable priced day-to-day functional clothes, aiming to reach the goal of helping customers to establish a connection between their apparels and nature. To do that, UNIQLO has tried to differentiate and identify its image through unified store designs and universal products. The case of Fast Retailing seeks to reveal how this Asian company, while retaining a unique contextual-based philosophy infused in its globally located subsidiaries and stores, has strived to become the world's best-selling apparel retailer, a goal that could not be easily achieved without a full adherence to its corporate principles throughout its head office and overseas offices.

To this end, Fast Retailing has adopted a corporate officer system to separate management decision-making and business-executions: the corporate board is responsible for making main strategic decisions, while various committees ensure the smooth execution of these decisions. Through its global area structure, committees are responsible for supervising the operations of global offices run by regional managers who possess local insights. These regional managers gather every six months at the Tokyo head office where they discuss their respective challenges and then return with guidance or decisions from Tokyo. They then communicate these decisions to their subordinates including store managers. In this way, corporate philosophy and business vision are fully diffused to each employee from head office to regional offices and to each and every store. But both regional managers and their regional store managers are empowered to decide and modify strategies based on their local needs.

This decentralized organizational structure serves well for customer-centred MNEs in the fashion industry where intelligence on customer and market needs is a determinant for business success, and it is more important for Fast Retailing because its products do not always reflect the most popular fashion trends but rather need valuable input from customers and feedback from each specific region. However, risks still exist within the corporate's heavy reliance on regional management, such as the 'spill-over' effect on the global business performance if regional officers or employees fail to perform their duties properly and are caught in local scandals, or the growing cost of labour in China where increasingly company production takes place.

In order to differentiate itself from its strong rivals and compete to become the industry's top seller, Fast Retailing's strategy has been to carry out its unique product philosophy throughout the corporate structure while realizing its business visions. A global area structure is essential for Fast Retailing because the controlling power of head office ensures the communication and transmission of corporate principles and the empowered regional offices guarantee good business performance. What is more important about this case is that Fast Retailing is one of the not-too-many great Asian companies that have succeeded in competing with non-Asian companies in fashion retailing, especially in non-Asian areas where customer tastes and needs differ from those of home markets. Other than its Asian attributes, the feat in balancing high-level decentralization with unifying corporate values and culture and maintaining consistent standards in products sold world-wide, is the key element among the many reasons for Fast Retailing to become successful.

REFERENCES

Bain, M. (2017) Nike is facing a new wave of anti-sweatshop protests. Quartz, 1 August. Available at: https://qz.com/1042298/nike-is-facing-a-new-wave-of-anti-sweatshop-protests (accessed 31 March 2020).

Barrie, L. (2018) How TAL Apparel is rebalancing for growth. Just-style, 22 August. Available at: www.just-style.com/interview/how-tal-apparel-is-rebalancing-for-growth-ceo-interview_id133486.aspx (accessed 31 March 2020).

Business of Fashion (2019) Without a soul, a company is nothing. Available at: www.businessoffashion.com/articles/professional/uniqlo-fast-retailing-ceo-tadashi-yanai-management-principles (accessed 28 December 2019).

CBS News (2015) McDonald's to simplify structure, focus on customers. Available at: www.cbsnews.com/news/mcdonalds-to-detail-latest-turnaround-plans (accessed 31 March 2020).

Chang, J. (2019) Research on laws of European, American and Japan fashion brands life cycle. Available at: http://www.dpi-proceedings.com/index.php/dtem/article/viewFile/31014/29595 (accessed 24 April 2020).

Christensen, C.M., Ojomo, E. and Dillon, K. (2019) How investment made Singapore an innovation hub. Available at: www.barrons.com/articles/how-investment-made-singapore-an-innovation-hub-51549458040 (accessed 31 March 2020).

DeBold, T., de Acosta, R., Lajoie, M. and Watts, J.M. (2015) Singapore celebrates 50 years of independence. Available at: http://graphics.wsj.com/singapore-50th-anniversary/?mod=e2f.

EDB Singapore (2017) The case for centralization in Asia. Available at: www.edb.gov.sg/en/news-and-events/insights/headquarters/the-case-for-centralization-in-asia.html (accessed 31 March 2020).

Estrin, S. and Meyer, K. (2013) How Different Are Emerging Economy MNEs? A Comparative Study of Location Choice. London: LSE mimeo.

Fast Company (2012) *Cheap, chic, and made for all: How Uniqlo plans to take over casual fashion.* Available at: www.fastcompany.com/1839302/cheap-chic-and-made-all-how-uniqlo-plans-take-over-casual-fashion (accessed 4 April 2020).

Fast Retailing (2019a) About Fast Retailing. Available at: www.fastretailing.com/eng/about/business/aboutfr.html (accessed 28 December 2019).

Fast Retailing (2019b) Annual report 2018. Available at: www.fastretailing.com/eng/ir/library/pdf/ar2018_en_08.pdf (accessed 28 December 2019).

Fast Retailing (2019c) Company website: Sustainability – Promotional framework (org structure). Available at: www.fastretailing.com/eng/sustainability/vision/organization.html (accessed 28 December 2019).

Fast Retailing (2019d) Company website: UNIQLO's strategy. Available at: www.fastretailing.com/eng/group/strategy/tactics.html (accessed 28 December 2019).

Fast Retailing (2019e) Corporate governance. Available at: www.fastretailing.com/eng/about/governance/corpgovenance.html#pagetop (accessed 28 December 2019).

Fast Retailing (2019f) Fast Retailing annual report. Available at: www.fastretailing.com/eng/ir/library/annual.html (accessed 28 December 2019).

Fast Retailing (2019g) Fast Retailing's growing path (1949–2003). Available at: www.fastretailing.com/eng/about/history/ (accessed 28 December 2019).

Fast Retailing (2019h) Industrial ranking. Available at: www.fastretailing.com/eng/ir/direction/position.html (accessed 28 December 2019).

Fast Retailing (2019i) Interview with the CEO. Available at: www.fastretailing.com/eng/ir/direction/interview.html (accessed 28 December 2019).

Fast Retailing (2019j) UNIQLO business model. Available at: www.fastretailing.com/eng/group/strategy/UNIQLObusiness.html (accessed 28 December 2019).

Fortune (2019) UNIQLO's secrets for building a global brand. Available at: https://fortune.com/2017/10/12/uniqlo-clothing-global/ (accessed 28 December 2019).

Ghosh, M. (2019) Royal Enfield sets up Thailand assembly unit. LiveMint, 23 March. Available at: www.livemint.com/auto-news/royal-enfield-sets-up-thailand-assembly-unit-1553315286434.html (accessed 31 March 2020).

Goto, A. and Kazuyuki, M. (2009) Technology policies in Japan: 1990 to the present. In *21st Century Innovation Systems for Japan and the United States: Lessons from a Decade of Change: Report of a Symposium*. Washington, DC: The National Academies Press. doi: 10.17226/12194.

HBRCHINA (2019) Fast retailing group President Tadashi Yanai: UNIQLO is bucking the trend. Available at: www.hbrchina.org/2020-0119/7712.html (accessed 28 December 2019).

Jiang, S. (2019) UNIQLO China organizational structure. Available at: www.jiangshi.org/523893/blog_1035042.html (accessed 28 December 2019).

Johanson, J. and Vahlne, J.E. (2009) The Uppsala internationalization process model revisited: From liability of foreignness to liability of outsidership. *Journal of International Business Studies*, 40(9): 1411–1431.

Jones, G. (2005a) *Renewing Unilever*. Oxford: Oxford University Press.

Jones, G. (2005b) Unilever: Transformation and tradition. *Harvard Business Review*. Available at: https://hbswk.hbs.edu/item/unilever-transformation-and-tradition (accessed 1 April 2020).

Koyanagi, K. (2017) Multinationals in Asia: For Unilever's chief, good business is found in helping the world be better. *Nikkei Asian Review*, 19 October. Available at: https://asia.nikkei.com/Business/Multinationals-in-Asia-For-Unilever-s-chief-good-business-is-found-in-helping-the-world-be-better (accessed 1 April 2020).

Lang, N., Khanna, D., Bhattacharya, A. and Chraïti, A. (2018) Why MNCs are still winning big in emerging markets. Boston Consulting Group, 15 March. Available at: www.bcg.com/en-in/publications/2018/mncs-still-winning-big-emerging-markets.aspx (accessed 31 March 2020).

Maljers, F.A. (1992) Inside Unilever: The evolving transnational company. *Harvard Business Review*. Available at: https://hbr.org/1992/09/inside-unilever-the-evolving-transnational-company (accessed 1 April 2020).

Marico (2019) About us. Available at: https://marico.com/about-us/marico-history (accessed 31 March 2020).

Martin Roll (2019) UNIQLO's strategy. Available at: https://martinroll.com/resources/articles/strategy/uniqlo-the-strategy-behind-the-global-japanese-fast-fashion-retail-brand/ (accessed 28 December 2019).

Maulia, E. (2017) Unilever Indonesia expands beauty products for Muslim women. *Nikkei Asian Review*, 27 September. Available at: https://asia.nikkei.com/Business/Unilever-Indonesia-expands-beauty-products-for-Muslim-women (accessed 1 April 2020).

Mehta, S. (2018) Available at: www.unilever.com/Images/investor-event-2018-sanjiv-mehta-unilever-south-asia_tcm244-529109_en.pdf.

NSS Magazine (2019) The Uniqlo's LifeWear. Available at: https://www.nssmag.com/en/fashion/18752/uniqlo-history-lifewear (accessed 24 April 2020).

Sim, A. and Pandian, J. (2003) An exploratory study of internationalization strategies of Malaysian and Taiwanese firms. In M.V.S. Usha and J. Brennan (eds), *Proceedings of the 2003 Academy of International Business Northeast Conference: Globalization in the Age of Technology*. USA: US Department of Education BIE, pp. 107–129.

Sina (2015) UNIQLO's leisure empire: Selling clothes began with storytelling. Available at: http://blog.sina.com.cn/s/blog_5db0e42d0102vx1w.html (accessed 28 December 2019).

Singhania, R. and Rao, D. (2018) Chinese investments in SEZ in India. *China Business Law Journal*, 6 July. Available at: www.vantageasia.com/sezs-in-india-incentives (accessed 31 March 2020).

SOHO (2012a) The entrepreneurial saga of Japan's richest man: Tadashi Yanai. Available at: http://roll.sohu.com/20120901/n352062383.shtml (accessed 28 December 2019).

SOHO (2012b) UNIQLO's 'Store Manager System'. Available at: http://roll.sohu.com/20120622/n346263326.shtml (accessed 26 January 2020).

SOHO (2017) How does UNIQLO train 4000 store managers in 7 years? Available at: hwww.sohu.com/a/132417676_163538 (accessed 26 January 2020).

SOHO (2019) Zara, H&M, GAP, and UNIQLO's respective competitive advantages. Available at: www.sohu.com/a/337606851_737523 (accessed 28 December 2019).

Southeast of Wealth (2019) UNIQLO's philosophy is the secret to Mr Yanai's success as Japan's richest man. Available at: https://baijiahao.baidu.com/s?id=1631420954109094839&wfr=spider&for=pc (accessed 28 December 2019).

Suder, G. (2016) The internationalization path and sustainability dynamics in emerging economies: The case of Indian SMEs. In J.R. McIntyre, S. Ivanaj, V. Ivanaj, R.N. Kar (eds), *Emerging Dynamics of Sustainability in Multinational Enterprises*. Cheltenham: Edward Elgar Publishing, pp. 134–163.

Thirawat, N. (2017) Internationalization theories: Applications to Asia-Pacific firms. In N. Thirawat (ed.), *Internationalization and Managing Networks in the Asia Pacific*. Cambridge: Chandos Publishing, pp. 53–78.

Unilever (2011) Unilever announces reorganisation to further drive growth. Available at: www.unilever.com/news/press-releases/2011/11-06-23-Unilever-announces-reorganisation-to-further-drive-growth.html (accessed 1 April 2020).

Unilever (2019a) 2010–present: Sustainable living. Available at: www.unilever.co.uk/about/who-we-are/our-history/2010-present.html (accessed 1 April 2020).

Unilever (2019b) Unilever announces leadership and organisation changes. Available at: www.unilever.com/news/press-releases/2019/unilever-announces-leadership-and-organisation-changes.html (accessed 1 April 2020).

UNIQLO (2019) Business model. Available at: www.uniqlo.com/sg/corp/model/ (accessed 26 January 2020).

Vanham, P. (2018) The story of Viet Nam's economic miracle. World Economic Forum, 11 September. Available at: www.weforum.org/agenda/2018/09/how-vietnam-became-an-economic-miracle (accessed 31 March 2020).

Vision Critical (2019) How UNIQLO plans to dominate the fashion retail world. Available at: www.visioncritical.com/blog/uniqlo-domination (accessed 28 December 2019).

World Bank (2018) Infrastructure gaps vary across East Asia and the Pacific – and between cities and rural areas. Available at: www.worldbank.org/en/news/feature/2018/03/28/infrastructure-gaps-vary-across-east-asia-and-the-pacific-and-between-cities-and-rural-areas (accessed 31 March 2020).

Wubs, B. (2008) *International Business and National War Interests: Unilever between Reich and Empire, 1939–45*. Abingdon: Routledge.

Yean, T.S. (2018) Chinese investment in Malaysia: Five years into the BRI. *ISEAS*, 11. Available at: www.iseas.edu.sg/images/pdf/ISEAS_Perspective_2018_11@50.pdf (accessed 31 March 2020).

Yu, J. and Kim, S. (2013) Understanding liability of foreignness in an Asian business context: A study of the Korean asset management industry. *Asia Pacific Journal of Management*, 30(4): 1191–1217.

4

MARKET ACCESS CONDITIONS AND REGIONAL INTEGRATION

4.1 MARKET ACCESS CONDITIONS: VARIATIONS AND MARKET INTEGRATION IMPACTS IN ASIA

This chapter provides key knowledge on market access conditions and it also explains the way in which they are shaped by regional integration. It covers:

- an introduction to market access conditions: what are the variations across key markets in Asia, and which forms of market integration impact business in Asia
- a case study that explores the New Hope Group – a long-term commitment for Asian expansions
- a case study focused on Toyota's market expansion across Asia: adapting to diverse macro-economic environments
- it concludes by analysing the resulting strategic implications.

The Asian business environment provides a variety of market access conditions, which differ sometimes from country to country and often from one form of market grouping – containing various member states – to another. As a basis to the understanding of what market access is granted to firms that operate across borders, it is important to first understand the business environment in a broad sense.

The basics of market access

The Asian macro-economic environment is highly diverse and shaped by a variety of conditions.

The analysis of a business environment

This macro-economic environment typically includes:

- the political and social environment
- the economic environment
- the natural environment
- the technological environment
- the legal environment
- and bilateral and regional market group contexts.

These environments and context are the basis on which international business and marketing decisions are shaped, and extend the PESTEL (Political, Economic, Social, Technological, Environmental and Legal) model or framework. This also allows firms to further monitor the macro-environmental conditions as they may change and differ in their impact on a business venture.

A firm's analysis of its Asian macro-environment is highly focused, and comparative.

- In regard to the political and social environment, one focuses on the stability or change emanating from legislation (local and international), government policies, political change, funding, grants and other initiatives, wars or conflicts, local and internal trading environments, as well as the social context impacting consumer and lifestyle trends (behaviour and attitudes), demographics (age, sex, gender, ethnicity, employment, home ownership), media, and ethical issues. For example, while Asia accounts for 60 per cent of the world population, its distribution is uneven with extremely young populations in conflict-torn parts of the continent while the most mature economies are challenged by an increasingly aging society.
- In the economic environment, factors are highlighted that influence consumer purchasing power and spending. This includes, among other, trends in income levels, income distribution, an emergence of the middle class, interest rates, savings, industry trends and local taxes. For example, Japan has a more equal wealth distribution than any other major country in Asia, in contrast to other countries such as Indonesia, which has the sixth-worst inequality in the world, according to Oxfam, warning that such gaps can cause an economic 'race to the bottom' (Oxfam, 2017). Today, on average, Singaporeans earn similar salaries as in the US. Salaries in Taiwan remained about 40 per cent lower, and in China they were about 10 per cent of the salary paid for a similar role in the US in 2011 (DBS, 2011: 13). On averaging, salary increases between 2018 and 2019 became significant in Indonesia, at 8.3 per cent, China at 6.9 per cent, the Philippines at 6 per cent and Hong Kong and Singapore at 4 per cent, catching up very quickly with mature Western economies if sustained.

- For the natural environment, the existing and changing physical and natural resource factors are scrutinized including commodities and raw materials, but also environmental and natural attitudes, disasters, and changes in government intervention. In raw materials, for example, we find that Indonesian coal and palm oil, Thai rubber and Pakistan's copper are major parts of the world's largest manufacturing supply chains. Yet resource abundance does not on its own translate into sustained economic growth and development.
- In the technological environment, changes in technology affect marketing and operational efforts including, among others, innovative skills, methods, systems and equipment such as automation, robotics, artificial intelligence and virtual reality. For example, while some western parts of Asia, such as Afghanistan, remain less prone to technology despite leapfrogging to the use of smartphones and some (yet limited) IT usage, we can find leading technology disruptors in other parts of Asia, among them, Southeast Asia's capabilities in areas of high tech and telecom, transportation and logistics, financial services, and healthcare, from Chinese tech titan Alibaba's e-commerce to Korean Favvrs' linking Instagram to shopping sites with machine learning capabilities.
- The legal environment includes factors shaped by all legal aspects including employment, labour, quotas, taxation, resources, imports and export regulations. For example, Malaysia's import duty rates range between 0 per cent and 50 per cent; the average duty rate is around 6 per cent. For Laos, for non-agricultural goods from countries outside the ASEAN, the import duties average 8.3 per cent. Legal systems and their enforcement vary greatly across Asian countries. For example, the Indian system is still based much on the British common law, as is that in Australia and New Zealand. Also, the legal systems of Bangladesh, Hong Kong, Myanmar, Nepal and Pakistan are built on common law. Chinese law blends various influences, including German civil law and Soviet-inspired socialist law. Customary law can be found in parts of Myanmar, Malaysia (using Sharia law for personal law as do, to some extent, Bangladesh and Pakistan) and Indonesia, which are also influenced by Muslim law. Religious law prevails to date in Afghanistan. Thailand, Laos, Cambodia and Vietnam mainly use civil law systems, which can also be found, for example, in Azerbaijan, Uzbekistan and Russia. Each system differs though in its interpretation and application. The representation of women in parliament remains low in Asia, with an average across Asian nations of 20 per cent (the global average is 24 per cent). As an example, less than 5 per cent of Thai parliamentarians are female and women remain vastly blocked from government and legal positions in much of Asia despite the growth of female education, due to a combination of factors: one key factor is the level (or lack) of democracy (Prihatini, 2019).

In most parts of Asia and Asia-Pacific, bilateral and regional market groups provide an important context for cross-border business conditions, such as the stability or change in preferential trade and investment (market access) conditions among countries within a region or as part of the international or global supply chain, including typically some form of reduction of customs duties for goods, the free or privileged movement of people, capital and/or services, inter alia. For example, Cambodia, Lao PDR, Myanmar, and

Vietnam have cut import duties among them, through ASEAN arrangements, to 0–5 per cent on 98.86 per cent of their tariff lines (compared to the 8.3 per cent average rate as above for non-ASEAN imports). This also applies mainly to the ASEAN-India tax rate since 2019.

Cross-border business and marketing decisions are engrained in the opportunity and cost analysis of the location (see Chapter 5) and need to fit with market access conditions emanating from the business environment.

Market expansion conditions: Trends and challenges in selected countries

Eastern Asia and Pacific constitute one of the world's fastest-growing developing regions, while growth in the western part of the region is typically slow, specifically in large economies including Russia, Kazakhstan and Ukraine (World Bank, 2019).

Asian economies have been growing for some time, and increasingly undergo constraints due to under-utilized rural labour supplies and skilled urban labour. This is a trend for the developed as well as all the emerging Asian economies, which underpins market expansion. Most Asian economies have moved (or are moving) from attracting production activities from internationalizing 'Western' firms to add the benefits stemming from increasingly advanced value chain contributions (including advanced manufacturing, R&D and services), and into strong bi-and pluri-country internationalization within the region. Just as is the case for the economies of other parts of the world, none of these economies has developed in isolation.

The IMF World Economic Outlook has forecasted economic growth specifically for India to continue for many years to come, driven by increased domestic demand, and an even better integration into regional and international trade and investment, and at the same time, stable consumer prices. China, for long known as the 'global factory' (Buckley, 2011), is predicted to become the world's largest economy before 2030 (World Bank, 2019), and has accelerated its knowledge and services capabilities in recent years. China continues to be able to keep rising inflation at reasonable levels (IMF, 2018) while its growth has become steadier, at a more sustainable pace due to population and productivity constraints. Similar trends as seen in China now are expected for India in the longer term.

The smaller and mid-sized Southeast and South Asian countries have been exposed to suffering from trade tensions, especially those between the USA and China, and they also suffer regularly from meteorological challenges. One example for the latter is Malaysia.

These economies have become more and more dependent on supply chain participation (see Chapter 6): countries that participate in higher value-added exports and experience sustained dynamic services demand are the main beneficiaries of regional growth. This is, for example, the case for Japan, South Korea, Singapore, and especially for Thailand and Taiwan. Over the past years, they have also increasingly traded with each other, in addition to trading with developed non-Asian countries (Barua, 2017).

The very low-income countries continue to suffer mostly from persisting economic inequality and weak market access demand, while economic inequality has declined across most of Asia. Afghanistan is one example of a low-income country; Mongolia classifies as lower middle income and Kazakhstan as upper middle income.

Some parts of developing Asia are less affected, in that the economies are increasingly becoming attractive for cross-border trade and investment, and many are determined to be part of free trade areas and currently show considerable growth. For example, in the ASEAN-5 (Indonesia, Malaysia, Philippines, Thailand, Vietnam), growth was expected to be 5.3 per cent in 2018 and 5.2 for 2019 at the time of writing (IMF, 2018: 40). Their companies' investments continue to target mainly other emerging or developing markets, yet there is growing interest in developed market investment from all of these counties, with varying capabilities.

Many economies in Asia have expanded thanks to commodity exporting activity, yet some countries continue to depend strongly on this one particular export. These economies have come to need substantial fiscal consolidation, are sometimes challenged by war and conflict, and are all hit by decreasing prices. This is the case, for example, for Indonesia and Malaysia. This means that these economies need to diversify to decrease commodity dependence. At the same time, they aim to increase other sources of revenue that can fund remaining development needs. This provides for market access opportunities. Malaysia, for example, increasingly offers foreign investment incentives in areas such as technology under conditions such as the creation of better-paid jobs.

Finally, some emerging countries such as Vietnam, Myanmar and Bangladesh have become or are on the way to becoming thriving locations for low-cost manufacturing and have attracted manufacturing formerly located in China; others, in the West of Asia, are still missing out on economic growth due to war, unrest or weak governments that do not provide the conditions favourable for internal growth of domestic industry nor for international investors or for value chain participation. These countries have yet to begin the path towards fostering both economic development and human capital.

Pham reports that 'identifying a nation's current position on the "value chain" (determined by development and human capital levels) will help you locate stocks about to thrive and tossing out those shares in industries about to croak. For instance, in nations with highly skilled workforces, such as Japan and South Korea, consider their advanced manufacturing and services industries. But for investment opportunities in nations with less developed workforces, like Indonesia or Vietnam, look into agriculture and low skilled manufacturing' (Pham, 2017).

The link between human capital and economic development

Typically, we will expect that an increase in human capital directly affects economic growth because it fosters productivity. Human capital, depending on levels of education and training, provides the key input into R&D and accelerates innovation, technological change and value added.

This diverse business environment is the main arena for Asian companies that do business across borders. It requires careful consideration of market entry conditions, to ensure the strategically most suitable cross-border location choice.

Market access: Variations across Asia

For companies that operate internationally, market access is essential in regard to tariff and non-tariff conditions, the latter encompassing possible variations in policies, regimes, regulations, processes that might increase transaction costs in cross-border business. International transaction costs are those costs that are incurred when buying or selling a good or service across borders, and represent the efforts required to bring the good or service to market.

A firm will typically assess those costs on the basis of conditions, upon or as part of their evaluation of location choices, and then decide on the main way in which to enter the market through its choice of an entry mode. The latter comprises a range of strategic options of investment. From low to high commitment, from low or shared risk to high risk, from less market and internationalization learning and returns, companies make decisions to access other markets that depend on their capabilities. These will be further explored and detailed in Chapter 5 of this book.

Setting the scene for this is the question of whether and how the Asian business environment welcomes access to its various markets. Due to the diversity of government and economic systems (cf. also Chapter 1), this market access is dissimilar. Cross-border operations may be a first move for the firm, or it may be part of an established strategy, to add to – or change – a location at any moment, for example due to geo-economic shifts. Examples of this, among many, are the tariff policies of world powers and more market integration – such as the Trans-Pacific Partnership (TPP11) – or less regional integration – such as Brexit, the United Kingdom's exit from the European Union.

Trade liberalization – the provision of preferential market access to partner economies – has been used as an effective development tool, and a means to achieve long-term political stability through economic collaboration. From a resource-based view, doing business within one's home region strengthens intra-regional locational production network strategies. This stems from region-bound firm specific advantages. This means that in a region, a firm excels through higher productivity of comparable assets (tangible and intangible) than competitors thanks to certain inherent capabilities that can help achieve scale economies, scope economies, exploitation of national differences in nearby markets as well as arbitrage and externality benefits. These benefits enable an 'evolutionary strategy of resource combinations' and 'platforms for future investments' (Kogut and Zander, 1993: 16) linked to knowledge bundling among more localized partners (cf. also Fan and Scott, 2003).

The combination of FSAs with location specific advantage (multiple country specific advantages) results in RSAs that are immobile; all firms have access to the location and its region and will differ in the capability to leverage its potential value-added activities.

The benefits from cross-border business activity consist of the leveraging of transactions organized within regional networks that may include:

- the ease of acquisition, processing and acting on information about labour supply opportunity and shared production networks
- the existence of close business links that provide for efficient exchange and spillovers of business knowledge
- regional cooperation that supports the formation of alliances between firms and the development of distinctive business cultures
- economies of scale that originate from sharing infrastructure, with efficiency derived from industrial linkages and subcontracting, the division of labour and sometimes common regional governance structures supporting the development of regional industrial hubs
- in trade flows, intra-regional demand for finished and unfinished intermediate products that increases steadily (Pula and Peltonen, 2009).

This capability, in the ideal case, allows firms to not only overcome country-to-country differences, but to also leverage these differences to create value. One example is the capacity to overcome the challenges of changing policies, for example in China. China's *Negative List for Market Access*, for example, published by the National Development and Reform Commission as a unified table of prohibitions and **licensing** requirements, applies to domestic and foreign companies across the country. This includes industry specific laws, regulations and administrative approvals for foreign investors, and is consulted in conjunction with the *Special Administrative Measures on Access to Foreign Investment* of the respective year (e.g. *2020 FI Negative List*) released by the Commerce Ministry. This provides insight into whether investment by a foreign entity is permitted and under what ownership structure, as well as further licensing or certification requirements. For example, the 2018 list prohibits internet-related business activities, and prohibits, among other industries, information technology and software. Doing business across several markets in the neighbouring Asia has the potential to offset potential disadvantages in this context, or to leverage partnerships.

The variations in market access conditions can hence hinder the applicability and efficiency of international strategy. Through preferential market access, such as free trade agreements, economies strengthen trade and investment ties between countries, and promote their industries' cross-border market access. While research continues to debate the most direct influence of FTAs, Baier and Bergstr (2007) found that the average impact of free trade agreements is to double the **bilateral trade** after a ten-year period. Magee (2008) estimated the anticipatory and long-run impact of FTAs and revealed that these have increased trade between members by an average of 90 per cent.

Intra-Asian FTAs: Ambitions in shaping privileged bilateral and plurilateral market access conditions

Table 4.1   Creating positive or negative integration

Positive integration	Negative integration
The commitment of FTA members to removing trade barriers is called *negative integration*, i.e. the removal of restrictions. This is, for example, the case for the China–Singapore FTA, and for the South Korea–Vietnam FTA.	Forming a 'common market' with appropriate institutions governing the group, and a policy framework that allows turning of commitment into practice, is called *positive integration*, i.e. policy integration and development and modifications for joint action. The ASEAN is working to become a common market.

Source: Adapted from Suder and Lindeque, 2018

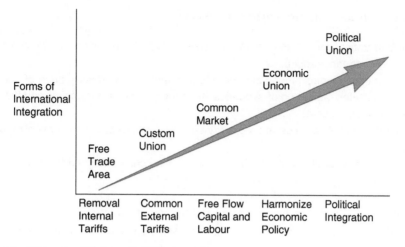

Figure 4.1   Degrees of international integration

Source: Suder, 1994

The various degrees of market integration are illustrated in Figure 4.1, which correlates degrees of market integration with the harmonization of policies, the intensity of the resulting correlation defining the level of integration achieved. The main form of market integration found in Asia is the bilateral or multilateral FTA, removing internal tariffs between signatories, and the common market, which allows for member economies to have one common external tariff also, and to opt for additional joint initiatives such as the free flow of capital and labour, in variations. The FTA focuses mainly (though not exclusively) on improving conditions for the cross-border flow of trade and services. Among this, tariffs are reduced or eliminated. Tariffs can be defined as customs duties on merchandise imports that provide price advantage to locally produced goods and increase import prices. This hinders international trade that is recognized as a source of competitiveness and hence economic welfare. Bilateral agreements, that is, between two countries, may reduce tariffs significantly and improve market access. Multilateral tariff negotiations, that is, among a number of countries, reduce the complexity that many bilateral agreements may cause.

In free trade areas and customs unions, trade creation emerges from consumption shifts from a high-cost producer to a low-cost producer, which means that trade expands. Trade diversion means that trade decreases when trade with non-members is replaced by trade with members of the union whether efficient or not, as it becomes cheaper.

The creation and diversion of economic flows allows for the application to all or some of the economic freedoms (goods, services, people, capital) of a single market.

Cost efficiencies result from market access by:

- reducing transaction costs in terms of currency losses, border patrols, customs procedures and red tape reductions
- reducing uncertainties among member states benefiting the relative price of currencies, which facilitates the selling of securities, the raising of funds and capital, and the recruitment of diverse labour
- increasing marketing, price and cost transparency, efficiencies and economies of scale effects
- improving of productivity and the international value chain (adapted to Asia from Suder, 2011: 36).

The analysis specifically of Eastern Asian free trade agreements (e.g. by Lee and Shin, 2006) finds an increase in trade among members as well as some trade diversion, depending on certain characteristics of member countries, however for the regional trade agreement of the ASEAN, only trade creation is found, with no trade diversion effects.

We will now review the key forms of market integration that facilitate market access across Asia.

APEC

APEC, the Asia-Pacific Economic Cooperation, is a regional economic forum founded in 1989. This is the largest market grouping in Asia. The 21 APEC members include Australia, Brunei Darussalam, Canada, Chile, China, Hong Kong-China, Indonesia, Japan, Republic of Korea, Malaysia, Mexico, New Zealand, Papua New Guinea, Peru, the Philippines, Russia, Singapore, Chinese Taipei, Thailand, the United States of America and Vietnam. They represent 2.6 billion people, about 60 per cent of world GDP and 47 per cent of world trade. APEC is increasing its degree of unification, although its core mission is to facilitate trade and FDI by removing barriers. Members agreed to a roadmap for a 'Free Trade Area of the Asia-Pacific' in 2014. When doing business within APEC, business also benefits from additional external market access through more than 21 bilateral free trade agreements that APEC has signed, including among others with Russia.

ASEAN

Most members of the ASEAN are members of APEC. APEC trade facilitation initiatives reduced 'transaction costs by a further 5 per cent between 2007 and 2010' (APEC, 2011) and continue to focus on the reduction of trade transaction costs including non-tariff measures and behind-the-border barriers.

The ASEAN's members are Indonesia, Malaysia, the Philippines, Singapore, Thailand, Brunei Darrussalam, Laos, Vietnam, Myanmar and Cambodia, with 590 million inhabitants in 2009, 633 million in 2017, and an expected 741 million people by 2035 (Suder and Lindeque, 2018). Timor Leste is expected to join under conditions of further growth developments and stability. The combined total GDP is estimated at about $2.5 trillion. The ASEAN was created to accelerate economic growth, social progress and cultural development and is equipped with a dispute settlement system. An ASEAN Free Trade Area, AFTA, was created in 1993, aiming to stimulate growth through a reduction of government control on national economies. This was a response to the EU's and NAFTA's regional peace and stability initiatives. It functions also through better market access through reduced intra-regional tariffs and non-tariff barriers significantly, i.e. through cross-notification mechanisms. AFTA does not apply a common external tariff on imported goods. There is no EU-style free movement of labour or common currency project. Most intra-regional trade in goods benefits from a 0–5 per cent tariff range, mainly among the ASEAN-6 comprising Brunei Darussalam, Indonesia, Malaysia, the Philippines, Singapore and Thailand. AFTA's trade relations extend to other regions in the world, for example within the Trans-Regional EU–ASEAN Trade Initiative (TREATI). AFTA has FTAs with China, Japan, South Korea, India, Australia and New Zealand and other countries.

Middle East

With parts of the Middle East located in Western Asia, it is important to be aware of the Gulf Cooperation Council (GCC), comprising Saudi Arabia, Kuwait, Bahrain, Qatar, the United Arab Emirates, Yemen and the Sultanate of Oman. In normal times, they constitute their own customs union, yet disputes with Qatar and the war in Yemen disrupt integration, stability and market access.

Working groups focus as much as possible on industry, energy and environment, university cooperation, business cooperation and the preparation of a free trade agreement. There used to be bilateral relations with Iran, Iraq and Yemen.

Trans-Pacific Partnership

The integration at the Pacific Rim level has specifically made very significant progress through the Comprehensive and Progressive Agreement for Trans-Pacific Partnership (CPTPP), which is one of the most relevant FTAs within the region and beyond. Since December 2018, it provides businesses with preferred market access across 11 mainly

Asia-Pacific-centric countries, including Australia, Brunei, Canada, Chile, Japan, Malaysia, Mexico, New Zealand, Peru, Singapore and Vietnam. The Trump Administration in 2017 decided that the USA would not participate in the TTP.

CPTPP countries account for 13.5 per cent of global GDP. This type of regional trade agreement is also a common form of reciprocal preferential access in which lower or zero tariffs are applied to products originating among members so as to foster trade cooperation.

Trade agreements can vary in strength, depending on the provided relative advantage.

The much-coveted 'most-favoured nation' provisions in FTAs

Most-Favoured Nation (MFN) clauses, when used in FTAs, are provisions which ensure that the FTA is upgraded to more favourable rates or conditions which any partner to the FTA may later agree with another trade partner that is not participating in the FTA. This goes well beyond the liberalization achieved through WTO membership. As an example, the provisions in the EU–Japan agreement can benefit the Australia–EU FTA if commitments are more favourable in that FTA and will then automatically apply without renegotiations. (Suder and Lindeque, 2018: 404)

4.2 Case study: New Hope Group – a long-term commitment for Asian expansions

Overview

In 2008, a locally produced tainted infant formula scandal in China enraged the entire nation and urged the industry and government to re-evaluate and enact new laws regarding food safety and related monitoring systems. Demands for imported baby food and other food and beverage (F&B) products have been steadily increasing in China ever since. Many Chinese agricultural and food processing companies have been fulfilling this need by accelerating foreign imports to China's market – a business activity that could not meet profit maximization without free trade agreements. New Hope Group, known as China's biggest agricultural and forage processing company, has been playing a leading role in participating and promoting such bilateral trading activities in China. Through various forms of foreign direct investment, the privately owned company has contributed to benefiting multiple players including foreign food producers and Chinese investors, while satisfying the market needs of the countries involved.

Learning outcomes

By the end of this case study, students should be able to:

1   Identify the drivers or motives for establishing FTA partnerships between countries in the Asian region.
2   Understand how FTAs benefit a country and business.

Introduction: The surge in demand for imported F&B products in China

When greater focus is placed upon infrastructure development and GDP growth, corporate social responsibility has been shown to get overlooked as the economy advances in developing countries. News such as the child slavery bust in the garment factory in Vietnam (*The Australian*, 2011) and premature deaths or severe illness caused by air and water pollution resulting from the rapid growth of the economy in India and China (Carnegie Endowment for International Peace, 2012; *The Hindu*, 2019) have never failed to shock the world. Reasons for these incidents could be laggard laws and regulations or malpractices in unethical companies with little penalty locally. Some of these incidents, for example food insecurity resulting from dubious food processing, may have serious impacts on society, causing life-threatening or life-taking tragedies, instigating angry and despairing families, decreasing or completely losing consumers' confidence in certain brands. On the brighter side, these incidents can trigger development of laws or systems, more rigorous control of industries and markets, and new demands from consumers. In 2008, there was such an incident that started an ascending trend of demand for imported F&B products in China, effectively boosting bilateral trade between China and its trading partners and manifesting the importance and value of FTAs.

In 2008 China's infant formula scandal received the most attention from the nation and the world among other food safety concerns in this country. Four years before the scandal, very sadly, half a dozen babies died of malnutrition in central China after

(Continued)

(Continued)

being fed tainted infant formula. Sanlu Group, a formerly trusted local infant formula producer in China, was later found to have kept selling its tainted infant formula even when it found melamine in its milk supply. Sales were only stopped after Sanlu's biggest **stakeholder**, Fonterra, a leading dairy producer and exporter in New Zealand, warned the New Zealand government, which in return informed Beijing about the issue. A government investigation was then launched. The investigation discovered the same issue in 21 other infant formula producers in China. Other than the aforementioned six deaths, over 300,000 babies had suffered from kidney stones and other complications in this scandal.

Since then, demand for foreign infant food from Chinese parents with young babies has gone viral. Parents believed that imported infant formula was safer no matter how promising the new marketing campaigns were about Chinese brands. Many foreign brands took this opportunity to raise their prices: at the time, China's media reported that the prices of some imported baby formula could be twice those of local brands (Marketplace, 2018). However, Chinese parents believed that the higher the price, the safer the products – after all, the rapid emergence of the middle class and growing disposable income rendered Chinese families more money to spend on the products that were perceived to be of higher value. According to the Chinese National Bureau of Statistics, China's urban household average annual income per capita rose from US$320 in 1990 to US$4,300 in 2012 (Asia Perspective, 2014). Chinese consumers' thirst for foreign baby formula only marked the beginning of the boom for foreign F&B products in China.

Increased needs met stricter regulations

Demands for imported products from China had spread into other F&B sectors such as dairy products, meat, and fresh vegetables and fruits; meanwhile Chinese consumers' price sensitivity also became higher due to their increased access to imported goods. Wider internet coverage in China raised exposure to foreign brands: consumers began to use e-commerce platforms such as Hai Tao, the global version of Tao Bao, China's biggest e-commerce platform by Alibaba, or to use *Daigou*, independent personal international shoppers, who sometimes encountered legitimacy and legal issues, to buy overseas F&B products. The amount of infant formula purchased through the internet grew to the extent that it caused anxiety among local supermarket owners and shoppers in the source countries and raised the attention of China Customs. In 2013, China Customs issued a limit of 5 kilograms on international mailing of infant formula: any international mailing package to China with over 5 kilograms of infant formula would be returned to the sender's address. In 2014, China approved **cross-border e-commerce** platforms, where customers could order overseas products at lower tax rates. According to the deputy director of Liaowang Institute's dairy research centre, the sale of imported infant formula on cross-border e-commerce platforms alone was US$960 million in China in 2014, and that figure tripled in 2017 to US$2.6 billion (Marketplace, 2018).

While more foreign brands were introduced to Chinese consumers through these unconventional channels, the survival conditions for properly imported foreign products in China became tougher. Some foreign F&B producers and their price fixing strategies for the Chinese market had already faced investigation from the government: in 2013, China's top economic planning agency fined six foreign infant food producers including Abbott Laboratories (US based), and more than US$100 million was charged for anti-trust and price fixing (Marketplace, 2018). Additionally, the launch of China's Food Safety Law in 2015 reinforced more rigorous controls and supervision for both domestic and imported F&B products. According to Teng Jiacai, deputy minister of the China Food and Drug Administration, even when nearly 99 per cent of all domestically produced infant formula met national standards in 2015, many Chinese consumers still favoured imported formula due to the lack of confidence in domestic brands (*China Daily*, 2016).

At the time, there was a large portion of Chinese consumers who were buying foreign branded infant formula and F&B products from the source countries instead of the Chinese market, driving a harsher competitive environment for F&B exports in China and increasing costs for Chinese consumers.

Facilitation from the 'history making' FTA

FTAs between China and its growing numbers of trading partners have grown in number, scale and scope. Australia has been a major source of imported F&B products for Chinese consumers with its exports to China's market increasing since the China–Australia Free Trade Agreement (ChAFTA) was signed. On 17 November 2014, the President of China and the then Prime Minister of Australia co-held a press conference in the Australian capital, Canberra, during the 2014 G20 Brisbane Summit to announce the end of the prolonged 21 rounds of ChAFTA negotiations. The negotiations had spanned the ten years of a joint feasibility study period and the duration of two terms of presidents in China or four terms of prime ministers in Australia (BBC News Chinese, 2014). The ChAFTA, which was officially signed in June 2015, covered more than a dozen areas including goods, services and investment, and is known for having the highest level of liberalization in trade and investment among all FTAs that China has signed with any country so far (Xinhua Net, 2015). The then Prime Minister of Australia, Tony Abbott, hailed the ChAFTA as 'history making' for both countries (ABC News, 2015a).

(Continued)

(Continued)

In 2015, tariffs of more than 85 per cent of Australian exports to China were eliminated. Once ChAFTA was fully implemented, 98 per cent of Australian goods were expected to enter China duty free, and 100 per cent of China's exports to Australia would enjoy zero-tariff treatment (Australian Government, Department of Foreign Affairs and Trade, 2016). Table 4.2 shows some of the sectors that would face tariff adjustments with the implementation of ChAFTA.

Table 4.2   Tariff adjustment to some sectors by Australia Sino FTA

Product	Current Tariff	Future Tariff	Years Until Fully Implemented
Dairy	Unclear	0	4–11
Infant formula	15%	0	4
Beef	12–25%	0	9
Lamb	23%	0	8
Barley	3%	0	Immediate
Sorghum	2%	0	Immediate
Live animal (cattle)	5%	0	4
Leather	Unclear	14%	2–7
Horticulture	Unclear	0	4
Marine foods	Unclear	(majority) 0	4
Drinks	14–30%	0	4
Mining	Unclear	0	Unknown

Source: Data compiled from iFeng Finance, 2015

A key outcome of these bilateral tariffs cuts was the opening up of two large markets. Thanks to ChAFTA, Australian products have become a vibrant force in the F&B sector of the Chinese market. According to World's Top Exports, China was Australia's top trading partner in 2018 with a total of US$74 billion (29 per cent of total Australian exports). The Department of Foreign Affairs and Trade of Australia also revealed that China was Australia's largest agriculture, forestry and fisheries export market, which was estimated to be worth AU$13.5 billion in 2017 (World's Top Exports, 2019).

Due to a similar economic structure as that of Australia, New Zealand's exports to China had shown a similar pattern. The China–New Zealand FTA was signed in 2008 and was the first FTA that China had signed with a developed country. The FTA had driven New Zealand's exports to China from US$1.8 billion in 2008 to US$9.38 billion in 2017 (Ministry of Commerce of China, 2018; *The Diplomat*, 2014b).

The number of New Zealand based formula producers who exported to China was once as many as 200 (NutraIngredients-Asia, 2017), however since the infant formula scandal, New Zealand's dairy products had experienced challenges on the Chinese market. Fonterra, the New Zealand based dairy producer and exporter, did not sell products through its own brands in China but through many other brands including Sanlu, which was 43 per cent owned by Fonterra. Even though Fonterra was the whistle-blower in Sanlu's tainted formula case, it was once suspected of complicity in this scandal because it did not expose the issue earlier and did not disclose the issue publicly but went through diplomatic channels (*Forbes*, 2008; *The Diplomat*, 2014b). After Sanlu's scandal was exposed, Fonterra and its many product brands in China, such as Anchor, had created a bad impression among Chinese customers and aroused attention from the Chinese government and regulators resulting in higher bars and stricter rules for importing baby food from New Zealand. In 2013, Fonterra announced that it had found bacteria that could cause botulism in its products. The contamination was claimed to originate from a dirty pipe in its New Zealand based factory. The company had to initiate a global recall of many of its partners' dairy products including those in China. China had thus instituted a temporary ban of all baby formula imports from New Zealand (BBC News, 2013). This botulism scare resulted in the resignation of Fonterra's milk products chief.

In 2017, the number of New Zealand infant formula producers on Chinese market had decreased to 13, but New Zealand's dairy products were still one of the top choices for Chinese consumers (NutraIngredients-Asia, 2017). A Mintel survey from 2017 revealed that 57 per cent of Chinese mothers perceived Australia and New Zealand branded infant food to be superior (NutraIngredients-Asia, 2017).

China's free trade agreements

Including Australia and New Zealand, China has so far signed 16 FTAs with 24 countries and regions. There are also ten new FTAs and several existing FTAs under negotiation for their ratification or upgrade.

Trading between China and its FTA partners has outnumbered trading with its non-FTA partners, even those who once set the highest trading records. For example, in

(Continued)

(Continued)

June 2017, the Chinese government reopened its imported beef market to the US after a 13-year 'mad cow disease' ban. This was exciting news for US beef producers because the US was once China's biggest source of beef imports, accounting for nearly two-thirds of China's imported beef market. However, China's import duty rate on US beef was 37 per cent in 2017, more than triple the 12 per cent for most of China's FTA trading partners. In the same year, tariffs for Australian beef exports to China were subject to a 7.2 per cent import duty (*BEEF Magazine*, 2018). In 2018, total beef exports from Australia to China were 17.31 metric tons, compared to 0.69 metric tons from the US (Sohu Finance, 2019).

At the end of 2009, the Ministry of Commerce of China worked with the Chinese Academy of Social Sciences to initiate a survey on the utilization of FTAs by Chinese enterprises. The results of this survey demonstrated that the utilization rate of China's FTAs within Chinese enterprises was generally low. The most frequently applied FTAs were those signed between mainland China and Hong Kong and China–ASEAN FTA at 16.3 and 20 per cent respectively. All the rest of China's FTAs were applied by fewer than 10 per cent of the Chinese enterprises. This was in striking contrast to the 80 per cent's utilization rate of North America's FTAs by its enterprises in general (International Centre for Trade and Sustainable Development, 2015). On further examination the government found out that the main cause of the situation was that enterprises generally did not have adequate knowledge or information about the FTAs that were initiated and signed between governments. Although most of the clauses in the FTAs were designed to bring benefits to enterprises, companies found them useless because they had not been adequately involved. To solve this problem, the Chinese government established an evaluation mechanism to assess the utilization, performance and execution of existing and future FTAs (International Centre for Trade and Sustainable Development, 2015), aiming to induce more enterprise to participate in the FTAs. In 2012, a more strategic layout of China's FTAs was officially proposed at the 18th Chinese Communist Party Congress and was presented again at the Party Congress's Third Plenum a year later in 2013. The proposal pointed out that China's previous FTAs lacked strategic focus and that future FTAs should emphasize big economies and higher levels of liberalization, trading not only in goods but also in other commercial segments such as services and investment. Although the FTAs had helped China in strengthening relationships with other countries, in 2012 China's trade with its FTA partners only accounted for 22 per cent of its total trade, indicating room for growth (*The Diplomat*, 2014a).

The 'history making' ChAFTA set an example for FTAs with a high level of liberalization. Besides having benefited Chinese consumers with greater choice of, and sometimes cheaper, imported products, ChAFTA has also greatly benefited the enterprises in Australia by eliminating trading tariffs and offering Chinese enterprises and investors better incentives to invest in Australia. Chinese investment in Australia therefore increased from AU$6 billion in 2007 to AU$65 billion in 2017. ChAFTA also facilitated private Chinese investment in Australia by liberalizing the Foreign Investment Review Board screening threshold for private Chinese investors in non-sensitive sectors from AU$252 million to AU$1,094 million (Australian Government, Department of Foreign Affairs and Trade, 2018). According to KPMG, private Chinese company investment in Australia grew to 83 per cent of total deal volume and 60 per cent of deal value in 2017 (KPMG, 2018: 10).

Investing in Australia and New Zealand

As a leading agriculture company in China, the New Hope Group has steadily increased its investment in multiple sectors in Australia. Not only that, it has been markedly involved in promoting cooperation between the two countries by initiating the Australia Sino One Hundred Year Agricultural and Food Safety Partnership, or ASA100. ASA100 aimed to promote, develop and unify Australian agriculture and food manufacturing sectors, through the advance of international trade in Australia with a focus on China. On 17 November 2014, the same day when the ratification of China–Australia FTA negotiations was announced, ASA100 was officially launched with the endorsement of the highest level of both Australian and Chinese government officials in Canberra (Sohu Finance, 2014).

As a non-government business initiative consisting of 30 to 50 leading agricultural companies from Australia and China, ASA100 was expected to further accelerate and facilitate long-term cooperation between the participants and the two countries by realizing its six objectives: branding Australian agriculture products and exports; non-tariff barrier removal to improve Chinese market access; developing and implementing food safety and supply chain programmes to increase bilateral understanding of Australian and Chinese food safety process, regulations and distribution channels; promoting agricultural infrastructure such as investment in infrastructural expansion; relationship building; and capability development (ASA100 Official Website, 2019). As Liu Yonghao, the CEO of New Hope Group, introduced ASA100 to the world, he also announced that it planned to finance the expansion of its agricultural value chain by investing AU $500 million in Australian farms and agricultural products (Sohu Finance, 2014). This decision was based on the satisfactory results of previous investment projects in Australia.

'The Australian governments are good; they welcome Chinese and international investors as long as the investors bring benefits to Australian people, they will support', Liu commented on his ASA100 initiation: 'I have found many investments made by Chinese enterprises in Australia, they have acquired this, or acquired that, but in this pattern, if we could develop with Australian partners, isn't it much better?' (ABC News, 2017).

(Continued)

(Continued)

In 2013, Hosen Capital, a private equity fund under New Hope Group, acquired Australia's fourth biggest beef processing company Kilcoy Pastoral Company (KPC). At the time it was acquired, KPC had 750 employees and its yearly cattle output capacity was around 250,000. This investment aimed to double the processing capacity and increase the number of employees (*ECNS*, 2016).

Noticeably, after the acquisition, Hosen Capital retained KPC's local management and operations and used its partnerships, capital and expertise to make KPC a global player in the beef industry: since the acquisition of KPC, its exports to China have risen from around 17 to 28 per cent of its total output. Even so, the Chinese market only accounted for roughly a quarter of KPC's production. This meant the majority of KPC's expansion in its output has been exported to other international markets. The expansion of KPC's production not only benefited other businesses in the Kilcoy region (the area within a 1610 kilometre radius of Kilcoy), but also significantly boosted local employment. Until February 2017, the acquisition had resulted in an additional 130 jobs at KPC, and it was estimated that the completion of facility expansion would eventually result in another 250 jobs (*ABC NEWS*, 2018). Furthermore, Deloitte's modelling estimated an average net increase in employment in the greater the Kilcoy region to be just under 900 fulltime equivalents each year over a ten-year period from 2015 to 2025.

Less than a year from the establishment of ASA100, in July 2015, New Hope Group made its second move in its value chain expansion in Australia: a partnership between the Perichs, one of Australia's biggest dairy farming families, and Freedom Foods, an ASX listed food processing company. Freedom Foods and New Hope Group, along with Perich Group, which was fully owned by Freedom Foods, formed to establish the Australian Fresh Milk Holdings (AFMH). An acquisition of Moxey farms made this consortium a four-way partnership. New Hope Group, the biggest stakeholder in AFMH, worked to provide distribution links through China and to fund investment in dairy farms across New South Wales and Victoria. It also worked with Freedom Foods to seek new market opportunities (ABC News, 2015b).

As Liu explained in a Chinese TV interview, *Dialogue*, in 2016, the reasons for him to develop and expand the relationship with Australia were mainly the following: 1) the abundance of grasslands in Australia made it possible to substantially lower production costs in the agricultural sector, 2) the protected and unpolluted natural environment made Australian dairy products highly competitive at a world level, and 3) the promises and commitments that he made via ASA100. AFMH has been one of the proud projects of ASA100 (New Hope Group Official Website, 2016a). The establishment of AFMH has allowed New Hope Group to invest in large scale intensive dairy farms in Australia. As with KPC, managers of Moxey and Perich farms continued to manage and operate their existing business. With the support of New Hope Group and the upstream and downstream connection brought by this partnership, AFMH was set to acquire more land. In May 2017, AFMH acquired Bruem farm (327 hectares) and North Logan farm (1,150 hectares), the biggest farmland in the upper river area of Moxey farm. As of 2017, AFMH owned 2,100 hectares of farmland and 5,500 head of cattle, compared to 3,700 head in 2015 (ACB News, 2017).

New Hope Group's investment also took the growing and changing needs of Chinese consumers and the Chinese market into consideration. In June 2016, New Hope Group fully acquired a 27-year-old vitamin and supplement company, Australian NaturalCare (ANC), arising from trendy needs for natural supplements from the Chinese market. New Hope Group stated that this was also part of its value chain expansion plan in ASA100 (Financial Review, 2016). This acquisition signified an official step into the healthcare sector for New Hope Group, and initiated the debut of ANC's natural, non-chemical and unpolluted products in China.

The latest investment of New Hope Group in Australia was its acquisition of Real Pet Food in November 2017. The acquisition turned New Hope Group into Real Pet Food's largest shareholder at the price of AU$1 billion. The deal was New Hope Group's foray in the pet food sector in Australia and was also an essential part of the Group's 'animal protein supply chain' project. 'New Hope Group is a known professional in the animal nutrition field, and the acquisition is an important strategy of the company in this sector', said Liu after the deal was revealed: 'Nowadays, more and more families take pets as their family members, which generates more diverse consumer demands. I am optimistic about the Chinese pet food industry in the next few years' (China Invests Overseas, 2018). As Australia's biggest pet food company, Real Pet Food's CEO, David Grant, stated that the company's new shareholder would be fully engaged to promote the brand in both the China and North America markets.

As an active Chinese investor, Liu Yonghao emphasized all the investment undertaken by New Hope Group had so far brought 'benefits to Australia', while also helping to expand his business, which therefore also 'brought benefits to China' (Financial Review, 2016). In an announcement in August 2017, Nick Dowling from New Hope Group explained why the company might be immune to criticism about investing in Australia and buying Australian companies: 'We invest into businesses, we don't acquire businesses. We look to work with great partners that have great businesses where we can bring our resources and market access to give life to opportunities that business wouldn't otherwise have – it's all about giving oxygen for those businesses to grow' (ABC News, 2017). In the same statement, New Hope Group revealed that the company planned to invest a furtherAU$1 billion by 2020 to help grow more businesses in Australia.

(Continued)

(Continued)

Besides Australia, New Hope Group also initiated multiple investments in New Zealand. As early as 2011, it had partially acquired PGG Wrightson (PGW), known as New Zealand's biggest agricultural supply and service company (Invest in NZ, 2011). On PGW's 2018 annual report, Agria Singapore, a fully owned subsidiary of New Hope Group, held a 50.22 per cent stake in the company (PGW, 2018: 99). This acquisition contributed to New Hope's completion of its long-term strategic development of the 'animal protein supply chain' due to PGW's leading industry technology and resources, while backing PGW's growth with capital support.

Further into technology and research expansion, in May 2015, New Hope Dairy of New Hope Group established a strategic cooperation agreement with AgResearch, an institute of the New Zealand government (New Hope Group Official Website, 2016b). The cooperation agreement served to enhance New Hope Dairy's own research into product improvement in areas such as infant formula and would deliver innovation in products and services to both New Hope and AgResearch.

A milestone for New Hope Group

After five years of investment and strategic cooperation in Australia and New Zealand, New Hope Group set up its Australian headquarters in Sydney in October 2016. This was an important step and milestone for the company's international expansion. In his headquarters' opening speech, Liu said: 'We greatly value the market complementarity between China, Australia and New Zealand, and because of that, New Hope Group has been increasing its investment and deepening its cooperation with Australia and New Zealand in the past few years' (New Hope Group Official Website, 2016c). The investment in Australia has been gradually completing New Hope Group's blueprint of a full value chain of its own and expansion with China's FTA partners, reflecting the objectives of ASA100. In the opening speech, Liu also disclosed that the land in St Leonards, which was successfully acquired by New Hope in 2015, would be developed into a 43-floor luxury apartment landmark, indicating its ambition and involvement in Australia's real estate business.

Case questions

1   Why has China been actively involved in FTAs with other countries?
2   How would a company benefit from FTAs? Does an FTA guarantee success? How and why? Please provide examples to illustrate your points.

4.3 Case study: Toyota's market expansion across Asia – adapting to diverse macro-economic environments

Overview

Toyota Motor Corporation (Toyota) is a Japanese multinational company that operates through three core segments – Automobile Business, Financial Services and All Others. The Automobile Business segment designs, manufactures and sells a variety of automotive vehicles. The Financial Services segment provides auto financing and leasing services. The All Others segment engages in housing, telecommunications and all other businesses. The Asian market has played a key role in Toyota's overseas expansion plans. This case study examines how the company's growth and expansion in different countries in the Asia-Pacific region was highly contingent upon their varied macro-economic environments. It focuses on Toyota's expansion strategies in its most pivotal Asian markets as filed with the Securities and Exchange Commission (SEC) – Japan, Thailand and China – and explains how Toyota adapted business decisions to best suit these countries' various business conditions including levels of market access, economic environments, natural environments, technological environments, and political and social environments. It outlines the opportunities and challenges these different environments presented and discusses their impacts on Toyota's cross-border business activities.

Learning outcomes

By the end of this case study, students should be able to:

1   Identify the characteristics of the diverse macro-economic environments in different Asian countries and understand how they have impacted Toyota's market expansion.
2   Understand the actions taken by Toyota in response to the opportunities and challenges embedded in the dynamics of the Asian markets and the business conditions of various countries.

Introduction and background

Toyota Motor Corporation (Toyota) was founded by Kiichiro Toyoda in 1933 initially as a division within Toyota Automatic Loom Works Ltd, a textile loom manufacturer. Toyota

(Continued)

(Continued)

produced its first automobile vehicle, the G1 truck, in 1935, and its first passenger car, the Model AA, in 1936. Nowadays, Toyota's primary businesses include the design, manufacture and sale of a wide variety of automotive vehicles ranging from passenger cars to commercial trucks. It has grown to be one of the top automobile manufacturers in the world over the years. In 2008, Toyota surpassed General Motors as the largest auto-maker in both production and sales. In many of the subsequent years, Toyota maintained its leading position in the global market. As a preeminent player in the automotive industry, Toyota sells its products in roughly 190 countries. The domestic Japanese market is Toyota's primary battleground. For the fiscal year ended 31 March 2019 (FY 2019), it recorded sales of 2.2 million vehicles in Japan, 25 per cent of total sales, and an operating income of 1.7 trillion yen, 69 per cent of its total operating income (Toyota, 2019b). In 2019, Toyota had six R&D centres in Japan, accounting for 38 per cent of all R&D facilities (Toyota, 2019a). While the firm had been shifting production overseas over the years, Japan remained the primary site for Toyota's R&D efforts to drive technological innovation and advancement. It started to expand businesses into other Asian markets in the late 1950s. In 1957, the number of vehicles exported jumped by 374 per cent to 2,010 compared to the prior year (Toyota, 2012b). According to Toyota's 2019 Annual Report as filed with the US SEC, in FY 2019, Toyota's vehicle sales in Asia totalled 1.7 million units, 25 per cent of its overseas vehicle sales and 19 per cent of total vehicle sales. Operating income in Asia was 453.7 billion yen, 56 per cent of the total overseas operating income and 18 per cent of its total operating income. As of March 2019, Toyota has established 24 plants and manufacturing companies and four R&D centres in Asia (excluding Japan), accounting for 36 per cent and 25 per cent of all manufacturing and R&D sites, respectively (Toyota, 2019a). As per the 2019 annual report, Thailand and China were Toyota's two principal markets in Asia. Thailand was among the first foreign nations in which Toyota set up plants. It continued to be a key production hub for Toyota and also provided strong sales figures over the years. In July 2018, Toyota 'reached a production milestone of 10 million units in Thailand' (*The Nation*, 2018). Reuters reported that it sold 315,113 cars in Thailand in 2018, accounting for one third of total Thai car sales (Reuters, 2019). As the largest automotive market in the world, China was another core battleground for Toyota. According to a *Financial Times* article, China accounted for 30 per cent of total global car sales in 2018, and Toyota recorded sales of 1.5 million vehicles in the Chinese market (Hancock, 2019b).

This case study aims to address these questions: What were the dissimilarities in the market access conditions in different Asian countries? What were the main macroeconomic factors influencing Toyota's growth in its key Asian battlefields? How did Toyota adapt its product offerings, marketing and operations to exploit the diverse opportunities and conquer the various challenges?

Leveraging various market access conditions

Toyota's penetration into Thailand started decades ago when it established a wholly owned subsidiary – Toyota Motor Thailand Co. Ltd. (TMT) in 1962, and Thailand has gradually become a key production and exporting hub for Toyota. Thailand's macro-economic environment has increasingly welcomed access to its market over the years, as it has been committed to removing trade barriers, improving market access and attracting foreign investments through both tariff and non-tariff measures. It was a founding member of the ASEAN, an intergovernmental organization promoting economic and market integration among the ten member countries and other nations in Asia created in 1967. In 1992, Thailand participated in the ASEAN Free Trade Area. In 2008, the Japan–Thailand Economic Partnership Agreement (JTEPA) went into effect. The JTEPA was an FTA between Japan and Thailand aimed to 'liberalize and facilitate trade in goods and services', and included the elimination of tariffs on auto-parts (Ministry of Foreign Affairs of Japan, 2007). Thailand exempted companies that relocated to Thailand from corporate income tax for eight years and slashed corporate taxes by up to 50 per cent. In 2018, Thailand established a special economic zone, the Eastern Economic Corridor (EEC), covering the provinces of Chonburi, Rayong and Chachoengsao, in order to attract FDI, particularly in the automotive industry which accounted for 10 per cent of Thailand's GDP (Rastogi, 2018). The Thai government would enhance infrastructure, extend land leases for up to 50 years, and allow a free flow of international currencies in the EEC area to strengthen connectivity and promote manufacturing. Thailand's favourable market access conditions reduced trade and investment costs for Toyota and supported its decision to expand production in Thailand. Therefore, Toyota relocated a significant portion of its manufacturing activities to take advantage of Thailand's investment stimulus packages, building three production plants there – two in the EEC Province Chachoengsao (Ban Pho and Gateway) for passenger cars and one in Samut Prakan (Samrong) for commercial vehicles. To enhance the productivity of the Thai workforce, Toyota-Daihatsu Engineering and Manufacturing expanded industry–academic partnerships in Thailand as well as provided advanced R&D training for Thai engineers. These R&D programmes not only increased production efficiency but also allowed the firm to take advantage of Thailand's R&D-based tax incentives such as additional periods of tax exemption. In 2019, with 14,900 employees, the combined full capacity at these plants was reported to be roughly 800,000 vehicles per year (Toyota, 2019a). While Toyota mainly emphasized Thailand's role in production, the Thai market also added to the company's strong sales. Toyota Motor Thailand and its affiliates have more than 100 dealers as well as 300 showrooms (*Dun & Bradstreet*, 2020). As of July 2018, Toyota had produced a total of 10 million vehicles in Thailand, 52 per cent of which were sold in the Thai market and 48 per cent of which were exported globally (*The*

(Continued)

(Continued)

Nation, 2018). Because the AFTA allowed car-makers operating in Thailand to pay zero or significantly slashed tariffs for exporting automobiles to member nations, effectively integrating the ASEAN auto industries into a single market, Toyota Thailand's main export markets were the ASEAN members to benefit from the tariff incentives (Kotani, 2017). An exemplary windfall from Toyota's expansion into Thailand was the Thai-produced Hilux pickup truck. This model gained a widespread reputation and was highlighted in various TV shows, including BBC's *Top Gear*, for its remarkable sturdiness and durability. In the first half of 2019, Toyota recorded 272,293 sales of the Hilux, which was the fourth best-selling pickup globally (Focus2move, 2019).

Unlike its penetration into Thailand, which promoted market integration and encouraged FDI in the auto industry, Toyota's expansion into the Chinese market was a unique experience because of China's distinctive forms of trade barrier. China has long been the largest car market in the world. The *Financial Times* reported that 23.8 million units of passenger vehicles were sold in China in 2018, approximately 30 per cent of total global sales (Hancock, 2019a). In order to protect local auto-makers from international competition, China enacted various policies that impeded access to its market. It placed high tariffs on imported vehicles and parts. Moreover, it required foreign car-makers to establish joint ventures with local partners to operate locally. The foreign auto manufacturer was permitted to own a maximum stake of 50 per cent in the joint venture. To gain access to the promising Chinese market without paying the high tariffs, Toyota conducted a joint venture with China FAW Group Corporation (FAW) in 2004 in which Toyota owned 50 per cent. This joint venture was named FAW Toyota Changchun Engine Co. Ltd. (FTCE). FTCE operated in three production sites, Tianjin, Changchun and Sichuan, to manufacture a variety of models: the Vios, the Land Cruiser Prado, the Corolla, the Crown, the Coaster and the RAV4. GAC Toyota Motor Co. Ltd. (GAC Toyota), a 50–50 joint venture between Toyota and Guangzhou Automobile Group Co. Ltd. (GAC), was established in the same year. GAC Toyota had three plants and produced and sold the Camry, the Yaris, the Highlander and the Levin. In 2018, Toyota produced roughly 1.16 million and sold 1.47 million vehicles (*South China Morning Post*, 2019). The widespread popularity of the Corolla, the Levin and the Camry contributed substantially to the strong sales. While China had instituted stiff trade barriers to foreign auto manufacturers, after it joined APEC in 1991 and the WTO in 2001, the nation was working towards completely opening its auto market in order to fulfil its accession commitments. China gradually eased restrictions on foreign capital. To facilitate its operations in China, Toyota started a marketing support company, Toyota Motor (China) Investment Co. Ltd., to provide sales and customer service training for employees as well as to manage matters related to advertising, sales and public relations. To further complement the operations of its joint ventures, Toyota established Toyota Motor Finance China Co. Ltd. to offer automobile finance services such as auto loans. Regarding the joint venture regulation, in 2018, China announced that it would fully eliminate the limit on foreign ownership in the next five years (PWC, 2018). To take advantage of the improved market access, Toyota decided to accelerate the push into China and would potentially raise its stakes in the joint ventures. In 2018, Bloomberg reported that Toyota aimed to triple its car production in China by 2030 (Sano, 2018). Toyota planned to invest an additional 242 billion yuan to boost production and increase sales in China. Reuters reported that its scheme was to build new assembly plants and expand sales networks, as well as develop cutting-edge electric vehicle (EV) technologies (Shirouzu, 2018). With regard to tariffs, in 2006, China reduced import tariffs for completed cars from 80–100 per cent to 25 per cent and for parts from 35 per cent to 10 per cent. On 1 July 2018, it further cut import tariffs to 15 per cent for vehicles and 6 per cent for parts. In response to the better market access, Toyota lowered the prices for its Lexus exported from Japan to China by roughly 27,000 yuan on the same day in an attempt to attract more customers, causing Lexus sales to climb nearly 40 per cent compared to June 2018 (Nakamura and Fukao, 2018).

While the improved market accesses to Thailand and China promoted Toyota's global expansion, beginning in the 1960s, the foreign trade and capital liberalization in Japan intensified the competition in the country's automotive industry and motivated Japanese car-makers to reorganize the industry and improve productivity to gain international competitiveness. On a wave of consolidations and collaborations, in 1966, Toyota established a cooperative partnership with Hino Motors (Hino) to enhance competitiveness and thereby expand market shares. Following the alliance, Hino and Toyota focused on large trucks and lighter vehicles, respectively (Toyoda, 1987). The two companies cooperated to plan and design new products, streamline procurement, manufacture and sales, and improve technologies. Toyota formed a similar alliance with Daihatsu Motor (Daihatsu) in 1967 (Toyota, 2012b). These partnerships made Toyota a well-rounded car-maker that provided a wide range of models, from mini vehicles to commercial trucks. In the twenty-first century, fierce competition in the global automotive industry and massive capital needs required for the R&D of innovative technology provoked another wave of restructuring. Toyota acquired full control of Daihatsu in 2016 (Kubota, 2016) and expanded strategic partnerships with a number of firms, such as Mazda Motor in 2017 and Subaru Corp in 2019 (Toyota, 2019a), to maximize resource utilization in research and production.

The impacts of economic environments

The overall trend in economic growth was a principal determinant of Toyota's performance. As people's disposable income and consumer spending correlated closely with

(Continued)

(Continued)

economic growth, the demand for Toyota's products fluctuated with the business cycle. Since the 1950s, Japan started to recover from World War II and a consequent economic recession. It grew at an astonishingly rapid pace – later referred to as the 'Japanese economic miracle'. The Korean War triggered the fast recovery as Japan, the nearest country to the battlefront, served as a main supplier of goods for the war. The government's effective economic reforms, including a policy of complete industrialization, also contributed to Japan's revival. After a period of fast expansion, Japan's economy continued growing steadily for the most part and remained one of the top economies in the world. In 2019, Japan was ranked the third largest economy by GDP by the **International Monetary Fund (IMF)**, following the United States and China. As a result of the booming economy, people's disposable income increased tremendously, and more people could afford cars – a once luxurious dream. To satisfy the continuously increasing car demand, Toyota endeavoured to enhance its production network, including building new plants such as the Teiho Plant in Toyota City, expanding existing capabilities, and introducing a flexible body line employing both general-purpose and specialized machinery. In the flexible body line, only specialized machinery needed to be switched when working on a new model, which substantially reduced the preparation time for production. Similarly, China's auto market expanded dramatically as the economy boomed after a series of economic reforms in the 1970s. In response to the growing demand in China, Toyota eliminated aged production lines and constructed new lines to increase production capacity and efficiency. In 2019, the combined annual capacity at Toyota's six plants in China was upgraded to over 1.36 million units as a result (Toyota, 2019a). Furthermore, to ensure prompt fulfilment of consumer demand, Toyota made joint investments with FAW and GAC to create a logistics network. The firm consolidated logistics operations to reduce cost and maximize efficiency.

While the steady growth of the economy and consumer spending supported Toyota's expansion, the company also faced severe challenges due to economic contractions. The aftermath of World War II devastated the Japanese economy and placed Toyota on the brink of bankruptcy. In 1949, faltering demand caused the financially distressed company to report a loss of 35 million yen (Daito, 2000). It was forced to cut personnel and delay wage payments. The special demand for Toyota's trucks, as a result of the outbreak of the Korean War in 1950, came to a rescue. The United States army's order of approximately 5,000 vehicles from Toyota, totalling 3.66 billion yen, saved the company from insolvency (Toyota, 2012b). At the G5 summit in 1986, central banks decided to intervene in currency markets to correct the trade deficit for the United States, and the yen over-appreciated significantly as a consequence. Subsequently, Toyota's products were less competitive in the global market and its operating profit suffered a severe hit. In FY1986, the company's operating income dropped by 34.9 per cent to 329.3 billion yen (Toyota, 2012a). Toyota responded to the crises through several cost reduction measures. For example, space-saving robots were employed to weld major parts, and spare parts were stored in a centralized inventory instead of at separate plants. Another major disruption to the Japanese economy was the 2008 financial crisis. In Q1 2009, Japan's GDP declined at an annualized rate of 15.2 per cent. The yen appreciated as investors rushed to purchase yen not only because they needed to unwind their yen short carry trade positions but also because they considered yen a safe haven (Takenaka, 2019). Toyota was under pressure to cut costs and improve profitability. The company scaled back production in Japan and planned to shift production away from Japan to overseas sites such as Thailand and China. Instead of permanently closing production facilities in Japan, Toyota suspended some assembly lines and ran some plants below full capacity (Soble, 2010). The yen buoyed again in 2019 due to the escalating trade tensions between the United States and China, causing Toyota to trim earnings forecasts and pursue cost reduction efforts (Tajitsu and Buckland, 2019).

Opportunities and challenges presented by natural environments

A major challenge for Toyota to operate in the Japanese market was that Japan lacked natural resources and relied greatly on imports. Between 2014 and 2019, raw material imports in Japan averaged 0.4 trillion yen (Trading Economics, 2019). Although the trade liberalization as part of the economic transformation removed some trade barriers and facilitated the supply of raw materials such as scrap metal, the heavy reliance on imports was still costly.

Therefore, Toyota was dedicated to maximizing the efficient use of limited resources. It developed the **just-in-time (JIT)** inventory system to eliminate waste, commonly referred to as the Toyota Production System (TPS). It purchased necessary quantities of raw goods only after receiving new orders from customers and did not hold a safety inventory. The JIT system maintained low levels of inventory and provided for cost-effective production (Low, 1997). It required less warehouse space for raw material storage, cut inventory costs thanks to less excess materials, and reduced waste from materials expiring or becoming outdated. It was later implemented at Toyota's overseas plants during its global expansion. In 2018, Toyota established the TPS group to administer the cost reduction measures in its production system. It was adopted by numerous global corporations like Dell and McDonald's (Singh and Kaur, 2018). One shortcoming of the JIT system was that it relied on supply chain resilience and efficiency to ensure timely delivery of adequate inventory. Severe flooding in Thailand

(Continued)

(Continued)

caused a significant disruption to Toyota's supply chain in 2011. Since Toyota did not hold safety inventory, it experienced a shortage of parts and suspended production at all three plants in Thailand for weeks. According to the *Financial Times*, Toyota estimated 150,000 units of lost production and its Q2 2011 net income plummeted by 18.5 per cent to 80.4 billion yen, significantly below analysts' forecast of 103.5 billion yen. Its share price dropped 22 per cent as a result (Whipp, 2011). Toyota resumed operations after 42 days.

Unlike Japan, China was known for its abundant natural resources. It dominated the supply of key materials used in the production of EV batteries like lithium. In order to secure stable access to the raw materials needed for lithium batteries, in 2019, Toyota partnered with the Chinese multinationals Contemporary Amperex Technology Co. Ltd. (CATL) and BYD Company Ltd. (BYD), the world's top lithium battery suppliers. To further strengthen the business tie, Toyota established a joint company with BYD to start researching and developing battery EVs and related parts in 2020.

Various factors related to the natural environment could impact a company's businesses. While resource abundance in China apparently facilitated Toyota's development of EVs, the firm was able to contain the negative impact of Japan's lack of raw material by implementing a cost-effective inventory system. On the other hand, an unanticipated natural disaster caused the unprepared company substantial damage.

Technological environments and Toyota's R&D efforts

A pivotal contributor to Japan's economic growth was the nation's dedication to technological innovation. The government supported private sector R&D through various measures, such as issuing R&D tax credits (Goto and Kazuyuki, 2009) and forming a national innovation system to promote university–industry partnerships (Kondo, 2009). Japan's R&D expenditure was 3.2 per cent of its GDP in 2017, higher than most of the top economic entities. Corporate expenditure accounted for 70 per cent of total expenditure (OECD, 2019). The technological environment in Japan encouraged Toyota to invest in in-house R&D to gain a competitive advantage and promote its image as a technological leader. In FY2019, Toyota spent 1.05 trillion yen – 3.5 per cent of its net revenue – on R&D (Toyota, 2019a). Some examples included the in-house development of electronic components and semiconductors that had historically been sourced to external suppliers and the invention of hybrid technologies that enhanced vehicles' fuel efficiency. In 2017, Toyota partnered with Panasonic to research and develop industry-leading high-capacity, high-output automotive prismatic batteries. As the development and application of AI technology progressed in Japan, in October 2019 Toyota introduced an AI programme named 'Yui', which delivered a personalized driving experience by learning the driver's facial expressions and through conversations with Yui and responding to his or her unique needs and preferences (Chang, 2019). As of September 2018, Toyota had approximately 260,000 granted patents and 940,000 patent applications, mainly in areas of semiconductor devices, pictorial communication, direct conversion of chemical to electrical energy, etc. Toyota's investment in in-house R&D promoted by the encouraging technological environment in Japan helped the firm gain a competitive advantage in the global market by introducing products with cutting-edge technologies.

Toyota's endeavours to innovate and advance industry-leading technologies were further supported by China's favourable technological environment. The massive amount of data on driving behaviour and road conditions gathered in the Chinese market greatly facilitated the development and testing of new technologies. For instance, training the aforementioned AI algorithm Yui required big data on numerous drivers' driving patterns. Moreover, support from the Chinese government for new energy vehicles (NEVs) also promoted R&D activities. China classified plug-in hybrid EVs, battery EVs and fuel-cell EVs as NEVs. The country was under pressure to meet its objective of achieving 2 million annual sales of NEVs by 2020 in its endeavours to reduce carbon emissions. NEVs were exempt from vehicle and vessel as well as purchase taxes, and the government provided direct subsidies for NEV manufacturers and consumers (Heller, 2017). Three of Toyota's four Asian R&D centres were located in China. Toyota and its local partners – GAC and FAW – jointly invested in the R&D sites. The principal R&D activities included the design, development and evaluation of EVs and EV components. Through the joint ventures, Toyota aimed to produce 400,000 eco-friendly cars per year (Kawakami, 2019). To strengthen its EV research and production, Toyota was also seeking to construct a new battery plant with an annual capacity of 100,000 batteries by 2021.

Trends and challenges in political and social environments

As motorization in Asia progressed, people's needs started to diversify. The change in consumer demographics and lifestyle trends once posed a major challenge to Toyota's market share in Japan. The percentage of young drivers and female drivers increased in the 1990s. Toyota's product offerings initially failed to attract these user groups and

(Continued)

(Continued)

its market share fell below 40 per cent for the first time in 1996. To remediate this issue, Toyota decided to customize its product design, marketing efforts and operations. The company adopted a principle of developing various models targeted at different consumer groups. For example, due to people's growing eco-awareness, the demand for fuel-efficient cars trended up in recent years. In response, Toyota has invested heavily in the research and development of environmentally friendly cars such as the Prius and the Aqua. These two models were ranked as the top two best-selling cars in Japan in 2016 (Bekker, 2017). Toyota used Thailand as the production base for EVs in order to benefit from the Thai government's substantial tax incentives for green vehicles. Investments in hybrid EVs would be entitled to 'an import tariff exemption for relevant machinery' (Rastogi, 2018). Investments in plug-in hybrid EVs could avail of three-year corporate tax exemptions, in addition to the tariff exemption for machinery. Investments in battery EVs were eligible for five to eight years of corporate income tax exemptions plus tariff exemption for key components. Further, for companies producing EVs and parts in the EEC zone, the corporation tax would be further reduced by 50 per cent for five years. In 2017, Toyota committed to an investment of 19 billion baht to produce hybrid EVs at its facility in Chachoengsao located in the EEC zone. The plants started production in 2018. In 2019, Toyota initiated a 21 billion baht project to produce plug-in hybrid and battery EVs (Maikaew, 2019). It planned to produce 7,000 hybrid EVs per year as well as manufacture 70,000 batteries and 9.1 million units of other parts. Another example was Toyota's plan for its fifth generation RAV4 debuted in 2018. Toyota offered 'gasoline-only and hybrid versions with two-wheel- and four-wheel-drive power trains targeting activity- and family-oriented people in their 30s to 40s' (*Japan Times*, 2019). In December 2019, the RAV4 won the 'Japan Car of the Year' award, the most prestigious car prize in Japan (Lyon, 2019). Moreover, the company ran television commercials and published advertising articles in women's magazines. Toyota's ongoing efforts to offer a wide range of high-quality, affordable passenger cars customized for different consumer groups helped establish its predominant market position in Asia. These measures successfully helped Toyota regain its pre-eminence in Asia amidst changing social environments.

A noteworthy obstacle for Toyota's expansion into China was the political relationship between Tokyo and Beijing. In 2012, the disputes over the claim of Diaoyu Island between the two governments provoked a boycott of Japanese goods in the Chinese market. Toyota suspended production at some plants. Its sales in September 2012 plunged by 48.9 per cent year-over-year (*The Guardian*, 2012). Since then, the company has endeavoured to mitigate risks stemming from the sporadic eruptions of anti-Japan sentiment among Chinese consumers. Toyota shifted its sales focus to southern China, as market analysis showed that anti-Japan sentiment was weaker in the south (*South China Morning Post*, 2013). This shift was practical as Toyota had a major production site in Guangdong Province. In the long run, Toyota sought to maintain a stable, friendly relationship with Beijing through various measures, such as granting royalty-free access to its patented hybrid car engine technologies and sharing expertise with Chinese car-makers.

Final remarks

The diverse macro-economic environments and market access conditions in different Asian countries required Toyota to enact different expansion strategies based on various scenarios. The firm formed alliances with regional partners to achieve economies of scale from sharing infrastructure and resources as well as to facilitate the efficient exchange of business knowledge. In order to fulfil surging demands, Toyota was prompt to upgrade its facilities and enhance its production capabilities. During an economic downturn, the firm halted production at selected plants and ran below full capacity in response to the dropping demand. When encountering shifting consumer demographics and preferences, Toyota introduced new products and specific marketing campaigns targeted at different consumer groups. To cope with dissimilar market access levels, the company enacted distinctive plans to enter foreign markets. For example, to take advantage of Thailand's auto industry investment incentives, it moved a substantial amount of manufacturing activities to Thailand and turned it into a key production and exporting hub. To gain access to the Chinese market and avoid the stiff tariff burden, Toyota established joint ventures with local car-makers to operate in China. As the market access conditions changed, it acted quickly to adapt its operations accordingly, e.g. expanding green-vehicle R&D investments in China to benefit from the tax breaks and government subsidies. The diverse market expansion conditions in Asian countries created different opportunities for Toyota, and Toyota successfully planned its cross-border business activities to exploit these opportunities and obtained pre-eminence in the Asian markets. While this case study focused on its largest three Asian battlefields – Japan, Thailand and China – Toyota also had a predominant presence in other Asian countries such as India, Malaysia, etc. In these countries, it also adopted different expansion strategies based on the trade and investment conditions.

Although Toyota's expansion had mostly been victorious, the company also encountered obstructions originating in the macro-economic environments. Toyota enacted effective strategies to cope with the predicted obstacles. For instance, to cope with the lack of natural resources and the high cost of imported raw materials, it developed the well-known and widely utilized JIT system to eliminate inventory waste and ensure cost effectiveness. However, in the face of unanticipated events such as the flooding in Thailand and the nationalist boycott of Japanese goods in China, it also suffered from significant losses.

(Continued)

(Continued)

Case questions

1   How did the diverse macro-economic environments in different Asian countries influence Toyota's expansion strategies? Please list some examples.
2   How did the market access conditions differ in Thailand and China? What were Toyota's strategies to enter these markets?
3   What were some of the challenges that the macro-economic environments in the Asian countries cause Toyota? What were the consequences and how did Toyota respond?

4.4 STRATEGIC IMPLICATIONS

This chapter has centred on how market access differs from one country to another and has demonstrated how free trade agreements and other forms of market integration impact firms' market expansion. We have explored the key aspects that define the business environment in Asia's main market and MNE locations. International business and marketing decisions are deep-rooted in the opportunity and cost analysis of the location. The continent's overall variations of economic inequalities are slowly reducing yet remain significant depending on where a company strategically positions it business, and to what extent that is based on motivations and capabilities: what would the firm like to do, and what is it capable of doing?

We have demonstrated that not every company looks to do business in highly developed wealthy markets, but there are many benefits from exploring less developed and emerging economies, and in particular, utilizing a multi-country strategy. The latter is increasingly facilitated through market integration, where economies get together to reduce tariff and non-tariff barriers and make cross-border trade and investment easier and more accessible to help business help economies to grow and thrive.

The New Hope Group case study illustrates the advantages and disadvantages of diverse regulatory environments that companies do business in, and how market integration through free trade agreements alters the opportunities and costs that shape international business, both on a macro and micro level. It also provides us with indications regarding the impact of the political and social environment on business strategy.

The case study focused on Toyota then provides an additional viewpoint on practices in adapting business decisions to best suit these countries' various business conditions including levels of market access, economic environments, natural environments, technological environments, and political and social environments. Again, how can companies best benefit from the dynamics of the Asian markets while dealing with the diversity of business conditions of a range of countries, and utilize the region as the backbone of its international operations?

The capacity to learn and adapt is a pivotal capability. There is no pan-Asian harmonized business environment. Yet there are more and more companies that extend their capabilities as they use Asia as their pivotal home or host region. Within a resource-based view of the multinational, we learn that valuable, rare, inimitable resources and organization (VRIO) lead to competitive advantage. Certain behavioural orientations towards integration, reconfiguration, renewal and recreation of a company's resources and capabilities throughout its internationalization, with continuous adapting of core capabilities to adjust to the changing environments, help a firm's competitiveness and survival. These capabilities are dynamic, to deal with the variations in the region.

Internalization theory and its application to the emerging market multinationals sheds even further light on strategic implications within this context. Internalization theory (introduced previously in Chapter 2, section 2.1) serves to describes multinationals' exploitation of outstanding, unique, rare knowledge directly abroad. EMNEs have been found to seek strategic assets while exploiting cost or political or financial advantages at home. Among other strategies, they will seek market expansion through often mid-level technology at fixed costs and prove their agility – at times through divestiture or relocation – when this cannot be maintained. Also, their competencies in operating in difficult institutional environments have been found to be particularly advantageous for market expansion across and beyond the region. The most recent research findings in the field of internalization theory indicate that companies can seek to internalize knowledge from abroad or foreign knowledge (Casson and Wadeson, 2018).

Both case studies in this chapter have demonstrated this to different extents. The case of New Hope illustrated how EMNEs accelerated their internationalization through bilateral trade activities. In China, the 2008 milk scandal painted a bad impression of domestic food products among customers, which tremendously increased the demand for foreign ones. Many local customers scrambled to buy imported commodities through cross-border e-commerce platforms or personal channels. These products were viewed as high-quality, safe and reliable, albeit with higher prices. To reduce product prices and regulate the food market, the Chinese government sped up negotiations and signed several FTAs with main trade partners including Australia and New Zealand. This also prompted Chinese companies to 'go global' and located their subsidiaries in developed countries to 'orchestrate' their global production network. New Hope was a typical example.

Compared to its advanced economy MNE (AMNE) counterparts, New Hope, as an EMNE pursuing geographic diversification, was inferior in terms of technological and managerial experience and lacked high-standard raw materials at home. But it had strong firm specific advantages based on abundant market experience. In international business, a firm's competitive advantages largely depended on its ability to recombine CSAs and mobilize its FSAs (Verbeke and Kano, 2015). China's FTAs with Australia and New Zealand opened a window for New Hope to exploit market complementarity and expanded its agricultural value chain. Investments in these two countries were important since they reduced the exposure to safety and quality risks and facilitated capturing advanced technologies. Accordingly, New Hope mainly invested in the up-stream industries, such as acquiring KPC and PGW, and agricultural technologies, such as acquiring ANC and cooperating with AgResearch.

However, it was not easy to enter into and survive in developed countries. EMNEs faced dual liabilities – 'liability of foreignness' and 'liability of origin'. These competitive disadvantages often led to investment failure. Specifically, the average success rate of **cross-border M&As** by Chinese companies was only 67 per cent, below that of AMNEs (BCG, 2015). But New Hope has successfully invested more than seven affiliations in Oceania. This could be attributed to the bilateral FTAs, a country-level trade protocol, and ASA100, an industry-level **strategic alliance**. ASA100 built a bridge between leading agricultural companies in Australia and China and, most importantly, promoted cooperation among these companies, which helped New Hope to build trust and mitigate liabilities in this region.

The New Hope case also provided an example of how AMNEs managed locality advantages in emerging markets. Because of the enormous market size and the rapid growth rate, emerging markets have attracted thousands of AMNEs to conduct business there. In certain situations, the traded products' country-of-origin (e.g. dairy products mentioned in the case) was a source of advantages that supported AMNEs' internationalization (Cuervo-Cazurra et al., 2018). This was referred to as 'country-of-origin advantages' (COAs). FTAs could augment such advantages as bilateral tariff cuts reduced the prices of imported products and then boosted their sales in host countries. Many foreign Australia and New Zealand-based companies gained substantially in China after tariff adjustment.

Doing business in emerging markets, however, was challenging because of the weak, variable institutions and complex economic environment. Many AMNEs collaborated with local partners, considering that their market knowledge was inadequate. Fonterra, for example, used to cooperate with Chinese partners including Sanlu, a 'protagonist' of the 2008 milk scandal. Any misconduct by the business partner could be magnified internationally and by association; Fonterra could bring unanticipated damage to its own brand name. Meanwhile, emerging markets have become new battlegrounds for international business (Peng, 2001), thus making the competitive environment harsher. Non-government bilateral trade initiatives, such as ASA100, acted as a funnel to sieve out better partners for AMNEs and advanced the flows of market knowledge. For example, New Hope has engaged to promote the brand of Real Pet Food in China.

Similarly, Toyota also benefited from FTAs. Since Toyota established its first wholly own subsidiary (WOS) in 1962, Thailand has gradually become a key production and exporting hub. The reasons for this location decision could be as follows. First, Thailand, as a founding member of the ASEAN, had CSAs in terms of **geo-politics**, labour costs and natural resources. Toyota effectively compensated its cost liabilities originating from high labour rates and a lack of raw materials such as scrap metal at home. Second, Thailand has been committed to removing trade barriers, improving market access conditions, and attracting foreign investments through a series of tariff and non-tariff measures (e.g. establishing the special economic zone EEC). The JTEPA signed in 2008 also optimized the investment environment. These favourable conditions reduced trade and investment costs and prompted Toyota to recombine its FSAs. Hence, Toyota paid more attention to R&D at home, while regarding Thailand as one of its manufacturing centres. Third, locating in Thailand was a 'springboard' to enter into other ASEAN markets. This was because the AFTA provided that car-makers operating in Thailand could pay zero or significantly reduced tariffs to export automobiles to other member nations.

The Toyota case was especially conducive to discussing the impacts of a dynamic and variable institutional environment in the emerging markets on AMNEs' entry modes. In 1962, when the ban was lifted, Toyota entered into Thailand with a WOS, a mode with a high degree of control that allowed Toyota to protect its core technologies. In contrast, before 2001, when China joined the WTO, there were high tariffs on imported vehicles and strict regulations governing foreign capitals. Conducting joint ventures with Chinese partners such as FAW and GAC became an appropriate strategic option. Products made by JVs – Corolla, Levin and Lexus, to name but a few examples – were popular due to the reduction in price and the COAs associated with Japanese auto manufacturing. With the relaxation of restrictions, Toyota built its supporting subsidiaries to complement the operation of JVs, raised its stake in JVs, and increased investments in both assembly plants and cutting-edge EV technologies in China. These actions accelerated its expansion in China and expanded its sales network.

Besides, this case provoked thought on the strategic agility for MNEs. According to internalization theorists, FSAs could be viewed as knowledge bundles that took the form of intangible assets (e.g. technology and know-how), innovation capabilities, and relationships with outside actors (Rugman and Verbeke, 2003). But FSAs were not fixed. MNEs needed to orchestrate or recombine their FSAs dynamically in a fast-moving business environment (Pitelis and Teece, 2018; Narula et al., 2019). Toyota to some extent demonstrated these. First, the company has formed stable and long-standing strategic alliances with Hino and Daihatsu respectively since the 1960s and has sought to expand strategic partnerships with a number of firms such as Mazda Motor and Subaru Corp. These alliances helped Toyota to focus on its core technologies, acquire new technologies and accelerate the commercialization of new products. Second, it created a set of manufacturing systems, commonly referred to as JIT or TPS and since adopted by many well-known global companies such as Dell and McDonald. Third, Toyota made efforts to maintain a stable, friendly relationship with Beijing. It made good sense noting the 'liability' of Toyota's 'country-of-origin' arising from the past Sino-Japan war (Gao et al., 2018). Also, some recent political events, like the China–Japan disputes over Diaoyu Island, intensified the national animosity and impeded Toyota's sales in China. But Toyota coped with these through patent license, **technology transfer** and relocation in South China.

Finally, the case of Toyota also indicated that national innovation systems and the technological environment in both home and host countries could effectively support MNEs' R&D activities and improve their technological capabilities. Japan was one of the most innovative countries in the world, with favourable conditions to engage in in-house R&D activities. It was thus unsurprising that Toyota still maintained Japan as its primary R&D site to drive important innovation. The distinctive and disparate market characteristics in emerging markets were also conducive for MNEs to enhance their innovation capabilities; Thailand and China were prime examples as shown in the Toyota case. AMNEs could also gain from the innovation policies in emerging economies. The Chinese government, for example, recently supported the development of NEVs through direct subsidies and tax cuts for both consumers and car-makers; this greatly strengthened Toyota's ability to research and produce EVs.

REFERENCES

ABC News (2015a) Australia and China sign 'history making' free trade agreement after a decade of negotiations. Available at: www.abc.net.au/news/2015-06-17/australia-and-china-sign-free-trade-agreement/6552940 (accessed 18 April 2019).

ABC News (2015b) Two of Australia's biggest dairy farming families, the Moxeys and Perichs, form a dairy consortium backed by Chinese investmnet. Available at: www.abc.net.au/news/rural/2015-04-28/moxey-farms-consortium-new-hope-dairy/6428248 (accessed 10 April 2019).

ABC News (2017a) New Hope Group backs Australian agriculture, plans to invest $1b by 2020. Available at: www.abc.net.au/news/2017-02-02/meet-the-chinese-billionaire-backing-australian-agriculture/8191408 (accessed 10 April 2019).

ACB News (2017b) AFMH acquires more farms: Mega dairy company expands aggressively. Available at: http://m.acbnews.com.au/html/2017/companynews_0515/18950.html (accessed 18 April 2019).

ACB News (2018) New Hope's first Australian beef project scored high. Available at: www.acbnews.com.au/azjujiao/20180125-22594.html (accessed 18 April 2019).

ASA100 Official Website (2019) Available at: www.asa100.net.au (accessed 1 April 2019).

Asia Perspective (2014) China's Increasing Appetite for Imported Food and Beverages. Available at: http://asiaperspective.net/2014/03/19/chinas-increasing-appetite-imported-food-beverages/ (accessed 10 April 2019).

Australian Government, Department of Foreign Affairs and Trade (2014) ChAFTA fact sheet: Agriculture and Food. Available at: https://dfat.gov.au/trade/agreements/in-force/chafta/fact-sheets/Pages/chafta-fact-sheet-agriculture-and-processed-food.aspx (accessed 10 April 2019).

Australian Government, Department of Foreign Affairs and Trade (2016) Guide to using ChAFTA to export or import. Available at: https://dfat.gov.au/trade/agreements/in-force/chafta/doing-business-with-china/Pages/guide-to-using-chafta-to-export-or-import.aspx [Accessed 18 April 2019].

Australian Government, Department of Foreign Affairs and Trade (2018) ChAFTA outcomes at a glance. Available at: https://dfat.gov.au/trade/agreements/in-force/chafta/fact-sheets/Pages/chafta-outcomes-at-a-glance.aspx (accessed 10 April 2019).

Banalieva, E.R. and Santoro, M.D. (2009) Local, regional, or global? Geographic orientation and relative financial performance of emerging market multinational enterprises, *European Management Journal*, 27(5): 344–355.

Barua, A. (2017) Asia's retail spending boom: Shoppers go on a frenzy and why not? *Asia Pacific Economic Outlook*, Deloitte University Press, 28 March. Available at: www2.deloitte.com/insights/us/en/economy/asia-pacific-economic-outlook/2017/q2-asia-retail-spending-boom.html

BBC News (2013) China bans New Zealand milk powder in botulism scare. Available at: www.bbc.com/news/world-asia-23565651 (accessed 1 June 2019).

BBC News Chinese (2014) ChAFTA: Praise outweights criticism from Australia. Available at: www.bbc.com/zhongwen/simp/world/2014/11/141117_world_australia_china_deal_opposition (accessed 18 April 2019).

BCG (2015) *Gearing Up for the New Era of China's Outbound M&A*. Available at: http://image-src.bcg.com/Images/BCG-Gearing-Up-New-Era-China-Outbound-MandA-Sep-2015-CHN_tcm55-127562.pdf (accessed 6 April 2020).

BEEF Magazine (2018) With import duty rate tripled, U.S. beef faces even tougher challenge in China. Available at: www.beefmagazine.com/exports/import-duty-rate-tripled-us-beef-faces-even-tougher-challenge-china (accessed 18 April 2019).

Bekker, H. (2017) 2016 (full year) Japan: 30 best-selling car models. Available at: www.best-selling-cars.com/japan/2016-full-year-japan-30-best-selling-car-models/ (accessed 6 April 2020).

Buckley, P.J. (ed.) (2011) *Globalization and the Global Factory*. Cheltenham: Edward Elgar.

Carnegie Endowment for International Peace (2012) Will emerging economies repeat the environmental mistakes of their rich cousins? Available at: https://carnegieendowment.org/2012/03/01/will-emerging-economies-repeat-environmental-mistakes-of-their-rich-cousins-pub-47307 (accessed 31 May 2019).

Casson, M. and Wadeson, N. (2018) Emerging market multinationals and internalization theory. *International Business Review*, 27(6): 1150–1160.

Chang, B. (2019) Toyota has created a car that uses AI to sense a driver's state, and can even wake them up using inflatable cushions or cold air if they're nodding off. Available at: www.businessinsider.com/toyota-has-created-a-concept-car-with-ai-called-yui-2019-10 (accessed 6 April 2020).

China Daily (2016) Infant formula imports skyrocket since scandals. Available at: www.chinadaily.com.cn/china/2016-06/30/content_25911336.htm (accessed 10 April 2019).

China Invests Overseas (2018) China's New Hope Group Acquires Australian Real Pet Food For $770M. Available at: www.china-invests.net/20180119/46300.aspx (accessed 18 April 2019).

Classora Knowledge Base. Ranking of the World's Richest Countries by GDP (1967). Available at: www.en.classora.com.

Cuervo-Cazurra, A., Luo, Y., Ramamurti, R. and Ang, S.H. (2018) The impact of the home country on internationalization. *Journal of World Business*, 53(5): 593–604.

Daito, E. (2000) Automation and the organization of production in the Japanese automobile industry: Nissan and Toyota in the 1950s. *Enterprise and Society*, 1(1): 139–178.

DBS (2011) Imagining Asia 2020: Make Way for the Asia Giant. Available at: www.dbs.com.sg/iwov-resources/article/DBS_IMAGINING_ASIA_2020.pdf (accessed 6 April 2020).

Dun & Bradstreet (2020) Toyota Motor Thailand Company Limited. Available at: www.dnb.com/business-directory/company-profiles.toyota_motor_thailand_company_limited.0d9a8400bbd6d30c1875c3e08337185c.html (accessed 24 April 2020).

Financial Review (2016) China's New Hope buys Australian NaturalCare vitamin group. Available at: www.afr.com/real-estate/chinas-new-hope-buys-australian-naturalcare-vitamin-group-20161006-grw7oq (accessed 10 April 2019).

Focus2move (2019) World's best selling pick-up: The top in 2019. Available at: https://focus2move.com/world-best-selling-pick-up/ (accessed 6 April 2020).

Forbes (2008) China's tainted baby formula scandal widens. Available at: www.forbes.com/2008/09/17/baby-milk-china-bizcx_pm_0917notes.html#76665b02fb7a (accessed 1 June 2019).

Fugazza, M. and Nicita, A. (2011) *On the Importance of Market Access for Trade: Policy Issues in International Trade and Commodities Study Series No. 50*. Geneva: UNCTAD. Available at: https://unctad.org/en/Docs/itcdtab51_en.pdf (accessed 6 April 2020).

Gao, G.Y., Wang, D.T. and Che, Y. (2018) Impact of historical conflict on FDI location and performance: Japanese investment in China. *Journal of International Business Studies*, 49(8): 1060–1080.

Goto, A. and Kazuyuki, M. (2009) Technology policies in Japan: 1990 to the present. In *21st Century Innovation Systems for Japan and the United States: Lessons from a Decade of Change: Report of a Symposium*. Washington, DC: The National Academies Press. doi: 10.17226/12194.

Hancock, T. (2019a) China car sales drop for first time since 1990. *Financial Times*, 14 January. Available at: www.ft.com/content/70d3db5a-17dd-11e9-9e64-d150b3105d21 (accessed 6 April 2020).

Hancock, T. (2019b) Why Ford is stalling in China while Toyota succeeds. *Financial Times*, 4 March. Available at: www.ft.com/content/6fd5a4c4-36c1-11e9-bd3a-8b2a211d90d5 (accessed 6 April 2020).

Heller, M. (2017) Chinese government support for new energy vehicles as a trade battleground. National Bureau of Asian Research, 27 September. Available at: www.nbr.org/publication/chinese-government-support-for-new-energy-vehicles-as-a-trade-battleground/ (accessed 6 April 2020).

iFeng Finance (2015) China and Australia officially signed FTA: 97% Australian exports to China face zero tarriff. Available at: http://finance.ifeng.com/a/20150617/13783122_0.shtml (accessed 10 April 2019).

IMF (International Monetary Fund) (2018) *World Economic Outlook*, October. Available at: www.imf.org/en/Publications/WEO/Issues/2018/09/24/world-economic-outlook-october-2018 (accessed 6 April 2020).

IMF DataMapper (2019) World Economic Outlook, International Monetary Fund. Available at: www.imf.org/external/datamapper/NGDPD@WEO/OEMDC/ADVEC/WEOWORLD?year=2019 (accessed 27 March 2020).

International Centre for Trade and Sustainable Development (2015) China's free trade zone strategy enters a new trend of dual tracks Available at: https://www.ictsd.org/bridges-news/%E6%A1%A5/news/%E4%B8%AD%E5%9B%BD%E8%87%AA%E7%94%B1%E8%B4%B8%E6%98%93%E5%8C%BA%E6%88%98%E7%95%A5%E8%BF%9

B%E5%85%A5%E5%8F%8C%E8%BD%A8%E5%B9%B6%E8%BF%9B%E7%9A%84%
E6%96%B0%E6%80%81%E5%8A%BF (accessed 24 April 2020).

Invest in NZ (2011) New Hope Group keen on joint bid with Agria Corp for a 50.1%
in PGG Wrightson. Available at: www.investinnz.co.nz/investmentNZ/2011/03/
new-hope-group-keen-on-joint-bid-with-agria-corp-for-a-50-1-in-pgg-wrightson/
(accessed 27 April 2019).

Japan Times (2019) Remodeled versions of Toyota's popular RAV4 SUV on sale again in
Japan. Available at: www.japantimes.co.jp/news/2019/04/11/business/corporate-
business/remodeled-versions-toyotas-popular-rav4-suv-sale-japan/#.Xffri2RKhaQ
(accessed 6 April 2020).

Kawakami, T. (2019) Toyota gears up to produce 400,000 green vehicles in China.
Available at: https://asia.nikkei.com/Spotlight/Electric-cars-in-China/Toyota-gears-
up-to-produce-400-000-green-vehicles-in-China (accessed 6 April 2020).

Kondo, M. (2009) University–industry partnerships in Japan. In *21st Century
Innovation Systems for Japan and the United States: Lessons from a Decade of Change:
Report of a Symposium*. Washington, DC: The National Academies Press. doi:
10.17226/12194.

Kotani, H. (2017) Toyota supply chain is Exhibit A of deepening ASEAN integration.
Available at: https://asia.nikkei.com/Economy/Toyota-supply-chain-is-Exhibit-A-of-
deepening-ASEAN-integration (accessed 6 April 2020).

KPMG (2018) Demystifying Chinese investment in Australia. Available at: https://
home.kpmg/au/en/home/insights/2018/06/demystifying-chinese-investment-in-
australia-june-2018.html (accessed 30 March 2019).

Kubota, Y. (2016) Toyota to take full control of Daihatsu for about $3 billion. *Wall
Street Journal*, 29 January. Available at: www.wsj.com/articles/toyota-to-take-full-
control-of-daihatsu-for-about-3-billion-1454053859 (accessed 6 April 2020).

Lee, J.W. and Shin, K. (2006) Does regionalism lead to more global trade integration in
East Asia? *North American Journal of Economics and Finance*, 17: 283–301.

Low, S.P. (1997) *Managing Productivity in Construction: JIT Operations and Measurements*.
London: Routledge.

Lyon, P. (2019) Toyota USA's top selling RAV4 wins Japan's biggest car award. *Forbes*,
7 December. Available at: www.forbes.com/sites/peterlyon/2019/12/07/toyotas-top-
selling-rav4-wins-japans-biggest-car-award/#7f80926e772d (accessed 6 April 2020).

Maikaew, P. (2019) Toyota sends EV plans to BoI. *Bangkok Post*, 23 January.
Available at: www.bangkokpost.com/business/1616042/toyota-sends-ev-plans-to-boi
(accessed 6 April 2020).

Marketplace (2018) Foreign infant milk formula still highly coveted in China 10 years
after the melamine scandal. Available at: www.marketplace.org/2018/10/24/world/

foreign-infant-milk-formula-still-highly-coveted-china-10-years-after-melamine (accessed 10 April 2019).

Ministry of Commerce of China (2018) Brief of trade and investment between China and New Zealand. Department of American and Oceanian Affairs. Available at: http://mds.mofcom.gov.cn/article/Nocategory/200210/20021000042985.shtml (accessed 10 April 2019).

Ministry of Foreign Affairs of Japan (2007) *Japan–Thailand Economic Partnership Agreement*. Available at: www.mofa.go.jp/region/asia-paci/thailand/epa0704/agreement.pdf (accessed 6 April 2020).

Nakamura, Y. and Fukao, K. (2018) Toyota emerges as winner in tariff war, for now. Available at: https://asia.nikkei.com/Economy/Trade-war/Toyota-emerges-as-winner-in-tariff-war-for-now (accessed 6 April 2020).

Narula, R. (2012) Do we need different frameworks to explain infant MNEs from developing countries? *Global Strategy Journal*, 2(3): 188–204.

Narula, R., Asmussen, C.G., Chi, T. and Kundu, S.K. (2019) Applying and advancing internalization theory: The multinational enterprise in the twenty-first century. *Journal of International Business Studies*, 50(8): 1231–1252.

New Hope Group Official Website (2016a) Integrating resources in competitive industrial belts. Available at: http://en.newhopegroup.com/az/index.html (accessed 28 April 2019).

New Hope Group Official Website (2016b) New Hope Group set up its Australia-New Zealand Headquarters Available at: www.newhopegroup.com/jtdt2016/Article/201610/ArticleContent_268.html (accessed 10 April 2019).

New Hope Group Official Website (2016c) Why did we go to Australia? Available at: www.newhopegroup.com/zt2016/Article/20166/ArticleContent_131.html (accessed 18 April 2019).

NutraIngredients-Asia (2017) Chinese infant formula boom: Kiwi exports to top NZ$1bn for the first time. Available at: www.nutraingredientsasia.com/Article/2017/10/09/China-infant-formula-boom-Kiwi-exports-to-top-NZ-1bn-for-the-first-time (accessed 10 April 2019).

OECD (Organisation for Economic Co-operation and Development) (2019) Gross domestic spending on R&D (indicator). Available at: https://data.oecd.org/rd/gross-domestic-spending-on-r-d.htm (accessed 12 December 2019).

Oxfam (2017) An economy for the 99%. Briefing Paper, January. Available at: https://d1tn3vj7xz9fdh.cloudfront.net/s3fs-public/file_attachments/bp-economy-for-99-percent-160117-en.pdf (accessed 6 April 2020).

Peng, M.W. (2001) The resource-based view and international business. *Journal of Management*, 27(6): 803–829.

PGW (2018) PGG Wrightson Limited Annual Report 2018. Available at: www. pggwrightson.co.nz/Investors/Company-Reports (accessed 24 April 2020).

Pham, P. (2017) Why is Asia's 99% so poor? *Forbes*, 18 October. Available at: www. forbes.com/sites/peterpham/2017/10/18/why-is-asias-99-so-poor/#1ba24b8023be (accessed 6 April 2020).

Pitelis, C.N. and Teece, D.J. (2018) The new MNE: 'Orchestration' theory as envelope of 'internalisation' theory. *Management International Review*, 58(4): 523–539.

Prihatini, E. (2019) There's no 'silver bullet' in bringing more women to parliament in Asia. *The Conversation*. Available at: https://theconversation.com/theres-no-silver-bullet-in-bringing-more-women-to-parliament-in-asia-108879 (accessed 6 April 2020).

PWC (PricewaterhouseCoopers) (2018) The opening-up of Chinese automotive industry and its impact. Available at: www.pwccn.com/en/industries/automotive/publications/chinese-automotive-industry-opening-up-impact.html (accessed 19 December 2019).

Rastogi, V. (2018) Thailand's automotive industry: Opportunities and incentives. Available at: www.aseanbriefing.com/news/2018/05/10/thailands-automotive-industry-opportunities-incentives.html (accessed 6 April 2020).

Reuters (2019) Thailand's total domestic car sales seen down 3.8 pct in 2019 -Toyota, Available at: https://www.reuters.com/article/toyota-thailand/thailands-total-domestic-car-sales-seen-down-38-pct-in-2019-toyota-idUSL3N1ZL3I5 (accessed 18 April 2019).

Rugman, A.M. (2005) *The Regional Multinationals: MNEs and Global Strategic Management*. Cambridge: Cambridge University Press.

Rugman, A.M. and Li, J. (2007) Will China's multinationals succeed globally or regionally? *European Management Journal*, 25(5): 333–343.

Rugman, A.M. and Oh, C.H. (2010) Does the regional nature of multinationals affect the multinationality and performance relationship? *International Business Review*, 19(5): 479–488.

Rugman, A.M. and Verbeke, A. (2003) Extending the theory of the multinational enterprise: Internalization and strategic management perspectives. *Journal of International Business Studies*, 34(2): 125–137.

Rugman, A.M. and Verbeke, A. (2004) A perspective on regional and global strategies of multinational enterprises, *Journal of International Business Studies*, 35: 3–18.

Rugman, A.M. and Verbeke, A.(2005) Towards a theory of regional multinationals: A transaction cost economics approach, *Management International Review*, 45(1): 5–17.

Sano, N., Inoue, K. and Buckland, K. (2018) Toyota to target tripling China production over next decade. Available at: www.bloomberg.com/news/articles/2018-08-28/toyota-said-to-target-tripling-china-production-over-next-decade (accessed 6 April 2020).

Sethi, D. and Judge, W. (2009) Reappraising liabilities of foreignness within an integrated perspective of the costs and benefits of doing business abroad. *International Business Review*, 18(4): 404–416.

Shirouzu, N. (2018) Toyota to increase production capacity in China by 20 percent: source. Available at: www.reuters.com/article/us-toyota-china/toyota-to-increase-production-capacity-in-china-by-20-percent-source-idUSKBN1L20MD (accessed 6 April 2020).

Singh, C.D. and Kaur, H. (2018) *Evaluating JIT Initiatives in Manufacturing Industry*. Munich: BookRix.

Soble, J. (2010) Toyota to expand overseas production. *Financial Times*, 27 July. Available at: www.ft.com/content/500774ca-99a3-11df-a852-00144feab49a (accessed 6 April 2020).

Sohu Finance (2014) ASA100 memo signed: New Hope Group plans to invest 5 billion in Australia. Available at: http://money.163.com/14/1119/08/ABDDC8M700253B0H.html (accessed 18 April 2019).

Sohu Finance (2019) Statistics of beef imports of China in 2018. Available at: www.sohu.com/a/291450394_100271841 (accessed 18 April 2019).

Sohu News (2013) Confirmed by the customs: Exceeding 5 kilo per package of overseas mailing of infant formula to China will face. Available at: http://news.sohu.com/20130315/n368965563.shtml (accessed 10 April 2019).

South China Morning Post (2013) Toyota weighs options to deal with anti-Japan sentiment in China. Available at: www.scmp.com/business/companies/article/1275293/lingering-tensions-prompt-toyota-mull-shifting-focus-china (accessed 6 April 2020).

South China Morning Post (2019) China's demand for Lexus cars lifts Toyota's third-quarter operating profit higher, but misses forecasts. Available at: www.scmp.com/business/companies/article/2185152/chinas-demand-lexus-cars-lifts-toyotas-third-quarter-operating (accessed 6 April 2020).

Suder, G. (2011) *Doing Business in Europe*, 2nd edn. London: Sage Publications.

Suder, G. and Lindeque, J. (2018) *Doing Business in Europe*, 3rd edn. London: Sage Publications.

Suder, G., Riviere M. and Lindeque, J. (2018) *The Routledge Companion in European Business*. London: Routledge.

Tajitsu, N. and Buckland, K. (2019) Stronger yen prompts Toyota to trim profit forecast, saps Honda. Available at: www.reuters.com/article/us-toyota-results/stronger-yen-prompts-toyota-to-trim-profit-forecast-saps-honda-idUSKCN1US0E2 (accessed 6 April 2020).

Takenaka, M. (2019) The forces fueling the yen's rises and falls. Available at: www.japantimes.co.jp/opinion/2019/05/23/commentary/japan-commentary/forces-fueling-yens-rises-falls/#.XfKEPuhKhaQ (accessed 6 April 2020).

The Australian (2011) Child slavery bust in Vietnam with Australian charity's help. Available at: www.theaustralian.com.au/news/latest-news/child-slavery-bust-in-vietnam-with-australian-chritys-help/news-story/fa70b870685ea7af5250354b86 67e370 (accessed 31 May 2019).

The Diplomat (2014a) China's FTA Strategy. Available at: https://thediplomat. com/2014/06/chinas-fta-strategy/ (accessed 18 April 2019).

The Diplomat (2014b) Feeding the Dragon: Lessons of the New Zealand–China FTA. Available at: https://thediplomat.com/2014/01/feeding-the-dragon-lessons-of-the-new-zealand-china-fta/ (accessed 1 June 2019).

The Guardian (2012) Japanese car sales plunge in China after islands dispute. Available at: www.theguardian.com/business/2012/oct/09/japanese-car-sales-china-islands-dispute (accessed 6 April 2020).

The Hindu (2019) In India, air pollution is the third-highest cause of death among all health risks. Available at: www.thehindu.com/sci-tech/energy-and-environment/over-12m-early-deaths-in-india-in-2017-due-to-air-pollution-report/article26719117.ece (accessed 31 May 2019).

The Nation (2018) Toyota marks Thai production milestone of 10m units. Available at: www.nationthailand.com/Auto_ADO/30349868 (accessed 6 April 2020).

Toyoda, E. (1987) *Toyota: Fifty Years in Motion*. Tokyo: Kodansha International.

Toyota (2012a) A 75-year history through data. Available at: www.toyota-global.com/company/history_of_toyota/75years/data/automotive_business/sales/activity/japan/region/1936.html (accessed 6 April 2020).

Toyota (2012b) A 75-year history through text. Available at: www.toyota-global.com/company/history_of_toyota/75years/text/index.html (accessed 6 April 2020).

Toyota (2019a) Annual Report 2019. Available at: https://global.toyota/pages/global_toyota/ir/library/annual/2019_001_annual_en.pdf (accessed 6 April 2020).

Toyota (2019b) FY2019 Financial Results. Available at: https://global.toyota/en/ir/financial-results/archives/ (accessed 6 April 2020).

Trading Economics (2019) Japan imports of raw materials. Available at: www.tradingeconomics.com/japan/imports-of-raw-materials (accessed 6 April 2020).

Verbeke, A. and Kano, L. (2015) The new internalization theory and multinational enterprises from emerging economies: A business history perspective. *Business History Review*, 89(3): 415–445.

Whipp, L. (2011) Thai floods erode Toyota's profits. *Financial Times*, 8 November. Available at: www.ft.com/content/74941cfa-09e4-11e1-85ca-00144feabdc0 (accessed 6 April 2020).

World Bank (2019) *Global Economic Outlook: Slow Growth, Policy Changes*. Washington DC: World Bank. Available at: www.worldbank.org/en/publication/global-economic-prospects (accessed 6 April 2020).

World's Top Exports (2019) Australia's top trading partners. Available at: www.worldstopexports.com/australias-top-import-partners/ (accessed 18 April 2019).

Xinhua Net (2015) Three minutes to learn about China FTA's liberalization. Available at: www.xinhuanet.com/world/2015-10/08/c_128294953.htm (accessed 18 April 2019).

5

MODES OF ENTRY AND INVESTMENT INTO ASIA

5.1 MODES OF ENTRY AND INVESTMENT

This chapter focuses on modes of entry and investment that companies use to enter Asia or venture across Asian markets. This includes:

- an introduction to modes of entry and investment
- a case study focused on the example of Mahindra & Mahindra, with its local optimizer strategy
- a case study on Volkswagen's Asia entry modes and its strategic responses to institutional influences
- a conclusion with final remarks about strategic implications.

Entry mode is the specific path chosen by MNEs to enter a foreign market. As you read in Chapter 2, choice of entry mode is a crucial strategic decision involving different degrees of resource commitment, organizational control, risks and expected returns. This chapter elaborates on the various issues faced by MNEs in making the choice of different modes of foreign market entry.

Modes of entry fall into three categories – trade-related, investment-related, and contractual or transfer-related entry modes.

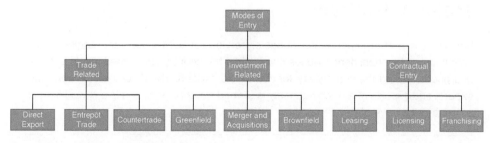

Figure 5.1   Modes of foreign market entry

Trade-related entry modes

Trade is usually the first step taken by an MNE to enter a foreign market. Trade-related entry modes refer to foreign market entry through the purchase and sale of goods and services across national borders. Traditionally, firms venturing abroad for the first time typically use trade as their mode of entry. Trade-related entry modes include exporting, entrepôt trade and countertrade.

Exporting

Exporting is the first step in a firm's international venturing in which it maintains its production facilities at home and sells its products abroad. This requires relatively low investment and, therefore, carries low risk as well. Trade operations help the firm to gain valuable experience about operating in an unknown international market and also specific knowledge in the context of the individual countries in which it begins operations.

Trade as a mode of foreign market entry may be used by firms of any size as compared to other entry modes which demand greater resources and are riskier. Over a period of time, accumulated experience with exporting helps a firm to consider more aggressive and involved forms of international venturing such as FDI. It is often seen that firms continue to use trade as a mode of entry, along with other higher forms of foreign market entry. For instance, Toyota (Japan) has used FDI as its mode of entry in several countries of Asia, where it established production bases, and it has then used these locations to export its cars to other neighbouring regions. Toyota made its India entry in 1997 through a joint venture with the Kirloskar group, which is among India's pioneering business groups (Toyota, 2019). It established two manufacturing units in the southern state of Karnataka and started the export of the Etios car and service parts and accessories to South Africa in 2012. It also began exporting automobile parts to Brazil and Indonesia in the same year using the manufacturing unit as its base (Toyota, 2012).

Trade definitions

Firms may export or import either goods or services or both. Goods are tangible products that can be seen; hence, goods coming into the country are termed visible imports and goods leaving the country are termed visible exports. The difference between the exports and imports of a given economy is termed trade balance and is a crucial item in a country's balance of payments.

Services are intangible products that form a large component of economic activity in both advanced and emerging markets. Services include transport, travel, communications services, insurance and financial services, computer and information services, royalties and license fees, other business services (merchanting, operational leasing, technical and professional services), and cultural and recreational services.

Source: Varma (2012)

Emerging economy service exports have grown at twice the rate of exports from advanced economies over the past few decades. This growth has been driven by the Asian region, in particular China, which is now the world's fourth largest services exporter. Hong Kong, India and the Philippines have also contributed to the rapid growth of exports and are net providers of traded services (Richards, 2019). Tourism, for instance, is a major foreign exchange earner for Asian countries like Thailand, Indonesia and Sri Lanka. The services sector has been responsible for the growth of India's GDP in the last two decades, primarily through the contribution of the knowledge intensive information technology sector.

Trade facts

Value of world merchandise trade: US$ 19.67 trillion
World's leading merchandise trader: China
Value of world trade in commercial services: US$ 5.63 trillion
Information and communication technology recorded the highest export growth (15 per cent) among services sectors, led by computer services
Growth in world exports of computer services: 17 per cent
China was the leading exporter of commercial services (by value) among developing countries, with exports increasing by 17%
Bangladesh and Myanmar have continued to remain in the list of the top five LDC merchandise traders from 2008 to 2018
Cambodia has remained in the list of the top five LDCs for commercial services.

Source: WTO, 2019

Direct exporting, in the initial stages of foreign market entry, is where the sales department of the firm simply handles foreign sales in addition to domestic sales. When the business grows sufficiently, a separate department or division is set up to handle sales in a foreign market. The firm may later set up a sales office or a subsidiary in the foreign market for marketing and distribution activities. Direct exporting gives exporters greater control over the export process and helps them to develop a close relationship with foreign buyers. It also needs a greater commitment of human resources, finance and time.

Indirect exporting is the sale of goods in foreign lands through different kinds of export, commission agents or intermediaries based in both the home and foreign market. Export intermediaries are third parties who specialize in facilitating imports and exports. Their services may be limited, such as transportation, documentation and customs claims, or they may perform more extensive services, including taking ownership of foreign-bound goods and marketing and financing functions. The local intermediaries serve as an extension of the exporting firm and help in local supply chain management, pricing and customer service.

Typical intermediaries include the export management company (EMC), which acts as the client's export department. Small firms often use an EMC to handle their foreign shipments, prepare export documents, and deal with customs offices and insurance companies. EMCs are generally more knowledgeable about the legal, financial, and logistical details of exporting and importing and, thus, help the exporter from having to develop in-house expertise. Exporters can also use the services of export agents, such as manufacturers' export agents who sell in a foreign market on behalf of a manufacturer; export commission agents who make overseas purchases for their customers; and export merchants who buy and sell for their own accounts. The use of these services comes in exchange for a commission.

Direct and indirect exporting are not mutually exclusive options and a firm may use a combination of both approaches for different foreign markets. The decision regarding which approach to use depends on the required resource commitment, strategic importance of the foreign market, a need for after sales service and the availability of intermediaries in the foreign market.

Terms of trade

Trading firms need to be familiar with different terms that are used for quoting the specific terms of sale or terms of price. These terms of sale are conditions stating the rights, responsibilities, costs and risks borne by both the exporter and importer. These terms are known as Incoterms and have been harmonized and defined by the International

Chamber of Commerce as standards, to ensure uniformity in export transactions (International Chamber of Commerce, 2019).

> **Free on board (FOB):** A term of price in which the seller covers all costs and risks up to the point where the goods are delivered on board the ship in a designated shipment (export) port, and the buyer bears all costs and risks from that point on. This means that the buyer is responsible for the insurance and freight expenses in transporting goods from the shipment port to the destination port. The seller clears the goods for export. Delivery takes place when the goods pass the ship's rail at the named port of shipment.
>
> **Free alongside ship (FAS):** A term of price in which the seller covers all costs and risks up to the ship at the designated shipment (export) port. The buyer bears all costs and risks thereafter, including the loading of goods. The buyer also arranges shipping.
>
> **Cost, insurance and freight (CIF):** A term of price in which the seller covers the cost of the goods, insurance and all transportation and miscellaneous charges to the final destination port in a foreign country. Delivery takes place when the goods pass the ship's rail in the port of shipment. At that point the risk of loss or damage to the goods is transferred from the seller to the buyer. The seller clears the goods for export.
>
> **Cost and freight (C&F):** This term of price is similar to CIF except that the buyer purchases and bears the insurance.

Payment methods for export

Export managers should also be familiar with different payment methods in exporting. Trade transactions are complicated since they involve foreign currency which may fluctuate in value during the course of the trade deal. There is an additional risk of change in government policy, and that all payment mechanisms such as credit cards and checking accounts do not work uniformly well across the world.

The key payment methods used in international trade are listed below – in order of most secure to least secure.

Cash in advance

Cash in advance refers to the payment that is received either before shipment or upon the arrival of the goods. This is the safest method of payment for the exporter, who receives money at the outset of the transaction. However, buyers are usually reluctant to use this mode of payment because it blocks a large amount of their working capital until the sale of goods takes place. Also, if buyers do not know the exporter well, they may fear that the goods may be delayed or not sent. The method is popular only where there is an order for custom-made goods.

Letter of credit

The **letter of credit** (L/C) is the most commonly used payment method in international trade. It is a contract between the banks of the buyer and the seller that ensures payment from the buyer to the seller on receipt of the export shipment. The system is popular because almost all banks across the world have established relationships with their counterpart banks in other countries.

It is a letter addressed to the seller, written and signed by the bank acting on behalf of the buyer, in which the bank promises to honour drafts drawn on it, if the seller meets the specific conditions that are given in the letter of credit. These conditions are usually the same as contained in an export contract or sales agreement. The letter of credit also specifies the documents that the exporter is required to present, such as the **bill of lading**, commercial invoice and certificate of insurance. Before making a payment, the buyer's bank verifies that all documents are according to the agreement between the buyer and the seller.

Documentary collection

Documentary collection is a method of payment under which the exporter retains ownership of the goods until payment is received or he is certain that it will be received. In this method of payment, the bank, acting as the exporter's agent, regulates the timing and sequence of the exchange of goods by holding the title documents until the importer either pays the draft, termed documents against payment (D/P), or accepts the obligation to do so, termed documents against acceptance (D/A).

The two principal documents used in documentary collections are a draft and a bill of lading (B/L).

1   The *draft* is a financial instrument that instructs a bank to pay a specific amount of a specific currency to the bearer on demand or at a future date. A draft is a negotiable instrument that normally needs to be physically presented as a condition for payment. The buyer must make the payment. A draft may be either a sight draft (payable upon presentation) or a time draft (payable on a specified future date).
2   A *bill of lading* is a document of title of the goods being shipped along with the documents for shipment and the carrier's receipt for the goods being shipped. A sight draft is commonly used for D/P payment. However, for export sales that take several months in ocean transportation, exporters and importers may agree to use D/P of 30, 60, 90 or 180 days.

In practice, D/A are usually accompanied by a time draft ranging from 30 days up to perhaps two years, which is why time draft-based collections are also viewed as an important commercial or corporate financing approach that is granted by the exporter to the importer. The disadvantage of this method of financing is the high risk of receivable collection for the exporter. D/A is a riskier collection method than D/P because the importer can claim the title of goods under the 'promise' of payment rather than actual payment. For this reason, most bad debts accumulated in international trade have been transactions that used D/A as terms of payment.

Open account

Under this method of payment, goods to be sold are first shipped and the importer is billed for them later. The method can be used only if the customer is reliable, as there is no guarantee of payment from the buyer and all risk is borne by the seller. Very often exporters who prefer less risky modes of payment lose business to competitors. In recent years, open account sales have increased because of the increase in international trade, more accurate credit information about importers, and greater familiarity with exporting in general.

Entrepôt trade

Entrepôt trade refers to the import of goods for the purpose of re-exporting them. Goods imported are simply re-exported without further processing, to another nation from a special zone or port. For instance, in the Gulf region, Bahrain was traditionally the major centre for the re-export of goods, a position now occupied by the free trade zone of Dubai in the United Arab Emirates, which is now an important centre for re-exporting goods to Iran and the countries that constituted former southern Russia. Hong Kong also played the role of the entrepôt (a trade post where merchandise can be re-exported without paying import duties) by intermediating trade between China and the rest of the world.

Countertrade

Countertrade is a form of trade where all or partial payments are made in kind rather than in cash. In the context of international trade, it often involves the substitution of developing country goods for foreign exchange to enable purchases from the developing country and is, therefore, also viewed as a form of flexible financing or payment in international trade. Countertrade takes the form of four distinct types of trading arrangements: (1) barter, (2) counter purchase, (3) offset and (4) buyback.

Barter is the oldest form of trade and involves the direct and simultaneous exchange of goods between two parties without a cash transaction. Barter in the modern context often involves governments and business firms. The Thai government has bartered fruit for Chinese-made locomotives, passenger buses and armoured cars. The Brazilian government entered into a barter deal with South Korea's major shipbuilders and the state-run oil developer Korea National Oil Corporation (KNOC). The arrangement essentially had Korea, the world's largest shipbuilder, providing Brazil with drill ships or floating production, storage and offloading platforms in return for stakes in its oil fields in the Santos area, which KNOC would manage (Barter News Weekly, 2010).

A *counter purchase* is a reciprocal buying agreement whereby one firm sells its products to another at one point in time and is compensated in the form of the other's products at some time in the future. Examples of this type of arrangement include the Russian purchase of construction machinery from Japan's Komatsu in return for Komatsu's agreement to buy Siberian timber.

An *offset* is an agreement whereby one party, usually the importer, requires that a portion of the materials, components or semi-manufactures be purchased in the local market. Unlike counter purchase wherein exchanged products are normally unrelated, products taken back in an offset are often the outputs processed in the original contract. The exporter often sets up a manufacturing assembly. For example, the Shanghai Aircraft Manufacturing Corporation of China entered into an arrangement for the purchase of jets from the Boeing Company, using its proceeds from manufacturing the tail sections of the jets for Boeing. Offset is particularly popular in sales of expensive military equipment or high-cost, civilian infrastructure hardware.

Buyback or compensation arrangement occurs when a firm provides a local company with inputs for manufacturing products (mostly capital equipment) to be sold in international markets and agrees to take a certain percentage of the output produced by the local firm as partial payment. Buybacks help developing country producers upgrade technologies and machinery and ensure after-sale service.

Investment-related entry modes

Foreign direct investment as a mode of foreign entry occurs when a firm establishes a physical presence through ownership of productive assets such as capital, technology, land, plant and equipment, over which it has effective control to certain degrees.

FDI involves a higher resource commitment, as compared to other modes of entry such as trade and contractual entry, and thus makes greater demands on the resources and capabilities of the firm and is therefore a high-risk mode of entry. FDI helps the MNE to acquire varied experiential knowledge based on its presence in different foreign locations and also helps it with further foreign market entry.

Firms use different kinds of FDI to enter different markets. Take an example from the beer industry – South African Breweries (SAB) became a key player in the US market through its acquisition of Miller Brewing in 2002, and was rechristened SABMiller plc. It subsequently acquired Bavaria SA in South America, and Foster's in India, getting a major share of the beer market in both these countries. It entered the Chinese market through a joint venture, which is a collaborative arrangement between two firms for doing business. SABMiller thus used a variety of FDI methods to enter different markets and attained the position of the world's third largest brewer. We examine the different types of FDI in the next section.

Types of FDI

FDI may be classified based on the form of investment (greenfield versus mergers and acquisitions), nature of ownership (wholly owned versus joint ventures) and level of integration (horizontal versus vertical).

Main form of investment

Greenfield investment is an investment process in which a firm builds a new manufacturing, marketing or administrative facility in the host country. It is a long-term investment in which an overseas production facility is set up from scratch.

A *merger* is the amalgamation of two existing enterprises. It is a voluntary and permanent combination of two businesses, which integrate their operations and identities with those of the other. The merged enterprise then functions as a new entity.

An *acquisition* is the purchase of an existing business venture in a foreign country. It is a mode of FDI entry that allows a firm to establish itself in a short period of time since it takes over a running enterprise. From a legal point of view, the target company ceases to exist, the buyer 'swallows' the business and the buyer's stock continues to be traded. It can be through the purchase of a minority stake (where a firm purchases 10–49 per cent of the company's stock) or a majority stake (where a firm acquires over 50 per cent stock). An acquisition can be hostile if the acquired company is unwilling to be bought, or it can be friendly and with the consent of the acquired enterprise. Significant recent deals in the Asian region include Berkshire Hathaway (USA) buying a stake in One97 Communications, India's largest digital payments company (*Forbes*, 2018). One of the largest Chinese acquisitions in 2018 was a bid by a consortium of five Chinese companies, including the Bank of China's investment unit, to acquire Singapore-based warehousing company GLP, formerly Global Logistic Properties, for 16 billion Singapore dollars ($11.9 billion) (Kishimoto, 2018).

Firms often find mergers and acquisitions the fastest route to internationalization. The acquisition of an existing company gives the MNE immediate access to valuable resources such as plant, equipment, staff, customers and suppliers. It also gives them immediate revenue and return on investment. However, there are several challenges in this kind of investment, in the form of differences in culture, corporate values, business environment and methods of operation.

The host country governments often prefer the greenfield form of investment since it helps to create new jobs and production, leads to the transfer of knowledge and technology, and creates global linkages for the home country.

Nature of ownership

FDI can also be classified by the desired degree of control in the venture. Firms may choose between a wholly owned venture and strategic alliances such as joint ventures, according to the nature of control it desires to have.

Strategic alliances or international collaborative ventures are a form of FDI in which two firms form across-border business alliance. The collaborating firms pool their resources and share the costs and risks of the combined new venture. Strategic alliances are an important mode of entry, and critical to the firm's survival and growth in the world of global business. They can be formal agreements with equity stakes or short-term contractual agreements for cooperation in a specific task. These agreements are aimed at sharing or co-developing products, technologies or services through exchange between firms. These alliances are of two types – equity joint ventures and cooperative joint ventures.

An *equity joint venture* entails establishing a new entity that is jointly owned and managed by two or more parent firms in different countries. To set up an equity joint venture, each partner contributes cash, facilities, equipment, materials, intellectual property rights, labour, or land use rights. These collaborative arrangements could have an equal ownership pattern, that is, a 50–50 ownership or in any other proportion, according to agreement between partners. Many large TNCs such as Motorola Inc. (USA), Siemens AG (Germany), Sony Corporation (Japan), and Toyota Motor Corporation (Japan) have used such alliances for market entry and expansion into the Asian region. Sony Corporation had set up two joint ventures in partnership with Shanghai Oriental Pearl Group to make and market PlayStation consoles and games in China. The alliance is a response to the suspension of the ban on game consoles within Shanghai's free trade zone and could be a challenge for Sony since the Chinese market is very different from traditional console markets like those of Japan, Europe and the United States. Piracy and smuggling of consoles are very common, and Chinese gamers prefer computer and mobile games as compared to console-based games (Reuters, 2014).

The *project-based non-equity venture* is a collaborative agreement between partners who come together for sharing profits from a project with a relatively narrow scope, which has a clearly defined timeline. This form of collaboration does not need the creation of a new legal entity. The partners combine resources and capabilities till the venture bears fruit and marks the end of the collaboration. This form of collaboration is commonly found in technology intensive industries. For instance, IBM (USA) entered into an alliance with NTT (Japan) giving it access to outsourcing services to reach the Japanese consumer (IBM, 2000). Sony (Japan) entered into an alliance with IBM (USA) and Toshiba (Japan) for developing the Cell chip as a more powerful substitute to Intel's Pentium chip. It was known as a 'supercomputer on a chip', incorporating advanced multi-processing technologies used in IBM's sophisticated servers, Sony Group's computer entertainment systems and Toshiba's advanced semiconductor technology (IBM, 2005). The increase in the number of such alliances among TNCs all over the world has transformed the global business environment as firms share fixed costs and risks as well as the advantages arising out of the synergies of complementary skills and assets. These alliances are gaining importance worldwide as global competition intensifies for access to markets, products and technologies.

A *wholly owned subsidiary* is an entry mode in which the investing firm owns 100 per cent of the new entity in a host country. This new entity may be built from scratch by the investing firm (greenfield investment) or through a merger and acquisition with a local business, both discussed above. Many MNEs choose this alternative only after expanding into markets through other modes that have helped them accumulate host-country experience. The current trade war between the USA and China has led several MNEs to shift their production base to Southeast Asian countries. These include Harley Davidson (USA), which is shifting part of its production to Thailand, and Panasonic Corporation (Japan), which shut up shop in the USA and moved to consignment production and exports from Malaysia (Yap, 2018). China focused its greenfield FDI at Southeast Asia across a wide range of sectors, including machinery and electronics in Vietnam and Malaysia, software and electronics in Singapore, metals and hydrocarbons in the Philippines and textile production in Kazakhstan and Bangladesh. US investment flows to developing Asia, excluding China, showed a similar trend, rising 71 per cent in 2018 (Kynge, 2019).

The decision over whether a multinational invests in greenfield FDI or uses the M&A route is not only determined by firm level considerations but also on the investment policy regime and domestic regulations of the host economy. In developing Asia, for example, domestic regulations in many economies – including the People's Republic of China (PRC), India and the Philippines – limit foreign ownership in various industries to joint ventures and create barriers for greenfield FDI.

Direction of FDI

Horizontal FDI takes place when a firm invests abroad in the same industry in which it operates in the home country. This represents a geographical diversification of the MNE's established domestic product line. Most Japanese MNEs, for instance, begin their international expansion with horizontal investment because they believe that this approach enables them to share experience, resources and knowledge already developed at home, thus reducing the risk of foreign market entry. The acquisition of Ranbaxy Laboratories Limited, a leading Indian pharmaceutical TNC, by Japan's Daiichi Sankyo, is an example of horizontal FDI.

Vertical FDI refers to investment in activities along the firm's existing supply chain to avail the benefits of vertical integration. It occurs when the MNE enters a foreign market to produce intermediate goods that are intended for use as inputs in its home country's (or in other subsidiaries) production process (this is called backward vertical FDI), to market its homemade products overseas, or to produce final outputs in a host country using its home-supplied intermediate goods or materials (this is called forward vertical FDI). An example of backward vertical FDI is offshore extractive investments in petroleum and minerals. For example, ONGC, which is in the business of petroleum refining in India, has purchased oil fields in South Africa. Similarly, Honda (Japan) owns both suppliers of car parts and dealerships for sales in various countries of the world.

Umbrella holding company

An umbrella holding company is an investment company that brings all the firm's existing investments such as branch offices, joint ventures and wholly owned subsidiaries under one umbrella in order to combine sales, procurement, manufacturing, training and maintenance within the host country. It is often seen that many large MNEs try to combine production divisions for different sub-units under a common umbrella in an important destination. For example, DuPont set up DuPont China Ltd as its holding company to unite various joint ventures in the pharmaceutical and plastics divisions under a common coordinated management.

Contractual entry modes

Contractual or transfer-related entry modes are those associated with transfer of owner-ship or utilization of specified property such as technology or assets from one party to the other in exchange for royalty fees. This category includes entry modes like interna-tional leasing, international licensing, international franchising and turnkey projects.

International leasing

International leasing is an agreement in which the foreign firm (lessor) leases out its new or used property – usually machines or equipment – to a local company in another coun-try. International leasing enables the lessee to use existing equipment that is idle but in good operational condition to be productively used in another country. It is beneficial for the lessee who may not have the financial capability for the development of new equipment. The foreign lessor retains ownership of the property throughout the lease period during which the local user pays a leasing fee.

The major advantages of this mode for TNCs include quick access to the target market, efficient use of superfluous or outmoded machinery and equipment, and accumulation of experience in a foreign country. From the local firm's perspective, this mode helps reduce the cost of using foreign machinery and equipment, mitigates operational and investment risks, and increases its knowledge and experience with foreign technologies and facilities.

International licensing

International licensing is a contractual entry strategy in which a firm that owns intel-lectual property (the licensor) grants to another firm (the licensee) the right to use that property for a specific period of time in exchange for a royalty fee. The intellectual prop-erty may be any kind of expertise, know-how, blueprints, technology and manufacturing designs to be used by the licensee in a foreign market.

Licensing is a popular mode of entry used by firms in both the manufacturing and service industry. High technology firms such as Intel (USA) engage in different licensing agreements for sharing technology. The Walt Disney Company (USA) has been the top global licensing brand for several years (Licence Global, 2019) and allows the use of its cartoon characters on apparel to manufacturers in Asian countries such as Hong Kong. PVH Corporation (USA) is another leading licensing firm, which owns brands such as Van Heusen, Tommy Hilfiger, Calvin Klein, IZOD and Arrow.

Licensing allows the firm to reap the benefits of exploiting its existing innovative technology for foreign expansion without any additional investment. This makes it suitable for use by SMEs and young firms like the born global. Licensing also allows a firm to enter foreign markets that restrict entry through tariff barriers and in strategic sectors such as defence. Swiss MNE Roche entered the Japanese market through a licensing agreement. This also helped it to acquire knowledge about the local market and the local drug approval process for further penetration into the Japanese pharmaceutical sector. For instance, it entered into a strategic alliance with Chugai Pharmaceuticals, and became a majority shareholder in the firm. Through the strategic alliance with Roche, Chugai gained the exclusive right to develop and market Roche products in Japan, and simultaneously got access to the global market for its in-house products by out-licensing them to Roche (Chugai Pharmaceuticals, 2002). The licensee also benefits through the technical collaboration as it is able to upgrade its technical capability and improve its competitiveness in the global market.

The licensor often faces difficulty in maintaining satisfactory quality control over the licensee's manufacturing and marketing operations, which can damage their trademark and reputation. Very often, a licensee ultimately becomes a competitor, especially if the original licensing agreement does not specify the regions within which the licensee is allowed to market the licensed product. For example, in the 1960s, Radio Corporation of America (RCA) licensed its cutting-edge colour-television technology to a number of Japanese companies including Matsushita and Sony. RCA considered licensing a good strategy for earning a return on its technical know-how in the Japanese market without the costs and risks associated with FDI. However, Matsushita and Sony quickly assimilated RCA's technology and used it to enter the US market and compete directly against it. As a result, RCA became a minor player in its home market, while Matsushita and Sony gained a much bigger market share.

International franchising

International franchising is an entry mode in which the foreign franchisor grants use of intangible property rights, such as a trademark or brand name, to the local franchisee. It usually includes strict and detailed instructions on how to carry out the business operation and often includes production equipment, managerial systems, operating procedures, advertising and promotional materials, and even loans and financing. Franchising originated in the 1850s when Isaac Singer provided detailed instructions about his sewing machine in order to popularize it. Leading franchising firms include McDonald's, Kentucky Fried Chicken (KFC) and Subway in the fast food industry, hotels such as Hilton Hotels, and business services such as the UPS Store. Leading Asian franchisers include Kumon (Japan) for child education, Jollibee (the Philippines) for fast food and Paris Baguette (South Korea) for bakery products (Franchise Direct, 2019). Compared to licensing, franchising involves longer commitments, offers greater control, and includes a broader package of rights and resources.

The franchisee operates the business under strict instructions from the franchisor and is bound under contract to follow the procedures and methods of operation laid down in the contract. In exchange for the franchise, the franchisor receives a royalty payment that amounts to a percentage of the franchisee's revenues. For example, Burger King and McDonald's require the franchisee to buy the company's cooking equipment, burger patties and other products that bear the company name.

International franchising allows the franchisor to maintain consistency in its products in different markets. It also allows the franchisor to tightly control the entire business, and provides a quick and easy avenue for leveraging assets such as a trademark or a brand name to establish a global presence.

However, the franchisee may harm the franchisor's image by not upholding its standards and can become a competitor by slightly altering the franchisor's brand name or trademark. The business may also suffer due to other disputes such as in the case of McDonald's in India. McDonald's entered India in 1995 via a 25-year agreement with a local franchisee partner, but it ran into trouble when the franchisee started defaulting on payment of royalty, leading to a termination of the agreement and prolonged litigation until both parties reached a final settlement after six years. During this period several restaurants across the country had to be shut down or served only a partial menu (Live-Mint, 2019).

Turnkey Projects

Turnkey projects, also called build-operate-transfer (BOT), is a form of foreign market entry in which a foreign investor assumes responsibility for the design and construction of an entire operation, and, upon completion of the project, turns the project over to the local purchaser. The subsequent management of the project is also handed over to local personnel who have been trained by the investing MNE. In return for completing the project, the investor receives periodic payments that are normally guaranteed. BOT is especially useful for very large-scale, long-term infrastructure projects such as power-generation, airports, dams, expressways, chemical plants, and steel mills. Managing such complex projects requires special expertise. Turnkey projects are mostly administered by large construction firms such as Bechtel (the United States), Hyundai (Korea), or Friedrich Krupp (Germany). Large companies sometimes form a consortium and bid jointly for a large BOT project.

5.2 Case study: Mahindra & Mahindra – the local optimizer strategy

Overview

Mahindra & Mahindra (M&M) is the flagship company of the Indian $20.7 billion Mahindra group, with predominant business interests in the automobile and farm equipment sector. The group's diversified business interests have a global presence in over 100 countries and 11 industries. Its most important products are automobiles (39 per cent) and farm equipment (16 per cent). The firm has used technological collaboration as a key strategic element for capability development and growth in both the domestic and foreign markets. It has also had a keen focus on developing its capabilities through research and development, by using technical and other collaborations.

It has followed the *local optimizer strategy* of capability development and enhancement using technological collaboration for optimizing local products and processes for the domestic market. It later utilized these products and processes to enter other emerging markets. It has also established joint ventures with leading global MNEs for progress in research and development and growth of innovative ideas to hone its production skills in items ranging from alloy steel to farm equipment, and later, across a range of automobiles.

M&M has used diverse modes of entry into different markets ranging from exports to acquisitions and greenfield ventures. It followed an unconventional internationalization path, as it began exporting to geographically distant countries such as Yugoslavia at the same time as it was selling in Asian markets such as Indonesia.

Learning outcomes

By the end of this case study, students should be able to:

1   Understand the local optimizer strategy followed by emerging market MNEs from Asia, which develop ownership advantages by optimizing products and processes for specific conditions of the domestic market, to be replicated for market entry in other emerging markets with similar conditions.
2   Understand that the internationalization path adopted by Asian MNEs does not always follow the sequential order of export–transfer–investment, in geographically proximate regions followed by geographically distant countries.

Introduction

M&M was incorporated by brothers J.C. and K.C. Mahindra and Gul Mohammed as a steel trading company in 1945 and got the name Mahindra & Mahindra (M&M) when its founder Gul Mohamed migrated to Pakistan in 1948. M&M is seen as a symbol of India's progress and industrial development in the post-independence era after 1947. Its growth and evolution are illustrative of the growth and progress of the Indian economy.

M&M became a public listed company in 1955 and was listed on the Bombay Stock Exchange in 1956. The aspiring MNE made its debut in international financial markets with a maiden GDR issue of US $75 million. In 1994 it went through a major reorganization, which led to the creation of six strategic business units: automotive, farm equipment, infrastructure, trade and financial services, IT and automotive components. The automotive and farm equipment business continue to function as its leading units in both the domestic and foreign markets.

M&M has manufacturing units in 12 countries outside India, research and development facilities in 11 countries and it gets 49 per cent of total revenue from foreign markets (Annual Review, 2018).

Domestic operations

M&M started as a domestic steel trading company, and later entered into the realm of automotive manufacturing. It had an international orientation from the outset but was aware that its capabilities were limited and insufficient for product development, since these were developed at a time when India was a closed economy. M&M therefore adopted a strategy of global technological collaborations to overcome this disadvantage for growth in both domestic and international markets.

Automobile division

M&M began domestic operations as a manufacturer of general-purpose utility vehicles. It entered into its first franchise agreement in 1947, to assemble the iconic WWII Willys Jeep, which was specifically developed for India's rugged terrain in rural and semi-urban areas. The venture started with a consignment of 75 Jeeps, which came from Willys Overland Export Corporation, USA (now part of the Daimler Chrysler group) in knocked down (CKD) condition, and were assembled at Mazagon, Bombay. The Jeep was perfect for the Indian market, which had a predominantly low-income consumer base in semi-urban and rural areas connected by under-developed infrastructure. M&M started manufacturing the Jeep in 1954 in Mumbai. This was the starting point for M&M's

(Continued)

(Continued)

automobile business, which has continued to be its leading business division, both in the domestic and international market.

The agreement with Willys was the starting point of M&M's strategy of capability development through collaborations and helped it to develop its firm specific assets, which were aimed at optimizing products and processes for the specific conditions of the Indian market to begin with. This is characteristic of the local optimizer strategy used by emerging market MNEs from countries such as India, where firms develop ownership advantages by optimizing products and processes to meet the specific conditions of the domestic market. The strategy targets two unique conditions of emerging markets at the beginning of their internationalization journey. The markets consist of low-income consumers who need low priced products that are specifically manufactured according to local conditions such as poor and rugged road conditions. The products also need to be designed with low maintenance features, since the after-sales service lacks quality which is provided by relatively low skilled technical staff (Ramamurti and Singh, 2009).

M&M continued with its strategy of technological collaborations with various international giants to hone its skills and develop its capabilities. In 1979 M&M became a licensee of automobile giant Peugeot (France) to manufacture XDP 4.90 diesel engines. It began the assembly of Peugeot engines at Ghatkopar in Mumbai.

Its collaboration with Ford in 1996 led to the creation of a joint venture named Mahindra Ford India Ltd, for the manufacture of two popular Ford passenger cars for the Indian market – the Escort and Fiesta. These capabilities helped in the manufacture of the Scorpio, which became M&M's best-selling sports utility vehicle (SUV), built for the global market.

Farm equipment

Farm equipment is also a leading business division of M&M. The entry and subsequent growth of M&M in this sector was also made possible by several strategic technological collaborations. In 1950 M&M entered into a deal with Mitsubishi Corporation (Japan) for sourcing 5,000 tons of steel for wagon building. This was followed by its collaboration with International Harvester, USA in 1961. The US firm was a manufacturer of agricultural machinery, construction equipment, trucks, automobiles, and household and commercial products and it had a tie-up with M&M for the manufacture of tractors.

This collaboration made M&M a key participant in India's agricultural transformation called the Green Revolution, through its contribution to the mechanization of agricultural processes. It also marked the beginning of M&M's entry into the farm equipment sector, which has been a key segment of its business along with automobiles.

Tractors became a key product of M&M's growth and its premier export item across the world. Its capabilities in this product were further strengthened through a joint venture with Ugine Kuhlmann, France, in 1962. This collaboration led to the creation of the Mahindra Ugine Steel Company (MUSCO), for the manufacture of alloy steel.

In 1963 M&M entered into a joint venture with International Harvester Company and Voltas Ltd. The JV was called the International Tractor Company of India (ITCI) and was formed with the mandate to manufacture 3,500 tractors. M&M currently has manufacturing facilities across the world in 12 global locations, including the USA, Brazil, Algeria, Turkey, Finland and Japan.

The farm equipment division MUSA made its first foreign market entry at Tomball, Texas, USA for the distribution of tractors in 1994. M&M tractors found consumers in both small hobby farmers and large landowners in the US market and has consistently remained in the top three positions in the market since then. MUSA became the first tractor company in the world to win the prestigious Deming Application Prize in 2003 and the Japan Quality Medal for customer focus in 2007.

The farm equipment sector continues to be an important contributor to the M&M business, in both the domestic and foreign markets. The sector saw total sales of 330,436 units in 2018–19, out of which 316,742 units were sold in the domestic market and 13,694 units were exported (Mahindra.com, 2019).

International ventures

M&M ventured into the foreign market by establishing its export division in 1969. It started exports to Indonesia and then to Yugoslavia in 1970. This was followed by exports to Nigeria and other African countries in the 1970s. Later M&M made South Africa its export hub for accessing other African countries. The group expected that its capabilities developed for the home market would be easily replicated in African conditions, since they closely matched market conditions in India. 'Mahindra is the world's largest tractor manufacturer by volume and many of our models are designed for markets that demand tough and efficient solutions which are also effortless to operate in harsh conditions. Our initial market study shows that these attributes are in high demand in South Africa as well and we trust that it will find favor with our customers', said Arvind Mathew, Chief of International Operations, Mahindra & Mahindra (*Economic Times*, 2019).

The replication of home-grown capabilities in foreign markets is also a characteristic of the local optimizer strategy. EMNEs enter other emerging markets by optimizing production methods developed at home through technological collaboration, to lower costs or increase reliability in similar operating conditions found in those markets. This is the result of using intermediate technology, which has been developed through

(Continued)

(Continued)

collaboration (Kobrin, 1977) and allows MNEs to set up production facilities quickly and in a cost-effective manner in other emerging economies (Amsden and Chu, 2003).

Using the capability development, learning and internationalization knowledge obtained through the early JVs, Mahindra based its own optimization strategy on cross-Asian strengths that it extended beyond the region. It began exporting to Nepal in the early 1990s and today it is one of its key markets. It also started exporting CKD units to other neighbouring countries of Sri Lanka, and subsequently to African countries such as Kenya, Namibia and Mozambique. It is interesting to note that M&M did not follow the traditional Western model of internationalization, which posits that firms begin exporting to markets in close geographical proximity first, and then tap markets that are geographically distant. It began internationalization with 'down market' exports and FDI, in a manner consistent with the product life cycle hypothesis.

M&M's farm equipment division MUSA had entered the US market in 1994 with the distribution of tractors. This presence was further strengthened through a joint venture with Rabobank Group to support the activities of dealer and retail financing options to enable the sale of tractors in the USA. Mahindra Finance was the outcome of the joint venture with De Lage Landen, a wholly owned subsidiary of the Rabobank Group and M&M, to serve as the primary financier for MUSA products in the USA.

By the early 2000s Mahindra had established its presence in neighbouring international markets such as Bangladesh and Sri Lanka, and also in the distant African markets of Tanzania, Congo, Madagascar, Mozambique, Ethiopia, Rwanda, Burundi and Nigeria. It also established a joint venture in South Africa, for the sale of its vehicles – the Scorpio and Bolero Pik-Up.

M&M's expansion across Asia and into the rest of the world continued to have typical elements of the local optimizer strategy. It successfully optimized products and processes using capabilities developed through collaboration, and then established itself in other emerging markets, using a combination of exports and local production, followed by acquisitions and several JVs. A clear case in point is the Scorpio, a stylish SUV that was developed from scratch using technology gained through collaboration. The vehicle was targeted at the Indian middle to upper income urban consumer, and leveraged M&M's reputation as a manufacturer of sturdy vehicles suitable for the Indian market.

It has preferred to use JVs as a vehicle of getting technology for upgrading its skills and developing its competitive advantage in the manufacture of vehicles and farm equipment. As these agreements expired, M&M absorbed their technologies and sold the products under its own brand name. The products developed through these technical collaborations were then exported to both neighbouring and other markets, which had similar operating conditions. Exports also paved the way later for establishing production facilities in these countries. This was followed by acquisitions, which helped to further strengthen its capabilities.

The acquisition of Ssangyong (South Korea), for example, led to developing capabilities on power trains. Its acquisition of Italian firm Pininfarina has resulted in collaborative design work on the Marazzo, a multi-purpose vehicle, and the Furio commercial vehicle range (Gopalan, 2018).

This is unlike the strategies of MNEs from developed, Western countries who merely make minor changes in existing products and processes for making an entry into emerging markets. M&M, on the other hand, developed its own capabilities and competitive advantages for use and exploitation in other emerging markets with similar income levels and an under-developed hard and soft infrastructure.

This points to the need for MNEs desirous of optimizing products and processes through collaboration, to have the necessary absorptive capacity for effective utilization of the foreign technologies that have been acquired. They also need to focus on developing production engineering capabilities through innovation for further growth.

R&D and the focus on innovation

M&M was a typical Indian MNE which built its capabilities as an assembler of multi-utility vehicles in the era of import substituting industrialization using licensed technology. The liberalization programme launched by the Indian government in 1991 forced M&M to focus on intensifying its R&D and innovation skills for product development to face potential competition from international players. It realized that it had limited skills as an assembler of multi-utility vehicles, and a limited brand image as a manufacturer of pick-up trucks and jeeps for the rural market.

The firm began its research efforts by establishing various departments for computer-aided design as well as engineering and vehicle design. The first product to emerge as a consequence of their R&D was a pick-up truck in 1997, followed by the Bolero, an SUV, in 2000, which replaced the Armada, which had been launched in 1993. The Bolero was the first product to be developed in-house, and it was done on a low budget investment plan of US$300 million and also used designs from the existing Armada's chassis, roof and door.

'Bolero's success was beyond our wildest dreams. More than 14 years later, it still sells one lakh [100,000] units a year', said Pawan Goenka, the senior designer from General Motors who was handpicked to enable M&M to re-invent itself to face foreign competition (Madhavan, 2013). Goenka had moved from General Motors which, in the early 1990s, had an annual budget of $1 billion as well as a team of 20,000 engineers spread across multiple locations. M&M's research facility, on the other hand, was a shed

(Continued)

(Continued)

and 50 engineers. Bolero also bolstered – and widened – the company's product range which had, thus far, included pick-up trucks and jeeps predominantly focused on the rural markets (Madhavan, 2013).

The firm thus began to consolidate its capabilities in automobile design, which led to the launch of the Scorpio, another SUV in 2002. The Scorpio has been hugely successful from its very inception and a source of major recognition for M&M. It was a stylish SUV, which targeted the Indian middle and upper-income consumer. It helped M&M consolidate its position as a manufacturer of sturdy vehicles suitable for India's rugged roads. Its design cost was a fraction of what its developed country counterparts in the US or Europe would have spent. This was possible since the Scorpio was developed by M&M's in-house low-cost engineers using low-cost Korean suppliers who were cheaper than the traditional suppliers used by developed country automobile manufacturers.

The capability to design and manufacture products at significantly lower costs than their Western counterparts despite operating at a much smaller scale became an important competitive advantage for M&M.

The success of the Scorpio in India gave a huge boost to M&M's global ambitions and the firm actively began looking to expand overseas. It began by targeting other emerging markets and started with initial sales to its neighbouring countries of Sri Lanka, Nepal and Bangladesh, followed by Iran and Kuwait in the Middle East and later Uruguay in South America. Its decision to target these countries was driven by the fact that they had operating conditions that were similar to those found in India.

The firm wanted to establish itself in different foreign markets with a local partner, as this was the key to long-term success and building trust with the customer. In 2005 it established Mahindra Europe as a subsidiary in Italy with the launch of the Scorpio and Bolero Pik-Up. It simultaneously entered several other markets of Europe in the same year. In addition to the Scorpio, Mahindra also developed the Mahindra Pik-Up, based on the Scorpio platform, exclusively for overseas markets in 2006. This helped M&M move into neighbouring markets like Bhutan and distant African markets such as Morocco, Algeria and Ghana. The Pik-Up also enabled its entry into the South African markets of Chile, Paraguay and Peru.

M&M had started exports into several other emerging markets by 2007, and it also had a modest presence in Europe. It gave exclusive distribution rights for its products in the US market to an American company.

M&M established a subsidiary Mahindra Automotive in Australia in 2008. The following years saw a consolidation of its farm and auto businesses and an expansion into other countries of South America such as Uruguay and Ecuador.

In 2011 M&M launched two SUVs for the global market – XUV 500 and Mahindra Genio, which was a newer version of the Pik-Up. This helped it to move into the South American countries of Uruguay and Ecuador and also into South Africa. The XUV 500 was yet another SUV designed for the global market and developed in-house by M&M's engineers, based on feedback on styling and development from customers across the globe.

In 2012 it further spread into the South American country of Colombia. In 2013, M&M established the Mahindra North American Technical Center (MNATC), as the North American headquarters of the Mahindra group's automotive division. It aimed to combine the M&M experience of developing rugged automobiles with the expertise of the best designers and engineers from global innovative organizations such as Tesla, Ford, Boeing and Apple in the conception and engineering of world-class Mahindra vehicles. The firm was later renamed Mahindra Automotive North America (MANA) and led to the establishment of a new manufacturing facility, with an investment of US$230 million in Detroit – the world's car capital in 2017. This was the first new automotive facility established in Detroit in over 25 years. The new investment created 250 new jobs in the region (*Economic Times*, 2017).

The GenZe (Generation Zero Emissions) electric scooters and electric assist bikes were among the earliest innovative products from MANA. The vehicles were conceived as zero emission, sustainable personal transportation for growing urban areas, and increased transit needs in Silicon Valley.

M&M established its subsidiary GenZein Palo Alto (USA) in 2012 and later moved to Fremont, which is the hub for electric vehicles and other clean technology companies. M&M's electric vehicles are manufactured, hand-assembled and road tested in Ann Arbour, Michigan. The electric scooter is meant to strengthen M&M's presence in rural parts of USA, where it already has a strong presence with its tractors. It is also visualized as a clean technology vehicle for quick commuting within the large urban spaces of the USA (Tilley, 2014).

M&M is the pioneer in the electric vehicle space in the domestic Indian market. Its vehicles include the electric sedan E-verito, and a newly launched electric three-wheeler Treo. It has collaborated with South Korea's LG Chen for setting up a lithium-ion battery manufacturing plant in Maharashtra. It has also made a huge investment for the development and manufacturing of electric power trains in Karnataka, which will be supplied to other auto-makers including its subsidiary Ssangyong Motor Co.

In 2018 it launched the Mahindra Roxor, an off-road vehicle with modern innovation. The launch of Roxor was significant for two reasons – it was the first vehicle to be made and launched in USA and it was also the first vehicle manufactured at the new auto plant in Detroit, after a gap of 25 years.

(Continued)

(Continued)

M&M established the Mahindra Research Valley (MRV) as an integrated product development centre with the intention of creating an innovative environment, infrastructure and people for R&D in the auto industry. Spread over 124 acres inside Mahindra World City (India's first special economic zone and an integrated business city), MRV has 500,000 square feet of built-up area housing 32 laboratories to physically make parts, do mock-up testing for use and abuse of various components, and design offices to virtually validate designs and test them.

With a view to strengthening its capabilities further, M&M established the Mahindra Agricultural Technology Center in the United States at Virginia in 2018. This research facility is visualized to create breakthrough technology products for the North American agriculture market to enable M&M to face global competition.

M&M further strengthened it capabilities through a series of strategic acquisitions. It obtained controlling stakes in the REVA Electric Car Company to create Mahindra Electric. It also acquired South Korea's SsangYong Motor Company in 2011 as well as the well-known Italian automotive design firm, Pininfarina S.p.A. in 2015

M&M was integrated across different functional areas such as design, production and marketing/distribution in both the home country markets and also foreign markets. It also covered different stages of the value chain and owned the brands under which

Table 5.1   Mahindra & Mahindra alliances

Year	Firm	Country	Outcome
1947	Willys Overland Corporation	USA	Manufacturing of the Jeep
1961	Ugine Kuhlmann	France	Manufacturing of alloy steel
1963	International Harvester Company of Chicago	USA	Manufacturing of farm equipment
1963	International Harvester Company and Voltas Ltd	USA	Tractors
1979	Peugeot	France	XDP 4.90 diesel engines
1986	British Telecom	UK	Entry into IT services space
1993	Mitsubishi Corporation and Nisho Iwai Corporation	Japan	Steel Service Centre
1996	Ford Motor Co.	USA	Manufacture of Escort and Fiesta
2011	De Lage Landen, Rabobank Group	USA	Mahindra Finance

it sold its products. This is another feature of the local optimizer strategy of emerging market MNEs. The scope of value chain activity is different for domestic and foreign markets. It is generally seen that scale sensitive production and R&D are concentrated in the home market, but final stage production or assembly along with marketing, distribution and after sales service are easily done in the foreign market (Ramamurti and Singh, 2009).

Final remarks

M&M is India's leading MNE in the automobile and farm equipment space. It started as a domestic steel trading company and adopted a strategy of capability development and enhancement using technological collaboration to develop itself into a manufacturer of utility vehicles. It has also had a keen focus on R&D and innovation to enhance its limited capabilities in product design and development.

M&M used the local optimizer strategy for entry into different markets across Asia by creating early alliances with major, innovative market leaders and mid-level players. It developed capabilities through alliances to expand across the region and rapidly into other global markets, to emerge as a leader in the automobile and farm equipment spaces. Its internationalization path has been based on the use of capabilities developed through collaborations and joint ventures in the domestic market to venture into other emerging markets. It has used a combination of modes – exports, collaboration and joint ventures, and acquisitions – to chart its evolution as a leading global MNE.

M&M's internationalization strategy did not follow the traditional Western model, of starting exports in proximate markets and then moving to distant regions. Its strategy followed the product life cycle theory, as it began internationalization with 'down market' exports and FDI. It started exports into distant countries such as Yugoslavia, followed by neighbouring Asian countries of Sri Lanka, Nepal and Bangladesh, and later Iran and Kuwait.

Case questions

1   What is the local optimizer strategy? Explain how this strategy helped M&M in its Asian expansion and how this has supported its global expansion.
2   Explain how M&M's focus on research and development in product design and other areas helped in its regional expansion.

5.3 Case study: Strategic responses to institutional influence – Volkswagen's Asia entry modes

Overview

When the automotive industry experienced declining car sales in Europe in the late 1970s, with their excess manufacturing capacity, the European automobile manufacturers began to seek opportunities elsewhere to compensate for the shortfall and increase their revenue and competitiveness outside their home markets (Directorate of Intelligence, 2012). Volkswagen Group (VW), as one of the leading players among them, took an early venture into Asia and set up what later became its second biggest production centre after Europe to support its ambitious global expansion. VW entered Asia almost 40 years ago. At the time both the industrial and institutional environment of the automotive industry were in an early and unstable state in most places in Asia. This greatly influenced VW's entry modes. VW derived revenues and expansion through its initial exploration of two distinctive Asian markets: South Korea and China. This experience rendered the company the knowledge of how to adopt diverse entry modes in other Asian locations. This case provides the background for discussing VW's essential entry modes to Asian markets and how VW's first-comer advantages in Asia may affect the growth of both the company and the automotive industry in its target Asian markets.

Learning outcomes

By the end of this case study, students should be able to:

1   Understand how government policies influence major industries in Asia and how the complex nature of institutional factors of Asian markets (including the importance of relationship with governments) could determine foreign companies' entry modes.

2   Understand that the entry modes adopted for Asia do not always follow a static sequential order such as export–transfer–investment, but rather need to be managed and modified based on the immediate practical circumstances and these may vary from country to country in Asia even though most of them are categorized as 'emerging markets'.

Introduction

While Europe was the birthplace of the automotive industry, it was the innovation of the automobile production systems by the USA and Japan that elevated this industry into key economic pillars for some nations. The key steps towards this predominance can be visualized through a timeline of developments in production systems, as illustrated in Table 5.2.

Table 5.2   Automotive production line development

Timeline	Production System	Initiating Country	Representative Company	Main Contribution
Late 19th century	Craft production system	Europe (Italy and France)	N/A	Division of labour, standardized manufacturing of components
1914	Mass production system	USA	Ford (Henry Ford) and General Motors (Alfred Sloan)	Assembly lines: Ford's standardized assembly lines and GM's more agile assembly line to meet diverse customer needs
1948–1975	Lean production system, or the Toyota Production System (TPS)	Japan	Toyota	Assembly lines that run optimally, without delays or issues, with minimum waste and maximum productivity

Source: BuntyLLC, 2019; Lee et al., 1996

On basis of their contributions to the automotive industry, a triad group was hence formed – Europe, the US and Japan – and their competitive edge differed from yet complemented each other. According to an intelligence report based on data from 1986 (Directorate of Intelligence, 2012: 5), after six consecutive years of loss, the medium-term prospect of Western Europe's automobile industry remained hazy, with challenging sales figures at the end of 1970s and early 1980s. Scholars found that the situation was aggravated by structural problems within the industry in Western Europe, primarily over-manning and excess capacity. To solve these problems and improve competitiveness, in addition to cost-savings through labour reductions, European car-makers looked to joint ventures (Directorate of Intelligence, 2012: 5). Particularly among the automotive triad, Japanese car-makers started charting their recovery path relatively

(Continued)

(Continued)

earlier than Europe and the US, starting in the 1970s not only by raising quality but also production efficiency (Donnelly et al., 2002; Directorate of Intelligence, 2012: 5). This gave much inspiration to the two other countries' automobile manufacturers, like VW, to investigate opportunities for seeking collaborations in Asia, i.e. to move closer to their strongest competitor, Japan, and increase their own learning and efficiencies. VW had been one of the earliest European automobile manufacturers to expand in Asia. Besides increasing competition from Japan in the 1970s, the Western European automotive industry also faced its global rivals from other places in Asia except for Southeast and Western Asia. The countries in Southeast Asia were believed to have more indigenous interest (Mukherjee, and Sastry, 1996), while Western Asia's economy largely depended on its abundant oil reserves. Among the remaining Asian countries, South Korea had also gradually grown into a major automobile exporter. This had shaped VW's motivation to initiate its Asia exploration and to narrow its location focus down to this particular region.

Where to garner VW's first-to-market advantages in Asia–South Korea or China?

The South Korean market

VW hence started to seek cooperation partners and opportunities with South Korea during the 1970s. The intention of VW to enter Asia was evidenced in the biography of Dr Carl H. Hahn, former CEO of VW, *Meine Jahre mit Volkswagen (My Years with Volkswagen)*. In the late 1970s, he reported, VW had planned to locate its second biggest production centre in Asia as an alternative to Europe to support local capability through international expansion (Hahn, 2005). At the time, the automotive industry had existed in South Korea for just over a decade, and was hence still young, growing and eager to tap into Western capabilities.

South Korea's own automotive industry emerged in the early 1960s when the government's first national economic development plan was implemented; this is perceived as the first period (1962–70) in Korean car manufacturing. Throughout this period, South Korea's automobile manufacturers produced cars under the so-called semi-knock down (SKD) model and rapidly gained experience and entered the completely knock down (CKD) stage.

- The SKD process was where the manufacturer partially broke down its finished car and sold the semi-finished parts to the importing factory, who would then reassemble these parts back into a complete car.

The CKD process was where the manufacturer broke down its finished car and sold this set of parts to the importing factory, who would then reassemble these parts, sometimes together with domestically produced parts, back into a complete car. With the gradual involvement of more original developed (OD) products and designs, South Korean manufactures were soon able to enter a mass production stage (Mukherjee and Sastry, 1996; Ebert and Montoney, 2007).

To encourage the development of the automotive industry further, the government lent support to several large, family-owned **business conglomerates**, namely the **Chaebols**, to facilitate their entry into the industry. For Chaebols, the incentive was the possibility to gain wider access to resources and raw materials for their diversified businesses and obtain significant additional funding that would be provided by the government (Ebert and Montoney, 2007). Besides participating in the national mission of advancing the economy, Chaebols could thus also use this opportunity to enrich their profile, reputation and business capabilities. Several Chaebols began developing or acquiring automobile businesses and slowly grew and consolidated their shares in this market. For example, Shinjin Motors was established during that time, focusing on passenger cars. So did Kia, which started assembling small trucks. Hyundai Motors and Asia Motors were the next to be established (Lansbury et al., 2012: 32).

The Automotive Industry Promotion Law published in 1962 served to protect this then-infant industry of South Korea: foreign automobile manufacturers were only approved to enter South Korea if forming JVs with domestic entities, and foreign automobile-makers were not allowed to possess more than 50 per cent of ownership (Liu, 2008). Although VW had not yet established an alliance or JV partnership with any South Korean companies, several other foreign car-makers did enter the market that way at this time. For example, Ford set up its Cortina producing lines by forming a technical alliance with Hyundai in 1968. Fiat also established a technical alliance with Asia Motors. Toyota had established a similar alliance partnership with Shinjin, and later GM, as the first American automobile manufacturer that entered the South Korean market and set up General Motors Korea via a 50–50 JV in 1972 (Lansbury et al., 2012: 32–3). This also marked the second national economic development plan implemented by the government. VW continued to watch these developments from afar.

The second period (1972–82) then illustrates the national government's drive to have the sector play a significant role in stimulating Korea's economy. Policies and regulations were adopted to promote this, including the introduction of mandating local content rules reaching 90 per cent by the early 1980 set for the automotive industry (Ebert and Montoney, 2007). As a consequence, companies decided to revisit their business models and to restructure and, for some, consolidate during this period: Asia Motors was purchased by Kia. General Motors Korea (the JV with Shinjin) was taken over by Daewoo. Hyundai maintained its position in the market. The Korean automotive

(Continued)

(Continued)

industry had just created a 'local triad', as of the end of 1970s, comprising Hyundai, Kia and Daewoo (Lansbury et al., 2012: 33). It is notable that about ten years later, i.e. in the 1980s, Samsung also established an automobile department named Samsung Motors, which was later acquired by Renault, the French car manufacturer.

This second period hence witnessed a rapid growth of South Korea's own automotive industry. The localization policy also showed a satisfactory result: from 1975 to 1981, local content of South Korean-made cars had increased substantially to an astounding 85 per cent (Lee et al., 1996). Collaborations with foreign automobile manufacturers had not only raised the technical expertise and experience of domestic manufactures but also helped South Korea to step into a mass production capability, that could serve the world. Even more importantly, the alliances helped South Korea to acquire the capability to design new cars and engineer efficient operation processes – leading them smoothly to the lean production stage, and therefore to enter the global automotive market and eventually become highly competitive. By 1993, the Chaebols had exported 38 per cent of their production to the world (Mukherjee and Sastry, 1996). The domestic along with the exporting demands stimulated South Korean automobile manufactures' expansion of scale and capacity.

VW entering South Korea: No easy path

Contrary to what one would expect, the South Korean market did not provide VW an easy entrance to Asia. Dr Hahn's biography indicates that VW's growing interest in South Korea never led to the establishment of a JV in that country, mainly due to communication issues (Hahn, 2005). As a matter of fact, by 1995, when some of the other world's leading automobile manufacturers such as Mazda, Mitsubishi, GM, Ford, Honda and Mercedes had entered South Korea (Mukherjee and Sastry, 1996), VW decided to come into the market through other modes of market entry.

Exporting

In the absence of automobile manufacturing in South Korea, VW chose to enter the market by selling finished products there. Foreign car-makers had to seek a strong tie-up relationship with local assemblers or distributors to sell their cars in the country. VW had to designate one or multiple dealers in Korea (Kim and Chang, 2019) to export its cars because they were manufactured overseas. To ease the process of finding sales agencies, foreign automobile manufacturers like VW often registered as members of the Korea Automobile Importers & Distributors Association (KAIDA). In addition to providing essential data and statistics of the South Korean market, KAIDA offered information and services for foreign car-makers to facilitate their sales and imparted a strong message that the South Korean market stayed 'open' to the world (KAIDA, 2019a). VW registered to become a KAIDA member in 1987 and started to export VW modelled cars to South Korea through Hyosung Trading Company (KAIDA, 2019b). Then, in 1998, Audi, which was majority owned by VW, also started to export cars to South Korea (Mukherjee and Sastry, 1996).

Fully owned subsidiary

The financial crisis in 1997–98 impacted South Korea's economy severely. Post-crisis, the Korean government started to review and adjust its economic development policies. It was aware that an export-oriented economy was not sufficient to underpin growth. The market hence started to open up to allow for and attract inward foreign direct investment. In 2000, the South Korean government liberalized its policy regarding merger and acquisition undertaken by foreign automobile manufacturers in South Korea, which further opened up South Korean's automotive industry (Park, 2003). A symbolic event occurred in this context, that is, the aforementioned acquisition of Samsung Motors by Renault, and then the launch of Renault Samsung Motors (Park, 2003).

Despite a long history of sales in South Korea through local agents, Audi (majority-owned by VW) formed 'Audi Volkswagen Korea' in 2004 and used a wholesale distribution model for motor vehicle supplies, accessories, tools and equipment (Bloomberg, 2019b). Models exported through Audi Korea to the South Korean market eventually included the Audi A series from 4 to 8, Audi Q 5 and 7, Audi TT, and Audi R 8, and proved highly successful.

The test phase was over: VW Korea was formally established in 2005 to make a 'full-fledged entry into the domestic imported car market' (VW Korea official website, 2019), emphasizing its positioning of an 'imported' car brand in the South Korean market and offering a higher-end option to South Korean consumers. In 2019, VW Korea operated 33 exhibition centres and 34 service centres in Korea, aiming to 'deliver the best vehicles' to customers. Models exported through VW Korea into the South Korean market included Arteon, Passat TSI and Passat GT, Tiguan and Tiguan Allspace. Data from 2014 revealed that a typical car dealership in the richest residential area of Seoul, Gangnam, at some stage could no longer absorb orders for the US$35,000 Tiguan because the demand largely exceeded supply. The Tiguan appeared to be the most popular imported automobile in South Korea in that year, and a significant success for VW's sales and services activity in the country. Among all imported auto brands in South Korea in 2014, 71 per cent were German branded. According to an analysis by *News China*, reasons for the popularity of German cars included the brand reputation, rising purchasing power of the middle class, and a trend of driving premium diesel cars. German-made cars constituted some the very few diesel-option cars in the South Korean market, and especially in the premium market. Improvements on noise and

(Continued)

(Continued)

emission levels, economical fuel consumption for longer distances and a reputation (tarnished some years later through the emissions scandal) of eco-friendliness had attracted many young consumers. German cars also sported wider choices of models, and sales benefited from the long-standing reputation of German engineering and German luxury automobile brands (*News China*, 2013). 'In the past, our domestic auto makers were small, and we had to support them (by buying them)', said a 40-year-old businessman from Gangnam. 'Now they are big enough and we are not obligated to give more support' (Sina Finance, 2014). This quote was prominently used by the publication to illustrate the growing interest in purchasing imported cars in South Korea. In 2018, the year-on-year growth of registered imported cars (by consumers) reached its historical peak at 16.7 per cent. The sales of VW branded cars including Audi exceeded 10,000 cars that year.

Acquisition

As well as VW's global expansion, its entry mode in South Korea also diversified, for example, through the acquisition of Scania, a world-famous Swedish truck brand. Scania had been producing and selling trucks in Korea through Scania Korea since 1998 (Sohu Auto, 2018). Through this acquisition, VW hence started producing in Korea, taking possession of Scania's production line in Busan to diversify its product offerings in South Korea (NY Times, 2014).

The Chinese market

In 1978, after VW's attempt to enter South Korea, the company seized the opportunity to enter China instead. Back then, China's economy had not yet recovered from the post-war recession and a domestic revolution that lasted close to ten years. Unlike the South Korean government's protection and centralized support of its domestic automobile manufacturers, the Chinese government provided significant autonomy to provincial and municipal governments regarding their collaboration with foreign industry, including automobile manufacturers. Nonetheless, the national government requested all activities to serve the main objective of acquiring technology and foreign capital (Mukherjee and Sastry, 1996). This policy led to a relatively fragmented automotive industry in China.

China's automotive industry developed with a focus on middle-sized trucks in the 1970s (Liu, 2008), when the country lacked basic techniques and skilled labour to produce passenger cars. The 'reform and open up' policy adopted by the Chinese government in 1978 confirmed the goal of reaching ambitious industrialization growth goals and attracting foreign capital. As part of this, manufacturing and exporting reputable foreign-branded cars were seen to meet such objectives.

Yet, as the Chinese government reached out to leading Western automobile manufacturers, after market research, many hesitated: they perceived China to have excessively low industrialization levels and almost no experience in advanced automobile manufacturing. In 1979, China had 130 assembly lines and produced only 186,000 vehicles with them. Most of these assembly lines only boasted a production capability in the hundreds. Also, unlike South Korea, passenger cars only accounted for a very small percentage among the vehicles produced and purchased (Mukherjee and Sastry, 1996). In addition, China, at that time, had no laws or regulations relating to the legitimacy of JVs or FDI in China. These conditions greatly hindered the negotiation between VW and the Chinese government for their collaboration in the 1970s. Yet there was opportunity to come.

VW entering China

Joint venture

In spite of these difficulties, the negotiation between VW and the Chinese government gained great support from the central government and indeed became a trigger for China to launch its first JV law (China Auto News, 2018b; EastDay.com, 2018). To make the cooperation feasible, a draft JV law was developed and proposed by the Shanghai municipal government to the central government. In 1979, the 'Law of People's Republic of China on Joint Ventures Using Chinese and Foreign Investment' was adopted (with its details added and further refined in its Implementation launched four years later) (Ford et al., 2010: 34). After years of negotiation, in 1982, an agreement to build a CKD assembly line for the VW Santana model was signed between VW and the Shanghai Tractor & Automobile Corporation, the then largest Chinese vehicle manufacturer, with the two partners equally involved. While some believed that this agreement successfully showcased the commitment of VW to enter the Chinese market, others thought it was an intentional obstruction to test China's car assembly and production capacity given China's considerably ineligible car assembly capability at that moment (EastDay.com, 2018). Either way, this agreement was a critical milestone for both partners, and for VW's increasing commitment to Asia in terms of sales and services as much as manufacturing. A year later, China's first CKD-produced Santana was unveiled in Shanghai. It became a vital stimulation for both partners to consolidate their partnership. Two year later, in 1985, a formal JV contract was signed creating the Shanghai-Volkswagen Automotive Company Ltd, later renamed SAIC-Volkswagen. The initial contract was signed for 25 years,

(Continued)

(Continued)

providing further evidence for a long-term commitment. The equity investment in this JV was composed of VW's 50 per cent; the Shanghai Tractor & Automobile Corporation's 35 per cent and now also the Bank of China with 15 per cent (Aggarwal, 2001: 171). The production line of SAIC-Volkswagen, initially built for the VW Santana, soon (in 1986) also served for an additional two models, namely the Passat Variant and Audi 100. At a steady annual growth rate of around 40 per cent, the SAIC-VW's production site was gradually expanded and upgraded.

Licensing

In 1988, a training and further education centre opened for SAIC-VW's workers who would not only be trained in China but also be sent to Germany to study other key technologies. This initiative was most appreciated by the Chinese government. As aforementioned, speedy and intensive industrialization was one of the key goals of the government. Therefore, any effective form of technology training would help the domestic workers to grow their skill sets and even restructure the industry, whether foreign-owned or locally emerging. Not only would it bring up 'a new generation of automobile workers and management personnel', but also bring 'a large number of enterprises in related industries to reconstruct their production to meet the new needs' (Aggarwal, 2001: 171). VW's establishment of such training centres and programmes further reinforced its good relationship with key connections in the central and local levels of the Chinese government: 'Our work in China was supported by government officials at the highest level', recalled by Dr Hahn in an interview: 'We strictly insisted on the VW standard for all our production in China, from the beginning of our corporation. Back then this country was going through a very tough period in terms of living, but we were lucky to have a group of motivated, down-to-earth, and visionary colleagues, with our focus fully concentrated on the work tasks. It has been proven by the history that our decision was right. Being part of the country that VW invested in was our philosophy which became the footstone of our success' (*China Auto News*, 2018a).

Having gained experience with its first JV, VW saw its second opportunity in this market from another prospective partner: First Automobile Works (FAW), which used to be a major truck producer in China. This time, before establishing a JV, a licensing agreement for production was signed between the two parties in 1988. With this, VW authorized FAW to produce the Audi 100 under a licensing of technology agreement and as a CKD production. The first term for this agreement was signed for six years (Auto Home, 2011). In the following year, 1989, a total of 1922 Audi 100 units were assembled by FAW. Three years after the signing, in 1991, VW and FWA decided to strengthen this relationship, through what became its second JV in China: the FAW-Volkswagen partnership, with 60 per cent owned by the Chinese government and 40 per cent by VW (Aggarwal, 2001: 172).

Technology transfer

In 1995 when the licensing agreement terminated, VW brought Audi into the FAW-VW partnership and the JV contract was changed into the following: 60 per cent owned by FAW, 30 per cent by VW and 10 per cent by Audi. At the same time, FAW and Audi signed an agreement of technology transfer which included: 1) multiple series of Audi models to the production of the new JV, and 2) Audi's comprehensive involvement in the production management, equipment purchasing and upgrading, marketing, and after-sales service of China-produced Audi cars (Auto Home, 2011).

In 1996, FAW-VW and Audi went a step further, signing a 'co-designing' agreement for the Audi A6 C5. The project was conducted in VW's German headquarters and ran for three years (Auto Home, 2011). Although it was the first time the Chinese side of the JV had participated in the R&D of the production, the auto industry in China showed no signs of adopting lean production. To the contrary, this was the case for South Korea. At this stage, the capacity of the Chinese partners to acquire design and product development skills was still reported to be weak (Mukherjee and Sastry, 1996).

Later in 2002, Volkswagen Group China extended its JV partnership with SAIC by 20 years. In 2014, Volkswagen Group China extended its JV partnership with FAW by 25 years (VW Newroom, 2019). Both instances reconfirmed its great commitment to Asia.

As of 2019, the two JVs' ownership structures were the following:

- SAIC-Volkswagen:
  - 50% SAIC, 40% Volkswagen Aktiengesellschaft (incl. ŠKODA AUTO a.s.), 10% Volkswagen (China) Investment Company Ltd.
- FAW-Volkswagen:
  - 60% FAW, 25% Volkswagen Aktiengesellschaft, 5% AUDI AG, 10% Volkswagen (China) Investment Company Ltd.

Source: VW News Room (2019) Volkswagen Group China.
Available at: www.volkswagen-newsroom.com/en/volkswagen-group-china-5897
(accessed 8 April 2020).

VW China had also provided an important contribution to the company's overall production capabilities. Table 5.3 lists the numerical capacity and models produced by the two JVs.

(Continued)

(Continued)

Table 5.3   Details of VW JVs in China as of 2019

JV Names	Total production (October 2019)	Models produced
SAIC-VW	Over 4.0 million vehicles	Volkswagen: Polo Family (Polo), New Santana Family (New Santana, Gran Santana), Lavida Family (New Lavida, New Gran Lavida, Lavida, e-Lavida), New Lamando, New Passat, Passat PHEV, PHIDEON, Teramont, Teramont X, Tiguan (Tiguan Silk Road, New Tiguan L, Tiguan L PHEV), Tharu, T-Cross, New Touran L ŠKODA: New OCTAVIA Family (New OCTAVIA, OCTAVIA Combi), 2019 RAPID, 2019 RAPID Spaceback, SUPERB, KAMIQ, KAROQ, KODIAQ, KODIAQ GT
FAW-VW		Volkswagen: TAYRON, TAYRON R-Line, T-Roc, CC, Magotan, Sagitar Family (New Sagitar, Sagitar R-Line), Golf Family (New Golf, New Golf GTI, New Golf R-Line, New Golf Sportsvan, e-Golf), C-TREK, Bora (New Bora, Bora Classic, e-Bora) Audi: Q2L, A3 Limousine, A3 Sportback, Q3, A4L, Q5L, A6L (A6LC8, A6LPHEV) JETTA: VA3, VS5

Source: VW News Room, 2019

VW expanding further across Asia – Is ASEAN the next horizon?

Riding on its successful expansion into Asian markets in South Korea and China, VW further planned its entry into other markets in Asia. In 2014, VW analysed its then sales numbers on a global scale. The result indicated that VW's sales in the mature markets such as the US were much smaller than in the emerging markets such as in Asia. It was also suggested by analysts, according to a Bloomberg report, that the company would expect consolidated growth in sales (by approximately 4.5 per cent every year) until 2018 should it expand its business to more emerging markets such as Indonesia, Thailand, Malaysia, the Philippines and other smaller countries (ICRA Online, 2014).

However, risks existed in the ASEAN for VW. As a precedent, Toyota, one of VW's major competitors, had suffered from declining sales in Thailand due to political unrest in the country in 2014. Toyota was the automobile industry's foreign-owned first mover into Thailand during the 1960s. Not only had Toyota historically owned the biggest market share, it was also the biggest car seller in the ASEAN in addition to Thailand. A decreasing demand from the market in addition to a withdrawal of first-time buyers' rebate and rising competition impacted Toyota with a 10 per cent decline in sales (ICRA Online, 2014), leaving the company with an excess capacity that would cause further issues.

The Thai market

The automotive industry in Thailand started during the 1950s as part of the government's economic development plan, aiming to upgrade its economy from mainly agricultural to industrial (*Bangkok Post*, 2019). In 1973, the Automobile Industry Development Committee was established, setting a minimum local content of 25 per cent (Chiasakul, 2004: 5). This represented the 'local promotion' period of Thai's automotive industry. 1992 to 1996 was termed the 'liberalization period' for the industry, which grew by 12 per cent until 1997 when Asia's financial crisis hit the country (Chiasakul, 2004: 5; The Economist, 2013). After that, Thailand rapidly nicknamed itself the 'Detroit of Asia', moving from a country that intended to develop an indigenous automobile industry to restrict outflow of foreign exchange and meet local demands (Mukherjee and Sastry, 1996) to a production hub for global automobile brands due to an industrial restructuring initiated by the government (Chiasakul, 2004: 8).

Thai-produced vehicles such as Honda, GM and BMW, pioneered by the first batch of Mitsubishi Motors' vehicles exported to Canada in 1988 (Kaosa-Ard, 1993: 3; Mitsubishi, 2005), were exported to many countries in the ASEAN and Australia and New Zealand (CNN Business, 2019). Yet the country had attained the ninth place for global vehicle production in 2012 and 2013 and on a regional level has become the largest automobile manufacturer in Southeast Asia (*Bangkok Post*, 2019). According to ASEAN Briefing, the market share of cars produced in Thailand was divided by: Toyota with 27.4 per cent, Isuzu with 19 per cent and Honda with 15 per cent, followed by Mitsubishi with 8 per cent and Nissan with 7 per cent, and the other global car brands sharing the remaining 24 per cent (ASEAN Briefing, 2018).

In 2014, the Thai government announced that it would offer tax exemptions for eight years to foreign automobile manufacturers who invested 6.5 million baht ($200 million) or more into manufacturing cars in Thailand (ICRA Online, 2014; CNN Business, 2019). VW was then reported to have applied to the Thai government to build a production plant in Thailand (AutoHuanqiu, 2014). Besides the tax incentives, analysts also hinted that VW was motivated to have a presence in Thailand to narrow its gap with Toyota (ICRA Online, 2014). By 2014, the luxury motorbike brand Ducati, which had become part of VW in 2012, was already produced in Thailand. It was reported that VW's application received approval in 2015 although there had been no sign of construction of a new VW production plant in that country as yet (Handelsblatt, 2018). Other than that,

(Continued)

(Continued)

VW also had cooperated with a Malaysian auto-maker, DRB-Hicom Bhd, to produce the Passat in Malaysia (AutoHuanqiu, 2014). It seemed that its accumulative experience in South Korea and China paid off, enhancing the company's regional market entry and operations capability.

At this time, several of VW's international competitors had started expanding into more locations through their existing businesses in the Asian region, mainly China or using China as a base to serve a number of markets across Asia – and beyond. General Motors (GM) had announced in 2017 that it had started exporting its Chevrolet Sail to Mexico and the Caribbean supported by its JV plant with SAIC. Volvo's S90 had also been exported from its China plant to Belgium and for onward shipment to other European countries (Automotive Logistics, 2017).

VW's expansion plan into the ASEAN was conceived in 2018 when it also planned to increase sales of its China-built vehicles through market entry into Southeast Asia, while supporting its Chinese partners FAW and SAIC to scale their capacity to export (*South China Morning Post*, 2014). The export activity was planned to start from March of 2019 and the target markets planned focused on the ASEAN markets (*People's Daily*, 2018). But it was alleged to be merely VW's 'first step' towards entering the ASEAN. 'Other emerging markets are soon to follow', said a VW spokesperson: 'It's not about competition between China and our other export facilities. It's about creating an additional source of supply' (Handelsblatt, 2018).

Aside from Thailand, other ASEAN countries also attracted the attention of VW, like the Philippines, where car sales had grown more than 15 per cent in 2017 (Handelsblatt, 2018). 'The market in the Philippines is growing very rapidly', said the same VW spokesperson (Handelsblatt, 2018). Other countries in this region would also see shipments of Chinese-made VW cars, but exporting from China was not to be VW's long-term solution.

Final remarks

VW currently owns 33 production plants in Asia, with 23 in China, one in South Korea (Scania), one in Taiwan, two in Thailand (Scania and Ducati), one in Malaysia (Scania), and five in India. Despite a challenging start, VW has already become one of the biggest and most successful European automobile manufacturers in Asia and has demonstrated particular commitment. Its entry modes for the diverse Asian markets have varied for a number of reasons. For example, its co-investment with Ford in Argo AI, a self-driving car start-up, was reportedly inviting an Asian partner to fill in Argo's void in Asia. This contributed to reaching VW's next major goal in applying artificial intelligence to self-driving vehicles (Bloomberg, 2019a).

Case questions

1   How did government policies and regulations influence MNEs' entry modes into Asia markets? Please give examples.
2   To what extent was VW's experience helpful to advance its decision to further deepen its investment in its major Asian markets: China and South Korea?

5.4 STRATEGIC IMPLICATIONS

This chapter has focused on the modes of market entry and investment that MNEs typically use, and how this is applied in the Asian context. This followed Chapter 4 coherently in which you learnt that the variations in the Asian business environment remain significant, though increasingly market integration allows for a reduction of transaction costs in cross-border trade and investment. This chapter, Chapter 5, that we are now concluding, has shown the options available for firms to choose from, and what impact this has on their market expansion and levels of commitment.

When MNEs consider new market entry modes or a change to an existing presence internationally, the expected or current performance of the firm's foreign subsidiary is a key determinant. Market entry into and across Asia is increasingly composed of foreign direct investment modes. Such investment modes are – as explained and illustrated in this chapter – illustrative of a multinational's commitment to the market and demonstrate greater engagement with the economy and society as a whole than we would find in trade. This is because trade-related internationalization typically tends to serve low-key internationalization objectives or supply chain requirements. The international success or failure of a firm's venture in a host market, or its need to upscale or downscale operations, is directly related to its subsidiary's performance.

However, altogether, two intra-organizational paradigms will typically be detrimental to the success in-country:

- externally: the international strategy may be misaligned to the host market potential and business environment
- internally: the management of the host market, its operational context and its challenges may be handled inefficiently.

Most recent research into foreign subsidiary (FS) success in Asia demonstrates that a number of characteristics drive success (Bai et al., 2018). These success factors are summarized and contextualized below.

Parent-firm characteristics

The parent MNE typically provides critical resources to the subsidiary (e.g. budget, technology, knowledge) that shape and re-shape (upscale or down scale) operations in the host country. This holds for MNEs investing into Asia, out of Asia and across Asia.

> *Parent-firm international experience* (in our previous chapter also named 'internationalization knowledge'): This holds specifically for cross-regional investment.

> *Parent-firm technological capability*: These have been found to be capabilities typically less imitable than other capabilities, and they incur low depreciation costs during their transfer into other markets. Bai et al. (2018) find this is the case for investments across Asia and from Asia.

> *Parent-firm size*: There is ample evidence in business literature that parent size correlates with available resources and capabilities in the host country. This holds for all types of Asia-centric investment directions.

Subsidiary characteristics

> *Technological resources*: These resources help the subsidiary in the absorption and deployment of resources transferred from the parent MNE, and the exploration and utilization of resources based in the host country. Also, these will determine research and development intensity, and hence a basis for influence of the subsidiary across the market and across the parent company. Some studies illustrate that these resources have the potential to promote the financial performance of the subsidiary. For Asian MNEs, it is important to note that they also compete on relationship-based capabilities, which we will discuss below.

> *Age*: Age defines host country experience and accumulated knowledge. This holds specifically for MNEs investing into Asia, and less so within and across Asia.

> *Size*: As one may assume, research evidences that parent structures typically provide more resources to a bigger rather than a smaller subsidiary. Yet this only holds significantly for MNEs coming into the Asian market.

Parent–subsidiary relationship

> *Entry mode and MNE ownership*: 'Some studies suggest that greater ownership control by the parent MNE is better for FS performance because greater foreign ownership reflects a higher commitment from the parent MNE, which will increase resource transfer, and that the MNE having greater control reduces the opportunistic behaviour of local partners (e.g. Dhanaraj & Beamish, 2009). However, other research suggests that greater ownership by the MNE may reduce the incentive of local partners to contribute to the focal FS, thus inhibiting collaboration, which could harm FS performance. Researchers also suggest that different entry modes represent different levels of investment irreversibility (versus

flexibility) (e.g. Belderbos and Zou, 2007; Song and Lee, 2014), and the costs and benefits of different entry modes may be largely conditioned on external uncertainty' (Bai et al., 2018). Benefits of relatively high degrees of ownership hold for Asian firms investing in their region, rather than non-Asian firms investing in Asia.

Subsidiary governance: 'Autonomy refers to the decision-making rights of subsidiaries in relation to their parent MNEs'. Despite a body of literature theorizing that a greater degree of autonomy may leverage subsidiary performance, there is no undisputable evidence for this to date.

Human-resources practice: The way in which the subsidiary is staffed, i.e. the MNE's expatriate strategy, influences the intensity of knowledge transfer between parent and subsidiary. This typically has a positive influence on performance in the host country.

Country-level factors

These factors determine the competitive advantage that can be obtained through access to and utilization of resources. The home country may, for example, provide access to capital and other advantages. The host country is even more instrumental, in that cultural and institutional 'knowledge gaps' need to be closed to attain a positive impact on performance. In addition, market attractiveness specifically drives performance when Asian firms invest across borders.

The case of Volkswagen in this chapter has provided an insight into this, and how the host country entry and investment path is adjusted accordingly. It focused on the co-evolution of MNEs' market entry strategies and business environment, through insights into the reported initial explorations of VW in Asia that began in South Korea. VW had sought to expand into this market before the early 1980s. Back then, the South Korean government encouraged foreign car-makers to collaborate with local partners. Several American and Japanese manufacturers, such as Ford, Toyota and GM, promptly captured this 'window of opportunity' to build close alliances or JV partnerships with local chaebols, which had already accumulated enough manufacturing and design experience there and stepped into a mass production stage.

Because of the failure in securing a desirable partner, VW however chose a 'wait-and-see' strategy that lasted until 1987, when it became a KAIDA member and then began exporting its products to South Korea. After that, the financial crisis of 1997–98 impacted South Korea's economy severely, eventually urging the government to ease protectionist tendencies and localization policies. The subsequent policy adjustments opened another important 'window of opportunity' for VW, this time to establish its own sale-focused subsidiaries – Audi VW Korea in 2004 and VW Korea in 2005. VW subsequently started local production in South Korea by acquiring Scania in 2018.

In contrast, when exploring and expanding the Chinese market VW chose a 'rolling the dice' strategy and adopted relatively high-commitment entry modes. Unlike the car-makers in South Korea, those in China had fairly meagre technological and manufacturing capabilities, making only a few partner options available for VW. What seemed even more challenging was that no formal laws regulated JV and FDI in China until 1979. It was therefore not surprising that leading Western automobile manufacturers would hesitate to enter this market.

In the VW case, we see how its entry into China coincided with the creation of institutional advantage viewed from a business perspective. The Chinese government, as well as taking new initiatives and engaging into policy changes, decided to delegate significant autonomy to local governments and state-owned enterprises, which dominated the Chinese economy at that time with their sophisticated ownership and funding structures, seen by scholars as similar to Chaebols in South Korea in many aspects. The conditions that VW could do business in were seen as favourable – and not only to reduce the time and cost of engaging with its multi-stakeholders. Also, this provided a potentially favourable context to engage in 'institutional entrepreneurial' activities. The 1979 JV law in China is hence seen as a trigger for the entry of VW, and thus marked a critical milestone for both VW's international expansion and the marketization of the Chinese economy. It is seen as a milestone in the shaping of the Chinese business environment and demonstrated that MNEs could have an impact on the business environment in a host country, and ultimately, its growth potential which would impact that of an entire region.

The entry modes undertaken by VW for the Chinese market, evolving from licensing to JV, also spotlighted the role of the host government. It has been reported that the Chinese government's primary objective for welcoming foreign cooperation was to acquire technologies. Indeed, VW initially collaborated with two partners, namely SAIC and FAW, through technological licensing. These initial market engagements also deepened the ever-important trust relationship needed to successfully do business in Asia (and specifically, in China) and gave rise to two JVs – SAIC-Volkswagen in 1985 and FAW-Volkswagen in 1991.

The institutional and business environmental factors in Southeast Asia also influenced the market entry decision of MNEs through other types of incentives. A typical example was Thailand, which offered tax exemptions for large automobile MNEs. This induced VW to build a Thai production plant in 2014. From technology and sales to manufacturing in different locations, this case has highlighted the range of conditions that companies study before making an entry and investment choice, that can vary – depending on those decisions and its own objectives– in terms of location, mode of investment or its evolution, and the timing thereof. The case also provided a view on the strategic implications for so-called 'Western', non-Asian companies entering, persisting and succeeding in Asia, and how they act upon their evaluation of conditions that help or hinder market entry and operational effectiveness with a regional view.

The second case study brings us back to an example of an Asian firm and its strategic plan to enhance the value of the region for its market reach and operations. The case study examined this through Mahindra & Mahindra Limited, an Indian multinational conglomerate holding company with predominant business interests in the automobile and farm equipment sector. M&M is the flagship company of the Indian $20.7 billion Mahindra group, which is known for its diversified business interests through a global presence in over 100 countries and in 11 industries. M&M started as a domestic steel trading company and adopted a strategy that focused clearly on capability development and enhancement. The company has pursued this through various tools, especially using technological collaborations to develop itself into a highly successful manufacturer of utility vehicles. It has also had a keen focus on R&D and innovation to enhance limited organizational capabilities in product design and development.

M&M has followed the local optimizer strategy of capability development and enhancement through the input of cross-regional learning and capability improvement. It has based its strategy of technological collaboration to optimize local products and processes for the domestic market. This is a particularly insightful case of the local optimizer strategy as a strategic tool used by emerging market MNEs such as M&M, where firms develop ownership advantages by optimizing products and processes to meet the specific conditions of the domestic (or regional) market. The MNE later uses these capabilities to enter other markets where the products and processes can be replicated. Those markets are typically foremost emerging markets, though not always. Indeed, M&M also used technological collaborations with various international giants to hone skills and develop its additional capabilities. This began with an alliance with Willys Overland Export Corporation (USA), for assembling the Jeep for India's rugged rural areas. This was followed by several other collaborations with MNEs across the world to support its objective to emerge as a leader in the automobile and farm equipment spaces.

M&M also established joint ventures with leading global MNEs to drive its progress in R&D and growth of innovative ideas to hone its production skills in other product areas, for items ranging from alloy steel, to farm equipment and later across a range of automobiles.

The case of M&M has illustrated the variety of motivations that shape strategic intent and impact in its Asian market entry and investments. This was combined with the firm using diverse modes of entry into different markets ranging from exports to acquisitions and greenfield ventures. It followed an unconventional internationalization path, as it began exporting to geographically distant countries such as Yugoslavia at the same time as it was selling in proximate Asian markets such as Indonesia.

Taking a 'birds-eye view' on Asia, that is, adapting the internationalization strategy to a regionalization level that goes well beyond a country-by-country approach, proves advantageous in the commitment to doing business in Asia.

REFERENCES

Aggarwal, V. K (2001) *Winning in Asia: European Style*. New York: Palgrave Macmillan.

Annual Report (2018) Available at: http://mahindra.com/annualreviewFY18.

Annual Review (2018) Available at: www.mahindra.com/resources/pdf/about-us/mahindra-rise-brochure-june-2019.pdf.

ASEAN Briefing (2018) Thailan's Automotive industry: Opportunities and incentives. Available at: www.aseanbriefing.com/news/2018/05/10/thailands-automotive-industry-opportunities-incentives.html (accessed 18 October 2019).

Auto Home (2011) 23 years' marching ahead: FAW-VW's development review. Available at: www.autohome.com.cn/news/201107/217532.html (accessed 4 August 2019).

Auto Huanqiu (2014) Volkswagen is about to launch production plant in Thailand to consolidate its market shares in South-East Asia. Available at: http://auto.huanqiu.com/globalnews/2014-04/4951967.html?agt=15438 (accessed 19 July 2019).

Automotive Logistics (2017) VW seeks to boost presence in emerging markets with exports from China. Available at: www.automotivelogistics.media/vw-seeks-to-boost-presence-in-emerging-markets-with-exports-from-china/20021.article (accessed 16 July 2019).

Bai, T., Du, J. and Solarino, A.M. (2018) Performance of foreign subsidiaries 'in' and 'from' Asia: A review, synthesis and research agenda. *Asia Pacific Journal of Management*, 35(3): 607–638.

Bangkok Post (2019) Automotive industry at a turning point. Available at: www.bangkokpost.com/business/1606570/automotive-industry-at-a-turning-point (accessed 4 August 2019).

Barter News Weekly (2010) Bartering with government. Available at: www.barternewsweekly.com/2010/02/bartering-with-government (accessed 8 April 2020).

Belderbos, R. and Zou, J. (2007) On the Growth of Foreign Affiliates: Multinational Plant Networks, Joint Ventures, and Flexibility. *Journal of International Business Studies*, 38: 1095–1112.

Bloomberg (2019a) Argo's tie-up with Ford, VW, leaves room for Asian automaker, Available at: www.bloomberg.com/news/articles/2019-07-12/argo-s-tie-up-with-ford-and-vw-leaves-room-for-asian-automaker (accessed 6 August 2019).

Bloomberg (2019b) Audi Volkswagen Korea Ltd. Available at: www.bloomberg.com/profile/company/AUDIZZ:TT?cic_redirect=3 (accessed 8 August 2019).

BuntyLLC (2019) The ultimate guide to car production lines. Available at: https://buntyllc.com/car-production-lines/ (accessed 8 August 2019).

Chiasakul, S. (2004) *Production Networks, Trade and Investment Policies, and Asian Regional Cooperation: The Thai Automotive Industry Case*. Bangkok: Asian Development Research Forum.

China Auto News (2018a) My 40 years with China Automobile: Starting from the establishment of SAIC-Volkswagen. Available at: www.ctoutiao.com/1231797.html (accessed 19 July 2019).

China Auto News (2018b) This was how VW was refined in China. Available at: www.yidianzixun.com/article/0KOiMYu5 (accessed 4 August 2019).

Chugai Pharmaceuticals (2002) Strategic alliance with Roche. Available at: www.chugai-pharm.co.jp/english/profile/strategy/roche_alliance.html (accessed 8 April 2020).

CNN Business (2019) How Thailand became the 'Detroit of Asia'. Available at: https://money.cnn.com/2018/07/10/news/world/thailand-auto-industry/index.html (accessed 4 August 2019).

Directorate of Intelligence (2012) Prospects for Western Europe's automobile industry. Available at: www.cia.gov/library/readingroom/docs/CIA-RDP89T00295R000400410001-1.pdf (accessed 18 July 2019).

Donnelly, T., Mellahi, K. and Morris, D. (2002) The European automobile industry: Escape from parochialism. *European Business Review*, 14(1): 30–39.

EastDay.com (2018) First passenger car JV: SAIC's 30 years of history. Available at: http://auto.eastday.com/a/180816142433198-2.html (accessed 4 August 2019).

Ebert, R.R. and Montoney, M. (2007) Performance of the South Korean automobile industry in the domestic and United States markets. *The Baldwin-Wallace College Journal of Research and Creative Studies*, 1(1): 12–24.

Economic Times (2017) Mahindra opens Detroit's 1st car making plant in 25 years. Available at: https://economictimes.indiatimes.com/industry/mahindra-opens-detroits-1st-car-making-plant-in-25-years/articleshow/61731936.cms?from=mdr (accessed 8 April 2020).

Economic Times (2019) Mahindra wants to make South Africa hub for its exports in the continent. Available at: https://economictimes.indiatimes.com/industry/auto/auto-news/mahindra-wants-to-make-south-africa-hub-for-its-exports-in-the-continent/articleshow/69173794.cms (accessed 8 April 2020).

ECNS (2016) New Hope Group opens Australian headquarters. Available at: http://www.ecns.cn/business/2016/10-08/229159.shtml (accessed 24 April 2020).

Forbes (2018) Berkshire Hathaway takes stake in India's Paytm. Available at: www.forbes.com/sites/gurufocus/2018/08/27/berkshire-hathaway-takes-stake-in-indias-paytm/#59a2d944984f (accessed 8 April 2020).

Ford, J.L., Sen, S. and Wei, H. (2010) FDI and economic development in China 1970-2006: A cointegration study. Available at: www.birmingham.ac.uk/Documents/college-social-sciences/business/economics/2010-papers/economics-papers-2010/10-24.pdf (accessed 18 July 2019).

Franchise Direct (2019) Top 100 franchises 2019. Available at: www.franchisedirect. com/top100globalfranchises/rankings?page=4 (accessed 8 April 2020).

Gopalan, M. (2018) For M&M to be truly global, we need a second home market. Available at: www.thehindubusinessline.com/specials/auto-focus/pawan-goenka-of-mahindra-and-mahindra-talks-about-industry/article24823139.ece# (accessed 8 April 2020).

Hahn, C.H. (2005) *My Years with Volkswagen*. Munich: Herbig, FA.

Handelsblatt (2018) VW to boost Asia sales by exporting cars out of China. Available at: www.handelsblatt.com/today/companies/made-in-china-vw-to-boost-asia-sales-by-exporting-cars-out-of-china/23580714.html?ticket=ST-36436029-ONw11lk9rc9LQdfnReMR-ap6 (accessed 18 October 2019).

IBM (2000) NTT Comware and IBM announce intention to form alliance to deliver IT services in Japan. Available at: https://www-03.ibm.com/press/us/en/pressrelease/1496.wss (accessed 8 April 2020).

IBM (2005) IBM, Sony, Sony Computer Entertainment Inc. and Toshiba disclose key details of the Cell chip. Available at: https://www-03.ibm.com/press/us/en/pressrelease/7502.wss (accessed 8 April 2020).

ICRA Online (2014) How does Thailand fit into Volkswagen's plans? Available at: www.fool.com/investing/general/2014/04/23/how-does-thailand-fit-into-volkswagens-plans.aspx (accessed 17 July 2019).

International Chamber of Commerce (2019) Incoterms® 2020. Available at: https://iccwbo.org/resources-for-business/incoterms-rules/incoterms-2020 (accessed 8 April 2020).

KAIDA (2019a) History of imported cars. Available at: www.kaida.co.kr/en/sense/history.do (accessed 19 July 2019).

KAIDA (2019b) Import car info. Available at: www.kaida.co.kr/en/sense/origin.do (accessed 30 September 2019).

Kaosa-ard, M. (1993) TNC involvement in the Thai auto industry. *TDRI Quarterly Review*, 8(1): 9–16.

Kim & Chang (2019) Automotive in South Korea. Available at: www.lexology.com/library/detail.aspx?g=e4532067-87b8-47b1-aa00-c1816e5e001f (accessed 18 July 2019).

Kishimoto, M. (2018) Chinese cash pushes Southeast Asia's M&A tally to record high. Available at: https://asia.nikkei.com/Business/Business-deals/Chinese-cash-pushes-Southeast-Asia-s-M-A-tally-to-record-high (accessed 8 April 2020).

Kynge, J. (2019) China triples investment in emerging Asia on trade war. *Financial Times*, 3 April. Available at: www.ft.com/content/b9b44cd6-55b0-11e9-91f9-b6515a54c5b1 (accessed 8 April 2020).

Lansbury, R.D., Suh, C.S., So, C.S. and Kwon, S.-H. (2012) *The Global Korean Motor Industry: The Hyundai Motor Company's Global Strategy.* Abingdon: Routledge.

Lee, D.O., Lee, K., Kim, J.J. and Lim, G.C. (1996) Executive insights: The Korean automobile industry – challenges and strategies in the global market. *Journal of International Marketing,* 4(4): 85–96.

Licence Global (2019) Licence Global's 2019 Top 150 Leading Licensors. Available at: www.licenseglobal.com/rankings-and-lists/license-globals-2019-top-150-leading-licensors (accessed 8 April 2020).

Liu, J. (2008) Enlightenment from comparing the automobile industry policies of China, Japan, and South Korea. *Economic Review,* Vol. 10.

LiveMint (2019) McDonald's, Vikram Bakshi working on out-of-court settlement. Available at: www.livemint.com/companies/news/mcdonald-s-vikram-bakshi-working-on-out-of-court-settlement-1557146222573.html (accessed 8 April 2020).

Madhavan, N. (2013) How Mahindra & Mahindra came to dominate the Indian automotive industry. Available at: www.forbesindia.com/article/boardroom/how-mahindra-mahindra-came-to-dominate-the-indian-automotive-industry/39141/1 (accessed 8 April 2020).

Mahindra (2019) Mahindra's farm equipment sector sells 3,30,436 units during FY-19. Available at: www.mahindra.com/news-room/press-release/mahindra-s-farm-equipment-sector-sells-330436-units-during-fy-19 (accessed 8 April 2020).

Mitsubishi (2005) Mitsubishi Motors releases new Triton pickup truck in Thailand. Available at: https://web.archive.org/web/20140427153627/http://www.mitsubishi-motors.com/en/corporate/pressrelease/products/detail1324.html (accessed 18 October 2019).

Mukherjee, A. and Sastry, T. (1996) Automotive industry in emerging economies: A comparison of South Korea, Brazil, China and India. *Economic and Political Weekly,* M75–M78.

News China (2013) Three reasons for Korean to favor German cars. Available at: http://news.china.com.cn/world/2013-12/28/content_31030000.htm (accessed 30 September 2019).

NY Times (2014) VW wins enough shares to take full control of Scania. Available at: https://dealbook.nytimes.com/2014/05/13/volkswagen-wins-enough-shares-to-take-full-control-of-scania/ (accessed 24 April 2020).

Park, B.-G. (2003) Politics of scale and the globalizaiton of the South Korean automobile industry. *Economic Geography,* 79(2): 173–194.

People's Daily (2018) VW plans to expand its Chinese business overseas: Focusing on Philippines and ASEAN markets. Available at: https://baijiahao.baidu.com/s?id=1595093207931127505&wfr=spider&for=pc (accessed 30 September 2019).

Ramamurti, R. and Singh, J.V. (2009) Indian multinationals: Generic internationalisation strategies. In R. Ramamurti and J.V. Singh (eds), *Emerging Multinationals in Emerging Markets*. Cambridge: Cambridge University Press, pp. 110–166.

Reuters (2014) Sony forms joint ventures in China for PlayStation, Available at: www.nytimes.com/2014/05/27/business/international/sony-forms-joint-venture-in-china-for-playstation.html (accessed 8 April 2020).

Richards, P. (2019) The international trade in services. *Reserve Bank of Australia Bulletin*. Available at: www.rba.gov.au/publications/bulletin/2019/mar/the-international-trade-in-services.html (accessed 8 April 2020).

Sina Finance (2014) S. Korean auto market stormed by German luxury cars. Available at: https://finance.sina.com.cn/world/20141117/182520841291.shtml (accessed 10 August 2019).

South China Morning Post (2014) Volkswagen sells China-made cars in Southeast Asia, helping partners scale export readiness. Available at: https://www.scmp.com/business/companies/article/2143201/volkswagen-sells-china-made-cars-southeast-asia-helping-partners (accessed 17 july 2019).

Sohu Auto (2018) Flagship S650's standardized curtain restraint system! Scania announced the new series of trucks to South Korea. Available at: www.sohu.com/a/222729086_754319 (accessed 19 July 2019).

The Economist (2013) Thailand's booming car industry: Detroit of the East. Available at: www.economist.com/schumpeter/2013/04/04/detroit-of-the-east (accessed 17 October 2019).

Tilley, A. (2014) Indian-backed electric scooter startup launches in US, poaches talent from Apple, Tesla. Available at: www.forbes.com/sites/aarontilley/2016/01/20/indian-backed-electric-scooter-startup-launches-in-us-poaches-talent-from-apple-tesla/#1eb9e87b50f8 (accessed 8 April 2020).

Toyota (2012) *Sustainability Report 2012*. Available at: www.toyotabharat.com/documents/environment/sustain-report/2012/sustainability_report12_fe.pdf (accessed 8 April 2020).

Toyota (2019) Legacy. Available at: https://www.toyotabharat.com/toyota-in-india/legacy/ (accessed 8 April 2020).

Ullatil, P. (2013) M&M scripts global strategy. Available at: www.business-standard.com/article/companies/m-m-scripts-global-strategy-103120201047_1.html (accessed 8 April 2020).

Varma, S. (2012) *International Business*. Delhi: Pearson Education.

Verband der Automobilindustrie (2017) Automobile production. Available at: www.vda.de/en/services/facts-and-figures/annual-figures/automobile-production.html (accessed 30 September 2019).

VW Newsroom (2019) Volkswagen Group China. Available at: www.volkswagen-newsroom.com/en/volkswagen-group-china-5897 (accessed 24 April 2020).

Yap, K.L.M. (2018) Southeast Asia has an investment boom, thanks to the trade war. *Bloomberg*, 22 October. Available at: www.bloomberg.com/news/articles/2018-10-22/thanks-to-the-trade-war-southeast-asia-has-an-investment-boom (accessed 8 April 2020).

WTO (2019) Highlights of world trade. *World Trade Statistical Review 2019*. Available at: www.wto.org/english/res_e/statis_e/wts2019_e/wts2019chapter02_e.pdf (accessed 8 April 2020).

6

ASIA'S GLOBAL VALUE CHAIN PARTICIPATION

6.1 THE CRUCIAL PARTICIPATION OF ASIA IN SUPPLY AND GLOBAL VALUE CHAINS

This chapter focuses on Asia's global value chain participation. It covers:

* an introduction to the reasons why and how participation in Asia's supply and value chains has become crucial
* a case study that explores Huawei's supply chain management amid US–China trade tensions – establishing collaborative partnerships with Asian suppliers
* a case study that then provides a different perspective on a similar sector, looking at Samsung's supply chain management – a unique blend driving capability development and adjustment
* it concludes with key highlights and their strategic implications.

Introduction: Defining supply and global value chains

Asia has enjoyed its pre-eminence in attracting production activities for more than two decades now. China specifically has been known as an outstanding contributor to the 'global factory' (Buckley, 2011) and is predicted to remain in that role as it is set to become the world's largest economy before 2030. Yet China's role, and that of the other Asian economies, has changed, not only in terms of value created but also due to shifts in its distribution across countries through supply chains, and through the strategic utilization of global and regional value chains. To various degrees, the Asian economies are interlinked across the production stages within and beyond Asia and add some of the most significant value to products and services provided every day, everywhere.

The analysis of supply and value 'chains' explores phenomena that are known under a variety of terms including 'production fragmentation', 'outsourcing', 'offshoring', 'production sharing' and 'vertical specialization'. All of these depict how high volumes of intermediate products or services (parts, components, intermediate services) are produced and supplied in stages across different countries, regions and boundaries. They then get exported to other countries for further production and/or delivery. This happens within Asia, through intra-Asian supply and value chains, and with the rest of the world when other suppliers or the focal firm (the firm that ultimately delivers the product or service) is located elsewhere.

Differentiating supply chains and value chains

It is essential for firms to consider two perspectives in this fragmented production, that is, supply chains and value chains. They refer to two interpretations of similar if not identical activities:

- GVCs focus on the process in which companies receive raw materials or service-specific information, add value to them through production, manufacturing, sophistication and/or other processes to create a finished product or service, and then sell to consumers. This is about the generation of value for the customer, as determined by this customer, and importantly includes activities such as design and branding.
- The SC is the flow of inputs and outputs, representing the steps it takes to get the product or service from raw material or innovation to the customer. The main difference is that the latter involves all parties in fulfilling a product or service order in stages from conception and design, customer request, for customer satisfaction – often mainly centred on the cost of materials and effective product delivery. Modifications in SCs include incremental changes in the physical movement and management of materials. Changes in SCs are overall less transformative to the company's place in the competitive market than GVC changes.

Multinationals play a key role in determining how cross-border trade and investment is conducted to serve their respective supply chains. Gartner, the global research firm, has repeatedly reported Unilever to score highest in SC leadership worldwide, obtaining the highest level of recognition ('master' level) in 2019, followed by top rankings for Inditex, Cisco, Colgate-Palmolive and Intel (Gartner, 2018). Among Asian firms, South Korea's Samsung Electronics is the SC leader in this ranking, at 17th worldwide overall, and it was the only Asian company in the firm's Top 25 list of 2018, which measures business performance and opinion. Samsung notes on its marketing supports that its 'competitive edge at Samsung Electronics comes from the competitive edge of our suppliers' (Samsung, 2019), which include approximately 2,500 suppliers across the globe, with an inherent strategy of spreading out production among Asian countries. This creates a direct impact on the economies in the region that are part of this chain: Samsung's Vietnam investment, for example, helped Vietnam to turn into the world's second biggest exporter of smartphones after China.

While SC are company-focused, the regional and GVCs are typically measured and reported by (inter-)governmental and multilateral organizations. This is because they also comprise an understanding of how the rise of value-added contributions on a macro-economic level increases development and competitiveness. The main sources of GVC data are the World Bank, the IMF, the OECD and others. GVCs are more developed across Asia than in any other region in the world (OECD, 2013).

Both approaches have in common that they scrutinize efficiencies through a staged approach, separated into upstream and downstream value chain activities. These stages are exemplified in Figure 6.1, and distinguished between 'upstream', i.e. pre-production, and 'downstream', i.e. post-production stages.

Value and supply chain steps

Supply chains are typically organized into stages that create, maintain or raise efficiencies. For multinationals, that takes place through the strategic location of where those stages take place: this is mainly determined through procurement and supplier relations, and put into locations that allow for cost advantages and quality benefits and adhere to other objectives that the firm pursues (e.g. reputation).

The allocation of these stages in strategic and geographic terms is based on market research, and on a firm's capabilities. This research is either conducted in-house (especially when intellectual property, IP, is important) or outsourced to research companies. The findings of this research then determine whether the stages can be fulfilled by an intra- or inter-firm supply chain network, that is, either by capabilities within the firm itself or by external suppliers, or a mix of the two options. While SC was traditionally more of a sub-category of procurement in most companies, this area has risen from the back office a C-suite level of decision-making since the start of the millennium. This is due to its central role today in gaining (and maintaining) competitive advantage. In particular, the most successful firms are capable of strategically integrating physical SC assets with digital innovation (advanced analytics, robotics, AI, **blockchains**, etc.).

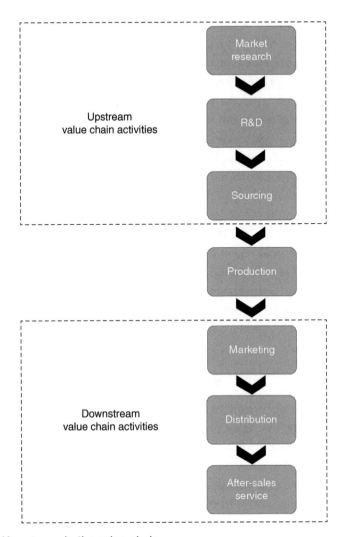

Figure 6.1   Key stages in the value chain

This leads to an integration of functions within the firm supporting effective, customer-centric SC, rather than SC supporting the strategy through a more simplistic approach to production and delivery. This is increasingly important for the survival of multinationals in a fast-moving environment, in which disruptions happen fast, for example, the computer, software and books sectors, which experienced disruption some years ago. At this moment, apparel, office products and other sectors are undergoing similar disruption.

Asia-Pacific consumers are the fastest adopters worldwide of new technologies and have the largest concentration of mobile and social media users. Some of the most impactful examples include: in China, Tencent, Alibaba, Baidu, Ant Financial or Xiaomi Corporation; in South Korea, Naver; in Japan, Rakuten and SoftBank. These are examples of firms that have already aligned and integrated their core strategy and digital technology, basing their business models on responsive, agile and customer-centric supply chains, and doing this more so than their competitors specifically through the adoption and effective utilization of new technologies.

Companies working across Asia typically use multiple suppliers (i.e. external suppliers are numerous), yet often one supplier (who is typically called the contractor, focus, flagship firm or principal) will choose another supplier (the subcontractor) to provide one or all parts of the product, service or sub-stage/component. The subcontractor, for example, takes care of the production design, or its processing or component's manufacture, or maintenance or services, in fulfilment of the contractor's specifications.

The multi-supplier strategy is used to add value to every one of the firm's business projects, keeping transaction costs low yet the quality of supplies at the desired level, using a network of most suitable suppliers who are aligned to a timeframe, no matter where they are. Technology is one of the key tools that allows internal and external products and services to be integrated throughout this complex system, allowing for SC efficiencies and value distribution at each stage through effective GVCs. When subcontracting takes place externally and in foreign markets, 'offshoring' is the term used. When the SC is mainly conducted in-house, i.e. through an intra-company supply chain, yet abroad, then we speak of 'captive sourcing' through foreign direct investment.

Flexibility and speed are at a premium: mitigating risk and bringing a product or service to market faster than the competition constitutes a crucial part of competitive advantage in most cases. To remain competitive, allocating the most value-adding stages of the SC in a way that retains ownership of the main factors of competitive advantage tends to be crucial, especially for companies that are dependent on keeping IP and other knowledge factors.

Seeking efficiencies through the understanding of value-added

In most cases, the principal firm retains core activities in the SC, including stages that add most value. For example, this includes some crucial part of production or assembly, or marketing, or a service that competitors do not provide or provide differently or less effectively.

This means that most often, the principal will mainly delegate the low-value supply stages and/or distribution or customer service to independent suppliers only. The principal and their intermediaries are seen as essential contributors to one or more value-adding activity: from a GVC perspective, they deliver value at different stages or holistically.

This value chain can be changed or adjusted when the SC is (re-)configured to achieve a certain level of quality and effectiveness, e.g. through technological innovation, automation or artificial intelligence. This may shorten value chains and even lead to the removal of previously important and/or costly stages. Examples of such changes include where customers:

- may prefer to acquire a product or service directly and/or online rather than via distributors (e.g. for convenience, price or as promoted through WEIBO, the Chinese microblogging system, Taobao, the virtual marketplace, or other platforms). For example, Mercedes-Benz's smart division in China has been an early mover and pioneer of auto brand in e-commerce when it sold 205 smart cars within four hours through group buying on Taobao, back in 2010.
- or may choose to follow new marketing channels, such as virtual influencers (KOL – key opinion leaders), very popular in China, who capitalize on their online popularity via live-stream apps to promote and sell anything from their own beauty product lines to wines and electronics.
- or may become increasingly aware of ethical issues in supply chains – e.g. human or animal welfare, or climate impact – and demand less packaging, or better crop resistance options or cosmetics advances, e.g. through microbiome technologies that remove certain stages of the supply chains in these industries, as for example explored by the Malaysian Palm Oil Board, Malaysia, or as already utilized for example by Unilever India.

At the same time, Asia is at the forefront of digital innovation for data collection. China's facial recognition systems are used, for example, in business applications by the Ant Financial Services Group, Alibaba's mobile payment unit, streamlining final delivery systems and pick-up of final products or services, while not only collecting buyer data but also matching it with biometrical information. Asian EMNEs also increasingly tend to bring these capabilities in through M&As with developed market firms.

Also, increasingly blockchains are used that alter supply chain efficiencies through better:

- product provenance and traceability, including authenticity of items for branding and for more accurate recalls, and hence improving bottom-line while enhancing trust
- streamlined operations through interoperability and end-to-end integration of data documentation, increased accuracy and timeliness (up to real-time synchronization) in collaborative planning and delivery
- accountability and integrity through full audit trails, increased accuracy in forecasting, with the potential to provide better control over ethical and environmental standards.

Producer or buyer driven?

Value chains are typically producer driven and buyer driven. The buyer is either a large wholesaler or distributor, the principal or the end-buyer. The principal aims to satisfy by providing a product or service along the desired specifications and marketing expectations.

- Producer-driven chains are mainly linked on intra-firm level across affiliates of multinational firms.
- Buyer-driven chains constitute networks between legally independent firms.

The latter is usually found for relatively simple products, such as apparel, home goods and toys, where generally innovation drives product design and marketing yet the principal firm outsources production. Product-driven chains are those mainly found for technology- and more capital-intensive items including cars and complex electronics.

This is when technological innovation and production capabilities are crucial components of competitive advantages and are deployed in-house or among captive suppliers only to keep control over IP and to maintain end-to-end visibility throughout the chain.

Governance and risk management challenges

Resilience, protection and risk management of the SC are essential as companies may lose B2B (business-to-business) or B2C (business-to-customer) customers if the SC is mismanaged, disrupted or hindered in its effectiveness in any way. The governance of value chains therein encompasses the ability to deal with and effectively manage the complexity of transactions, the codifiability of information and the capability of suppliers.

The objective of keeping risk assessable and manageable, and of ensuring SC resilience, includes the ability to maintain resilience to natural or human-made disaster (drought, flood, accidents, terrorism, etc.), through various techniques.

They typically include:

- the diversification or increase of suppliers
- the shortening of supply chains to reduce uncertainty
- the protection of materials and contracts
- the agility to take and implement timely strategic decisions that enable GVC reconfiguration.

Shortened or diversified supply chains allow for better control, visibility, and faster adaptation, while complex chains require multi-layered mitigation. For example, Diageo plc, the global manufacturer and distributor of premium spirits, wine and beer, imports more than 60 per cent of the product it sells in Asia from Scotland; tailors its distribution and inventory practices to each product segment; and uses local manufacturing or postponement to minimize the impact of any supply chain disruption on its Asian business; and dramatically reduces its SC through less inventory (see, for example, Cooke, 2018). Yet shorter supply chains may result in loss of efficiency and higher transaction costs. Also, shorter supply chains are more vulnerable to impacts stemming from recession.

Still, in the year 2010, sources such as the Asian Development Bank Institute noted that strategizing the SC in Asia was a 'relatively new topic' (Banomyong, 2010).

Today, Asian SC management is highly sophisticated, and highly integrated with the global markets. In addition, it is in Asia that one can observe the most successful cases of combining physical and digital capabilities of SC stakeholders, to leverage the strength of the network through integrating it effectively.

This may include increasingly, among others:

- sophisticated automatic storage and retrieval systems (ASRS), that typically have a payback period of five to seven years, such as, for example, provided by Daifuku throughout Singapore
- the likes of the modular AutoStore type system such as, for example, used by Yusen Logistics, the logistics provider headquartered in Laos, provided by Swisslog, that allow for bins to be stacked high and tight on a grid served by high-speed robots
- connectivity between small parts warehouses and production through automated guided vehicles (AGVs) such as driverless forklifts provided by Toyota
- KIVA robots as used by Amazon or the similar AI-centric Geek+ robot development by Alibaba. This is core to the evolution of business to Industry 4.0, the intelligent interconnection of people, machines, systems and products.

Asia-based logistics providers play a critical role in facilitating this supply chain integration. Yet it is infrastructure investments that drive the physical connectivity between neighbouring countries, as well as their digital connectivity, coupled with market grouping/integration.

This impacts the direct cost of SC management, i.e. costs of the logistics service provided, and indirect costs originating as a consequence of the service provided, such as delays, insurance premiums, etc. A 2019 report by Korn Ferry reports that 'Shippers are increasingly aware that if they do not have the technological capabilities to accomplish their goals, they should partner with those that do' (Korn Ferry, 2019: 4). Through the disruptive nature of digital innovation, e-commerce and business-to-consumer shipping, the SC has transformed over the past decade and allows for real-time visibility into production and shipments, and traceability of the origin and nature of components. With this, data integration between SC stakeholders helps facilitate network optimization and agility, finding the best option for SC stages at a given time, making timely decisions that keep the SC moving, and providing checks and balances to leverage order and shipment accuracy.

Resilient SCs are based on the evaluation of the principal's markets and suppliers, which determines the selection process for suppliers, which is then formalized and implemented through agreements. These agreements set the basis that helps to monitor, evaluate, review and revise the supplier relationship, and are hence crucial elements in SC risk reduction.

For example, at certain moments in time, management may decide on the repatriation of SCs to safe-haven countries with low geo-political and geo-economic risk and uncertainties, and/or by constituting inventory buffers. The agreements will define how agile and cost-effective this process is, and the degree of risk, for example in terms of quality, delivery, or distribution changes. The latter constitute the warehousing of inventory or components at one or more stages of the chain yet tend to increase costs compared to just-in-time delivery or similar cost-efficient solutions.

Another example is the potential risk stemming from importing, which needs to be mitigated considering its advantages that include cost benefits, access to talent, faster corporate growth, productivity, service and technological innovation. The risks may encompass the vulnerability to exchange rate fluctuations, uncertainty stemming from supplier/partner selection, with potential qualification, monitoring and managing operations costs, and potentially IP and reputational costs.

A final example is the risk that originates from SCs not adhering to sustainability expectations.

Transport is responsible for 18 per cent of global emissions, and total CO_2 emissions continue to increase despite climate change. Innovation and automation in SCs have the potential to reduce these dramatically.

Agility and standardization

The agility and flexibility of SCs across Asia are crucial, because of:

- fast-growing markets that result in uncertainty of future locational advantages
- exposure to political, geo-political and geo-economic shifts (with shifting competitiveness of countries), which results in concerns over the long-term nature and reliability of locational advantages
- exposure to tariff risk with non-Asian markets, yet decreasing tariffs result in more regionally focused SC capabilities and intra-Asia centric Third party logistics (TPL) competence

- increasing product complexity and service expectations within Asia, which require on-going innovation capacity
- sustainability, ethical and safety issues, which are increasingly important to consumers and require ever-increasing SC diligence and responsibilities
- changing labour costs, infrastructure investments, short product developments, talent shortages, which change SCs specifically as they become increasingly digitalized.

At the same time, the standardization of SCs is applied as much as is feasible. Standardization is 'the process of establishing a compatible and interchangeable concept, design, specification, procedure (practice), and doctrine that can increase commonality of products, processes, and systems' (Min et al., 2014: 360). This is usually driven by information technology and digital innovation that provides competitive advantage through cost-efficient logistics operations. Standardization takes place from the most basic standardization of pallets, to intermodular boxes, to container sizes; also packaging and label standards through governmental regulations can induce efficiencies.

Variations in market limit the standardization potential in SCs. For example, the ASEAN Cosmetic Labelling Requirement asks producers to label products locally with the name and address of the company or person responsible for placing the product in the local market. In Malaysia, labelling in Bahasa Malaysian and/or English is possible, while in Thailand, Thai language on the labels is compulsory, and in Taiwan, traditional Chinese characters need to be used.

Third party logistics

Third party logistics (abbreviated 3PL or TPL) can play a crucial role in the design and provision of client-focused supply chains, as a one stop shop service that may provide (as per contract) the management function of, for example, inbound freight, customs, warehousing, order fulfilment, distribution, and/or outbound freight to customers.

The origins of TPL

When using a TPL, the principal typically seeks to focus only on producing and selling and on service, that is, outsourcing part or all of a firm's distribution and fulfilment services. In 1996, Accenture registered '3PL' as a trademark, explained as: 'A supply chain integrator that assembles and manages the resources, capabilities, and technology of its own organization with those of complementary service providers to deliver a comprehensive supply chain solution' (Accenture, 2019). It is no longer a registered term.

Almost all Asian SCs converge at some stage through China, India and Southeast Asia. This is where we find TPLs to be most active. Some of the players present in Asia's TPL market are Asian, some non-Asian. They include Deutsche Post AG, Nippon Express Co. Ltd., C.H. Robinson Worldwide Inc., Kuehne + Nagel International AG, XPO Logistics Inc., DB Schenker, DSV A/S, Geodis, Sinotrans Co. Ltd., and UPS Supply Chain Solutions, among others. The TPL market is estimated to reach US$55.7 billion by 2025 (The Insights Partner, 2019) with Asia being one of the most attractive markets worldwide. Warehousing services are the fastest growing segment. In Southeast Asia specifically, we continue to find an extremely fragmented industry with a significant number of smaller players with deep local knowledge and connections. They are frequently used by the larger TPLs as sub-contractors to leverage local coverage, or (mainly in China) as joint venture partners.

In essence, the TPL moves goods from one end of the supply chain to the other within the constraints imposed by both clients and the commercial environment. Within the SC, the greater the distance between the manufacturer of components, the final assembly, and the distributor or retailer, the more important it is to manage both material and information flows in the SC effectively.

This requires the ability of TPL to receive and act upon complex information and instructions from principals, which requires a high degree of competence because:

- the degree of control that a company exercises over its TPL is contingent on the TPL's competence, especially when acting cross-border
- international SCs are more complex than national SCs and require special attention also in regard to location choice and modes in the supplier network, and to how they organize R&D, product sourcing, marketing and customer service activities, in addition to stages of production
- flexibility is required to manage various country and region specific risks and opportunities – SC leads may prefer contractual relationships with independent suppliers and distributors in one location while engaging in direct investment in another
- they must continuously learn to ensure efficiencies through new technical, digital and managerial know-how, product and service ideas, and improved R&D capabilities – this learning capability needs to flow effectively through the SC.

However, on-going changes in the business environment make TPLs in Asia highly exposed to risk. Their market suffers from:

- increasing numbers of competitors
- increasing labour costs without productivity gains
- more capital-intensive contract logistics, e.g. end-to-end cold storage
- more complex SCs, which result in difficulty controlling the quality of service and delivery.

This leads to consolidation trends in the industry, for example through increasing mergers and acquisitions such as Danish DSV and Swiss Panalpina in 2019, boosting DSV's Asia-Pacific footprint as fourth largest forwarder in the world: 'Acquiring Panalpina will increase DSV's revenues in the Asia-Pacific region from 10 to 17 percent of its total. Andersen said Asia is a faster growing region than Europe, the Middle East and Africa (EMEA) where DSV currently earns most of its revenue' (American Shipper, 2019).

Final remarks: The evolution of intra-Asia value added

In a sample comprising China, Japan, Korea, Taiwan, Singapore, Malaysia, Thailand, the Philippines and Indonesia (Suder et al., 2015), the changing roles of Asian economies regarding the location of value chain activity can be observed. In 1990, the main international trade flows were still centred on Japan: most Asian countries depended on Japan's exports and imports in the Asian region. By 2005, significant changes had taken place, as China had taken Japan's role, and turned into a dominant hub for Asian international trade: almost all Asian developing countries strengthened their presence in international trade and their role in SCs at this time. Especially, increasing interactions and SC complexity across China, Korea, Japan and Taiwan emerged, as well as an increasing interdependence between East Asia and the ASEAN. From being relatively isolated in its role as 'global factory', China now became a regional actor, creating cross-border Asian production networks to include all developed and lesser developed economies in the region.

China at the same time took on the role of high value final products receiver and continues to strengthen this through increasingly advanced production technologies, engaging in the vertical production process (such as the production of manufacturing parts and components) through effective production systems and logistics. Most other Asian economies are at some stage of advancement within this technological trajectory, resulting in a 'shift away from being a mere assembler of final products to the more sophisticated production of intermediate items. As a result, [a firm] becomes a key supplier of important parts and components to other countries in the region which guarantees its dominant position in the value-added payoff across the regional production networks' (Suder et al., 2015). This goes hand in hand with improved cross-border collaboration on a political level. The box below provides an example.

Cross-border SC facilitation through government agreement: The Greater Mekong Subregion (GMS) Cross-Border Transport Facilitation Agreement

An increasing number of initiatives across parts of Asia aim at facilitating regional supply chains. This includes, for example, the Greater Mekong Subregion Cross-Border Transport Facilitation Agreement. This subregion has come to collaborate through a 1992 development programme by the Asian Development Bank, promoting the connection of six states: Cambodia, China (with a focus on the Yunnan Province and Guangxi Zhuang Autonomous Region), Laos, Myanmar, Thailand and Vietnam. Among them, Laos, Thailand and Vietnam agreed on facilitation measures to stimulate road and rail transport and logistics. The agreement specifically simplifies and harmonizes legislation, regulations, procedures and requirements relating to the cross-border transport of goods and people. For example, two adjacent national authorities carry out their inspections jointly and simultaneously. As another example, road traffic regulations, is brought in line with common rules, and a Free Market for Transport Services is gradually established. The Asian Development Bank, upon impact analyses, found that the agreement brought 'positive effects of the development of economic corridors on intra-GMS trade in intermediate goods, especially for electric machinery. This implies that cross-border transport infrastructure in the GMS has contributed to lower service link costs and facilitated vertical integration across borders in this industry' (Fujimura, 2017: 24).

In summary, three key trends shape the increasing sophistication of value chain participation in Asia:

- the focus on perceived customer experience: avoiding disappointment by creating resilience within the broader regional value chain participation
- the scale of digital SC capabilities: leveraging automation in manufacturing, logistics and customer service
- the shift to circular/life-cycle SC designs, with environmental sustainability and ethical impact analysis across the value chain.

6.2 Case study: Huawei's supply chain management amid US–China trade tensions – establishing collaborative partnerships with Asian suppliers

Overview

Huawei Technology Co. (Huawei) is a Chinese multinational technology company whose core businesses include constructing telecom networks, providing equipment and software to enterprises, and manufacturing consumer electronics. Since Huawei initiated its expansion outside China in the late 1990s, it has gained a predominant presence in the broader Asian market and transformed into a global leader. As of 2019, Huawei has become the world's biggest telecommunications network and solution provider and has surpassed Apple as the second biggest smartphone-maker behind Samsung. As a technology-focused and consumer-centric company, Huawei developed its core technologies and assembly lines in-house and implemented a producer-driven supply chain system. While firms with producer-driven supply chains typically rely on vertically integrated contractors, Huawei largely sourced production to external partners and purchased finished components from global suppliers, roughly 36 per cent and 60 per cent of which were based in the US and Asia, respectively. Due to a ban by the US government on exports to China, however, Huawei started to diversify its sourcing away from the US and hunted for more suppliers in Asia. This case discusses Huawei's supply chain management and its strategic actions to boost self-reliance by investing in R&D and collaborating with suppliers in Asia in response to the US ban.

Learning outcomes

By the end of this case study, students should be able to:

1   Identify the characteristics of Huawei's supply chain management and understand how the diversification of sourcing with an increasing focus on Asia has mitigated Huawei's supply risks amid the trade turmoil between the US and China.
2   Identify the opportunities and challenges within Huawei's decision to reduce its reliance on American technology by investing in R&D and switching the focus onto Asian markets.

Introduction

On 19 September 2019, Huawei released its latest Android-based flagship smartphone: Mate 30 Series. This Android phone series came with an announcement that all of Google's Android apps would not be pre-installed, including the Google Play Store which serves as the official app store for the Android operating system. This announcement, although it was seen as disappointing to some Huawei fans, did not come as a surprise: just a month before the launch of Mate 30 Series, Google had disclosed this intention on its official sources (The Verge, 2019). The full Huawei sensation, however, really only began when the US Department of Commerce added Huawei to its Entity List on 15 May 2019, officially 'blacklisting' the company as far as US corporations were concerned (Android Authority, 2019). Following this announcement, a number of US American tech companies, like Google, announced they would hence discontinue their business relationships with Huawei. In addition to the risk of now getting barred from using Google's Android due to its own business decision, Huawei also faced potential loss of access to US supplies of cyber security tools and semiconductors due to their compliance with a political decision of the US government.

The following case study introduces how Huawei's globally scaled supply chain management has helped the company to leverage a leading competitive position. It also provides a basis to reflect upon the capability of entering and exiting locations to adjust supply chains with a shift to Asian markets and a reduction of prior dependence on global suppliers for the benefit of closer, Asian suppliers.

Background

Huawei was founded in 1987 in Shenzhen, which is seen by many to be China's Silicon Valley. The company started its business as a rural sales agency for phone and cable network businesses, which gradually expanded into metropolitan areas of China (Martin Roll, 2018). After 30 years, Huawei's business incrementally grew into three main branches: the Carrier Business, the Enterprise Business, and the Consumer Business. The Consumer Business and the Carrier Business were the main contributors to the company's revenue, accounting for 89.2 per cent of Huawei's 2018 annual revenue (Huawei, 2019: 20). In 2018, the company was reported to have sold 203 million phones globally, overtaking Apple as the second biggest smartphone-maker just behind Samsung (Cnet, 2018). At the same time, the Carrier Business experienced an annual decline of 1.3 per cent caused by weak demand for Huawei's 5G network equipment in the US and certain European markets. In the Asia-Pacific region, however, Huawei maintained strong momentum and earned CNY454,080 million in revenue. It invested heavily

(Continued)

(Continued)

in in-house core technology R&D for its smartphones, 5G deployment and other services. At the same time, the company aimed to source globally, providing world-class technology and skillsets to continuously drive technological advancements in its products and services. The majority of Huawei's key suppliers were leading Asian and US corporations. As reported, one of its flagship smartphone models, P30 Pro, with its CPU and radio/audio transmitter designed in-house, was built using approximately 31 external suppliers covering chip and device parts including storage, fingerprint reading, cameras, screens, speakers and cooling systems, etc. Table 6.1 shows some of P30 Pro's global suppliers as published in May 2019. As a result of the Huawei ban, the proportion of Asian suppliers increased as Huawei sought to diversify sourcing and turned to more Asian manufacturers in order to reduce its reliance on the US.

Table 6.1   Examples of Huawei P30 Pro's global suppliers

Products/ Components	Company	Region
Original equipment manufacturer (OEM)	TSMC	Taiwan
OLED screen	Samsung	South Korea
CIS chip	Sony	Japan
VCSEL	Lumentum	US
Lens	Sunny Optical	China

Source: Sohu (2019a)

Huawei's SCOR-based supply chain system

To efficiently operate and manage its global supply chain, Huawei has worked hard to implement a Supply Chain Operations Reference (SCOR)-based Integrated Supply Chain (ISC) system.

By 1999, Huawei had never actually used any modern supply chain management. The communication among Huawei's major departments was conducted through a unit called the 'Manufacturing Department', whose main duty included managing the company's manufacturing and procurement (Sohu, 2019b). Soon, an apparent lack of efficiency in strategic planning with regard to demand forecasting, operational planning and product manufacturing had led to a number of problems. Before 1999, Huawei had a low product annual delivery rate of 50 per cent, compared to an average of 94 per cent among other international telecommunication providers. Also, before 1999, it had a low inventory turnover of 3.6 times a year with the international average being 9.4 (Ni, 2018), and low efficiency in communication between the planning department and the procurement department (Sohu, 2019b). To improve efficiency in its supply chain operations, Huawei worked with its consulting partner IBM and launched a tailored ISC system in 1999. In this 'ISC reform', the leadership decided that the company would integrate all SC elements throughout its internal departments and external partners from designing a product to delivering the product to the consumer. Even more importantly, it launched a central 'planning' department for this process. SC management had become a strategic feature of Huawei's strategy. The concept of its ISC was to centre around three segments: the suppliers, the consumers and the 'in-between processes', which included R&D, sourcing, manufacturing (product assembly) and logistics (Kokemuller, 2019). During the early stage of building this ISC system (between 1999 and 2003), Huawei was deeply engaged in developing a system that would ensure accurate 'planning' or 'forecasting' for business operations such as production and logistics. The core of this system was deeply data-dependent with data-referenced features, which was called Supply Chain Operations Reference, requiring data transparency and sharing among involved departments. Figure 6.2 illustrates SCOR.

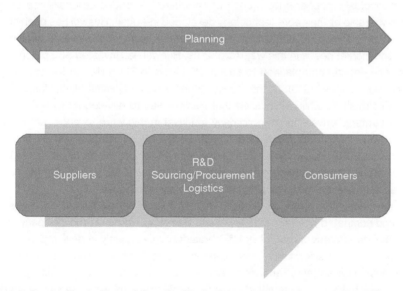

Figure 6.2 An illustration of Supply Chain Operations Reference (SCOR)

(Continued)

(Continued)

Ever since the ISC was implemented, Huawei has gradually established its partnership with numerous suppliers globally through years of cultivating an ecosystem advocating shared success. Major milestones during this journey include:

- 1999–2003, constructed thorough supply chain infrastructures and connected IT systems by implementing ISC
- 2005–2007, implemented a GSC to support global expansion, gradually laying out global supply chain networks
- 2008, combined GSC management and product and service delivery management, completing the establishment of global multi-functional centres and global supply chain networks
- 2012, implemented a business continuity management (BCM) system to improve efficiency of the GSC
- 2018, announced a 'Strategic Procurement' era – a procurement system that featured strategy, value-orientation and transparency. (iFeng, 2018; Sohu, 2019b)

Building up R&D capability

As with a typical producer-driven supply chain, where the producers ideally possess and retain ownership of their core technology developed in-house, Huawei has been striving to invest in R&D and advocate constant innovations to meet the ever-changing consumer and market needs in this way. As of 2019, Huawei had invested $60 billion in R&D across one decade and planned to spend $15 billion to $20 billion in the coming year (*Nikkei Asian Review*, 2019). At the Huawei Global Analyst Summit 2018, Huawei's then acting Chairman Xu Zhijun explained that Huawei was to develop its own CPU chips, and the strategic drivers for the company to invest in this were to 'construct Huawei's own hardware infrastructures, differentiate its products and competitiveness, and lower costs' (Sohu, 2018). Huawei's decision to develop CPU chips was partly prompted by the US ban on the Chinese telecom equipment manufacturer ZTE. Huawei felt the need to increase self-reliance by developing core technologies in-house.

In its Consumer Business section, Huawei had positioned itself as a premium brand and competed head on with Apple and Samsung. To do so, the company used a differentiation strategy through key R&D breakthroughs, mainly in device performance (such as battery performance and response speed), photography, communication capabilities (such as faster and more stable telecommunications), and design. These foci on which Huawei committed to have breakthroughs were identified through comprehensive end user research. For example, in 2018, through the studies of the behaviour and preferences specifically of female and young users, it was decided to combine technology with fashion and art. Huawei's P30 Pro models received an overwhelming welcome from fashion-conscious consumers with its revolutionary Leica triple camera design and exclusive AI computing for colour optimization and unique aesthetic vision options. These functions enabled users to stand out in their phone-taken photos in a digital social media era.

Aside from developing chips, Huawei was also in the process of launching a solution project that applied AI technology to raise productivity and enhance user experience. Huawei constructed an 'all-scenario' AI infrastructure portfolio to provide a connected, intelligent lifestyle across a full range of scenarios – from consumers to enterprises, from homes to devices, etc. The 'all-scenario' AI concept had already been applied by Huawei's major rivals such as Google, Apple and Samsung. The ultimate goal of the leadership was to obtain a connection of all digital devices through data synchronization. Similarly, Huawei's 'all-scenario' solution provided its clients with a customized, intelligent user experience while using Huawei products. The key technology to accomplish this was AI and the AI-driven computing and storage system – the Cloud technology. Huawei Cloud was attached to its phones, via which complementary connection and remote operation services (Huawei Mobile Services) could be extended to its other products, in a way to promote more and complementary Huawei's products to the market other than merely smartphones.

In the twenty-first century, data had come to be recognized as one of the fundamental resources that empower a much broader customer centricity through digitalization, especially AI. The Asian markets were coming to the foreground of data collection for digital innovation, with scant data privacy protection in place for consumers. The now-extensive network of Huawei product users in the Asia-Pacific region enabled Huawei's AI systems to become more intelligent via staff training on increasingly rich databases. In turn, a customized, smart user experience fulfilled by the powerful AI algorithms attracted more clients.

In order to build an 'all-scenario' AI solution, in June 2018, Huawei launched the Shining-Star programme to attract global developers. Unlike in-house R&D, this programme encouraged external organizational and individual digital developers to self-invite and establish partnerships with Huawei and was designed to create mutual benefit. In 2018, registered developers of Huawei's Consumer Business already exceeded as many as 560,000, and the revenue of Huawei's partners was reported by the company to have more than doubled year-on-year (Huawei, 2019: 37: no external source available).

Huawei was dedicated to developing core technologies in-house to optimize cost effectiveness and keep ownership of key capabilities. Yet the strategy also included the purchase of components and technology from external sources, especially for its mid- and lower-end products. For instance, Huawei's two flagship high-end models, 'Mate' and 'P' series, incorporated its own chipset – Kirin. Its Mate series phones were claimed

(Continued)

(Continued)

to have more advanced processors than other phones; and P series phones targeted users who cared more about design. Like many companies working across Asia with the presence of numerous external suppliers, Huawei used a 'multi-supplier strategy': while Huawei had developed Kirin, Xu revealed that nonetheless and in addition, some of the world's biggest Android phone chip suppliers such as America's Qualcomm and Taiwan's Media Tek, were on Huawei's supplier list and the reason was stated to 'keep the company growing healthily' (Sohu, 2018).

Also, as the cost for developing CPU chips was relatively high, Huawei purchased mid- and lower-ranged chip series from external suppliers for its mid- and lower-end smartphones, like the Huawei Maimang models, and Huawei's sub-brand Honor's mid- and lower-end models (Tencent, 2019). When some of Huawei's Carrier Business clients required their contracted phones to use US chips to match local telecommunication standards and comply with US mandates, Huawei also had to order chips from its US suppliers. The numbers from 2017 indicate that the deployment percentage of its own chips on Huawei's phones was 45 per cent (CCTime, 2018), meaning a rather large proportion of chips still came from US suppliers.

Ongoing R&D investment made Huawei a leading patent holder. Data showed that it ranked first for two consecutive years in terms of global Patent Cooperation Treaty patent applications from 2015 to 2016 (Martin Roll, 2018). As of 31 December 2018, its total number of patents exceeded 87,000, among which nearly 13 per cent were granted in the US (Huawei, 2019). In terms of UN patents, Huawei led the pack with Asia accounting for more than half of the international applications at the World Intellectual Property Organization in 2018 – an all-time record set by anyone (Reuters, 2019).

Sourcing/Procurement

As a latecomer in the industry who had set Apple and Samsung as its benchmark, Huawei aspired to grow into one of the top global players in the world. As a critical following step in its supply chain management, Huawei strengthened its phone manufacturing to complement its expanding R&D capabilities. Its collaborative multi-sourcing strategy became key, beginning with its comprehensive supplier selection system and the philosophy of 'openness, collaboration, and shared-success' to safeguard long-term partnerships with qualified suppliers.

Industry conferences and expositions were usually where the supplier selection process began. Each year, cross-departmental Commodity Expert Groups (CEGs), which were created by Huawei's Procurement Department, attended these expositions globally to source and purchase specific types of materials. The selection process evaluated suppliers through seven criteria for respective purposes: quality, technology, response, cost, delivery, social responsibility, and environmental protection (Ni, 2018). One measurement for its suppliers was the Huawei Supplier Social Responsibility Code of Conduct. This code embodied, in a coherent manner, some of the universally adopted sustainability guidelines, such as the Responsible Business Alliance Code of Conduct and JAC Supply Chain Sustainability Guideline. Once the initial contacts were conducted, experts from the CEGs worked with the client representatives to select potential suppliers based on the needs of the company and suppliers' adaptability potential for regional markets. These CEGs engaged multiple suppliers for different materials and invited suppliers to participate in the early stages of Huawei's R&D procedures to inspire shared value creation and collaborative innovation (NEPCON Asia, 2019; Sohu, 2019a). Huawei also invited suppliers to attend its regular training and coaching programmes to learn about industry best practices and enhance operation efficiency. The added expertise through the learning and collaboration contributed to Huawei's long-term commitment to technological enhancement. Huawei also adopted mechanisms to guarantee the fairness and openness of the process and to ensure that the suppliers' capabilities were consistent with its long-term expansion goal (NEPCON Asia, 2019; Sohu, 2019b). Huawei positioned itself as a technological leader and aimed to promote its brand globally, particularly in emerging Asian markets where it perceived lucrative opportunities. The rotating chairman Xu Zhijun was heard to anticipate that Asia and Middle East would have the largest demand for Huawei's next-generation mobile broadband hardware (*South China Morning Post*, 2019). The meticulous, responsible supplier selection system provided quality assurance to upscale in this region and shaped the basis for Huawei's branding campaign. This selection system was the foundation of its cooperation with over 13,000 supplier partners globally.

Huawei maintained a list of highly diversified suppliers in terms of their locations. According to Bloomberg's data in 2017, only 41 per cent of Huawei's suppliers were located in China, with US suppliers taking the second-place accounting for 24.7 per cent (*South China Morning Post*, 2018). At its 12th Core Suppliers Convention in 2018, Huawei unveiled a list of 92 core suppliers. All companies on this list were leading or reputable players in their respective field, offering what it considered to be the most advanced hardware components and software solutions for smartphones. Location-wise, 33 companies from this list were based in the US, 25 in China, 11 in Japan, 10 in Taiwan, 4 in Germany, i.e. 46 (50 per cent) of its key suppliers were based across Asia (iFeng, 2018).

Yet Huawei's procurement activities were to increasingly move towards finding more Asia-based suppliers, mainly due to the US ban. Because of concerns over cybersecurity risk and electronic espionage, the US Department of Commerce blacklisted Huawei and its affiliates in May 2019, requiring US firms to acquire special approval prior to

(Continued)

(Continued)

conducting business with Huawei. It was subsequently reported that it had promised its existing and potential suppliers to raise the utility rate of non-US suppliers, mainly Asian suppliers, to 80 per cent in the next two years and started to urge its suppliers to move production to China (C-Fol, 2019; *Financial Times*, 2019). The stock market performance of several related suppliers experienced a positive result from this: the valuations of two of its suppliers who were listed companies, Novatek (Taiwan) and Everwin Precision (China), had both soared by 10 per cent between May and June 2019; the stock price of Huawei's main chip producer, TSMC (Taiwan), had gone up 4 per cent; and the stock price of Sony (Japan), Huawei's most important transmit supplier, had increased by 2 per cent (Sohu, 2019d).

The shortening and, at the same time, diversification and repatriation of its supply chain on a local and regional level did not only reduce the impacts of the US ban, but also helped Huawei to reduce dependency on a limited number of suppliers, thus reducing risk and guaranteeing a better more resilient supply.

This was especially the case when the suppliers were both Huawei's partners and major competitors. Samsung, the South Korean conglomerate (see section 6.3), had been one such supplier since 2012 when Huawei purchased the 'Super AMOLED' touch screen from it for Ascend P1 phones. Samsung had been the world's largest smartphone manufacturer and the most advanced OLED screens provider, supplying Huawei with components such as the CMOS sensor, screen and RAM. Samsung's highly vertical-integrated supply chain model seemed to determine its strategic fulfilment for its own demands before its clients', in Huawei's view. Hence, the leadership held that the company seemed to gain considerable influence over Huawei's phone production capabilities, which appeared to be one aspect decreasing its own supply chain resilience.

Huawei's Ascend P1 had encountered continuous inventory management problems after its debut because of a screen supply shortage (Qianzhanwang, 2015). In 2017, when Huawei launched its first model for its flagship Mate series, the Mate 9 Pro, which had used Samsung as its sole supplier for OLED screen, the supply shortage happened again. It was reported that, with increasing demand from Huawei resulting from the success of Mate 9 Pro in both China and overseas, Samsung announced unexpectedly that it was unable to upscale its supply of screen shipments to meet Huawei's demand without jeopardizing its own needs. As a result, from March 2017, the production of Huawei's Mate 9 Pro started to stagnate (East Day, 2017) due to its over-reliance on those supplies. Learning from this, subsequently, Huawei started to seek and purchase more screens from other suppliers on the market. This was the year when Huawei officially included LG (South Korea) and BOE (China) as its OLED screen suppliers (Baidu, 2017; Sohu, 2019a). Huawei had now diversified suppliers to improve availability and reduce its reliance on limited supplies. Among the two, BOE was a China-based LED manufacturer and Huawei's screen order in 2017 was the company's first OLED order.

Huawei now remained resolutely driven by leveraging the technological strengths and core capabilities of Asia.

After two years as a major supplier to Huawei, BOE had grown into a global company and also achieved satisfying results in its own R&D in regular and bendable OLED screens. After having encountered several passive exclusions from partnership with its American suppliers due to the US ban, Huawei and BOE co-announced that BOE was the designated, exclusive supplier of bendable OLED screens for Huawei's next-to-launch 5G smartphones (Sohu, 2019c). Huawei's decision to switch from American suppliers to Asian sourcing mitigated possible supply disruptions resulting from the ban and made the supply chain more resilient.

This type of partnership was common in Huawei's 'collaboration and shared-success' practices. Huawei, as a professional ICT multinational from an emerging economy in Asia, had encountered numerous challenges in competing against the global industry's giant Samsung yet benefited from its home country's size and support. A 'growing with suppliers' strategy was both a necessity and a sensible tactic, which enhanced Huawei's productivity and performance in its 30+ years of existence.

In addition, Huawei's cooperation with the afore-mentioned TSMC, one of the world's largest semiconductor OEM companies based in Taiwan, formed Huawei's first and key OEM partner strategy for its CPU chips. TSMC also had been the co-producer for Apple's chips since 2014. Following the co-production of A9 chip phase with Samsung in 2015, TSMC had become the exclusive A-series chip supplier for Apple since 2016 and had won that exclusivity until 2020 (Apple Inside, 2018; iPhone Hacks, 2018). Apple, as Huawei's major target rival, had been regarded as the industry benchmark exercising high standards on its suppliers. Further, TSMC's clients had also included the world's other leading chip design companies such as Qualcomm and AMD.

The cooperation between Huawei and TSMC had started many years prior to an official strategic collaboration in 2013, the year that Huawei decided to enter the world's premium smartphone market relying on its newly debuted CPU chip, Kirin 950. October 2013 marked the initiation of Huawei's Kirin project with TSMC, and in April 2014, the first chip was produced. During the six months of production collaboration, the two companies worked together to solve technical problems and pursue technological enhancements in both product design and manufacturing. After a long period of technical research, in January 2015, Huawei was able to improve Kirin 950's performance by 40 per cent and energy efficiency by 60 per cent compared to its predecessor, Kirin 920, when Kirin 950 could finally be brought to market with an aim to mass-produce in the near future. Later that year the first batch was shipped out. TSMC was retained as an OEM supplier for Huawei's upgraded Kirin series, 960 and 980. But to meet Huawei's growing needs, another Taiwan- and three China-based OEM companies became additional CPU OEM suppliers for Huawei.

(Continued)

(Continued)

Logistics: A key driver for Huawei's success

'I believe Huawei's development of supply chain was a success and had achieved great effects, as of 2004', said Yu Donghai, former Director of Operation Supporting Team at Huawei's Supply Chain Management Department: 'But what about its overseas market?' (Sohu, 2019b).

Huawei's expansion into global markets started in 2005. Transportation of products before then was done by its intra-firm logistics department – a first-party logistics support system. This logistics department was responsible for delivering products nation-wide and only within China from its Shenzhen base. 'The first question came to us was: how do we design our *global* network?' said Yu (Sohu, 2019b). The essential strategic decision to support Huawei's global expansion was how to construct a layout for its global supply chain network, including a globally efficient, resilient, modern logistics network. In 2008, Huawei introduced the concept of 'pan-delivery' – the integration of GSC and the final product delivery processes. The company had mainly established five global supply centres (China, Mexico, India, Brazil and Hungary), three logistics centres (China, Netherlands and Dubai), and five procurement centres (China, the US, Japan, Germany and Taiwan). The centric role of Asia remained. Huawei carefully designed the layout of its supply chain network across Asia. Among Huawei's 13 logistics centres: over half were located across Asia from Far East, to Central, and to the West. A wide geographical coverage of these Asia-based logistics hubs was meant to play a critical role in Huawei's integration of its global supply chain. Its immediate impact was its improved capability to respond promptly to stores' and sales agents' needs for product delivery and efficient inventory management all over the world and meet the requirement of just-in-time delivery.

Each regional hub was designated to distribute products to areas in the most efficient and economical way. For example, the global centre in Dubai was responsible for delivering products to some rural areas in Africa where the transportation infrastructure was poorly constructed. In addition, the layout of the procurement centres took into account the set-up of other components in the supply chain network to maximize cost efficiency. Most of the company's core suppliers were located in China, Japan and Taiwan. Since there were existing logistics hubs for Huawei's carrier clients, the additional cost for setting up procurement centres was considerably reduced and hence, cost-efficient. Moreover, the three countries had been chosen to be the location of procurement centres to lower the risk from centralized sourcing and tap into a range of innovation potential. As Yu put it:

> We set up our procurement centers here because of these regions' advanced semiconductor industries or good electronic device supplying opportunities. This reflected our 'decentralized procurement' strategy. (Sohu, 2019b)

Huawei's risks and Asia's opportunities

Over the years, the supply chain for Huawei's smartphone business has faced several risk factors, among which the risk of supply continuity was significant. Supply chain disruptions due to a shortage of technology and skills for production and major macroeconomic forces could threaten Huawei's sustainable growth and thus undermine the-market position that had been pursued by Huawei.

As Huawei ran a typical producer-driven supply chain, its GSC was highly sensitive vis-à-vis two key factors: core technology and skills for components production. The list of its 92 core suppliers demonstrated Huawei's high dependency on both Asia and some US-based suppliers, due to a need for highly advanced technology and specific skills as well as globally adopted US standards imposed on the industry. Adding to Huawei's predicament was its vulnerability when external factors hindered its existing connection to the provision of US standardized technology. Huawei's Mate 30 Pro's debut with the ban on pre-installation of Google apps and software was just one such example. In May 2019, Huawei was removed from multiple key global technology standards-setting groups, such as IEEE, the dominant developer of telecommunications and information technology standards. The curtailment of its access to standards-setting bodies could put Huawei at disadvantage against competitors. Reporters at the *Financial Times* indicated that the ban was the outcome of the escalating trade war – China retaliated with new tariffs after Trump increased tariffs on Chinese goods (Sevastopulo et al., 2019). This ban hindered Huawei's premium smartphone strategy and restricted its capability to compete against its target rivals, such as its strategic goal to surpass Samsung in smartphone sales, which was just set at the beginning of 2019 (*LA Times*, 2019a), and its devoted efforts in 5G technology development. Meanwhile, the US urged other countries to ban Huawei from 5G mobile networks due to concerns over electronic espionage. Australia and Japan joined the US. New Zealand also expressed concerns and blocked Spark, one of New Zealand's largest telecommunications company, from using Huawei equipment. However, Spark kept Huawei on its preferred suppliers list. The company stated that its approach to 5G was 'multi-vendor' and it would submit another application to use Huawei's equipment (Nainan and Ramakrishnan, 2019). Germany, Norway, UK, Italy and France resisted US pressure and left the door open for Huawei's involvement in their 5G rollouts. The US ban was largely ignored in Asia – Japan was the only Asian country to bar Huawei. Analysts estimated that its products were often 20 per cent to 30 per cent cheaper relative to those of comparable quality produced by Western companies. According to John Ure, Director of the Telecommunications Research Project at the University of Hong Kong, Huawei's established reputation for 'value-for-money equipment' was highly attractive to emerging markets (*LA Times*, 2019b). In addition, some countries stated that they had welcomed Huawei partly due to their

(Continued)

(Continued)

strong ties with China. For example, nations such as Myanmar relied on China's cash to finance infrastructure like high-speed railways (*South China Morning Post*, 2019).

As introduced earlier, Huawei's main businesses covered Consumers (through offering smart devices to individual users), Carriers (through providing telecommunication equipment and services), and Enterprises (through building data storage and processing and Cloud services). Although this case has focused on the supply chain of its smartphones, remember that these three businesses of Huawei were highly entangled with mutual impact. The 5G technology for which Huawei has been given major recognition by the industry has an enormous impact on at least two of its businesses if not all three: its carrier business and consumer products. The 5G technology or network not only promised faster data speed but also greatly improved data transfer stability and with lower latency, based on which many innovations can be further envisioned and used, such as robots and the internet of things (IoT) including its extended utility in virtual reality (VR) and self-driven vehicles. All these became possible because connectivity would be majorly improved with a 5G network. Just as all existing networks must be standardized to be universally unified and used, 5G, as a newly emerged technology, needed to be given its own industry standards. Two American organizations released the standards for the two most important networks used currently: the Institute of Electrical and Electronics Engineers (IEEE) released standards for Wi-Fi networks in 1997 and the 3rd Generation Partnership Project (3GPP) released standards for the 3G network (including 3G, 4G/LTE) in 2008. Owners of 5G technology standard essential patents (SEPs) would become technology and market leaders more easily (IP Lytics, 2019). While Huawei might have been seen as limited in power to influence the development of 5G technology standards, it was reportedly in possession of the biggest share of 5G SEPs in the world with 28 per cent of the 5G SEP family (IP Lytics, 2019; *Wall Street Journal*, 2019). Other than Huawei, its Chinese rival in tech segment, ZTE, was reported to hold some 5 per cent of the SEPs in the 5G family (IP Lytics, 2019). Together Chinese companies held about 34 per cent of 5G SEPs as of March 2019, followed by South Korea's 25 per cent and 14 per cent each for the US and Finland (VentureBeat, 2019). If Huawei applied its 5G technology the way it had planned, its Carrier Business would be greatly enhanced because the telecommunication stations built by Huawei would be able to provide a 5G network. Its smartphone business would also be improved once its 5G technology was engineered into its processors on phones and other smart devices. The 5G technology once seemed like a golden ticket and voucher for Huawei to reach future domination of the technology market. However, the US ban had dragged down the process of Huawei redeeming this voucher and its impact was already evident. For example, Huawei once reported that it had finished the tests for a 5G network in September 2018, and it was estimated by the press that Huawei would be first in China to launch a 5G smartphone by June 2019, surpassing other phones using Qualcomm's SoC (Huanqiu, 2018). However, the fact was that until June 2019, not only had Huawei not launched its 5G smartphone, its direct Chinese rival in the smart device market, Xiaomi, which had not been moved onto the Equity List by the US and which had been abundantly supplied by its US-based suppliers, had launched its 5G smartphone instead: the Mi 9 Pro came out ahead of Huawei in September 2019. Mi 9 Pro carried Qualcomm's flagship 'best-in-class' processor, representing the latest 5G technology in China (Bloomberg, 2019).

The odds that the company had faced, led to an opportunity to rethink its existing business model and strategies and generated new positive outcomes. For example, Huawei was reported to have started production of its 5G telecom stations without US parts (ITNews, 2019) and its initiative of issuing national debts as a private company, spreading a reassuring message to the markets that the company had support from the country and would continue to grow. The public could also sense Huawei's stand with respect to its unprecedented challenge, in the statement from its founder, Ren Zhengfei, that the company had been considering licensing its 5G technology to an American company. In this way, according to Ren, a US company would be able to 'compete with us around the world' (Fortune, 2019). 'I don't see competition as a threat, but as a driver of further progress,' he said (Fortune, 2019). What's more, despite the adverse effect on its 1,200 US suppliers, Huawei's Asian suppliers were reported to see more benefits because of this event. TSMC, one of the most important partners for Huawei, had vowed to continue producing and shipping Huawei's Kirin chips, but was reported to have been put under much pressure, including a lawsuit filed by Globalfoundries, the world's second biggest chip factory behind TSMC. In August 2019, Globalfoundries accused TSMC of infringing 16 patents used in manufacturing computer chips. A series of lawsuits was filed in both the US and Germany, in addition to a complaint from Globalfoundries to the United States International Trade Commission. Although it was not directly stated, analysts wrote that Globalfoundries might had been emboldened by the Trump administration's comments about the trade war with China: 'It's almost like someone in the US State Department gave them the green light for this suit' (*New York Times*, 2019). As a counter move, TSMC was reported to have filed a series of lawsuits against Globalfoundries for violation of the former's 25 patents in its five chip production lines, taking place in multiple judiciary courts in countries including the US, Germany, and Singapore in October 2019 (Baijiahao, 2019).

Other Southeast Asian suppliers of Huawei confirmed again that their relationship with Huawei would continue regardless of the ban (*Japan Times*, 2019). According to the suppliers, Huawei was too important as a player in the industry, with its technology strength and well-established ties with firms in Southeast Asia. It had also cultivated close business ties with its clients and a strong brand image in Southeast Asia. 'Technology comes first', said a consultant of the security and command centre in the provincial government of Pangasinan in the Philippines: 'Our concern is disaster

(Continued)

(Continued)

management and crime prevention, international concerns like the trade war between the US and China are not really our concern' (*Japan Times*, 2019). On the other hand, Singapore, which was in the process of selecting its 5G system and accompanying equipment by 2020, noted that the situation was 'really tricky at the moment' due to close US–Singapore relations too. 'Singapore does not want to choose sides', said the official (*Japan Times*, 2019).

Case questions

1   From the case, what strategies had been adopted by Huawei in its supply chain and what values have been created through its globally sourced products?
2   How have the trade tensions between the US and China influenced Huawei's strategies regarding supply chain management, and what were the subsequent effects on its Asian ecosystem?
3   What capabilities has the Asian region provided Huawei with during its challenges and successes?

6.3 Case study: Samsung's supply chain management – a unique blend driving capability development and adjustment

Overview

Samsung is a South Korean company founded in 1938 that has grown over the past decades into a vast conglomerate. Its businesses – strongly oriented both towards the present and the future – have over time expanded to include textiles and food, machines and automobile, financial services and insurance, retail and real estate, leisure, bio and medical. Its 'crown jewel' and certainly best-known business is Samsung Electronics (SEC), spanning in product range from entertainment and household appliances, to world leadership in smartphones, flat panel TVs and DRAM memory. This is the world's largest maker of smartphones and semiconductors. This case focuses on Samsung Electronics, and in particular its smartphone business. Samsung Electronics ranked 6th in Interbrand's Best Global Brands 2018. In the mobile technology world, Samsung was ranked 15th place in the Fortune 500 ranking for 2019, right after Apple. Despite a number of issues in recent years, Samsung excels not only in its business altogether but is particularly recognized for its supply chain management that is profoundly embedded in the Asian region while serving the global market.

Learning outcomes

By the end of this case study, students should be able to:

1   Identify the main strategies that drive Samsung's supply chain within a hybrid Asian-Western management orientation.
2   Understand how the inter-relation between physical and digital capabilities benefits the resilience of supply chains across Asia and beyond.

Introduction

Samsung is a South Korean company founded in 1938 that has grown over the past decades into a vast conglomerate. Its businesses have over time expanded to include textiles and food, machines and automobile, financial services and insurance, retail and real estate, leisure, bio and medical. Its 'crown jewel' and certainly best-known business is Samsung Electronics (SEC), spanning in product range from entertainment and household appliances, to world leadership in smartphones, flat panel TVs and DRAM memory. Samsung (translated 'three stars') includes more than 78 businesses. This is the world's largest maker of smartphones and semiconductors. This case focuses on Samsung Electronics.

As of the 1950s, Samsung had become one of the top ten South Korean firms, already engaged in cross-border trade: first through imports fuelling its mass production strategy of the time, and then followed by exports.

Samsung's entry into the electronics industry officially started in 1968, through the foundation of Samsung Electronics (SEC). This was at a time of growth for major Japanese players, whose business models strongly influenced Samsung's initial processes.

In its past, SEC underwent four important phases: first, an emphasis on mass production, reliance on foreign technology, and a follow-the-leader strategy much dependent on government support. This led to continuous improvements in product engineering and assembly capabilities, foreign sourcing of technology in management,

(Continued)

(Continued)

production and marketing, and the creation of several joint venture companies with foreign technology suppliers.

By the end of the 1970s, thanks to the weight of its mass-production capability and the South Korean government's support for exports, SEC was able to seize a fairly large share of international markets, specifically the US market. By this time, Samsung had standardized its quality control systems, which developed into a 'New Management' mantra in the 1990s, accelerating attention to profit and quality rather than growth of sales, and on customer-centricity, seconded by quality management focused on the right timing of decisions and investment into the future. A 120 per cent rule was reported, which indicates 20 per cent of the workforce employed beyond current business needs to focus on the future of the business.

Samsung again increased its manufacturing capability through intensive training of employees, particularly shop-level technicians. Yet Samsung Group's development of market knowledge was not facilitated well enough, it appeared, by its internal organization: a greater need to focus on marketing capabilities was recognized, as well as brand development and innovation potential. There was little organizational support for links between production (knowledge accumulated in South Korea) and international marketing.

In the 1980s, Samsung's widening network of partners included mainly OEM suppliers, that is **original equipment manufacturers**. Its OEM strategy was successful, yet it appears to have held back some of the development of own design and marketing capabilities for mass-production goods further: the company increasingly depended on foreign sources of product design and distribution. The group's internal organization needed to strengthen organizational learning, it was found. As a result, the company opted for a focus on integrated circuit operation with a mass production goal of relatively low-end cost products and, at the same time, it started to build international infrastructures to increase internal capacity through the expansion of South Korean R&D centres, the creation of the 'Samsung Advanced Institute of Technology' and foreign-based R&D centres founded on continued collaboration with SEC with immediate sales goals.

Asia remained the most important market in terms of cost-effectiveness and low-cost resources and the Samsung supplier and investment network began to spread rapidly.

In the 1990s, Samsung had been cementing its rapid expansion of offshore production and had improved its own R&D capabilities. SEC's in-house R&D operations were centralized. Yet the hierarchical integration failed to provide researchers and engineers with satisfactory R&D conditions, it was reported, which needed to be aligned on the increasingly rapid pace of innovation across the sector. Indeed, the Japanese competition was fierce, and increased overseas production was part of the answer from Korean firms. Samsung decided to establish and strengthen centres in each of Samsung's main market regions to help develop products better suited to local needs, yet to make certain they would also collaborate to ensure cross-fertilization. In 1991, a Singapore-based purchasing office had also been established, leading to another increase in internationalization, and a vertically integrated operation in China. Samsung's cross-border cross-Asia footprint had increased significantly.

The 1990s were marked by the introduction of a 'New Management' strategy supporting quality management and high productivity, which were identified as the main weaknesses of its prior mass production approach. Key strategies were improvement in procurement, fair management and social trust management; implementing a Corporate Procurement Strategy that was to include transferring innovation methods to suppliers, such as process innovation, and education on Six Sigma; improving the manufacturing sites, and supporting the establishment of IT infrastructure across the partnership network.

Such investments challenges the internal and external suppliers to become crucial with increasingly fierce international competition, accelerated by the introduction of global standards, and the growth of Apple in particular. This also put supplier relations under more competition. Additionally, Samsung started to support suppliers' 'innovative capability through financial support, plant advancement, technology development, and human resource development', an approach implemented increasingly from 1998 to 2008 (Lee et al., 2015: 5).

'New Management' also helped leverage the quest for technological convergence emerging in the early 2000s. This was the 'golden era' of globalization, during which telecommunications became easier and cheaper, as well as transport, and international trade and investments boomed. 'Commerce soared; cost of shifting goods in ships and planes fell; phone calls got cheaper; people became mobile; tariffs were cut; the financial system liberalized; firms set up around the world, investors and consumers were affluent'. Samsung at that moment started to establish 'a unique and flexible SPS (Samsung Production System), a system of developing and producing a variety of models to meet the global demand as quickly as possible' (Lee et al., 2015: 3) and maintaining the Japanese-inspired just-in-time delivery model. This today includes an integrated purchasing information system for current and advance planning and forecasting.

Especially when Apple launched its iPhone in South Korea, major disruptions truly hit the Korean communications technology sector at home and globally. Samsung succeeded in what is now known as its 'leap to global first-class status'. Its focus on global competency, transparency, and establishment of a trust-based culture was enhanced. Partner support became systematic across its global SC, run through a partner collaboration centre. It became more and more attractive for suppliers to work with SEC, which supported their growth by classifying supplier firms into three

(Continued)

(Continued)

categories: Innovative Companies Association, Samsung Partners Association, and Global Hidden Champions. 'Vertical integration has become a major advantage under New Management. Samsung Electronics not only has accelerated the development of new products, it has reinforced the competitiveness of its overall ecosystem through technology and management advice to subcontractors' (Lee et al., 2015: 3). This enabled the development and introduction of the innovative Galaxy series, and the further stimulation of international market growth.

Altogether, over time, Samsung was able to incrementally build technological capacity and marketing momentum thanks to foreign linkages throughout the process of internationalization. Much of this happened in response to the need for adequate standards in mass production, through re-orienting internal production towards low-cost operation in peripheral areas and focusing innovation on high ends. Consequently, Samsung started to create significant strength in matching capabilities with its network structures. Moreover, through acquisitions, it fostered design development. Moving to an increasingly decentralized business model to capture such capabilities, Samsung's supplier network became increasingly global, vast and diversified over time. Today, more than 2,500 direct key suppliers are part of Samsung's ecosystem. Samsung's Venture Investment Corporation (SVIC) plays a main role to provide financial resources to start-up companies in the areas of information technology, communications, semiconductors, electronics and biotechnology. Education through, for example, its Samsung Advanced Institute of Technology (SAIT) and Seoul Comtech helped develop products from raw materials to finished goods, boosting cross-fertilization opportunities in multi-functional businesses.

Samsung's international footprint was accelerated through a strong regionalized cross-Asian basis. Singapore, host to a number of leading international consumer electronics players, quickly became one of the main regional hubs for Samsung Electronics. Samsung, just like Nokia, established assembly facilities in northern Vietnam, with Japanese and other parts suppliers clustering around them. Vietnam is today the world's second biggest exporter of smartphones after China, reported to be a direct outcome of that investment. Leading vendors such as Samsung, just like Apple, have large assembly operations in China. The most international of Samsung's characteristics is certainly its customer base as much as the range of its suppliers.

Samsung supply chain features

Samsung uses a supply chain with a very high vertical integration of parts production. The products' components are sourced as much as possible from existing Samsung plants or else from affiliates. They are typically only sourced from external partners if they are not available through this route. This extensive use of its own internally manufactured parts features in the supply chain for its phones, typically display and touch-screen modules, as well as the apps processor and power management integrated circuit; and to some extent only for its DRAM and flash products, especially for key high-value parts. Keeping the high value-added part of the chain under control is reported to have strengthened the innovation objectives set to drive product development, and to quickly and reliably get products to market in significant volumes. It also helps Samsung to manage multiple global channel partners and hence, to manage and diversify risk and keep better control over part design and costs (APEC, 2013:29). The historic influence of and benchmarking to the Japanese industry is noticeable in the supply chain speed and quality control. This influence fuses with Western management styles, resulting in what has been termed by researchers a 'hybrid management' (Khanna et al., 2011), which has leveraged the operation of a lean and integrated logistics system over time (Suh and Kim, 2009).

The Japanese management influence is seen in market share orientation, unrelated diversification, vertical integration, the focus on manufacturing competitiveness and operational efficiency, organizational discipline, great attention to employee loyalty, internal and seniority-based promotion and rewards, and in promoting participation by workers and shareholders in management. The Western style, largely influenced by a US American management scholarship, is seen as reflected in levels of risk taking, attracting and retaining core talent, important performance-based incentives, driving creative organizational culture, and maintaining a high speed (Blizard, 2017).

The supply chain system was strongly modernized and digitalized over the past years, from manufacturing operational enhancement through utilizing a global supply chain management (GSCM) system, to ensure the use of a product's platform in several operations, reduce inventory, line and manufacturing lead time, and to work systematically on continuous improvement of product launch speed. A flexible production system, which mixes cellular manufacturing and modular production systems for each product, has been refined over time. Initially developed around the 1990s, modular manufacturing systems 'enable skilled workers to use the simplest integrated combination of processes, machine systems, tooling, people, organizational structures, information flows, control and computer systems necessary to perform a given task' (Rogers and Bottaci, 1997). Through on-going modernization, it allows Samsung to yield benefits including productivity, relatively less expensive facility investment, cost-efficiency, effective model change, and so forth. Cellular manufacturing runs the group technology-driven focus on just-in-time manufacturing and lean manufacturing to maintain and increase speed, and coordinate the production of a wide variety of similar products, while allowing for as little waste as possible. This synchronization hence covers key aspects (Lee et al., 2015) of resource management, production planning, and manufacturing execution; it is combined with an on-line bilateral information system,

(Continued)

(Continued)

Glonet, to deliver requirement plans and execution information to suppliers. It also receives the key information on supply capacity, inventory and payment. A monitoring system that is combined with the Surface Mount Device (SMD) – where the components are mounted or placed directly onto the surface of printed circuit boards – and that tracks products' assembling processes, detects defective products, executes factorial analysis, and provides countermeasures on a real-time basis.

Samsung's R&D and design for smartphones today is managed through a multitude of R&D centres. It is noteworthy that the solution divisions in Korea prepare intermediate products not only for its own purposes but also for external customers including, for some time, Apple.

Product development and design constitute primary activities for Samsung, which was pointed out as unusual in that this is unlike Porter's original value chain model, which classified these as support activities. This serves the capability needed to develop new products and improve existing products, such as connected cars and mobile phones, and to remain efficient when cross-fertilizing the same technology. On the other side of the value chain, the assembly is almost exclusively completed by Samsung itself, which increases the ownership advantages of value-adding value chain activities and effectiveness advantages through standardization. In smartphones, for example, Samsung's own input constitutes about two-thirds of a phone's materials cost. In contrast to many other international companies, the company's components businesses started as profit centres, not cost centres – differentiating and innovating on components as much as for the end product.

For other stages of the production and of the value chain stages holistically (upstream and downstream), Samsung engages closely within the procurement process with external suppliers and seeks to replicate the intra-firm system and support mechanisms to obtain quality, speed, efficiencies and loyalty. Once inside the 'ecosystem', new benefits are offered increasingly within a support-driven ecosystem. Vertical integration is also not uncommon. For example, the vertical integration with important component businesses such as semiconductors and display panels facilitated the efficient, timely development of the Galaxy smartphone series. Integration for hardware also helps to be resilient to competitive pressures. While this does not compete with Apple's great advantage of a differentiated ecosystem on the services and content side, it does provide Samsung with considerable supply chain embedded power.

Asia-bound and rooted

At the time of writing, Samsung reports owning 217 worldwide operation hubs, including the HQ in Suwon, South Korea, plus manufacturing subsidiaries, sales subsidiaries, design centres and research centres, and operating 15 regional offices in Korea, North America, Europe, Southeast Asia, Africa and other regions of the world. Its 2,436 first-tier suppliers are located around the world in 73 countries. Its own production sites are located in Korea (6), China (11), SE Asia (8), SW Asia (2) and CIS (1), i.e. 28 in total. This compares with Latin America, North America and Europe (3 respectively), the Middle East and Africa (1 respectively), and illustrates the ongoing production-focused embeddedness in its wider home region. R&D centres are similarly distributed, with global spread yet a strong Asian basis.

The triangular importance of location, management skill and simultaneous investment into human resources for both internal teams and external suppliers was found to constitute a crucial backbone characteristic of SEC's holistic approach to supply chain management as a strategic tool. Among other more recent initiatives, field management showcases how to create future global leaders: by training locally sourced talent into regional Asian and global managers and leaders across functions and business as well as geographies.

In this, Samsung remains strongly Asia-bound and rooted, gaining many of its physical, digital and innovative capabilities from across the region. From the very start, founder Lee Byung-chul had been inspired by his education in Japan, where he spent several years. We have seen above that the systems driving Samsung's operations have reflected a hybrid between Japanese and Western management mantras for decades. Samsung's network is built on the company's past history of an OEM relationship with Japanese companies: the presence of the Japanese reduced the related risks of starting capital-intensive production overseas. Indeed, local joint ventures mirrored those established in Korea during the 1970s with and by Japanese companies. The training programmes had always been provided in Korea, or by Korean core staff.

Its production network in Asia has spread rapidly, especially since 1989 when the company opened its own TV assembly plant in Thailand. Asia is (and has always been) the major destination for Samsung's direct investment. In the 1990s, production networks in Asia came to extend beyond the ASEAN region to China and India, covering a range of activities from production in Asia of components to final consumer products. Still today, Southeast Asia and China represent Samsung's most important sub-production networks with the two central nodes located in Singapore and Beijing. Samsung remains the largest foreign investor in Vietnam and is one of the largest foreign investors in China. In both locations, this includes extensive investment in production facilities, research and development, and marketing and sales. It is currently significantly increasing its India investments (where the company has an R&D centre since 1996) especially in components for mobile phone display and batteries – and its venture capital arm, Samsung Venture Investment Corp, supports specifically the start-up community.

(Continued)

(Continued)

Challenges, issues or opportunities?

The local and international nature that supply chain disruptions may take is part of the highest risks to an MNE's revenue drivers. This is no different for Samsung than for its competition.

Specifically, in the complex and multi-layered nature of supply chains, actual and perceived levels of control and responsibility are potentially skewed in a manner different (and more challenging) from in traditional crises.

The recall of its Galaxy Note 7, a month after its release in 2016, was illustrative of the issues that can emanate within the increasingly multi-faceted supply chain-dependent delivery to market of innovative products and the potential resulting reputational risks. The recall was made necessary by reports of fires caused by the lithium-ion battery. Samsung blamed the issue on one of its battery suppliers while it was found subsequently that the issue originated in one of its subsidiaries, Samsung SDI. In the meantime, having re-launched replacement devices that remained faulty even without that supplier's input, the fire-risk that came from the devices also caused major safety concerns.

This crisis led to significant financial losses. Also, it highlighted the importance of establishing and using suitable digital capabilities to enhance visibility and traceability within increasingly complex supply chains, and to undertake quality control earlier (including design review and testing) and systematically. It was also found that the over-reliance in the supply chain on mainly one supplier hampered the availability of options when in crisis; in this specific case, 60 per cent of the batteries came from one supplier. This case highlights the limitations that the supply chain strategy developed and refined by Samsung over many years may suffer from. It also provides evidence for the need for continuous improvement, and the most appropriate use and combination of physical and digital capabilities at a given moment in time.

Today, other challenges and opportunities may arise from unpredictable international trade conditions: Samsung Electronics has been reported to lose ground as demand for memory chips and smartphones decreases in the face of a trade war, and as the re-emergence of tariffs as key negotiation tools between some of world powers changes production strategies from intermediaries being traded along supply chains, to investment to produce closer to the market. Geo-political issues are riveting the tech industry, which accounts for about 20 per cent of world stock markets. In addition, the average tariff rate on all US American imports rose to 3.4 per cent on average in 2019, its highest for 40 years. Most firms have passed the cost on to customers, yet in the highly competitive smartphone business, this remains a major challenge. This is even more so when introducing lower-priced phones as a reaction to competition from brands such as China's Xiaomi, Huawei, Oppo and Vivo.

In addition, the success of Samsung's parts sales business includes its contribution to the supply chain of the iPhone and of Huawei's smartphone business – about a third of Samsung's revenue comes from companies that compete with it – which raises the question of how to moderate dependencies if Samsung's own smartphone business suffers.

Savings are expected to come increasingly from further digital innovation and application. Blockchains are increasingly used to alter supply chain efficiencies especially given SC pressures during the Covid-19 pandemic. Samsung is reported to consider using blockchain technology more systematically to realize significant returns from its SC efficiencies (Bloomberg, 2019). As a digital ledger that can be used to track and verify whatever is needed, its utilization needs to be managed to accurately automate many of the current functions that are still exposed to much slower and more costly human interaction. Yet which ones they are, may need to be refined. In the shipping industry, blockchain already effectively reduces the time needed for red-tape and to coordinate with port authorities, and eliminates bottlenecks.

Other digitally driven strategies to consider originate from the changing nature of consumer influence, and the role that analytics and machine learning play to capture the needs in marketing and beyond.

Finally, Samsung's dependence on its internal innovation and its partnership with sub-suppliers have led to strong partnerships with an advantageous internalization of subparts assembly and process technology. Will the slowdown of globalization alter the social trust network that is at the core of Samsung's objectives of keeping its networks close?

Case questions

1   How and why is Samsung foremost Asia rooted and focused, while globally oriented?
2   How does Samsung's supply chain reflect a hybrid of Asian and Western management orientations? Why is this combination important?

6.4 STRATEGIC IMPLICATIONS

This chapter has focused on the global value chain participation of Asian economies and a more hands-on approach for corporate management, on supply chain efficiencies.

Asia had experienced a major transition over the past two decades in the way in which GVC participation is distributed, and in which its geographical economy has been altered into a network of increasingly high value-added, especially around Japan, China, India and other industrialized, service or increasingly developed economies. Economies in their peripheries provide important further supplies of lesser value-added, yet often with the ambition to increase that value as part of their path to greater development. The region has hence seen major shifts especially among the big players, which have evolved increasingly from 'factory' functions of their industries to turning into 'knowledge' centres. This trend has taken place simultaneously with the major evolution of emerging market multinational companies.

As a reminder, GVCs are typically measured, analysed and reported through (inter-) governmental and multilateral organizations. They provide an important way to track how the rise of value-added contributions on a macro-economic level increases and impacts both economic development and industry competitiveness. Value-added is assessed across data that distinguishes, among others, upstream, i.e. pre-production, and downstream value chain activities, i.e. post-production stages.

On a macro level, this allows organizations to gain a refined understanding of trade in intermediaries, that is, components within the supply chain being moved from one country to another to finally constitute one final product (or service). This takes places as intra-company trade (where entities or subsidiaries produce parts that they then send on to be refined or completed elsewhere, often in many stages and countries) or inter-company trade (where the components come from suppliers other than one's own).

On a micro level, for the internationalized company that operates across Asia, this means that within its networks, a given subsidiary or partner will play a part in value-adding. This happens through the production of a part, component or service in a foreign country, as an entity that is owned in full or in part by a multinational firm.

If this happens through its own subsidiaries, the overall organization of that subsidiary's role and its part in the supply chain for a given product or service allows for the strategic configuration of what happens where across borders. This means that the company uses the location and relocation of high value-added activities to attain its objectives, and so does each subsidiary or country manager within it. Those activities encompass business planning and strategy for a given proportion of international markets, their role and influence on global and regional strategy, and the role that functions such as research, development and innovation play: the distribution of subsidiaries and/or suppliers across regions of the world reveals the geographic scope of a multinational firm's strategy. We have seen in this chapter that Samsung's scope is held traditionally more closely to the Asian home region that used to be the case for Huawei, yet also that geo-economic and political pressures can cause companies to tighten their geographical scope in that sense.

The nature of the multinational's structure and depth of investment defines the ownership and control that ultimately determine the strength of the network. When it comes to its own subsidiaries, it is their research and development, manufacturing, assembly, distribution and marketing functions that precondition the product scope and functional orientation of its strategy, and the decision of how much value-added a given location is expected to provide. To make this even clearer: if a company runs a sales office or a trading office in a given location, its value-added will be lesser (and it will be considered a less strategic part of the value chain) than a facility that provides some essential part of manufacture or service, or service as a knowledge centre or innovation hub.

Multinationals hence develop local, regional and global strategies that are intertwined especially with their SC management. We have also demonstrated in the two case studies that, to maintain and strengthen competitive advantage, focused strategy-formulation and execution needs to include a focus on continuous long-term innovation and productivity gains including in SC management. What this looks like, clearly depends on whether the company is mainly market seeking, resource seeking, efficiency seeking, and/or strategic asset seeking in a given location or region. The case studies reveal how different the motivations are to use Chinese suppliers versus South Korean or Japanese suppliers. You will have learned how firms use various locations in that they balance where more or less value is added, and efficiencies reside.

The case studies provide interesting material on how two major players in the Asian telecommunications sector differ in managing their supply chain strategy and how this evolved over time. Both do have in common that they retain core competences for product fulfilment at 'home', hence keeping a degree of control and ownership to themselves. However, the degree and method by which they handle their intricate supply chains across Asia differ, with Samsung illustrating a more inherent pattern of embedding its SC in Asia historically, also relating to its marketing strategy. Huawei's approach was more mixed, given its developed-market strategy, yet shows the strategic decision made to repatriate and shorten the SC into Asia in times of crisis rather than selecting alternative suppliers from outside the region.

The multi-supplier strategy was found to be the prevailing strategy used by multinationals across Asia. But supplier relations in Asia are increasingly competitive, both through global and regional demand. Some companies, as in the cases presented, strive to counterbalance that competition by cultivating close relations and fostering engagement, sometimes including training and job perks, which keep suppliers and their own subcontractors loyal to the firm to secure fulfilment. This helps mitigate the risk of supply chain disruption, can be used to source important innovation capabilities, and brings a product or service faster to market than the competition, which constitutes a crucial part of competitive advantage in most cases in an increasingly mature, connected and digitalized region.

In particular, business leaders and strategists direct more future investment to the APEC part of Asia, as it increasingly integrates its markets. A recent CEO survey by PricewaterhouseCoopers showed 71 per cent of the 1,400 Asian leaders interviewed were stating they will increase investment in one or more of these 21 economies in their home region rather than elsewhere, and only 29 per cent in the rest of the world (PWC, 2018).

Most-favoured locations outside their home market were noted as Vietnam, China, Indonesia and Thailand. These locations are also those that boast the greatest increase in value-added capacity in the past decade. This coincides with a measurable perception by strategists that the global business environment has changed over the past years, particularly when it comes to barriers to employing foreign labour and barriers to cross-border services provision or delivery.

Both trends are limitations to the capacity also to bring knowledge and innovation capabilities into a given economy and to drive up its value-adding capacity. Strategic implications resulting from this include a trend to diversify yet shorter supply chains, and to conduct more value-added activities domestically or in the home region rather than globally. Also, company leaders state they adapt cross-border strategy and supply chain preferences to doing business in economies with bilateral ties or within regional free trade agreements, and in conjunction with loyal partners, joint ventures or bringing them closer through M&A – especially when this improves additional digitalization tools that the company can leverage.

REFERENCES

American Shipper (2019) DSV to acquire Panalpina. Available at: www.americanshipper. com/news/dsv-to-acquire-panalpina-for-46-billion?autonumber=847609&origin=relate darticles (accessed October 2019).

Android Authority (2019) Huawei and the Trump debacle: The story so far. Available at: www.androidauthority.com/huawei-google-android-ban-988382/ (accessed 19 September 2019).

APEC (2013) Global Supply Chain Operation in the APEC Region: Case Study of the Electrical and Electronics Industry. APEC Policy Support Unit, July, Singapore.

Apple Inside (2018) TSMC will continue to be Apple's sole chip producer for the 2019 'A13' processor. Available at: https://appleinsider.com/articles/18/10/12/

tsmc-will-continue-to-be-apples-sole-chip-producer-for-the-2019-a13-processor (accessed 19 September 2019).

Baidu (2017) Huawei became BOE's first OLED client, offering solution for its supply chain difficulties. Available at: http://baijiahao.baidu.com/s?id=15810268148467018 90&wfr=spider&for=pc (accessed 17 September 2019).

Baijiahao (2019) TSMC fights back: Suing Globalfoundries for 25 patents' violation and permission to the cessation of sales of chips. Available at: http://baijiahao.baidu. com/s?id=1646201095901266128&wfr=spider&for=pc (accessed 10 October 2019).

Banomyong, R. (2010) Supply chain dynamics in Asia. ADBI Working Paper Series, 184. Tokyo: Asian Development Bank Institute.

Blizard, S. (2017) *The Samsung Way*. Roxburgh Securities, 16 September. Available at: https://roxburghsecurities.wpcomstaging.com/2017/09/16/the-samsung-way/ (accessed 3 August 2019).

Bloomberg (2019) Xiaomi Launches Big 5G Challenge to Huawei in China. Available at: www.bloomberg.com/news/articles/2019-09-24/xiaomi-unveils-first-5g-phone-for-china-in-challenge-to-huawei (accessed 8 October 2019).

Buckley, P.J. (ed.) (2011) *Globalization and the Global Factory*. Cheltenham: Edward Elgar.

Canadian Embassy in the Republic of Korea/Commercial Section (2012) Global Value Chain Analysis on Samsung Electronics. Available at: https://unstats.un.org/unsd/ trade/events/2016/newyork-egm/documents/background/Canada%20-%202012% 20-%20GVC%20Analysis%20of%20Samsung%20Electronics.pdf (accessed 3 August 2019).

CCTime (2018) Usage of Huawei HiSilicon chip might exceed 50%, covering more mid- and lower-ranged phone models. Available at: www.cctime.com/html/2018-2-23/1362043.htm (accessed 8 October 2019).

C-Fol (2019) Huawei promised Asian Suppliers an 80% utility rate and urged them for production. Available at: www.c-fol.net/m/news/view.php?id=20190912124425 (accessed 8 October 2019).

Cnet (2018) Huawei exceeds 200 million smartphone shipments, setting company record. Available at: www.cnet.com/news/huawei-exceeds-200-million-smartphone-shipments-setting-company-record/ (accessed 10 September 2019).

Cooke, J. (2018) How Diageo reduced risk in Asia. Available at: https:// supplychainminded.com/diageo-reduced-risk-asia/ (accessed 1 February 2019).

Doffman, Z. (2019) Huawei's 'secret plan' to defeat Trump: New report. Available at: www.forbes.com/sites/zakdoffman/2019/09/11/huaweis-secret-plan-to-defeat-us-blacklist-exposed-new-report/#761fa169e39a (accessed 9 April 2020).

East Day (2017) The real reason for Huawei's lacking Mate 9 Pro inventory: Samsung stopped offering OLED. Available at: https://mini.eastday.com/mobile/170318192815961.html (accessed 23 September 2019).

Fan, C.C. and Scott, A.J. (2003) Industrial agglomeration and development: A survey of spatial economic issues in East Asia and a statistical analysis of Chinese regions. *Economic Geography*, 79(3): 295–319.

Financial Times (2019) Huawei tells suppliers to move production to China as US ban looms. Available at: www.ft.com/content/c47a93c6-25ec-11e9-8ce6-5db4543da632 (accessed 8 October 2019).

Fortune (2019) Huawei CEO has an elaborate plan to create a 5G rival in the US. Available at: https://fortune.com/2019/09/28/huawei-ceo-5g-license-competition/ (accessed 8 October 2019).

Fujimura, M. (2017) *Evaluating Impacts of Cross-Border Transport Infrastructure in the Greater Mekong Subregion: Three Approaches*. ADBI Working Paper Series, No. 771. Available at: www.adb.org/sites/default/files/publication/352026/adbi-wp771.pdf (accessed 9 April 2020).

Gartner (2018) *Gartner Announces Rankings of the 2018 Supply Chain Top 25*. Phoenix, 17 May. Available at: www.gartner.com/en/newsroom/press-releases/2018-05-17-gartner-announces-rankings-of-the-2018-supply-chain-top-25 (accessed 9 April 2020).

Guillaume, Y., Dawson, J., Otaye-Ebede, L., Woods, S. and West, M. (2017) Harnessing demographic differences in organizations: What moderates the effects of workplace diversity? *Journal of Organizational Behavior*, 38(2): 276–303.

Harbert, T. (2013) The secret to Samsung's ascent. Mobile Devices. Electronics 360 – Global Spec, 30 April. Available at: https://electronics360.globalspec.com/article/133/the-secret-to-samsung-s-ascent (accessed 3 August 2019).

Huanqiu (2018) Huawei: Done 5G network most critical tests, launch of 5G phone will be brought ahead. Available at: https://tech.huanqiu.com/article/9CaKrnKcwCs (accessed 9 October 2019).

Huawei (2019) *Huawei Investment & Holding Co., Ltd. 2018 Annual Report*. Available at: www-file.huawei.com/-/media/corporate/pdf/annual-report/annual_report2018_en_v2.pdf (accessed 9 April 2020).

iFeng (2018) Huawei revealed its 92 core suppliers' list for the first time. Available at: http://wemedia.ifeng.com/90756706/wemedia.shtml (accessed 20 August 2019).

iPhone Hacks (2018) TSMC to exclusively fabricate Apple's A-series chips until 2020. Available at: www.iphonehacks.com/2018/08/tsmc-exclusively-fabricate-apple-a-series-chips-until-2020.html (accessed 19 September 2019).

IP Lytics (2019) Who is leading the 5G patent race? A patent landscape analysis on declared SEPs and standards contributions. Available at: www.iplytics.com (accessed 8 October 2019).

ITNews (2019) Huawei already producing 5G base stations without US parts. Available at: www.itnews.com.au/news/huawei-already-producing-5g-base-stations-without-us-parts-531566 (accessed 8 October 2019).

Japan Times (2019) US ban on Huawei largely ignored in Southeast Asia. Available at: www.japantimes.co.jp/news/2019/08/19/business/u-s-ban-huawei-largely-ignored-southeast-asia/#.XaBzCOczbOQ (accessed 10 October 2019).

Khanna, T., Song, J. and Lee., K. (2011) The paradox of Samsung's rise. *Harvard Business Review*, July–August: 142–147.

Kim, C., Lee, K. and Choi, J. (2010) The study of building a learning organization and cross evaluation between companies applied DLOQ: Focusing on Samsung electronics F team practices. *Journal of the Korea Safety Management & Science*, 12(1): 83–96.

Kim, Y. (1998) Technological capabilities and Samsung Electronics' international production network in East Asia. *Management Decision*, 36(8): 517–527.

Kokemuller, N. (2019) What is integrated supply chain management? Available at: https://bizfluent.com/about-6690370-integrated-supply-chain-management-.html (accessed 30 August 2019).

Korn Ferry (2019) *2019 Third-Party Logistics Study: The State of Logistics Outsourcing. Results and Findings of the 23rd Annual Study* (C. John Langley, Jr., PhD, and Infosys). Available at: https://dsqapj1lakrkc.cloudfront.net/media/sidebar_downloads/2019-3PL-Study.pdf (accessed 9 April 2020).

LA Times (2019a) Will Huawei's loss be Samsung's gain in the China-U.S. trade war? Available at https://www.latimes.com/world/asia/la-fg-huawei-ban-samsung-20190530-story.html (accessed 24 April 2020).

LA Times (2019b) Why a ban on Huawei is being ignored by some of the oldest U.S. allies in Asia. Available at https://www.latimes.com/world/la-fg-philippines-huawei-southeast-asia-20190610-story.html (accessed 24 April 2020).

Lee, J., Lee, K. and Heo, J. (2015) Supplier partnership strategy and global competitiveness: A case of Samsung electronics. *Eurasian Journal of Business and Management*, 3(4): 1–12.

Li, T. (2019) Huawei to deploy ultra-fast 5G telecoms network coverage at Shanghai's railway hub in world first. Available at: www.scmp.com/tech/big-tech/article/2186610/huawei-deploy-ultra-fast-5g-telecom-network-coverage-shanghais-railway (accessed 9 April 2020).

Loten, A. (2016) Samsung recall puts supply-chain oversight in spotlight. *Wall Street Journal*. Available at: www.wsj.com/articles/samsung-recall-puts-supply-chain-oversight-in-spotlight-1476224149 (accessed 4 August 2019)

Lucas, L. and Fildes, N. (2019) Google suspends Huawei from Android services. *Financial Times*, 20 May. Available at: www.ft.com/content/d8b3d6e6-7aaa-11e9-81d2-f785092ab560 (accessed 9 April 2020).

Martin Roll (2018) Huawei – Transforming a Chinese technology business to a global brand. Available at: www.martinroll.com/resources/articles/strategy/huawei-transforming-chinese-technology-business-global-brand/ (accessed 28 August 2019).

Meng, B., Yamano, N. and Fang, Y. (2012) International economic interdependence and global value chains: An international input-output analysis. *IDE Discussion Paper*, 362, Chiba.

Min, H., Ko, H.-J., Lim, Y.-K., Park, J.-W. and Cho, Y.K. (2014) Challenges and opportunities for logistics standardisation in Asia-Pacific countries: A descriptive case study. *International Journal of Logistics Systems and Management*, 17(3): 357–380.

Nainan, N.K. and Ramakrishnan, S. (2019) Spark New Zealand keeps Huawei on preferred suppliers list but leads 5G rollout with Nokia. Available at: www.reuters.com/article/spark-nz-huawei-tech/update-2-spark-new-zealand-keeps-huawei-on-preferred-suppliers-list-but-leads-5g-rollout-with-nokia-idUSL5N27X0CU (accessed 9 April 2020).

NEPCON Asia (2019) How does Huawei handle their suppliers? Available at: www.nepconasia.com/en/News-Center/Industry_Press_Releases/Huawei-handle-suppliers/ (accessed 1 September 2019).

New York Times (2019) Lawsuit over computer chips invokes trade war with China. Available at: www.nytimes.com/2019/08/26/technology/globalfoundries-tsmc-lawsuit-computer-chips.html (accessed 10 October 2019).

Ni, Y. (2018) Analysis of Huawei's global supply chain. 2018 International Conference on Sports, Arts, Education and Management Engineering (SAEME 2018), Atlantis Press, Vol. 1999.

Nikkei Asian Review (2019) Why Huawei values collaboration with universities. Available at: https://asia.nikkei.com/Opinion/Why-Huawei-values-collaboration-with-universities (accessed 4 September 2019).

OECD (2013) *Interconnected Economies: Benefiting from Global Value Chains*. Paris: OECD Publishing.

Pula, G. and Peltonen, T. (2009) Has emerging Asia decoupled? An analysis of production and trade linkages using the Asian international input–output table. *European Central Bank – Eurosystem, Working Paper Series*, No. 993, Frankfurt.

PWC (PricewaterhouseCoopers) (2018) A World in Transition: 2017 APEC CEO Survey Key Findings, Hong Kong.

Qianzhanwang (2015) How badly was Huawei jeopardized by Samsung's short in supply of AMELOD screen? Available at: https://t.qianzhan.com/ind/detail/150805-036d015f.html (accessed 11 October 2019).

Reisinger, D. (2018) Why Samsung might turn to Blockchain for its global supply chain. Fortune. Available at: https://fortune.com/2018/04/16/samsung-blockchain-supply-chain/ (accessed 4 August 2019).

Reuters (2019) Huawei leads Asian domination of U.N. patent applications in 2018. Available at: https://www.reuters.com/article/us-usa-china-ip/huawei-leads-asian-domination-of-u-n-patent-applications-in-2018-idUSKCN1QZ2PP (accessed 24 April 2020).

Rogers, G.G. and Bottaci, L. (1997) Modular production system: A new manufacturing paradigm. *Journal of Intelligent Manufacturing*, 8: 147–56.

Sako, M. (2003). Modularity and outsourcing: The nature of co-evolution of product architecture and organization architecture in the global automotive industry. In: *Proceedings of the 11th GERPISA International Colloquium*. Paris.

Samsung (2019) Responsible management of supply chain. Available at: www.samsung.com/au/aboutsamsung/sustainability/supply-chain/ (accessed 9 April 2020).

Scott, A.J. (1988) *Metropolis: From the Division of Labor to Urban Form*. Berkeley, CA: University of California Press.

Sevastopulo, D., Stacey, K., Politi, J., Liu, N. and Hille, K. (2019) US chipmakers hit after Trump blacklists Huawei. *Financial Times*, 16 May. Available at: www.ft.com/content/ea36fade-7784-11e9-be7d-6d846537acab (accessed 9 April 2020).

Shin, W. and Kim, C. (2015) Samsung's journey to excellence in quality. *International Journal of Quality and Service Sciences*, 7(2/3): 312–320.

Sohu (2018) Why did Huawei make Kirin? Available at: www.sohu.com/a/228839554_808479 (accessed 15 September 2019).

Sohu (2019a) A list of Huawei smartphones' suppliers and 33 US supplier list. Available at: www.sohu.com/a/315789601_659777 (accessed 17 September 2019).

Sohu (2019b) Huawei ISC growing path. Available at: www.sohu.com/a/306480675_653366 (accessed 29 August 2019).

Sohu (2019c) Today, Huawei + BOE announced a war. Available at: www.sohu.com/a/294765555_632543 (accessed 18 September 2019).

Sohu (2019d) After the temporary ban relieve, Huawei had other options? Opportunities for Asian suppliers. Available at: www.sohu.com/a/324262734_334198 (accessed 8 October 2019).

Song, J. and Lee, K. (2014) *The Samsung Way: Transformational Management Strategies from the World Leader in Innovation and Design*. New York: McGraw-Hill.

South China Morning Post (2018) Huawei is in better shape to withstand US pressure, thanks to industry's largest research budget. Available at: www.scmp.com/business/companies/article/2143569/huawei-better-shape-withstand-us-pressure-thanks-industrys (accessed 8 October 2019).

South China Morning Post (2019) Huawei ban: Why Asian countries are shunning Trump's blacklist despite concerns about China's influence. Available at: www.scmp.com/news/asia/southeast-asia/article/3012820/huawei-ban-why-asian-countries-are-shunning-trumps (accessed 9 April 2020).

Suder, G., Liesch, P.W., Inomata, S., Mihailova, I. and Meng, B. (2015) The evolving geography of production hubs and regional value chains across East Asia: Trade in value-added. *Journal of World Business*, 50(3): 404–416.

Suh, J. and Kim, Y. (2009) Logistics lean integration strategies: Case study of Samsung electronics, LCD inbound logistics. *Journal of International Logistics and Trade*, 7(1): 107–116.

Tencent (2019) Why does Huawei purchase from Qualcomm when it has Kirin? Available at: https://new.qq.com/omn/20190612/20190612A0FCHK.html?pc (accessed 19 September 2019).

Thakur, A. and Sen, A. (2018) Samsung India: The bigger picture. Fortune India. Available at: www.fortuneindia.com/enterprise/samsung-india-the-bigger-picture/102822 (accessed 4 August 2019).

The Insights Partner (2019) The South East Asia third party logistics market. Available at: www.theinsightpartners.com/pr/south-east-asia-third-party-logistics-market (accessed 30 January 2019).

The Verge (2019) Huawei confirms the new Mate 30 Pro won't come with Google's Android apps. Available at: www.theverge.com/2019/9/19/20873690/huawei-mate-30-series-phones-google-android-ban-apps-block (accessed 19 September 2019).

VentureBeat (2019) China dusts the US, Finland, and South Korea with 34% of key 5G patents. Available at: https://venturebeat.com/2019/05/02/china-dusts-the-u-s-finland-and-south-korea-with-34-of-key-5g-patents/ (accessed 8 October 2019).

Wall Street Journal (2019) Where China dominates in 5G Technology. Available at: www.wsj.com/articles/where-china-dominates-in-5g-technology-11551236701 (accessed 8 October 2019).

White, E. (2018) Three charts explaining who is most exposed to Huawei. Available at: https://www.on.ft.com/2KFPxYA.

7
DIVERSITY AND CULTURES: FURTHER CONSIDERATIONS AND CONCLUSIONS

7.1 CROSS-CULTURAL MANAGEMENT

This concluding chapter of this book on doing business in Asia focuses on the key aspects of diversity and culture in Asia. It provides insights, combines them with the learning from previous chapters and discusses further considerations. The chapter covers:

- an introduction into **cross-cultural management**
- in-depth insights into cultural differences and commonalities across Asia
- key learning about cultural challenges and opportunities when doing business with Asia
- reflections about the diversity of this continent, analysing potentials and uncertainty impacts
- it then provides some concluding remarks.

> Culture should be regarded as the set of distinctive spiritual, material, intellectual and emotional features of society or a social group, and ... it encompasses, in addition to art and literature, lifestyles, ways of living together, value systems, traditions and beliefs. (UNESCO, 2001)

Asia has a complex and diverse cultural profile, triggered by intensive migration movements and settlements over centuries throughout the region, mainly from west to east and into the south-east.

A focus on culture necessitates the exploration of shared ideas, norms, behaviours and values in the region. Those are acquired often since childhood, or at a minimum over a lengthy period of time (if change of residence, for example), through 'experience in a given environment' (Redding et al., 2014: 258).

Behaviours are hence learned. They are derived from the social environment and may evolve over time due to experience that may be conditioned by societal, religious, economic, geographic or other influences. This leads to an understanding of how to appreciate and most suitably function in a specific context, in the most constructive case, and potentially to preconditioning resulting in prejudice and stereotyping, in its poorest attribution.

Culture is expressed through a variety of signs. Among them, verbal and non-verbal signs can lead to a variety of interpretations: these are some of the most visible expressions of cultural similarity or difference, as well as the perception of time and space, or the expression of agreement. If different, the successful business will be seen neither as right or wrong: culture is relative and there is no universal cultural absolute. If behaviours differ, it may well be because people and societies of different cultures perceive the world differently.

At the same time, it is important to remember that individual behaviour does not necessarily reflect culture but may simply show a certain personality. Indeed, we speak of culture only when groups exhibit certain collectively shared values and meanings.

Key aspects of cross-cultural management: Definitions

Behaviours: The range of mannerisms, actions and reactions towards one's environment.
Norms: A mean, average or median (derived from mathematics) establishing a pattern of behaviour.
Values: One's judgements about good or bad, acceptable or unacceptable, important or unimportant and what is 'normal'.
Attitudes: Similar to opinions, yet often unconsciously held and not necessarily rational.
Prejudices: Rigidly held attitudes, usually negative, not constructive and focused on particular groups of people.
Manners and customs: Manifestation of habitual ways of behaving and conducting oneself, including traditions.

Cultural differences and commonalities across Asia

Managing business across borders requires cross-cultural skills to create value stemming from the diversity of internal and external stakeholders. At the very basis, this means trusting in and understanding work-related behaviour that may vary from one's own, which is a positive and inclusive mindset. Variations can range from more or less formalistic negotiation styles to behaviours in the workplace itself, for example when getting familiar with the Chinese power-nap, or the Ngan in Thailand translating into work and play, where work days may be divided into a focus on work and a focus on short yet frequent periods of *sanuk* ('fun', relaxation in informal groups).

The Dutch cultural anthropologist Geert Hofstede's significant work on cultural clusters helps illustrate and comprehend business-relevant traits. His work was developed first in 1980 and refined ever since with numerous additional research data and analyses. This research is probably the most cited and influential business culture research to date. Though regularly criticized, it provides an interesting starting point to better understand culture across Asia for our purposes. We will focus on the historic core dimensions found by Hofstede (2019).

In particular, compared to the so-called Western cultures, we can report that:

- most Asian cultures are found to exhibit high **power distance** (though less so in Japan, South Korea and Taiwan) and collectivism
- in clustering data from across Asia, **uncertainty avoidance** scores high (except for Singapore and less so Hong Kong).
- overall, femininity prevails across most of Asia (except for findings for Japan and more recently China)
- long-term orientation (also named Confucian dynamism, a dimension elaborated by researcher T. Bond) is found in various expressions across Asia, and is seen as the most distinctive trait of China with a dominant capacity to adapt to a changing environment rather than static planning for the future. India also shows a high long-term orientation, yet this is expressed differently. The Korean long-term orientation is often reported as most visible in buyer–supplier relations, including their internalization (see also: Samsung case study, section 6.3).

Hofstede's dimensions briefly defined

Power matters: An expectation and acceptance that power is unequally distributed.
Individual or group matters: A preference to focus on oneself vs the group or society.
Assertiveness: An expectation that a gender or other sub-group is assertive vs nurturing.
Reliance on certitude: A preference for certainty vs uncertainty.
Future perspectives: A focus on the short term vs the long term.

Anthropologist Edward T. Hall (1976) elaborated concepts further and proposes also, among others, an interesting view of 'polychronic' versus 'monochronic' time orientation, in the interpretation of time as it varies across cultures.

In cultures prone to monochronic orientation, people tend to do one thing at a time, preferring to deal with one issue at a time, and along deadlines. Activities are typically sequenced in a linear manner and promptness is frequent. Polychronic tendencies in cultures are characterized by multiple tasks undertaken simultaneously, with flexible timeframes and roles, as reported for example for the Philippines. Time is hence spent often in recursive sequencing, and the perception of the importance of time worth spending focuses on building and maintaining relationships.

This is important in business because time dictates expectations about planning, scheduling, profit streams and what constitutes lateness in arriving for work and meetings, and hence the ever-important perception of engagement. For instance, Japanese managers tend to prepare strategic plans for extended periods, such as a decade. The planning time frame of Singaporean companies on the other hand spans several years. Altogether, compared to the rest of the world, Asian cultures are seen to prefer a steadier pace of work and are prone to more forward thinking. Yet there are nuances: Chinese, Indian and Indonesian employees, for example, are found to be forward thinking and competitive; Chinese staff were measured as less vigorous while Indian staff were found to be more data-rational and controlling, and less democratic. Indonesian employees are seen as inclined to follow rules more than their international peers, yet slower in accepting stakeholders as trustworthy. Singaporean staff show traits that are very similar to Hong Kong employees' though less proactive; the latter also applies to the Malaysian culture scores. The Thai employee culture is reported to be more flexible yet with a tendency to feel concerned (the latter often also reported for South Korea) rather than relaxed and less socially confident.

The interpretation of and need for context also differs between cultures, and has an impact on business conduct, team management, internal and external negotiation and employee behaviour. On-the-job behaviour in low context cultures tends to be focused on gathering and following rather explicit information. These cultures are those in which people will require much detail and background information before communication can be effective. Negotiators as much as managers need to be mindful of this to be heard and make an effective impact. High context, more implicit cultures, such as Japan and most of East Asia, rely heavily on socialization (continuously learning, and applying rules and behavioural patterns appropriate to one's given society) so they effectively do not need a lot of written and verbal information to work effectively.

Finally, in East Asia for example, the leader is often a person who gives directions and employees execute these as a sign of respect. Self-initiative is hence not self-evident in some Asian cultures.

Cultural challenges and opportunities when doing business with and within Asia

Employees evolve within three cultures:

- National culture: norms, behaviours, beliefs and customs shared across the population of a sovereign nation.
- Professional culture: which is determined by a profession and/or a sector and the content of the job.
- Corporate culture: which is characterized by an organization and defines its nature.

Working with and across cultures is challenging yet opens unique opportunities embedded in a variety of collective divergence. The complexity of working for multinational and cross-border business relies on the effective combination of the three dimensions listed above. Yet we focus on the national and regional culture in this chapter. Together, it can create new and powerful ideas and applications, innovation and problem-solving capabilities. Multicultural teams and initiatives are meant to increase market reach, research opportunity or innovative capabilities for organizations and are a reality for multinationals. When well managed, projects comprised of members from one single culture or organization tend to be of average effectiveness yet slower at problem-solving. What counts is making diversity a value, that is, by valuing one's own and the others' background on an equal level.

As trust is typically seen as partly etic, i.e. general or universal, and partly emic, i.e. culture specific, at least one part is typically straightforward to achieve. What creates trust in a quasi-universal manner relies on certain attributes and their perception: this includes clear communication, characterized by listening, questioning, giving and receiving feedback and recognition of the needs and concerns of others. Assertiveness and empathy help in acknowledging others' concerns and aspirations, understanding their point of view, perspective and reality. Doing so with integrity supports a team's understanding that one is acting honestly, fairly and ethically, expecting the best of others and providing encouragement.

Respect is crucial in valuing and acknowledging the contribution of others; being a team player helps working in cooperation with others and enhances consultation, collaboration and continual improvement. Finally, dealing positively with conflict builds another piece of trust when different goals and needs within a team result in conflict, yet a constructive approach will increase understanding and group cohesion.

Inclusive leadership promotes agile, flexible, intuitive management skills with clear processes, based on a broad and holistic vision, strategy and action across an organization and beyond.

Through acculturation, the process of adjusting and adapting to a culture different from one's own, it is possible to extend one understanding of cultural diversity and the value of inclusiveness across borders and cultures further. It is commonly experienced by people who live in other countries for extended periods, for example 'expatriates'. Through such socialization, acquiring cultural norms and patterns can be accelerated given this is typically a slow and complex process as one's own behaviour, the capacity to process information and interact with others, adapts.

The research presented above is core yet not exhaustive in regard to the studies that attempt to categorize cultural traits that are important for business. They provide reference points about cultures, and can be used to detect both differences and similarities. This assists the development of strategy and action in cross-border or cross-team multicultural management. Judging from the example of the Philippines with its high power-distance score, one will expect a hierarchical system with strong senior leaders who are the main decision-makers. By logic, you can hence prepare, for example, for negotiations (whether intra-firm or external) with Philippine teams that will likely require the involvement of those leaders. You can also expect that you will need to use some very clear communication and instructions when speaking to other staff, given that at that level, one will find relatively little habit of own initiative-taking.

Yet the scores only tell part of the story: middle-management tends to be well educated and most likely will be used as the main link to non-Philippine teams. Recognizing communication styles and channels is hence crucial, as are preferred styles to collaborate and to make decisions collaboratively or authoritatively.

7.2 THE DIVERSITY OF A CONTINENT: POTENTIALS AND UNCERTAINTY IMPACTS

The diversity of Asia results in a range of impacts, some more positive than others, some revealing great potential, and some uncertainty in how to best proceed. While it is possible to take a cluster approach to some of the cultural traits, as demonstrated in section 7.1

above, one would be mistaken to believe that there is one exact cultural norm across such a cluster or the region or parts of it.

The diversity of cultures results in an additional complexity to doing business in Asia, and across Asian locations. While it is commonly known that doing business across Asia holds a significant promise of innovation, growth and productivity, it is essential to know of potentials and uncertainties stemming from the diversity too. Cultural variations can, for example, influence attitudes in negotiation of agreements or in the handling of intellectual property.

In negotiation styles, for one, we find, for example, that Singapore typically uses a more sequential style, while China uses holistic decision-making – having agreed on one step of the negotiation does not necessarily mean moving on to the next step but may need to be revisited after other matters are discussed. In addition, in Singapore one may detect more results-orientation in the negotiation, while in China the focus is often given to processes: this process-orientation is based on the logic that if the process is right first and foremost, then one should be in the best place possible. Yet another illustration of such culturally biased attitudes in negotiation is that of 'straight-talking' versus 'circumlocution', both of which can make the other negotiator uncomfortable if unprepared. And in some cultures, issues can become absolutes, i.e. deal-breakers or ultimatums, while others will typically favour relative positions, that is, seeking compromise and face-saving solutions. Preparations and training are hence the keys to success in multicultural negotiations.

To take our example further, cultural difference may also lead to variations in the interpretation, management and control of IP rights, especially reported between China and other Asian countries. It was in 1982 that China set up its first IP laws together with a trademark law, yet it has taken a couple of decades to cover the essential IP policies and rules. The first IP treaty was signed in the PRC in 2012, and the first IP courts were established only since 2014. Protecting one's IP before doing business in China has become one of the key elements of market entry by foreign businesses, who have learned to register for IP in the country. With its 'first to file' system, any company entering the market, participating in trade shows, discussing with potential suppliers or distributors, has learnt to remain cautious to avoid fakes or counterfeits under their brands, trademarks or patents. In copyright, for example, protection may be declared to be automatic, yet it needs to be registered in China to enforce or license. Importantly, respect of one's business is typically based also on *Guanxi*-type relationships (Hitt and Xu, 2016). *Guanxi* is characterized by network relationships that are built through the exchange of gifts and favours to attain mutual benefits upon the principle of reciprocity. Reciprocity can also be found in Japan, known as *on*, and in most other Asian cultures in various degrees.

In addition, when the application of Western style non-disclosure agreements is signed, their scope of use and disclosure to third parties remains fragmented in some parts of Asia and their language may need cultural as much as literal translation.

Yet another example of the variety of culturally defined attitudes can be found in conflict management. Detecting and managing conflict is important in that a conflict that is not clearly recognized is unlikely to be solved before it harms productivity and performance, and hence management seeks to address conflict constructively. For examples of difference in approach, it is reported that business conflict in Japan and Vietnam will typically be managed in a more competitive manner than in Thailand and in Hong Kong. Both Thailand and Hong Kong, however, also prefer to avoid conflict altogether if possible, which was not found for Japan or Thailand.

These examples illustrate just some of the factors that may induce a certain degree of uncertainty in cross-border business in Asia. It is hence important to be prepared to accept a longer timeframe for success. Unrealistic timeframes are a well-known reason for failure when doing business across Asia. Other key factors for failure or delay of business results in this context include the failure to develop multilevel relationships within local companies, regulators and government; poor stakeholder management with shareholders, partners and regulators; a loss of the ability to influence within joint ventures or other partnerships; and prominently the failure to adapt to local work culture by trying to enforce one's way (also called **ethnocentricity**). It won't work (though a blend might!).

7.3 CONCLUDING REMARKS

The importance of understanding cultural differences among Asian nations has risen in the past decade along with the growth of foreign direct investment of Asian nations such as Japan, Taiwan, Korea, and Singapore in other Asian countries (e.g. China, Malaysia, Indonesia, Thailand). Today, in fact, a Japanese manager is more likely than an American, German, or English manager to be supervising a Thai employee of a multi-national in Thailand. The same pattern holds true in Malaysia and Singapore as well (Glassberg, 2005). Thus, cross-cultural management of Asians by Asian managers of various nationalities is an increasingly common occurrence. (Onishi and Bliss 2006: 204)

Management and leadership skills across the Asian cultures allow business to address the current ways of managing onshore and offshore-based employees and equip executives with the right tools to effectively manage local and non-local resources, and staff from various backgrounds and cultures.

The aim is to work effectively in teams abroad but also at home where a multinational will typically increase the diversity of origins and cultures on all levels of staff while aiming to leverage opportunity from diversity and inclusion. Effective intercultural exchange significantly determines the success of international transactions, the performance and productivity of a culturally diverse workforce, and the achievement of any global business mission.

Multicultural engagement goes way beyond the etiquette that many basic business books list, which barely scratches the surface of cultural dimensions, such as how to greet people, how to hand out business cards, how to handle titles or a handshake, the seating order at meeting tables, or at the negotiation or dining table. It is effective communication that plays the essential part of leaders' and managers' duty of engagement and inclusion. Knowing who has influence in a culture versus who has authority, and communicating with both, and how to do so, is key. It needs to be effective, inclusive, confident and audience-focused. Poor communication skills mean that leaders fail to inspire their teams, products fail to sell, entrepreneurs fail to attract funding, and careers fail to soar.

Working with different cultures means managing that:

- people show differences in causal reasoning
- and, accordingly, in making predictions
- and in their needs to ensure social integration, performance and well-being.

Engagement with multicultural stakeholders, whether internally or externally, is hence best geared towards:

- raising awareness: the key is an appreciation of one's own and others' cultures
- recognizing valuable differences
- recognizing valuable similarities
- highlighting the most relevant bridging mechanisms for your teams onshore and offshore.

The current trends towards increasing regionalization (and a less stable global political economy) also increase dependencies and connectivity across the company's home region. This means dealing with ambiguity close to home yet within a different culture and changing from ethnocentricity to openness with a view to benefiting from cultural flexibility.

As a best case, cultural diversity and inclusion will trigger advantages including:

- more innovations
- faster and more effective learning (and hence strategic renewal capabilities)
- better decision-making
- a larger talent pool, talent acquisition and retention
- a wider customer base.

In the worst case, this would mean:

- low employee engagement, low employee morale
- more conflicts
- poorer job performance
- less access to talent, less talent retention, and less internationalization knowledge
- reputational damage.

This is specifically so because intergroup bias engendered by group members may be perceived as dissimilar by others and as a threat or challenge to a positive and distinct self-image (Guillaume et al., 2017).

Let's illustrate these remarks with some final examples, which blend the above cultural traits to demonstrate the way in which they may interrelate. Consider similarities and differences, and how they may be bridged:

> Within Australian organizations, hierarchy is established for convenience, superiors are often accessible, and managers rely on individual employees and teams for their expertise. Managers and employees expect to be consulted and information is shared frequently; employees are expected to be self-reliant and display initiative, and there is a pronounced 'winner takes all' attitude. A short-term orientation, which is particularly nuanced in urban Australia, focuses on achieving quick results yet is relatively immobile on traditions and routines.
>
> In India, we find a greater and more explicit appreciation for hierarchy and a top-down structure; power is centralized (sometimes implicitly so, and not obvious to outsiders), and attitudes towards managers are formal even if one is on first name terms. Directive communication prevails. Collectivism and loyalty to the organization are important.
>
> In Indonesia, leaders are rather directive, management controls and delegates. Employees generally expect to be told what to do and when. Communication is indirect and negative feedback hidden. There is preference for a strongly defined social framework in which individuals are expected to conform to the ideals of the society and the in-groups to which they belong. It is not always material gain that brings motivation. Often it is the position that a person holds. This also means that maintaining workplace and relationship harmony is very important in Indonesia, and no one wishes to be the transmitter of bad or negative news or feedback: 'Asal Bapak Senang' (Keep the Boss Happy)!
>
> China again is a society that believes that inequalities among people are acceptable. Staff often act in the interests of the group and not necessarily of themselves. This is a society that is success oriented and driven, and at the same time displays a very pragmatic culture, which is comfortable with ambiguity. Many Chinese will sacrifice family time and leisure priorities to education and work. A long-term orientation persists with a noted perseverance in achieving results yet an ability to adapt traditions easily to changed conditions.

These traits might seem confusing at first. Yet there are factors that organizations and managers have control over to bridge cultures and combine their traits to create significant value for the multinational doing business across Asia: they have control, at a minimum, over corporate culture, strategy, unit or team design, human resources and training, leadership and indeed communication. There are hence sufficient grounds to turn diversity into inclusion, i.e. becoming part of a group or structure: what counts is making diversity a value, by valuing one's own and the others background on an equal level. Inclusive leadership and management behaviour that foster this multicultural value creation encompass, among others, leader and manager openness, leader and manager diversity beliefs, and empathy. Success when doing business in and across Asia depends on it.

REFERENCES

Guillaume, Y., Dawson, J., Otaye-Ebede, L., Woods, S. and West, M. (2017) Harnessing demographic differences in organizations: What moderates the effects of workplace diversity? *Journal of Organizational Behavior*, 38(2): 276–303.

Hall, E. (1976) *Beyond Culture*. New York: Anchor Books.

Hitt, M. and Xu, K. (2016) The transformation of China: Effects of the institutional environment on business actions. *Long Range Planning*, 49(5): 589–593.

Hofstede, G. (2019) *Compare countries*. Available at: www.hofstede-insights.com/country-comparison/ (accessed 11 August 2019).

Hwang, J., Chung, J. and Jin, B. (2013) Culture matters. *Asia Pacific Journal of Marketing and Logistics*, 25(5): 721–744.

Onishi, J. and Bliss, R. (2006) In search of Asian ways of managing conflict. *International Journal of Conflict Management*, 17(3): 203–225.

Redding, G., Bond, M. and Witt, M. (2014) Culture and the business systems of Asia. In G. Redding, M. Bond and M. Witt (eds), *Oxford Handbook of Asian Business Systems*. Oxford: Oxford University Press.

Souza, C. (2003) An inference of gift-giving within Asian business culture. *Asia Pacific Journal of Marketing and Logistics*, 1: 27–38.

Suder, G. (2012–2018) Multicultural management: Professor Suder's teaching material and notes. SKEMA Business School and University of Melbourne.

UNESCO (2011) Universal Declaration on Cultural Diversity. Available at: http://portal.unesco.org/en/ev.php-URL_ID=13179&URL_DO=DO_TOPIC&URL_SECTION=201.html (accessed 21 July 2020).

GLOSSARY

Acquisition Purchase of an existing business venture in a foreign country.

Asia-Pacific Economic Cooperation (APEC) An inter-governmental forum whose primary goal is to promote free trade and sustainable development throughout the Pacific Rim economies.

Asset exploitation strategy Strategy used by MNEs who leverage their existing firm specific advantages (FSAs) in new locations for international venturing.

Asset seeking/augmenting strategy Strategies of latecomer EMNEs to seek resources and capabilities to overcome their competitive disadvantages.

Association of Southeast Asian Nations (ASEAN) An inter-governmental bloc in Southeast Asia, which promotes economic, political, security, military, educational and socio-cultural cooperation among its ten member countries and other countries in Asia.

Belt and Road Initiative To co-build the infrastructure and accelerate the economic integration of countries along the route of the historic Silk Road, the Chinese government first proposed this ambitious policy and investment plan in 2013, which combines the land-based Silk Road Economic Belt and the 21st Century Maritime Silk Road.

Bilateral trade Cross-border transactions that occur between the two countries.

Bill of lading A document of title of the goods being shipped along with the documents for shipment and the carrier's receipt for the goods being shipped.

Blockchain Expanding list of data records, called blocks, linked by use of cryptography to create a digital ledger. Each block contains a cryptographic hash of the previous block, a timestamp and transaction data.

Born global SMEs that almost bypass internationalization as a process as they start and operate from day one in global markets as global players, servicing their customers wherever they are to be found.

Brownfield investment A combination of greenfield investment and mergers and acquisitions.

Business conglomerate A combination of multiple business entities, usually consisting of a parent company and many subsidiaries that engage in entirely different industries.

Business model The firm elaborates upon the rationale of how it creates, delivers and captures value for customers.

Chaebols A sizeable family-controlled business group in South Korea, which often consists of many diversified affiliates. Among the largest Chaebols are Samsung, LG, Hyundai and SK Group.

Collectivism Cultural value under which people emphasize cohesion among individuals and prioritize the group over the self.

Competitive advantage A firm is said to have a competitive advantage when it implements a distinctive value-creating strategy and gets more return than current and potential competitors.

Competitiveness The ability of a firm or a nation to offer desirable products that meet the quality standards of the local and world markets and get adequate returns on the resources used to produce them at a competitive price.

Contractual entry mode Contractual or transfer-related entry modes are those associated with transfer of ownership or utilization of specified property such as technology or assets from one party to the other in exchange for royalty fees.

Corporate social responsibility A series of organizational practices that aim to improve the welfares of employees, the community and civil society and protect the eco-environment.

Cost, insurance and freight (CIF) A term of price in which the seller covers the cost of the goods, insurance, and all transportation and miscellaneous charges to the final destination port in a foreign country.

Countertrade Countertrade enables a seller and a buyer from different countries to exchange merchandise with little to no cash or cash equivalents changing hands.

Counter purchase A reciprocal buying agreement whereby one firm sells its products to another at one point in time and is compensated in the form of the other's products at some time in the future.

Cross-border e-commerce A kind of online transaction conducted by customers from different countries through the e-commerce platform.

Cross-border mergers and acquisitions (M&A)   Firms wholly or partially acquire the ownership of a target company outside their home country.

Cross-cultural management   The management of differing and shared ideas, norms, behaviours and values, for the sake of effective human collaboration. Includes, among others, national, professional and corporate culture.

Dragon TNCs   Dragon TNCs (also called latecomers) are a cluster of firms, which originated from the peripheral regions of the global economy (such as the Asia-Pacific region) in a phase of catch-up industrialization.

E-commerce platform   E-commerce platforms, such as Amazon and Taobao, provide an application through which you can buy and sell many kinds of products on the internet.

Efficiency seeking motive   Locating investment to take advantage of different factor endowments, economic systems, policies and market structures to concentrate production in a limited number of locations.

Emerging market   A group of countries, such as China and India, which grew rapidly but did not satisfy the criteria of developed countries because of weak market institutions and unequal development.

Entry mode   The strategic decision about how to enter an international market, commonly including exporting, licensing, franchising, acquisition and greenfield venturing.

Entrepôt trade   The import of goods for the purpose of re-exporting them.

Ethnocentricity   Belief that one's own culture or ethnic group is superior to another's, highly unproductive in cross-cultural management.

Export   Cross-border transactions where goods or services produced in one country are directly sold to any other country.

First mover advantage   Benefits of using proprietary technology which has not been used elsewhere, including scale and scope economies in the new market.

Foreign direct investment (FDI)   A mode of foreign market entry through long-term investment in the productive assets of a company.

Foreign portfolio investment   Investment in financial instruments such as stocks and bonds through the stock exchange and other financial markets.

Free alongside ship (FAS) A term of price in which the seller covers all costs and risks up to the ship at the designated shipment (export) port.

Free on board (FOB) A term of price in which the seller covers all costs and risks up to the point where the goods are delivered on board the ship in a designated shipment (export) port, and the buyer bears all costs and risks from that point.

Free trade agreement (FTA) A treaty between two or more countries to reduce trade barriers to imports and exports among them through tariffs or non-tariff measures.

Free trade zone (FTZ) Geographic and economic areas where goods can be purchased, sold, manufactured, reconfigured, imported and exported without trade barriers.

Geo-economics The combination of economic and geographic factors relating to international business.

Geo-politics The combination of political and geographic factors influencing or delineating international relations and international business.

Global area structure An organizational arrangement with a highly decentralized structure. The primary operational responsibility in this organizational form is delegated to area managers, each of whom is responsible for a specific geographic region.

Global functional structure An organizational structure built around the basic functional tasks of the organization, such as production, marketing and finance.

Globalization The process during which a firm locates its production, R&D and marketing at multiple nations and regions.

Global value chain Chain of process in which companies receive raw materials or service specific information, add value to them through production, manufacturing, sophistication and/or other processes to create a finished product or service, and then sell to consumers.

Greenfield investment Investment in a foreign market which results in the creation of new assets and production facilities in the host country.

Import Cross-border transactions where domestic customers or companies purchase goods or services produced in any other country.

Incremental process model/stage model An evolutionary process involving a series of incremental decisions during which firms increase their commitment to a foreign market by shifting from low- to high-commitment entry modes.

Intellectual property (IP)   Intangible creations of the human intellect, which are protected by, among others, copyrights, patents, trademarks and trade secrets.

International franchising   An entry mode in which the foreign franchisor grants use of the intangible property rights, such as trademark or brand name, to the local franchisee.

International leasing   An agreement for foreign market entry in which a foreign firm (lessor) leases out its new or used machines or equipment to a local company.

International licensing   An entry mode in which a firm (the licensor) grants to another firm (the licensee) the right to use any kind of expertise, know-how, blueprints, technology and manufacturing designs for a specified period of time in exchange for a royalty fee.

In-house R&D   A firm conducts its research and development activities by itself rather than outsourcing these to other companies.

International Monetary Fund   An international finance organization that aims to foster global monetary cooperation, secure financial stability, facilitate international trade, promote economic growth and reduce poverty around the world.

Joint venture (JV)   A business entity created by two or more parties, generally characterized by shared ownership, shared returns and risks, and shared governance based on a particular task and objective.

Just-in-time (JIT)   A set of inventory management system created by Toyota to reduce cost and increase efficiency by aligning raw material orders from suppliers directly with production schedules.

Leapfrogging strategy   Leapfrogging strategy helps latecomer MNEs to catch up with early mover MNEs through the use of radical technological innovations.

Letter of credit(L/C)   A contract between the banks of the buyer and the seller that ensures payment from the buyer to the seller on receipt of the export shipment.

Liability of foreignness   The disadvantage suffered by the MNE in the host country due to its non-native status.

Licensing   A low-commitment entry mode under which a foreign entity is allowed to use the focal firm's brand and sell its products in an individual market.

Linkage, Leverage, Learning (LLL)   Strategy used by EMNEs, of leveraging the linkages on existing global value chains and using the learning from these networks to establish themselves as successful players in the global economy.

Market seeking motive   FDI driven by the need to protect an existing market or exploit new markets, motivated by prospects for growth and large market share.

Matrix structure   A geocentric organizational arrangement that blends two organizational responsibilities such as functional and product structures or regional and product structures.

Merger   Amalgamation of two existing enterprises. It is a voluntary and permanent combination of two businesses which integrate their operations and identities with those of the other.

Micro MNEs   Micro MNEs/Infant MNEs are a body of smaller MNEs in terms of resources, staff and capital which originate from the industrial countries and use vigorous, innovative strategies to enter the global market.

Monochronic   People tend to do one thing at a time, preferring to deal with one issue at a time, and along deadlines. Contrasting to polychronic.

Multinational corporation/enterprise (MNC/MNE)   A business organization that has business operations or investments in two or more countries.

Natural resource seeking motive   FDI associated with firms in the primary sector, motivated by their need for cheaper resources including transport and communication infrastructure.

Non-tariff barrier   All barriers that restrict international trade in a form other than tariffs, including export subsidies, anti-dumping duties, quotas, embargoes and sanctions.

Original equipment manufacturer (OEM)   A firm produces and assembles the final goods based on the unique design and requirements of other companies.

Ownership, Location, Internalization (OLI) theory   Theory of FDI which explains investment as determined by ownership, location and internalization advantages.

Parental networks   Strategic networks which provide member firms with access to information, knowledge, resources, markets and technologies, which enable their internationalization.

Planned economy   A type of economic system where the production factors of an economy (such as labour, capital and natural resources) are subject to the government based on a comprehensive plan.

Polychronic   In a polychronic time system, engagement and completion of human actions are far more important than schedules.

Power distance   (in cross-cultural management)   The degree of distribution of power between the lowest and highest power actor in a society, indicating how equality is perceived and handled.

Pull factors   Proactive motivations which provide the stimuli for a domestic firm to explore a foreign market.

Push factors   Reactive motivations arising out of environmental factors which provide a domestic firm with the stimuli to move abroad.

Short-term vs long-term orientation   Linkages persisting over time into the future, from quarterly to long-term business objectives and reporting patterns. In cross-cultural management also from protecting 'face' in short-termism to order by status, sense of shame and a sense of persistence in long-termism.

Special economic zone (SEZ)   Special purpose enclaves which give preferential treatment for taxation, land use, infrastructure access and government assistance to MNEs, to promote foreign trade and investment.

Springboard strategy   Springboard strategy uses international expansion as a springboard to acquire critical resources for improving a firm's global competitiveness.

Stakeholders   People with direct or indirect influence on the success of an organization, including shareholders, customers, part or all of society and/or others, affecting or being affected by its activities.

State-owned MNEs   Business entities established or acquired by governments to engage in commercial activities, including FDI operations, by way of having affiliates abroad or engaging in non-equity modes.

Strategic alliance   An arrangement between two or more companies pooling their resources to undertake a mutually beneficial project while each retains its independence.

Strategic asset seeking   Investment made to get assets such as R&D, technical know-how, patents, brand names, local permits, licenses and supplier and distribution networks.

Supply chain management   The process in which a firm inputs its raw materials and/or innovation and transforms these into final products, with the flow of inputs and outputs representing the steps it takes to get the product or service to the customer.

Tariff barrier   A tax imposed upon imports to protect local industries and companies.

Technology transfer   The focal firm transfers its accumulated knowledge to another one and allows this receiver to benefit from such knowledge.

Trade   Foreign market entry mode through the purchase and sale of goods and services across national borders.

Transnational network structure   An international organizational arrangement which combines elements of the functional, product and geographical organizational structures.

Turnkey project   Also called build–operate–transfer (BOT), is an investment in which the entire design and construction of an operation are done by a foreign investor who hands it over after completion, for management to a local team.

Uncertainty avoidance   Uncomfortable with uncertainty, in need of certainty.

Unicorn company   A startup company having a net value of over $1 billion.

Value chain   A series of activities that a firm needs to conduct to create and deliver valuable products for the market, including R&D, manufacturing, marketing and human resource management.

Wholly owned subsidiary (WOS)   An independent legal entity which is controlled and managed by a parent company with 100 per cent ownership.

INDEX

Page numbers in *italics* refer to figures; page numbers in **bold** refer to tables.